Authoritarian Capitali

MW00611078

After the Second World War, the liberal-democratic model of capitalism spread across the globe, ultimately prevailing over communism. Over the past two decades, a new statist-authoritarian model has begun diffusing across Asia. Rather than rejecting capitalism, authoritarian leaders harness it to uphold their rule.

Based on extensive research about East Asia's largest corporations and sovereign wealth funds, this book argues that the most aggressive version of this model does not belong to China; rather, it can be found in Malaysia and Singapore. Although these countries are small, the implications are profound because one-third of all countries in the world possess the same type of regime. With an increasing number of these authoritarian regimes establishing sovereign wealth funds, their ability to intervene in the corporate sectors of other countries is rapidly expanding.

RICHARD W. CARNEY is a faculty member of the China Europe International Business School (CEIBS). His articles have appeared in journals such as the *Journal of Financial Economics, Business and Politics*, and the *Review of International Political Economy*. He is also the author of *Contested Capitalism: The Political Origins of Financial Systems* (2009) and editor of *Lessons from the Asian Financial Crisis* (2009). Prior to CEIBS, he held faculty positions at the Australian National University and the Nanyang Technological University in Singapore. He was also a Jean Monnet Fellow at the European University Institute in Florence, Italy.

Business and Public Policy

Series Editor:

ASEEM PRAKASH, University of Washington

Series Board:

Vinod K. Aggarwal, University of California, Berkeley
Tanja A. Börzel, Freie Universität Berlin
David Coen, University College London
Peter Gourevitch, University of California, San Diego
Neil Gunningham, The Australian National University
Witold J. Henisz, University of Pennsylvania
Adrienne Héritier, European University Institute
Chung-in Moon, Yonsei University
Sarah A. Soule, Stanford University
David Vogel, University of California, Berkeley

This series aims to play a pioneering role in shaping the emerging field of business and public policy. *Business and Public Policy* focuses on two central questions. First, how does public policy influence business strategy, operations, organization, and governance, and with what consequences for both business and society? Second, how do businesses themselves influence policy institutions, policy processes, and other policy actors and with what outcomes?

Other books in the series:

TIMOTHY WERNER, *Public Forces and Private Politics in American Big Business*

HEVINA S. DASHWOOD, *The Rise of Global Corporate Social Responsibility: Mining and the Spread of Global Norms*

LLEWELYN HUGHES, *Globalizing Oil: Firms and Oil Market Governance in France, Japan, and the United States*

EDWARD T. WALKER, *Grassroots for Hire: Public Affairs Consultants in American Democracy*

CHRISTIAN R. THAUER, *The Managerial Sources of Corporate Social Responsibility: The Spread of Global Standards*

KIYOTERU TSUTSUI & ALWYN LIM (Editors), *Corporate Social Responsibility in a Globalizing World*

ASEEMA SINHA, *Globalizing India: How Global Rules and Markets are Shaping India's Rise to Power*

VICTOR MENALDO, *The Institutions Curse: Natural Resources, Politics, and Development*

JEROEN VAN DER HEIJDEN, *Innovations in Urban Climate Governance: Voluntary Programs for Low Carbon Buildings and Cities*

LILIANA B. ANDONOVA, *Governance Entrepreneurs: International Organizations and the Rise of Global Public-Private Partnerships*

MICHAEL P. VANDENBERG AND JONATHAN M. GILLIGAN, *Beyond Politics: The Private Governance Response to Climate Change*

Authoritarian Capitalism

Sovereign Wealth Funds and State-Owned Enterprises in East Asia and Beyond

RICHARD W. CARNEY
China Europe International Business School

CAMBRIDGE
UNIVERSITY PRESS

CAMBRIDGE
UNIVERSITY PRESS

University Printing House, Cambridge CB2 8BS, United Kingdom

One Liberty Plaza, 20th Floor, New York, NY 10006, USA

477 Williamstown Road, Port Melbourne, VIC 3207, Australia

314-321, 3rd Floor, Plot 3, Splendor Forum, Jasola District Centre, New Delhi - 110025, India

79 Anson Road, #06-04/06, Singapore 079906

Cambridge University Press is part of the University of Cambridge.

It furthers the University's mission by disseminating knowledge in the pursuit of education, learning and research at the highest international levels of excellence.

www.cambridge.org
Information on this title: www.cambridge.org/9781108741880
DOI: 10.1017/9781108186797

© Richard W. Carney 2018

This publication is in copyright. Subject to statutory exception and to the provisions of relevant collective licensing agreements, no reproduction of any part may take place without the written permission of Cambridge University Press.

First published 2018
First paperback edition 2018

A catalogue record for this publication is available from the British Library

Library of Congress Cataloging in Publication data
Names: Carney, Richard D., author.
Title: Authoritarian capitalism : sovereign wealth funds and state-owned enterprises in east asia and beyond / Richard Carney.
Description: New York : Cambridge University Press, 2018. | Series: Business and public policy | Includes bibliographical references and index.
Identifiers: LCCN 2017055356 | ISBN 9781316510117 (hardback)
Subjects: LCSH: Capitalism – Political aspects – East Asia. | Authoritarianism – East Asia. | Globalization – East Asia.
Classification: LCC HB501 .C2487 2018 | DDC 330.95–dc23
LC record available at https://lccn.loc.gov/2017055356

ISBN 978-1-316-51011-7 Hardback
ISBN 978-1-108-74188-0 Paperback

Cambridge University Press has no responsibility for the persistence or accuracy of URLs for external or third-party internet websites referred to in this publication, and does not guarantee that any content on such websites is, or will remain, accurate or appropriate.

For Michelle

Contents

Preface

The global balance of power is shifting. Emerging economies, many of which host authoritarian regimes, are benefiting from their economic and political ties with China to rapidly develop while bolstering the stability of their political rulers. In contrast to the liberal-democratic world order that has persisted since 1945, a new statist-authoritarian world order is on the rise. The sudden retreat of the United States from globalization has accelerated this transition and amplified the need to make sense of how authoritarian regimes work with their state-infused corporate sectors.

Singapore is a fascinating example of how these two systems can coexist. The city-state embraces many of the liberal economic arrangements advocated by the West while maintaining strong ties with China and a highly stable, semicompetitive authoritarian regime. Next door is Malaysia, which manifests a variation of the Singaporean liberal market–authoritarian model. But Malaysia's Borneo neighbor, Brunei, is different. It has a strongly authoritarian political system with an economy dominated by the state – even more than China. Just as democracies vary both in the structure of their political arrangements and in their market economies, authoritarian systems vary. This book offers fresh insights into this variation and draws implications for how these authoritarian regimes intervene in foreign markets and thereby propagate a state-infused economic model.

The origins of this book can be traced to a workshop I organized in Singapore just as the global financial crisis began riveting the world economy. The workshop brought together a distinguished group of academics alongside senior government and business leaders, many of whom were directly involved with the crisis that jolted the East Asian region ten years earlier, such as Soedradjad Djiwandono (Central Bank Governor for Indonesia during the crisis), Hubert Neiss (Director of the Asia-Pacific for the IMF during the crisis), and Anwar Ibrahim (Finance

Minister and Deputy Prime Minister of Malaysia at the start of the crisis).[1] During the workshop, it became clear that one of the challenges with identifying the consequences of the crisis was the lack of data about who exactly wound up owning the region's biggest corporations in the years afterwards.

Not long after the workshop, Temasek, one of Singapore's sovereign wealth funds (SWFs), announced that it had lost US$4.5 billion on its 3.8 percent stake in Bank of America when it sold its position in March 2009. On a per capita basis, this was equivalent to every Singaporean losing US$1,500. To put this in perspective, a comparable loss in the United States would amount to US$450 billion if we assume that every US citizen were to lose the same amount (300 million population × US$1,500). But this financial hit came on the heels of another significant loss of US$1.5 billion when Temasek sold its near 2 percent stake in Barclays just a couple of months earlier (December 2008 and January 2009). Despite these staggering losses, Singapore's political system remained stable, and the economy quickly rebounded, mirroring its spectacular performance during the Asian financial crisis.

These events revealed not only the carefully calibrated control that Singapore's ruling party maintained but also the enormous power that SWFs and, by extension, the governments that control them can wield. Indeed, SWFs can dramatically magnify the global reach and power of otherwise nonthreatening nation-states. In 2010, this potential was further manifested when Khazanah, Malaysia's SWF, successfully completed a hostile takeover of a Singapore-based firm, Parkway, as detailed in the opening section of Chapter 1. This event did not make headlines in the West, but it marked a first clear demonstration of the aggressive power that these financial titans could wield on behalf of their political masters.

The need to map how corporate ownership had changed across East Asia, coupled with the rise of SWFs, provided strong motivation to spend the time and resources necessary to identify exactly who owned the region's major corporations and how the landscape had changed since 1996. The frequent desire for opacity on the part of the owners made it all the more compelling. Anecdotes about the rise of foreign

---

[1] The contributions of many of the participants were published in an edited volume, *Lessons from the Asian Financial Crisis* (Carney 2009).

state ownership suggested that there was the potential to unveil an important new trend, with SWFs playing an outsized role. Moreover, understanding these phenomena could yield important insights into the transition of power between the West and East and the emergence of a new statist-authoritarian order. This led to a multiyear effort compiling ultimate ownership data about the region's largest companies, culminating in a paper that was published in the *Journal of Financial Economics*.[2] The paper was the first to systematically document the prevalence of foreign state ownership of listed corporations across East Asia in addition to detailing how corporate ownership had changed within individual economies.

The paper argued that the most significant changes to corporate ownership within specific countries were attributable to whether those countries experienced regime change. This formed the beginnings of the argument for this book. Some of the early ideas linking the structure of political regimes to state ownership arrangements were developed in a follow-up paper that was published in the *Review of International Political Economy*.[3] I am grateful to have had the opportunity to present that paper to University of California San Diego's Graduate School of International Relations and Pacific Studies (now known as the School of Global Policy and Strategy), Stanford's Asia-Pacific Research Center, the Balsillie School of International Affairs, the Institute for Advanced Studies in Vienna, and the Manchester Business School. Constructive criticism at this early stage was very valuable to the development of this book's argument, and I would especially like to thank Miles Kahler, Stephan Haggard, Takeo Hoshi, John Ravenhill, Eric Helleiner, Johannes Pollak, and Xiaoke Zhang.

Subsequent work relating to corporate governance in China took shape through a chapter that appears in an edited volume about China's business-government relations.[4] I am grateful to Xiaoke Zhang and Zhu Tianbiao for the opportunity to present my ideas to workshops at Peking and Zhejiang Universities and for their thorough and insightful comments. These workshops proved to be excellent forums for thinking about China in relation to the political economies of the other East Asian states that I focused on in my aforementioned papers.

[2] Carney and Child (2013).   [3] Carney (2014).   [4] Carney (2017).

To have the time to think about, refine, and turn these ideas into a book, I am grateful to the Crawford School of Public Policy. I thank Llewelyn Hughes, who gave me the opportunity to present some of the early ideas at Crawford's Research Seminar series, where I received valuable feedback. For their support and encouragement at various stages in the development of this project, I also thank Andrew MacIntyre, Veronica Taylor, Jenny Corbett, Fariborz Moshirian, and Dave McKendrick.

I am especially grateful to Travers Barclay Child, my coauthor for the *Journal of Financial Economics* paper, who provided insightful comments on several chapters of this book at different stages of their development. Many other individuals generously took time out of their busy schedules to read early (and sometimes later) versions of some of the chapters, and their constructive criticism was particularly helpful to the project's final form. I especially thank Terence Gomez, Krislert Samphantharak, Natasha Hamilton-Hart, Stephen Howes, Jong-Sung You, Andy Kennedy, and John Ravenhill.

Comments during presentations at the China Europe International Business School (CEIBS) pushed my thinking about how SWFs influence target firms and led me to further refine the theoretical model. I am particularly grateful to Sam Park and Daniel Chng for their helpful suggestions. A presentation at the Institute of Asian Research at the University of British Columbia offered a valuable opportunity to present an updated version of the project to East Asia experts. I especially thank Yves Tiberghien for hosting my visit and Kai Ostwald for chairing the session. In the latter stages of this book's development, CEIBS proved to be a very supportive environment, and I am grateful to the terrific group of faculty members in the Strategy and Entrepreneurship Department for welcoming me.

At Cambridge University Press, I have been very fortunate to work with an excellent and supportive editor, Sara Doskow, who consistently offered prompt and thorough answers to my numerous queries throughout the entire process. I also thank the two anonymous reviewers who offered extensive and incisive comments.

Finally, I owe those closest to me special acknowledgment. My parents have maintained amazingly steadfast support and encouragement despite the numerous time zones that frequently separated us. My father also offered particularly helpful ideas that drew on his own professional background working with a large

Chinese state-owned enterprise. I also owe a special debt of gratitude to my partner, Michelle Zheng Xue. Despite numerous speed bumps that appeared on the path to the project's completion, she maintained unwavering support, offered extremely valuable suggestions, and was remarkably generous with her time. I am very fortunate to have her by my side. For these reasons, this book is dedicated to her.

1 | *Introduction*

On May 27, 2010, Malaysia's sovereign wealth fund (SWF) Khazanah initiated a hostile takeover of Asia's largest healthcare chain, Singapore-based Parkway.[1] The surprise move was implemented through Khazanah's newly established healthcare firm, Integrated Healthcare Holdings (IHH). Such an aggressive move by a SWF was nearly unheard of, and it was the first time that a SWF attempted a hostile takeover of a foreign firm.[2]

The acquisition was provoked by the actions of two billionaire brothers, Malvinder and Shivinder Singh, who controlled the largest private hospital chain in India through their firm, Fortis.[3] Two months earlier, Fortis bought just enough shares in Parkway to overtake Khazanah's dominant ownership position.[4] On hearing that the Singh brothers were sending out feelers to other stakeholders about selling their shares, Khazanah initiated its hostile takeover.[5] But before Khazanah's offer could be finalized, it would require approval by the shareholders, creating the potential for a bidding war.[6]

---

[1] Mathew (2010).

[2] Venkat, Holmes, and Tudor (2010). According to Dealogic, the only previous hostile bid by a SWF was a failed bid by Temasek for United Overseas Bank's property arm in 2004.

[3] Mathew (2010).

[4] The stake was bought from US buyout firm TPG for $685 million. Fortis, the firm owned by the Singh brothers, bought a 23.9 percent stake at $3.56 per share, a 14 percent premium over its closing price of $3.12. This amount was just enough to overtake Khazanah's 23.32 percent stake, which was bought in 2008.

[5] Hun (2010). At $3.78 per share, Khazanah's offer for a 51.5 percent ownership stake was committing the SWF to an additional $835 million.

[6] The *Edge Financial Daily* (2010). Most of the other shareholders were asset management companies, including Bank of New York Mellon Corp. (5.94 percent), Franklin Resources, Inc. (4.01 percent), Matthews International Capital (3.21 percent), BlackRock Investment Management LLC (1.69 percent), Ocean, Inc. (1.4 percent), and Mellon Global Management, Inc. (1.05 percent).

At stake was a big and rapidly growing medical tourism market.[7] In the eyes of Fortis and Khazanah, Parkway was worth fighting for as the only Pan-Asian medical care provider, making it an ideal foundation for a regional healthcare platform.[8]

After a series of offers and counteroffers, Khazanah finally prevailed.[9] The deal was the fifth-biggest acquisition of a Singaporean company in history.[10] Parkway would now be owned by Khazanah via IHH. About a month later, a new chairman and two non-executive directors were appointed to Parkway, leading to the departure of numerous top managers in subsequent months.[11]

This episode illustrates an important new trend in the global economy – state-owned entities that engage in increasingly aggressive foreign investment behavior. The government entity that has attracted the greatest attention is the SWF. SWFs are state-owned investment vehicles that invest globally in various types of assets ranging from financial to real to alternative assets. Notable examples include Singapore's Temasek, the China Investment Corporation, and Norway's Pension Fund Global.[12]

---

[7] Huifen (2010). After Thailand, Malaysia, India, and Singapore were the top destinations in Asia for medical tourists. Over the previous five years, the number of medical tourists to Asian countries had increased by approximately 20 to 30 percent each year, and medical tourism in Asia was estimated to be worth $4 billion by 2012 (Confederation of Indian Industries and McKinsey 2002).

[8] Hun (2010). Parkway had a network of sixteen hospitals in Singapore, Malaysia, China, India, Brunei, and the Middle East. Outside of China, Parkway was the largest healthcare group by market cap with a capitalization of S$3.4 billion (US$2.44 billion). Other major healthcare service providers in the region included Bangkok Dusit Medical Services PLC with a market cap of US$970 million, followed by Apollo Hospitals Enterprise in India (US$973 million), Fortis (US$989 million), and Bumrungrad International Hospital, also in Bangkok (US$688 million). Khazanah already held stakes in Pantai, Malaysia's largest hospital chain, and Apollo, the main rival to Fortis in India. Khazanah also owned IMU Health, which owns the International Medical University in Kuala Lumpur.

[9] Venkat, Holmes, and Tudor (2010). On July 1, the Singhs made a counteroffer to acquire 100 percent of Parkway at $3.80 per share, 2 cents more than Khazanah's offer of $3.78. The thin margin between the offers provoked Khazanah to raise its price. On July 26, Khazanah responded with an offer of $3.95 per share, prompting the Singh brothers to abandon their takeover efforts and relinquish control of the company. Fortis sold its stake to Khazanah for a profit of $84 million.

[10] Dealogic.   [11] Dow Jones International News (2010); Khalik (2011).

[12] The International Working Group of Sovereign Wealth Funds provides a more detailed definition of SWFs: SWFs are "special-purpose investment funds or arrangements that are owned by the general government. Created by the general government for macroeconomic purposes, SWFs hold, manage, or administer

In 2000, SWF assets amounted to approximately US$1 trillion. By 2007, they had increased to over US$3.3 trillion, with shares held in one of every five listed firms worldwide.[13] By 2015, SWF assets had risen to US$7.2 trillion. Moreover, seventeen of the twenty largest SWFs, accounting for approximately 75 percent of total SWF assets, are currently located in authoritarian regimes.[14] By comparison, private equity firms managed assets of around US$2.4 trillion, while hedge funds managed about US$3.2 trillion in assets in 2015, and they are primarily located in the United States and the United Kingdom.[15] Figure 1.1 shows the surge in the number of SWFs initiated since the late 1990s.

SWFs becoming more, rather than less, prominent in the global economy is both surprising and puzzling because such growth contradicts theories about the global diffusion of liberalizing reforms, as manifested by several waves of privatization since the 1980s.[16] According to this line of argument, regimes of all stripes should be reducing the state's role in the economy, including in the corporate sector, as liberalizing reforms spread across the world. However, many states have used the diffusion of liberalizing reforms to expand state investment. For example, from 2001 to 2012, governments acquired more assets through stock purchases ($1.52 trillion) than they sold through share issue privatizations and direct sales ($1.48 trillion),[17] with much of this state investment channeled through SWFs.[18]

---

assets to achieve financial objectives, and employ a set of investment strategies that include investing in foreign financial assets" (International Working Group of Sovereign Wealth Funds 2008). General government includes both central government and subnational government. The definition was developed in the context of drafting the Santiago Principles, which delineate generally accepted principles and practices for SWF activities.

[13] Fernandes (2009); Alhashel (2015). The average size of their stake is 0.74 percent of the outstanding shares of a firm.

[14] The top ten SWFs by assets control approximately 75 percent of total SWF assets, and nine of the ten are located in authoritarian regimes. Data come from the Sovereign Wealth Fund Institute (updated November 2017).

[15] Preqin (2016), Global Private Equity and Venture Capital Report; Preqin Global Hedge Fund Report, 2016.

[16] On the diffusion of liberalization, see Elkins and Simmons (2004), Simmons, Dobbin and Garrett (2006), Büthe and Mattli (2011), and Bach and Newman (2010).

[17] Reported in Megginson (2013), based on data from the Thomson Reuters SDC Platinum M&A database and Privatization Barometer, available at www.privatizationbarometer.net.

[18] Megginson and Fotak (2015).

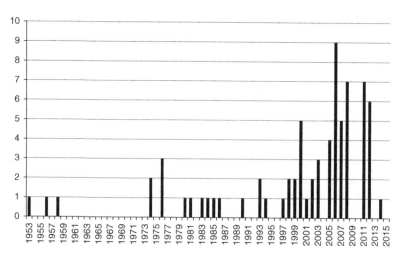

Figure 1.1 Number of SWFs established over time, 1953–2015.
Sources: Sovereign Wealth Fund Institute (2016) and Preqin Sovereign Wealth Fund Review (2016).

The rise of SWFs and other state-owned entities poses serious risks because of the tremendous scale of the assets they control, the risk that political objectives might influence their management, and their potential to influence or even control the most economically important corporations of foreign countries. Among advanced and most emerging economies, the firms of greatest importance to the national economy are usually publicly listed. Large-scale capital requirements lead these firms to sell shares to raise financing, in addition to other benefits associated with listing on a stock market (e.g., adopting market-oriented reforms to improve corporate governance and performance). However, this situation can also create the opportunity for investors with sufficient capital to buy a large enough stake in the firm to alter how it is governed. Because of their vast resources, SWFs are uniquely positioned to engage in these types of activities with regard to the world's largest firms. Understanding what drives this type of state investment behavior is this book's core research question: why do some states engage in more aggressive corporate intervention in foreign listed firms than others?

The hostile takeover initiated by Khazanah, Malaysia's SWF, is a prime example of aggressive state intervention. This type of investment behavior is indicative of the strategies employed by private equity firms.[19] Such firms purchase large stakes in target companies in order to implement value-enhancing strategies over the course of several years, often through management changes, streamlining operations, or expansion. Immediately following its takeover of Parkway, Khazanah appointed a new chairman and directors and integrated Parkway into its regional healthcare network. However, most SWFs act in a passive manner that involves exiting the investment when the SWF disagrees with management decisions. For example, the Brunei Investment Agency, which is headquartered next door to Malaysia, rarely takes large ownership positions and consistently adheres to a passive investment strategy.[20]

To explain the investment behavior of state entities such as SWFs, we must consider both the *capacity* of the state that owns them to engage in aggressive corporate interventions and whether the state possesses the *motivation* to do so. The capacity of a state to intervene aggressively in a foreign company depends on three attributes. First, the state must have a vehicle capable of initiating large ownership stakes that are held over an extended period of time, thereby enabling the implementation of major changes to target firms. This normally occurs either via SWFs or state-owned enterprises (SOEs; often owned by a SWF), but SWFs can facilitate this process by centralizing control over the activities of sprawling corporate assets, pooling resources and information, and identifying and assisting with investment opportunities on behalf of SOEs. But as I will discuss below, not all SWFs are equally suited to engaging in large, long-term holdings of foreign corporations. Second, the state must provide adequate transparency about the vehicle initiating the investment so that private investors can properly value the risk associated with co-investing with it and so that host country officials can decide whether to permit the investment. Third, the state investment vehicle must be capable of and willing to manage its ownership stake alongside other private investors (in a public-private co-ownership arrangement). This setup can be challenging for some states and private investors when the state entity seeks to intervene in firm governance.

State capacity is a necessary, but insufficient, condition. For example, some SWFs may take a large position in a listed firm but are unwilling to

---

[19] Armour and Cheffins (2011).
[20] Chapter 2 provides a detailed discussion of the range of activist tactics that SWFs (and SOEs) can deploy.

put pressure on managers to alter firm strategy. States must also be motivated to intervene aggressively. The most fundamental motivation driving state investment behavior regards leaders' desire to remain in power. For democratic leaders, institutional constraints normally restrict the duration of their position, granting an opportunity for members either of the same party or an opposing party to hold the position. For authoritarian rulers, institutional constraints are normally weaker, thereby granting political incumbents the opportunity to hold on to power for a longer, potentially indefinite, duration. Thus the strongest motivation to intervene arises from threats to authoritarian rulers' hold on power.[21] To the extent that such authoritarian leaders rely on state ownership of large corporations to maintain their rule, two threats are of particular salience – the crowding-out effects that accompany economic development and economic liberalization. Both of these threats enhance the ability of private capital to challenge incumbent rulers and the SOEs they rely on to preserve their rule. To account for the varying capacity and motivation of states to intervene aggressively in foreign listed firms, I offer a novel political explanation.

A New Political Explanation

I argue that the propensity for a state to engage in aggressive foreign corporate interventions depends on the structure of its political regime. My argument differs from the existing literature on SWFs and SOEs in two important ways. First, I focus on common underlying political determinants of SWFs and SOEs. Because both of these entities are controlled by the government, with SOEs often owned by a SWF, similar political pressures influence their behavior. Yet the literature on the political determinants of SWFs examines them separately from SOEs.[22] Moreover, the literature on SOEs largely developed before the rise of SWFs.[23] A common political explanation is therefore lacking.

The second difference concerns the political determinants themselves. The literature on both SWFs and SOEs has overlooked an important political development since the end of the Cold War – the

---

[21] For discussions on autocrats, see Tullock (1987), Wintrobe (1998), and Haber (2006); on democracies, see Mayhew (1974).

[22] For a review of the literature on SWFs, see Megginson and Fotak (2015) and Alhashel (2015).

[23] For an overview of the literature on SOEs, see Megginson and Netter (2001).

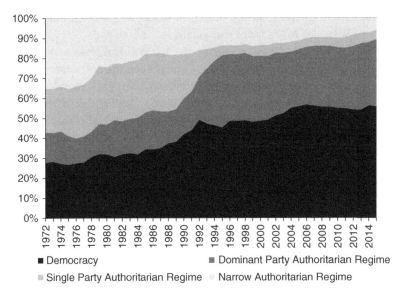

Figure 1.2 The prevalence of political regimes, 1972–2015.

Note: Narrow authoritarian regimes have an *ifhpol* score lower than 7 out of 10 without the representation of multiple parties in a legislature; single-party authoritarian regimes have an *ifhpol* score lower than 7 and a legislature with a single party; dominant-party authoritarian regimes have an *ifhpol* score lower than 7 and a legislature with multiple parties; democracies have an *ifhpol* score of 7 or above. The *ifhpol* score combines the Freedom House and Polity IV scores to generate a democracy index that encompasses more countries than either index alone. It comes from Hadenius et al. (2007), Authoritarian Regimes Data Set, version 5.0. Whether countries have a legislature with multiple parties is based on the *lparty* variable from Cheibub, Gandhi, and Vreeland's (2010) Democracy and Dictatorship Revisited data set for data from 1972 to 2008. Both variables have been updated to 2015. For additional details, see Chapter 3.

rise of dominant-party authoritarian regimes (DPARs). Few would have predicted that the "third wave" of democratization, which came to a halt in the mid-1990s, would be eclipsed by the diffusion of DPARs into the first decade of the twenty-first century.[24] However, DPARs are now the most common type of authoritarian rule, constituting one-third of the total number of regimes in the world, as illustrated in Figure 1.2. Given the contemporary importance of DPARs, it is critical

---

[24] Huntington (1991).

to understand the relationship of these regimes to the corporate sector and to SWFs and SOEs more specifically.

I argue that characteristics specific to each political regime affect the capacity and motivation of a state to intervene in the corporate sector. I place political regimes into one of four categories: (1) narrow authoritarian regimes (NARs), (2) single-party authoritarian regimes (SPARs), (3) dominant-party authoritarian regimes (DPARs), and (4) democracies.[25] NARs are those in which no meaningful competition for political office occurs, such as a monarchy or those ruled by the military (e.g., Brunei and Myanmar until 2012). To secure their rule, political elites in these regimes monopolize the control of information and resources – unlisted SOEs are one manifestation of this. SPARs are those in which a ruling party monopolizes the political arena by occupying all the seats in the national legislature and proscribing political opposition (e.g., China, Vietnam, and Laos). Competition for political office occurs within the party but not between parties, yielding a modest loosening of the control over information and resources. Consequently, partially state-owned enterprises are more likely to arise. DPARs hold elections in which competing political parties vie for public office, but rarely do these elections result in the handover of power. The usual result is a dominant ruling party with opposition parties holding a small minority of legislative seats (e.g., Malaysia and Singapore). The ruling party dominates the control of politically sensitive information and resources, though opposition parties also gain limited access, which corresponds to an increased reliance on partially state-owned enterprises. Finally, democracies are those in which competitive elections occur between candidates from multiple parties. Access to politically sensitive information and resources is not restricted to members of any single group or political party, and this corresponds to relatively few corporations with state ownership (e.g., Japan, South Korea, and the Philippines).

I argue that among the four political regimes, DPARs have the greatest capacity and motivation to intervene aggressively in foreign listed firms. With regard to capacity, DPARs are relatively more likely

[25] For discussions on the classification of democratic regimes, see Lijphart (1999), Przeworski et al. (2000), and Golder (2005). On the classification of authoritarian regimes, see Geddes (2003), Gandhi and Przeworski (2006), Gandhi (2008), Hadenius and Teorell (2007), Magaloni (2008), and Magaloni and Kricheli (2010).

to host mixed public-private corporations, corresponding to their semirestricted control of information and resources. Because of their capacity to host hybrid SOEs in the home market, DPARs can more easily engage in public-private ownership in foreign markets. Compared with other authoritarian regimes (i.e., SPARs and NARs), DPARs can also meet the transparency requirements of a larger set of foreign countries in order to acquire a large position in a target firm. Additionally, DPARs are more likely to have a strong motivation to intervene in the corporate sector compared with other regimes because they permit opposition parties to compete in elections but are unwilling to hand over power. As the threat of political opposition rises, DPAR leaders will engage in more aggressive tactics to protect their rule. An implication of this argument is that China's SOEs and SWFs are not as aggressive with their foreign investments as they can be; instead, Malaysia's SOEs and SWFs display more aggressive behavior compared with any other state entities in East Asia. This behavior is attributable not only to their regime differences but also to China's lack of a fully functional savings SWF. To appreciate why this matters, we must consider the varying types of SWFs and their role in mediating government involvement in the corporate sector.

The Importance of Savings SWFs to State Intervention

SWFs are conventionally categorized as foreign exchange reserve funds, stabilization funds, pension reserve funds, or savings funds.[26] As the name suggests, foreign exchange reserve funds are funded by foreign exchange reserves. Their purpose is to invest these funds overseas to reduce the negative carry costs of holding reserves or to earn higher returns on ample reserves through sizable allocations to equities and alternative investments.[27] However, a stockpile of reserves must be available at short notice to defend the value of the currency; thus these funds generally do not take large positions to be held for a long period. Therefore, reserve funds are invested in a relatively passive, diversified

---

[26] These categories are based on IMF and Santiago Principles taxonomies. Development funds are sometimes identified as a separate category, but following IMF economists (Kunzel et al. 2011), I group them together with savings funds. See IMF (2007, 2008).

[27] For example, up to 50 percent of reserves in South Korea and 75 percent for Singapore's GIC.

manner that generally maintains a small ownership stake in any one company.[28]

The purpose of stabilization funds is to buffer the economy – usually the financial markets – from external shocks. To this end, stabilization funds will invest in equities to buffer stock market volatility (e.g., Taiwan's Stabilization Fund), but this is normally short-lived because it is simply intended to stabilize the market. When they are not invested in domestic equities, stabilization funds invest primarily in a highly liquid portfolio of assets, such as fixed-income and government securities, that are not strongly correlated with boom/bust cycles.[29]

By comparison, the purpose of pension reserve funds is to invest so as to meet future expenditures associated with an aging population. In essence, pension reserve SWFs act as a commitment mechanism for politicians who might prefer to spend their countries' wealth today instead of saving it for future generations (e.g., Australia, Ireland, and New Zealand). These funds are more likely to initiate long-term ownership positions through equities purchases, but they are unlikely to pursue political objectives at the expense of prudent portfolio allocation. They differ from traditional pension funds in that they have no designated claimants on the available assets; rather, the legal or beneficial owner is the institution that administers the public pension system (social security reserve funds) or the government (sovereign pension reserve funds). This feature exposes them to potentially greater state influence than pension funds,[30] but because the purpose of these funds is specifically intended for the aging population and they are located primarily in Organisation for Economic Co-operation and Development (OECD) countries, pension reserve funds exhibit the highest levels of transparency and compliance with the Santiago Principles concerning SWF best practices compared with other types of SWFs.[31] Hence discretionary investment strategies are significantly curtailed.

The aim of savings funds is to share wealth across generations. This objective leads to investments via a high risk-return profile, including

---

[28] Al-Hassan et al. (2013).
[29] The IMF Global Stability Report (2012) indicates that fixed-income securities occupy 80 percent of the portfolio of these funds, with government securities consisting of around 70 percent of total assets.
[30] Yermo (2008).   [31] Bagnall and Truman (2013).

a high proportion of equities and other investments.[32] But because these funds are not specifically targeted for pension payments or other funding obligations, officials have more freedom to choose how they invest. Although many seek to transform commodities assets into diversified financial assets, this condition is a relatively minor restriction that grants significant freedom to decide how investment allocations are made. Consequently, savings funds are the most capable of taking large, long-term corporate ownership positions.

As shown in Figure 1.1, the number of SWFs has increased since 1997, suggesting that the Asian financial crisis may have spurred their creation. Although the crisis led to "profound changes in the demand for international reserves, increasing over time the hoarding by affected countries," more reserves did not necessarily equate to more SWFs.[33] The new reserve SWFs that have been created in Asia since 1997 (e.g., Korea Investment Corporation and China Investment Corporation) are relatively few in comparison with the number of countries that have accumulated them without also creating a reserve SWF (e.g., Malaysia, Indonesia, Thailand, and the Philippines). Indeed, most of the SWFs created since 1997 are savings funds rather than reserve funds.[34] Worldwide, more than half of all SWFs are savings funds, followed by stabilization funds at approximately 30 percent, with pension (9 percent) and reserve funds (7 percent) being relatively few in number. Savings funds therefore deserve close scrutiny both because they are the most capable of taking large, long-term corporate ownership positions and because they are the most prevalent type of SWF.

The Existing Literature with Regard to SOEs and SWFs

Because SWFs are a relatively recent phenomenon, the existing literature has mainly focused on SOEs to explain the varied nature of state intervention in the corporate sector. I therefore begin by discussing the literature on SOEs.

---

[32] Their equity allocation commonly exceeds 70 percent (Al-Hassan et al. 2013). Development funds are another class of SWF established to allocate resources to priority socioeconomic projects, usually infrastructure. I follow Al-Hassan et al. (2013) in grouping them together with saving funds.

[33] Aizenman and Glick (2009).

[34] See Al-Hassan (2013) and Megginson and Fotak (2015). Since 2008, most of the new SWFs were created in relation to the management of natural resources, usually oil (Megginson and Fotak 2015).

State-Owned Enterprises

There are two dominant views regarding the state's role with regard to SOEs. The first perspective emphasizes the public benefits that SOEs can generate, including a welfare role and their capacity to compensate for institutional voids. The second perspective considers the political benefits to business owners or politicians from state participation. The first public benefit that SOEs can serve occurs via a welfare role. For example, governments may force SOEs to reduce unemployment, invest in geographically remote areas, cater to less-profitable customer segments, or keep prices low.[35] State ownership may also be desirable when some quality-based dimensions are difficult to measure and enforce, as with pay-for-performance contracts to promote effective student learning in schools.[36] Finally, state ownership may be necessary for the successful financing and completion of long-term projects that private investors are unwilling or unable to fund.[37]

State ownership can also help to overcome institutional "voids" in product, labor, and financial markets that reduce the potential productive efficiency of a country.[38] Such voids are likely to occur among countries in the early stages of development. The state can step in to compensate for these voids by providing capital in cases where financial markets are underdeveloped or by coordinating the local deployment of complementary resources where product markets are underdeveloped.[39] The early industrial development of many countries was often associated with massive state involvement through SOEs or state-owned development agencies.[40]

However, the public benefits view of SOEs fails to explain a wide range of state interventions. On the one hand, this gap arises from questions about how the state reconciles competing welfare demands or how it chooses which institutional voids to fill. With limited resources, the state must make political decisions about how to allocate them. On the other hand, empirical questions arise as to why some countries with few institutional voids maintain high levels of state ownership, such as Singapore, or why countries with low development

---

[35] Bai and Xu (2005); Shirley and Nellis (1991).
[36] Hart, Shleifer, and Vishny (1997).   [37] Kaldor (1980); McDermott (2003).
[38] Khanna and Palepu (2000); Peng et al. (2009); Musacchio and Lazzarini (2014).
[39] Cameron (1961); Gerschenkron (1962); Aghion (2011); Mazzucato (2011); Rodrik (2007).
[40] Wade (1990); Haggard (1990); Evans (1995); Amsden (2001).

have so few SOEs compared with countries at comparable or higher levels of development, such as the Philippines in comparison with Malaysia.

The political view posits that politically connected firms can benefit from state intervention in the corporate sector. By acting as intermediaries for the distribution of state resources, SOEs may grant politically connected firms preferential access to government contracts or financing. For example, in a study of emerging markets, state-owned banks were found to lend more than private banks during election years.[41] The moral hazard accompanying this practice magnifies the problem, also known as the *soft budget constraint*.[42] The provision of abundant capital by the state will increase the likelihood of misallocation and inefficient bailouts. This is likely to result in bad investments and the use of public funds to rescue failed projects. Additionally, politically connected firms may successfully lobby government officials for the selective enforcement of costly regulations, giving them a competitive advantage over their rivals. Thus the political view predicts that state ownership and state strategic support for private firms will be more common in countries with weak institutions where corruption and cronyism can flourish.[43]

Politicians with authority over SOEs can likewise use these firms for direct political gain.[44] As a result, SOE managers are often poorly selected and lack the necessary incentives to pursue efficiency and profitability relative to private firms.[45] In some cases, direct conflicts of interest arise when SOE managers may themselves be appointed politicians or political allies. Consequently, compensation schemes are often not linked to economic performance but instead follow bureaucratic criteria such as hierarchy and seniority.[46]

However, focusing only on political benefits to political leaders and their cronies fails to explain a wide variety of state interventions. Specifically, this view disregards the capacity for political institutions to reduce investment risks such as expropriation risk and contracting

---

[41] Dinç (2005).   [42] Kornai (1979); Lin and Tan (1999).
[43] Ades and Di Tella (1997); Megginson and Netter (2001)
[44] Chong and López-de-Silanes (2005); Cui and Jiang (2012); La Porta and López-de-Silanes, (1999); Shleifer (1998).
[45] Boardman and Vining (1989); Dharwadkar et al. (2000); La Porta and López-de-Silanes (1999); Vickers and Yarrow (1988).
[46] Dixit (2002).

risk, thereby decreasing the inefficient allocation of state resources or selective regulatory enforcement. For example, political institutions can be designed to constrain the self-serving behavior of politicians. If threats to the survival of the regime are severe enough, then political leaders may implement new political arrangements that limit their rent-seeking capacity and thereby reduce expropriation risk. North and Weingast illustrate how the English parliament, under severe pressure to deal with crushing sovereign debt, successfully curtailed the expropriation powers of the king, yielding declines to the cost of capital and the subsequent development of stock and bond markets.[47] Stasavage further demonstrated that the benefits associated with the addition of parliamentary veto power over the executive were contingent on the heterogeneity of policy preferences among members of parliament.[48]

In addition to successfully reducing expropriation risk, political institutions can also help reduce a second type of investment risk – contracting risk.[49] Jensen et al. find that authoritarian regimes with legislatures and multiple parties yield improvements to investor protections by creating a forum for agreements that can reduce contracting risk.[50] Even though the executive retains confiscatory powers (i.e., expropriation risk), legislatures still serve a useful function by permitting nonstate/private actors to negotiate, monitor, and enforce agreements among themselves, thereby reducing the potential for selective or discriminatory regulatory enforcement.[51] Although Jensen et al. explicitly say that their argument does not apply to SOEs, there are good reasons to think that it might have traction with respect to *partially* state-owned enterprises whose performance depends on a properly functioning marketplace. By extension, SWFs with equity stakes in publicly listed firms will also value the reduction of contracting risk.

Sovereign Wealth Funds

A surge of recent research seeks to explain SWF investment behavior from different disciplinary perspectives, including finance,[52] strategy,[53]

[47] North and Weingast (1989).   [48] Stasavage (2002).
[49] North (1991); Acemoglu and Johnson (2005).   [50] Jensen et al. (2014).
[51] Ibid.   [52] Megginson and Fotak (2015).
[53] Johan et al. (2013); Vasudeva (2013).

political economy,[54] economics,[55] international law,[56] and organizational theory.[57] These studies recognize that SWFs can potentially have a tremendous impact on the firms in which they invest. SWFs' control of vast resources allows them to take sizable ownership positions in listed companies, thus allowing the SWF to intervene in the management of the firm and force changes such as initiating mergers and acquisitions or divestitures, expanding the firm's business prospects by partnering with other firms also owned by the SWF, or even changing the CEO and top management team.[58] As mentioned earlier, Malaysia's SWF, Khazanah, initiated a hostile takeover of Parkway Health in 2010. It subsequently replaced the top executives and integrated the firm into Khazanah's regional healthcare network (i.e., IHH).

Despite the propensity toward activism by some SWFs, most SWFs follow more passively oriented investment strategies.[59] SWFs employing a passive strategy usually acquire a relatively small ownership stake in a target firm and then sell the stake if they disagree with the strategic decisions of the firm. Brunei's SWF, the Brunei Investment Authority, is typical of SWFs with a passive strategy – it rarely takes large ownership positions in listed firms. Passive SWFs may sometimes take a large stake (>5 percent) simply because the target firm is perceived to be a good investment, illustrating that the size of the SWF's position is a necessary, but insufficient, condition for governance activism. For example, the China Investment Corporation occasionally takes ownership stakes greater than 5 percent but refrains from intervening in the invested firm.[60] However, some SWFs engage in limited forms of governance activism despite owning a small stake (<5 percent), such as engaging in informal discussions with management or submitting shareholder proposals for the proxy statement. Such proposals can include a range of corporate governance requests such as separating the chairman and CEO, placing alternative board candidates on the

---

[54] Clark et al. (2013); Gelpern (2011); Musacchio and Lazzarini (2014).
[55] Balding (2012); Gelb et al. (2014); Das et al. (2009).
[56] Bird-Pollan (2012); Epstein and Rose (2009); Gilson and Milhaupt (2008).
[57] Bagnall and Truman (2013); Clark et al. (2013). See Aguilera et al. (2016) for a review of the literature.
[58] Dewenter et al. (2010); Rose (2014).
[59] Kotter and Lel (2011); Bortolotti, Fotak, and Megginson (2015); Megginson and Fotak (2015).
[60] Koch-Weser and Haacke (2013).

company's proxy card for the company's annual shareholder meeting, or requesting the firm to address social/environmental issues. Norway's Government Pension Fund Global has recently engaged in these kinds of tactics.

The prevailing view is that domestic political arrangements have the greatest influence on SWF activities.[61] For example, in a special issue about SWFs in China, Singapore, Saudi Arabia, and Norway, Helleiner concludes that "the political logic that drives [SWFs'] behavior is much more often *domestically* than internationally focused."[62] While Clark, Dixon, and Monk point to the importance of both domestic and international legitimacy as influencing the governance of SWFs, a critical dimension of this governance – transparency – seems to be determined primarily by domestic factors.[63] If foreign regulations were the primary determinant of SWF transparency, then such high variance would not exist; we would instead observe uniformly high levels of transparency as SWFs cater to foreign regulators. Aizenman and Glick, for example, identify a strong correlation between the domestic governance indicator "voice and accountability" and SWF transparency.[64] Other studies corroborate this view. For example, Bernstein, Lerner, and Schoar find that SWFs invest more in firms headquartered in the home country (45 percent) versus firms headquartered in foreign countries (31 percent).[65] In another study, Bortolotti, Fotak, and Megginson find that SWFs take director board seats in only 6.74 percent of foreign investments compared with 30.3 percent of domestic investments.[66] Finally, Dewenter, Han, and Malatesta report that SWF activist tactics are twice as common for board representation, senior management turnover, and government influence when the target is a home-country firm.[67] Thus there is a growing body of work suggesting that the home country is of primary importance to SWF investment behavior.

---

[61] For a comprehensive review of the literature on SWFs, see Megginson and Fotak (2015).

[62] Helleiner (2009). On China and Singapore, see Shih (2009); on Saudi Arabia, see Smith Diwan (2009); on Norway, see Tranoy (2009).

[63] Clark, Dixon, and Monk (2013).   [64] Aizenman and Glick (2009).

[65] Bernstein, Lerner, and Schoar (2013). They use a sample of twenty-nine SWFs with 2,662 transactions between January 1984 and December 2007.

[66] Bortolotti, Fotak, and Megginson (2015). Their sample includes 1,018 investments by nineteen SWFs over the January 1980 to November 2012 period.

[67] Dewenter, Han, and Malatesta (2010). Their sample includes nineteen SWFs from January 1987 to April 2008, including 227 SWF purchase events.

However, this emergent literature has four limitations. First, it often treats SWFs as a homogeneous group. Without considering the limitations imposed on SWF activities due to their investment objectives (as with savings, stability, reserve, and pension SWFs), making comparisons among them can be problematic. Second, the literature either identifies broad correlations between SWF characteristics and political regimes (e.g., transparency and the level of democracy), or it focuses on individual country cases. Consequently, important patterns regarding SWF activities specific to certain political regimes have been overlooked. Third, as mentioned earlier, much of the SWF literature is divorced from the SOE literature. But because SOEs increasingly mix public and private ownership, with the public component frequently administered by a SWF, considering them together is necessary. Fourth, neither the SOE nor the SWF literature considers the rise of DPARs since the mid-1990s and how the impact of this type of regime differs from that of other regimes. To explain the varied nature of state involvement in the corporate sector while addressing these shortcomings in the existing literature, I now turn to my argument.

Summary of the Argument

I argue that the aggressiveness of state intervention in foreign listed firms is determined by the capacity and motivation of the home state to intervene. State capacity to intervene is determined by the type of political regime and the extent of control over information and resources that rulers depend on for regime survival. The motivation to intervene arises from efforts of rulers to reduce risks to regime survival, which is also determined by the structure of the political regime.

State Capacity to Intervene

As mentioned earlier, I place political regimes into one of four categories. Political leaders in these regimes engage in varying degrees of control over information and resources to uphold their rule. Such controls are tightest in NARs and loosen as one proceeds toward democracy. SOEs manifest these varying degrees of control with regard to their level of transparency and the nature of state ownership (i.e., wholly state owned, partially state owned, or no state ownership).

Regimes with a predominance of state ownership – authoritarian regimes – are more likely to host a savings SWF because these have the greatest capacity for large, long-term ownership stakes, and they facilitate the centralized administration of the state's sprawling corporate assets. Democracies will be more likely to have foreign exchange reserve, macro-stability, or pension SWFs.

With regard to the implications for state capacity to intervene in foreign corporations, NARs will have a relatively low capacity because of their preference for wholly state-owned enterprises coupled with low transparency. Private investors will be reluctant to co-invest with a state entity that discloses little information. Host governments will also be reluctant to permit investments in local firms without a sufficient level of transparency about the investing entity. Democratic states will also have a reduced capacity to intervene in foreign corporations because state ownership will be relatively low (many types of activist shareholder tactics require a large ownership stake). SPARs and DPARs will have the greatest capacity to intervene in foreign firms because they will be the most likely to host partially state-owned enterprises, and they will be more inclined than NARs to meet the disclosure requirements of host governments. However, DPARs possess a greater capacity than SPARs because their SOEs have more balanced public-private ownership, which is favorable to private investors, and because DPARs can meet a higher transparency threshold, which allows them to access more foreign markets.

State Motivation to Intervene

Among the three types of authoritarian regimes, incumbent leaders of DPARs face the most persistent threats to regime stability.[68] These regimes permit multiparty elections that commonly yield legislative representation for opposition parties even though competition is

---

[68] I refer to the persistence of electoral threats that DPAR leaders confront in contrast to the frequently unexpected and violent uprisings common to other forms of authoritarian rule and that contribute to their greater instability. Like democratically elected representatives, DPAR leaders are continually concerned with their popular standing at election time. The regularity of these elections coupled with the opportunity for political opponents and citizens to voice (in a limited fashion) their opinions, in addition to other institutional features, makes DPARs more stable. See Magaloni and Kricheli (2010) for a review of the literature on the threats these different regimes confront and their varying capacity to deal with them.

restricted. From this toehold, opposition parties can pose an increasing threat to the ruling party. One source of threat emerges from the institutional capacity of DPARs to reduce investment risk, which yields a larger presence for private capital. As the economy develops, tensions will increase with regard to the state's presence in the corporate sector – the ruling party must balance the need for political control via SOEs with the need to maintain popular support by reducing SOEs' crowding-out effects. Opposition parties can tap into private capital's desire for a reduced state-sector presence in the economy.

Economic liberalization magnifies the opportunities for private capital, thereby producing more powerful business owners who will seek more political representation to voice their preference for a reduced role for the state. But when political opponents threaten to depose the ruling party, I expect incumbent leaders of DPARs to react in two ways: (1) they will aggressively intervene in the domestic corporate sector to strengthen the state's control of vital resources and information, and (2) they will aggressively pursue higher investment returns in foreign markets to maintain the support of voter-investors and attempt to alleviate crowding-out effects to placate domestic business.

The story about Khazanah and Parkway matches this prediction. In 2008, Malaysia's ruling party coalition, Barisan Nasional (BN), suffered its worst electoral outcome since the country's independence in 1957. Following this election, the government engaged in a range of aggressive tactics via state-owned entities (SWFs and SOEs) to bolster the BN's support from strategically important groups and to aggressively improve investment returns. Khazanah's hostile takeover of Parkway is one manifestation of this.

Organization of This Book

Chapter 2 elaborates the argument more fully and systematically. It develops the theoretical model to be tested in subsequent chapters with global, regional, and individual country evidence. Chapters 3 and 4 focus on measures for the *capacity* of different regimes to engage in aggressive interventions in foreign listed firms, including the scope of public-private ownership, state- and corporate-sector transparency, and SWF indicators. Chapter 3 engages in quantitative tests of the predicted relationships with global data. In this chapter, I use a measure for state ownership of corporations that captures the extent of government intervention in the economy through both listed and unlisted firms. Although this general measure fails to identify specific ownership positions for the state in relation to families and other shareholders, it is useful for gauging the overall importance of SOEs to all types of regimes (i.e., including those that do not have a stock market and therefore lack SOEs with public-private ownership). I also examine various measures of political, corporate, and SWF transparency in addition to the prevalence of different SWF types across political regimes.

Chapter 4 narrows the focus to East Asia. This region is of intrinsic interest because it is the fastest growing in the world with the largest contribution to global gross domestic product (GDP). Methodologically, this region is well suited for this research topic because East Asian countries offer sufficient heterogeneity to examine regimes from each of the four categories. The chapter presents a descriptive overview of states' "capacity" characteristics from before to after the Asian financial crisis. This includes detailed assessments regarding the prevalence of state ownership of large firms in each country in relation to private ownership and how this public-private ownership balance changed over time. I also examine various cross-national state- and corporate-sector transparency measures over time. Finally, I survey the types of SWFs that states have established, their transparency, and their propensity for large corporate holdings both domestically and in foreign markets.

Chapters 5 through 7 present analytic narratives of countries that typify each regime type. The aim is to establish whether the necessary capacity conditions are met and then examine whether states have sufficient motivation to aggressively intervene in foreign listed firms. Chapter 5 studies a NAR, a SPAR, and a regime that transitioned from a SPAR to a democracy. For the case of a NAR, I examine Brunei, which has a savings SWF – the Brunei Investment Agency. Brunei is a useful NAR to study because it experienced an economic crisis in 1998 that illustrates how this type of regime responds to the risks associated with economic liberalization. Neither North Korea nor Myanmar experienced a comparable shock. Brunei is also an interesting case because its political regime resembles many of those located in the Middle East, a region that hosts many large SWFs. Through the investigation of Brunei, we can draw useful insights for these other oil-rich monarchies.

For a SPAR, I examine China, which has several SWFs, including the China Investment Corporation, the State Administration of Foreign Exchange, and the National Social Security Fund. Focusing on China is also beneficial because it has liberalized its economy far more extensively than the other two SPAR candidates – Vietnam and Laos – enabling comparisons to be drawn for other authoritarian regimes in the region that have also liberalized their economies, such as Singapore and Malaysia. I also choose to focus on China because of its intrinsic importance both globally and regionally.

Finally, I study a country that transitioned from a SPAR to democracy – Taiwan. Taiwan underwent regime change over the last several decades while retaining a commitment to openness, especially with the United States. Thus we can assess whether regime change exhibited corresponding changes to the nature of state involvement in the corporate sector. I focus on Taiwan rather than Japan because the latter did not experience a financial crisis in 1997–98, making it difficult to draw comparisons with the reactions of other regimes in the region. I also choose to focus on Taiwan rather than South Korea because the former hosts political parties that are strong and more capable of overcoming coordination problems. As discussed in Chapter 2, a regime's coordination capacity influences its ability to implement nontargeted goods and services such as a SWF. In comparison with the Philippines, a country with weak coordination capacity, Taiwan's political system provides a cleaner test for this argument than South Korea's.

Chapters 6 and 7 examine two DPARs – Malaysia and Singapore. These regimes are of interest because they share several important features in common while differing with respect to one key dimension that can account for their varying levels of state intervention. The features that they share in common include (1) well-established stock markets where they have listed most of their SOEs, (2) large, economically significant savings SWFs, (3) a sustained high level of growth over a long period of time, which allows for examination of how these regimes have coped with the rising pressures associated with the state's crowding-out effects, (4) the early implementation of liberalizing reforms that permit a longer time span to be examined to test the theory's predictions, and (5) having the distinction of being the two oldest DPARs in the world (Malaysia and Singapore gained independence in 1957 and 1965, respectively), thus granting sufficient time for each regime's institutional arrangements to produce regularized patterns concerning state involvement in the corporate sector. The key dimension of difference between them regards the level of threat to each regime's ruling party since the Asian financial crisis. Malaysia's ruling party became weakly dominant following the 1997 crisis, and it has confronted a growing threat from political opponents ever since, whereas Singapore's ruling party has remained strongly dominant.

I conclude in Chapter 8. I begin by concisely summarizing the argument and evidence. I then discuss this book's theoretical contributions to several additional literatures and to the SOE and SWF literatures mentioned in this chapter, including the role of the state to spur economic development in the presence of weak institutions, the stability and growth of DPARs, comparative corporate governance, and the global diffusion of liberalizing reforms. Finally, I offer some thoughts about areas for future research, including additional work on SWFs, the role of SWFs as institutional intermediaries, state-owned business groups within and between countries, the nature of state investment between countries with large state sectors, and extending the framework developed here to other aspects of "economic statecraft."

2 | Theory

This book's core research question is: why do some states engage in more aggressive interventions in foreign-listed firms than others? To answer this question, I begin by classifying states according to four regime types, including narrow authoritarian regime (NAR), single-party authoritarian regime (SPAR), dominant-party authoritarian regime (DPAR), and democracy. Each regime type possesses institutional characteristics that differentiate it from the others. As shown in Figure 2.1, these regime characteristics influence each state's capacity and motivation to intervene in the corporate sector, and these, in turn, influence whether that intervention is more passive or aggressive.

I develop the core theoretical framework by first explaining how regime characteristics influence a state's *capacity* to intervene. This first step allows me to narrow the list of political regimes with the potential to engage in aggressive corporate intervention from four down to two – SPARs and DPARs. I then explain how regime characteristics influence incumbent rulers' *motivation* to intervene, that is, those regimes that are the most likely to confront persistent and severe threats to their survival. This further narrows the list from two regimes down to one – DPARs.

The core theoretical framework assumes that each regime type has a similar capacity to establish a sovereign wealth fund (SWF) and that SWFs are equally effective in implementing investment strategies. At the end of the chapter I offer an extension to account for states' varying capacity to establish a SWF within each regime type as well as their varying effectiveness at initiating foreign investments – *coordination capacity*. This extension provides a more complete picture of how regime characteristics determine state investment and governance strategies.

The Dependent Variable

The dependent variable is the extent of state intervention in foreign listed firms. State intervention is composed of two parts – shareholder

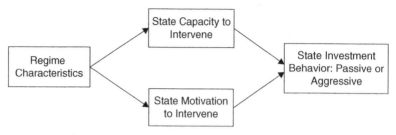

Figure 2.1 Theoretical model.

activism and extra-shareholder tactics.[1] *Shareholder activism* specifically refers to actions that the co-owner of a firm, alongside other shareholders, can deploy to alter a firm's governance and/or behavior. Because shareholding involves the ownership of stock in a company listed on a stock market, shareholder activism applies to publicly listed firms. For this reason, shareholder activism is a subset of the full range of state intervention tactics that a state can pursue in its dealings with the corporate sector. For example, state intervention can also extend to unlisted firms and a host of activities that do not depend on owning stock in a company, such as industry regulations, tariffs, government procurement initiatives, and development programs. I label these *extra-shareholder tactics*. The extent of shareholder activism that a state entity (SWF or state-owned enterprise [SOE]) pursues may be supplemented by extra-shareholder tactics.

Shareholder Activism

In the context of the existing literature on state involvement in the corporate sector, shareholder activism is a relatively recent addition. The global spread of privatization since the 1980s, coupled with financial crises among emerging economies during the 1990s and 2000s, expanded interest in the topic of corporate governance, contributing to an increase in the prevalence of shareholder activism among state-owned corporate entities (SWFs and SOEs).[2]

Shareholder activism applies to a range of activities that fall along a continuum with regard to whether they are passive or highly activist.

[1] See Megginson (2016) for an overview of state ownership and state capitalism.
[2] Megginson (2016).

Passive behavior simply involves selling an ownership position in a listed firm. As one proceeds toward the opposite end, more activist tactics become available, and these typically require larger ownership stakes to implement. The types of behaviors and tactics that fall along this continuum are best enumerated with reference to the institutional investors that typically deploy them.

Mutual funds and pension funds commonly engage in a limited range of activism due, in part, to legal constraints on their investment activities to ensure the preservation of capital on behalf of their clients. Their activist behaviors are confined to discussions with company management or directors, submitting shareholder proposals for the proxy statement (ballot), and voting on the proxy statement. With regard to shareholder proposals, these can include a range of corporate governance issues such as separating the chairman and CEO or placing alternative board candidates on the company's proxy card for the company's annual shareholder meeting (i.e., proxy access). Shareholder proposals can also include issues regarding executive compensation such as executive-compensation clawbacks or limits to executive compensation. Shareholder proposals may also concern social/environmental issues. Although these tactics are available to all shareholders, institutional investors with small stakes are unlikely to pursue them because of the time and resources necessary for such behavior.[3] However, investors with long-term holdings, such as pension funds, do display a greater propensity for shareholder engagement.

In contrast to mutual funds and pension funds, hedge funds can deploy a wider range of activist tactics. These may involve seeking board representation, suing the company for breach of fiduciary duty, launching a proxy contest to replace board members or the CEO, or taking control of the company with a takeover bid. Hedge funds usually aim to achieve an investment objective within one to two years[4] and implement their strategy with an ownership stake that falls between 5 and 10 percent.[5] Thus, taking control of a company with a takeover bid is rare (about 5 percent of the sample studied by Brav et al.).[6] Some hedge funds have gained notoriety for their hostile tactics, such as suing the firm, replacing the board or CEO via a proxy

---

[3] McCahery et al. (2016).   [4] Brav et al. (2008); Boyson and Mooradian (2007).
[5] Brav et al. (2008); Boyson and Mooradian (2007); Greenwood and Schor (2009).
[6] Brav et al. (2008).

contest, or implementing a hostile takeover. Hedge funds that engage in these kinds of hostile activities maintain larger ownership stakes in target firms and greater capital commitments.[7]

The investor class with the greatest capacity to alter firm governance is private equity funds. In contrast to hedge funds, which primarily take minority ownership positions, private equity funds typically acquire 75 percent or more of all outstanding shares and aim to control 100 percent of the votes. Based on a sample of sixty-six deals, Acharya et al. find that the median duration of a private equity (PE) fund investment is 3.5 years, with a minimum of 1.2 and a maximum of 7.3 years.[8] This high level of control and longer time span allows the PE fund to implement major changes. For example, Acharya et al. find that the composition of the board is usually split between the management team and the PE staff, the CEO is replaced 69 percent of the time, acquisitions occur in 24 percent of the deals, and in 9.7 percent of the deals a divestment occurs.[9]

An important conclusion to draw from this discussion is that larger ownership stakes are required to implement more aggressive shareholder tactics. Because this book examines states' propensity to influence foreign *listed* firms, state ownership levels play a critical role.

Extra-shareholder Tactics

State influence on foreign listed firms via SWFs and/or SOEs extends beyond shareholder activism to other activities such as network transactions and government influence. Network transactions involve the target firm engaging in some business-related contact with the SWF's or SOE's network of businesses.[10] Related business transactions include cases where the target firm enters into a major business agreement with another firm that is partially or wholly owned by the same SWF (i.e., an SOE). A SWF or SOE taking an equity interest in another firm that is wholly or partially owned by the target firm can also be included. A target firm purchasing an equity interest in another firm partially owned by the SWF or SOE can also be involved.

---

[7] Ibid.; Klein and Zur (2009); Greenwood and Schor (2009); Clifford (2008); Mietzner and Schweizer (2014).
[8] Acharya et al. (2013).   [9] Ibid.   [10] Dewenter et al. (2010).

Government influence includes efforts to alter the policies of the target firm's home government or to influence the target firm itself.[11] Tactics to influence the target firm's home government could include a range of policy options such as the easing of regulatory restrictions on foreign investment, an agreement to permit the acquisition of a firm located in the home country in exchange for permission to acquire a firm in the host country, trade agreements, or the creation of free trade zones. Tactics aimed at the target firm could include the home government reducing the cost of capital to the acquiring firm or SWF, granting preferential regulatory treatment to the target firm, awarding government contracts to the target firm, or a range of other perquisites that only a government could offer.[12]

Finally, SWFs and SOEs may have an inherent advantage relative to non-state-owned firms because state ownership can help to overcome institutional "voids" in product, labor, and financial markets.[13] Countries in the early stages of development are the most likely to have such voids and would be expected to welcome foreign state investments that can help address them. Through the acquisition of a foreign firm, a SWF or SOE could step in to compensate for these voids by providing capital where financial markets are underdeveloped or by coordinating the local deployment of complementary resources where product markets are underdeveloped.[14]

Passive or Aggressive State Intervention

The full scope of these shareholder and extra-shareholder tactics indicates whether a state, via a state-owned vehicle (SWF or SOE), intervenes passively or aggressively in a foreign listed firm. Passive intervention simply involves selling shares in a target firm without any extra-shareholder tactics. The most aggressive intervention not only includes a majority ownership stake in a target firm coupled with shareholder tactics like those used by a private equity firm but would also involve the use of extra-shareholder tactics such as network transactions and/or government influence.

[11] Baron (1995); Hillman, Keim, and Schuler (2004).   [12] Baron (1997).
[13] Khanna and Palepu (2000); Peng et al. (2009); Musacchio and Lazzarini (2014).
[14] Cameron (1961); Gerschenkron (1962); Aghion (2011); Mazzucato (2011); Rodrik (2007).

A final, important difference between state entities (SWF and SOEs) and their non-state-owned competitors (e.g., other institutional investors or nonfinancial corporations) regards the former's larger potential supply of capital and the potentially longer timeframe to achieve their investment objectives. These attributes enhance their ability to target large listed firms and implement changes to them.

Theoretical Framework

I assume that the primary interest of political leaders is to hold on to political power within the institutional constraints of the regime in which they are located. These institutional constraints allow leaders to exercise a particular level of control over information and resources to preserve their hold on power. Table 2.1 places political regimes into four categories, along with the salient regime characteristics that correspond to the varying controls over information and resources.

Regime Characteristics

Limitations on leaders' control over information and resources arise from institutions governing the extent of political competition, as well as institutions that reduce investment risk. As competition increases, more limitations are imposed on political leaders' unilateral control of information and resources. Institutions that protect private investors also enhance their access to resources, tilting the balance away from the state.

Political Competition and the Control of Information and Resources

At one end of the spectrum of political regimes are those with virtually no political competition – NARs. These regimes explicitly forbid political opposition and actively target citizens who speak critically of incumbent rulers. In these regimes, information and resources are monopolized by the incumbent ruler, thus denying opportunities to potential opponents to criticize, spread information about, or mobilize opposition against it. Examples include North Korea, Myanmar until 2012, and Brunei.

SPARs and DPARs have two important institutional differences with NARs. First, SPARs and DPARs have an institutionalized party system; second, they have a legislature. Authoritarian regimes ruled

Table 2.1 *State Capacity to Intervene: Regime Characteristics Determine the Control of Information and Resources*

| Regime type | Regime characteristics | | State capacity for corporate intervention: control of information and resources |
	Institutions that promote political competition	Institutions to reduce investment risk	
NAR	None: no competition	None: no legislature	Tight controls by a narrow group of political elites
SPAR	Modest: highly restricted competition (intraparty only)	Weak: populated by ruling-party members	Controls widened to elites within the ruling party
DPAR	Limited: restricted competition (intra- and interparty)	Moderate: legislatures with modest party heterogeneity	Controls widened relative to SPARs, but ruling-party elites retain residual rights of control
Democracy	Extensive: competitive	Strong: legislatures can effectively constrain the executive	The monopolized control of information and resources is prevented by the institutionalized separation of powers within different branches of government

by one party broaden access to state resources and information by including a wider group of individuals in the regime's membership as well as by institutionalizing mechanisms for attracting and retaining new members.[15] Often party systems will develop institutional

[15] Geddes (1999, 121–34); Boix and Svolik (2013); Bueno de Mesquita (2005); Gandhi (2008); Gandhi and Przeworski (2006, 2007); Lust-Okar (2005); Magaloni (2008); Malesky and Schuler (2010); Svolik (2009, 2012).

mechanisms to co-opt potential elite rivals either through the distribution of economic transfers and rents[16] or through institutions that produce credible intertemporal power-sharing deals.[17] One-party regimes are also more likely to institutionalize promotion criteria and to enable individuals to pursue a career with the party.[18] In NARs, career and promotion criteria are less institutionalized and more subject to the personal preferences of individual rulers, thereby weakening incentives for individuals to maintain long-term loyalty to the regime.

The second institutional difference between SPARs and DPARs in relation to NARs is the existence of a legislature. For both SPARs and DPARs, the legislature normally acts as a rubber stamp for the executive. Nevertheless, it can also reduce investment risk, and its effectiveness in this regard will be discussed further below.

However, an important difference between SPARs and DPARs is that political competition is restricted to party members in SPARs. Opposing parties are forbidden, and critics of the party are targeted and silenced. Examples of this type of regime include China, Vietnam, and Laos.

The ruling party in a DPAR must contend with both the intraparty competition found in SPARs as well as semicompetitive interparty politics. Interparty competition via regular elections for the legislature and the executive is restricted by the ruling party's limits on press freedom, the manipulation of electoral rules, and restrictions on who is eligible to run for office. While there is greater institutionalization of the political system to guarantee political opposition a minimal amount of representation, critical information that could be used by political opponents is curtailed (e.g., information about the ethnic distribution of home owners in Singapore). Access to resources is closely monitored and tightly controlled by the ruling party as well. Examples of this type of regime include Singapore and Malaysia.

In democracies, political competition is relatively unrestricted and characterized by a high degree of institutionalized rules governing political competition. Heterogeneous interests gain representation in the legislature, and checks and balances ensure that no single actor or party monopolizes control over politically sensitive information and

---

[16] Wintrobe (1998); Bueno de Mesquita (2005).

[17] Lazarev (2005); Brownlee (2007); Gehlbach and Keefer (2011); and Magaloni (2008).

[18] Geddes (1999).

resources. Examples include the Philippines, Taiwan, Japan, and South Korea.

These sketches of political competition across regime types are stylized accounts. In reality, countries vary within each of these regime categories as party and legislative institutions vary in strength or the executive's power varies with regard to the legislature. The important point is that a gradual increase in political competition corresponds to an increase in the formal institutionalization of the political regime. This permits more heterogeneous interests to gain representation, reducing the capacity for one group or party to monopolize access to state-controlled resources and information.

Institutions to Reduce Investment Risk

The capacity for a state investment entity to hold a large, long-term ownership position in a publicly listed firm depends on private investment capable of co-investing alongside the government. For private investment to take off, investment risk must be reduced, and this, in turn, depends on institutions that reduce investment risk. As these institutions become stronger, the control of resources will tilt away from the state and toward private capital.

There are two types of investment risk that must be addressed in order for private investment to occur and enable public-private co-investment – *expropriation risk* and *contracting risk*. These risks are associated with the protection of vertical and horizontal property rights, respectively.[19] Expropriation risk arises from the fact that any government strong enough to protect and adjudicate property rights is also strong enough to abrogate them. Out of fear that the government could arbitrarily expropriate investments, asset holders will be reluctant to invest.[20] Contracting risk regards the protection of property rights from other nonstate actors.[21] Failure to secure private property rights from encroachments by other private parties will also diminish investment. Thus a political regime's capacity to reduce expropriation risk and contracting risk influences the level of private ownership and the capacity for public-private co-investment.

---

[19] North (1991); Acemoglu and Johnson (2005).
[20] North and Weingast (1989).
[21] La Porta et al. (2000); Bebchuk and Neeman (2010).

Reducing Expropriation Risk. Regimes can reduce expropriation risk through the construction of institutional constraints on executive decision-making power. As North and Weingast demonstrate in the context of seventeenth-century England, the emergence of veto power over the king by the parliament effectively reduced expropriation risk.[22] This credible constraint subsequently led to the rapid development of England's capital markets and a fall in the cost of capital because lenders were more confident about repayment. Legislatures populated by representatives with heterogeneous preferences who vote together as a unified block strengthen the power of this constraint because they prevent the executive from aligning with the legislature.[23] Thus credible institutional constraints on executive power exist and can reduce expropriation risk when a parliament is populated by multiple political parties with veto power over executive decisions.

Democracies tend to have the most effective institutional arrangements for reducing expropriation risk because they have parliaments with multiple political parties that wield potential veto power over executive decisions. NARs have the weakest institutional constraints because they normally lack a legislature, let alone one with the power to constrain executive decisions. While SPARs do have a legislature, such as China and Vietnam, opposition parties are not represented, thereby undermining their capacity to constrain executive decisions. In such regimes, parliaments simply rubber stamp the policies introduced by the executive, although there may be scope for limited influence on the policymaking process via officeholders in the parliament. Additionally, the regime's control over information and resources will be widened to include a wider swath of party members, many of whom may have interests in strengthening and upholding protections governing private property.

Between SPARs and democracies are DPARs. They have parliaments in which multiple political parties may be represented, but their constraints on executive decisions are weaker than those found in democracies for two reasons. First, DPARs have a variety of mechanisms designed to preserve an entrenched majority of seats for the ruling party, resulting in limited or no effective power to opposition parties. As a result, the policy preferences for the majority of representatives are homogeneous and aligned with those of the executive. Second, the

[22] North and Weignast (1989).   [23] Stasavage (2002).

parliament usually wields little power to check executive decisions even if a disagreement arises; for example, the executive may simply dissolve the parliament and call for new elections in an effort to replace opposing members. However, the regime may be disinclined to engage in such heavy-handed actions in relation to corporate ownership because of concerns about reputational risks for attracting and maintaining popular support among private capital. The need for popular support differentiates DPARs from SPARs because the former engages in semi-competitive elections. This forces greater respect for the property rights of private capital. Thus expropriation risk will be highest in NARs, followed by SPARs, then DPARs, and will be lowest in democracies.

Reducing Contracting Risk. In regimes with effective checks and balances, as in democracies, parliaments pass laws to protect private property rights from encroachments by other non-state actors, and courts impartially and effectively enforce these rights. In regimes that lack checks and balances, as in NARs, there are no state-sanctioned forums for private actors to engage in public bargaining and reach self-enforcement agreements.

In regimes with a parliament that does not effectively constrain the executive, as with SPARs and DPARs, private actors can reduce contracting risk due to private agreements and self-enforcement.[24] Although the executive may not enforce bargains reached in the parliament, the mere existence of a legislative body can nevertheless reduce contracting risk by (1) reducing transactions costs of negotiations among interested parties,[25] (2) permitting regular repeated interactions that promote cooperation over the long term,[26] and (3) enabling monitoring and punishment via public "naming and shaming" possibilities that would not otherwise exist in an authoritarian regime characterized by secrecy.[27] The parliament must enforce investor protections through self-enforcement because control over the use of force will remain in the hands of the executive office unless it agrees to enforce parliamentary agreements. Asset owners who violate investment agreements will therefore have difficulty attracting investments in the future. To promote the maintenance of these agreements, corporate governance rules will be strengthened through such mechanisms as the mandatory disclosure of accounting and financial statements and by adopting internationally

[24] Jensen et al. (2014).   [25] Coase (1937).   [26] Williamson (1975).
[27] Jensen et al. (2014).

recognized corporate governance rules such as independent directors. Because courts are likely to be politically controlled and may therefore be ineffective, regime support for strong investor protections could act as an effective enforcement tool by permitting the ability to sue in the case of wrongdoing by corporate insiders.[28]

However, SPARs and DPARs are more likely to have an executive that will agree to the enforcement of parliamentary agreements regarding investor protections because these regimes are more likely to engage in public-private co-investment, thereby reflecting the loosening of regime controls over information and resources. SOEs that are partially state owned depend on a well-functioning marketplace in which private property rights are effectively enforced so that private investment occurs. Accordingly, strong incentives are created for the executive to participate in parliamentary negotiations, to abide by those which are struck, and to enforce them. However, the capacity for SPARs to reduce contracting risk is lower than for DPARs because the heterogeneity of actors with representation in the parliament is smaller (e.g., representatives of small and medium-sized enterprises).

Contracting risk is lowest in democracies because these regimes have parliamentary bodies in which multiple parties bargain and pass laws to protect property rights from other market participants. Moreover, the executive office of the government enforces these laws and is held accountable by the parliament. Courts also impartially and effectively enforce private property rights.

State Capacity to Intervene: The Control of Information and Resources as Manifested by SOE and SWF Characteristics

A critical manifestation of regimes' control of information and resources occurs through SOEs and state investment agencies, such as SWFs. As displayed in Table 2.2, specific manifestations of these controls include SOE and SWF transparency, the balance of public-private ownership, and the type of SWF that regimes choose to establish.

---

[28] Djankov et al. (2008).

Table 2.2 *Regime Characteristics Determine State Capacity to Intervene as Manifested by SOE and SWF Characteristics*

Regime type	Regime characteristics		State capacity to intervene: control of information and resources as manifested by SOE and SWF characteristics		
	Institutions that promote political competition	Institutions that reduce investment risk	SOE and SWF transparency	Public-private ownership: prevailing type of SOE	Prevailing type of SWF
NAR	None: no competition	None: no legislature	Low	Public dominance: dominant state ownership, often unlisted	Savings
SPAR	Modest: highly restricted competition (intraparty only)	Weak: populated by ruling-party members	Moderately low	Public oriented: state ownership dominates for strategically important firms	Savings
DPAR	Limited: restricted competition (intra- and interparty)	Moderate: legislatures with modest party heterogeneity	Moderate	Public-private balance: hybrid SOEs	Savings
Democracy	Effective: competitive	Strong; legislatures can effectively constrain the executive	High	Private dominance: relatively few SOEs	Mostly specific purpose (macro-stability, foreign exchange reserve, pension)

SOE and SWF Transparency

Transparency is necessary for public-private co-investment, such as state investment in foreign listed firms, because private investors require information regarding the state entities with which they are co-investing. Additionally, transparency is important to address concerns raised by foreign officials when a state-owned entity enters a foreign market.

NARs will be the least likely regime to address these needs because they favor withholding information from the public due to the opportunities it may create for political opponents.[29] The press will also be owned and controlled by the political elite and therefore refrain from independently monitoring and reporting on questionable government activities.[30] The lack of an independent judiciary further enables the maintenance of these arrangements.[31] This opacity not only matches the political incentives to deny information and resources flowing to political opponents but also permits political rulers to engage in rent seeking for themselves and direct patronage to key allies to maintain regime stability. SWFs and large SOEs are vital instruments by which leaders exercise their authority, so these information controls will naturally extend to these state-run entities.

As political competition increases and becomes institutionalized, information becomes more widely available. The pressures for greater information disclosure may occur either from external pressures on the regime, which acquiesces in order to hold on to power via limited concessions,[32] or from internal pressures in order to bolster the credibility of the regime's promises to supporters to share in the rents and thereby promote regime stability.[33] In either case, greater institutionalization of political competition yields more access to information about the regime and the resources it controls, including SOEs and SWFs. SPARs, which permit intraparty competition, open up information to a wider group of elites than NARs. DPARs, which permit both intra- and interparty competition, disclose even more information to a wider set of actors. Democracies have the highest transparency, which is entrenched by institutions that preserve the separation of powers so that no single political actor monopolizes access to all politically sensitive information and resources. Accordingly, SOEs and SWFs in democracies are more transparent and maintain greater accountability to the public for how their assets are used in comparison with those located in authoritarian regimes.

---

[29] Barros (2011).   [30] Kern and Hainueller (2009); Norris and Inglehart (2009).
[31] Moustafa (2014).   [32] Levitsky and Way (2010).
[33] Gehlbach and Keefer (2011).

Public-Private Ownership: Prevailing Type of SOE

The control of resources by a political regime is manifested by the balance between public and private ownership of the country's largest corporations. At one end of the spectrum are large firms wholly owned by the state (i.e., pure public ownership). At the other end are large firms completely owned by private investors, such as families, institutional investors, or individual shareholders. Between these two extremes are firms with a mix of public and private ownership.

Wholly state-owned corporations are likely to be most common to NARs. Wholly owning a corporation allows political rulers to maintain their stranglehold on both the resources controlled by the corporation and information concerning the use of those resources. Only when the corporation becomes publicly listed must the state disclose sensitive financial information in order to attract private investors. The lack of accountability to outside investors eases the capacity for incumbent rulers to use SOE resources for priorities that do not necessarily improve firm performance, such as denying business opportunities to potential challengers, co-opting elites via rent sharing, or directing funds to projects designed to maintain mass quiescence.

In the context of a SPAR in which a wider set of actors has political influence, control over the economy's vital economic resources will be modestly broadened. To reduce the state's crowding-out effects, private capital will be granted more opportunities to participate in the economy. Depending on how promotion incentives are structured for party members, they may push for the loosening of such restrictions themselves in order to boost investment and growth in their local political jurisdiction.[34] But to contain the political influence of private capital (or other political challengers), SPARs prohibit opposition parties that may represent interests independently of the ruling party while also maintaining state control over those firms and industries that are vital to downstream economic activities, such as banking and construction. This approach is effectively conveyed by Chen Yun's "birdcage theory" of the Chinese economy before its opening up in 1978. He proposed that the free market in China should have just enough freedom to fly like a bird inside the bars of a planned economy.[35]

---

[34] Carney (2012).
[35] Chen Yun was a Chinese Communist Party elder who supported Deng's liberalizing reforms (Paulson, 2015).

By comparison, the ruling party in DPARs will retain a dominant ownership stake in a smaller set of firms and industries in addition to a diminished presence across the rest of the economy. But an important political incentive that arises with partial privatization in the context of DPARs, as compared with SPARs, is for the ruling party to generate positive returns on the public's savings that are invested in SOEs, either directly via shareholdings or indirectly via a national savings program. Because DPARs hold regular elections in which opposition parties compete, the ruling party must maintain popular support. In the absence of process legitimacy, as with fully competitive elections, the ruling party must depend on output legitimacy via economic performance and rising incomes. Putting shares of SOEs in the hands of citizens can offer a particularly effective means to bolster popular support for the ruling party. This strategy worked spectacularly well for Thatcher's privatization program, which sold shares in state-owned companies in the 1980s to Britain's middle class, yielding broad-based political support for her party's economic policies.[36] Another example comes from the US National Football League – the Green Bay Packers. Among all the professional sports teams in North America's four traditional major leagues (football, baseball, basketball, and hockey), this team is the only one owned by individual shareholders in the community. This has yielded one of the most enduring and fiercely loyal fan bases among all of professional sports. The Green Bay Packers clearly illustrate that ownership in an organization heightens citizens' sense of loyalty to that collective enterprise so long as they trust that their investment is well managed. Ruling parties in DPARs can, and do, use this phenomenon to their advantage.

Finally, in democracies, the state faces pressure to further reduce its control of all firms and industries except for those which are best held by the state for economic reasons, such as a natural monopoly or projects that would not otherwise be funded by private investors. The reliance on popular support at election time requires that the state minimize its crowding-out effects and its drain on state finances (via taxes), thus leading to a decline in SOEs.[37] Such pressures to reduce state ownership become magnified in the context of economic globalization, which will be discussed later.

---

[36] Moore (1991).

[37] While greater political competition may grant opportunities for interest groups that favor a larger state presence, such as labor to boost state ownership, such factors are assumed to be held constant.

Prevailing Type of SWF

In authoritarian regimes, a state investment vehicle can offer an effective means for the centralized administration of sprawling corporate assets. This permits incumbent leaders to centralize their control of information and resources, implement directives in an efficient manner, and effectively monitor the deployment of state resources.

The type of SWF that authoritarian regimes favor will reflect the desire to control information and resources. Although authoritarian regimes vary with respect to the extent of their control over information and resources, a preference for a savings SWF will remain among all the authoritarian regime types. Savings SWFs will be preferred by rulers of authoritarian regimes because they match the need for a centralized agency to control the regime's ownership stakes in firms spread across the economy. The investment purpose of savings SWFs makes it the most appropriate type of SWF for this task because it permits large corporate ownership stakes for long periods of time. Other types of SWFs may also exist depending on the supply of financial resources (e.g., foreign exchange reserves) or political, social, or economic needs the regime confronts (e.g., a rapidly aging population that requires social security or pension funds).

In democracies, however, savings SWFs will be relatively less likely, *ceteris paribus*. Instead, SWFs will maintain specific, well-defined investment objectives that match the high level of transparency and accountability of the political system, coupled with the numerous checks and balances that prevent the concentration of power in a single party or branch of government. Pension, macro-stability, and foreign exchange reserve SWFs are therefore more likely to be established than savings funds. Savings SWFs may be established when there are surplus savings that require investment, as with commodities sales, but these will also be managed in a highly transparent manner that ensures accountability to voters/taxpayers and prevents crowding-out of private capital.

State Motivation to Intervene

State capacity to intervene is a necessary but insufficient condition for states to initiate aggressive investment behavior toward foreign listed firms. It is also necessary for states to be *motivated* to do so. The strongest motivation for a state to intervene comes from threats to incumbent rulers' hold on power. In this regard, authoritarian rulers are likely to confront the greatest threats. Two sources of threat are of particular salience to the maintenance of a large state sector – crowding-out effects and economic liberalization. Both threats enhance the ability of private capital to challenge incumbent rulers. Of course, these two threats do not exhaust all potential sources of threat that incumbent rulers may encounter. Table 2.3 shows how state motivation to intervene corresponds to each regime type and the state investment behavior implications.

Risks Due to Crowding-Out Effects

Crowding out occurs when government involvement in a sector of the market economy substantially affects the remainder of the market. With regard to SOEs, crowding out occurs when these firms provide a good or service that would otherwise be a business opportunity for private industry.[38] Risks to regime stability arise as private business gains economic and political influence yet crowding-out effects remain substantial. While these effects most directly impact business owners, they can also generate elevated costs to citizens who pay elevated taxes for inefficient state-owned firms and may have fewer employment opportunities. To sustain SOEs that lack a natural monopoly or fulfill an economic need private capital would not fund, governments must raise taxes or increase borrowing, thereby forcing interest rates to rise and depressing economic activity, further worsening output and employment.[39] As an economy develops and opportunities for private business grow, crowding-out effects become more significant; that is, the opportunity costs to private business owners arising from the presence of state-owned corporations become more severe.

In democracies, risks to regime stability are low because voters can voice their preference for a policy change at the ballot box. Risks to regime stability are greatest for authoritarian regimes because ruling elites are unwilling to hand over power to a political opponent or fully privatize because the control of information and resources via the state sector is crucial to regime stability. In NARs, SOEs dominate the economy, leaving few opportunities for private business. The weakness of private business owners coupled with zero tolerance toward political opponents keeps the risks to regime stability at a low

---

[38] Cumming and MacIntosh (2006).   [39] Garrett (1998).

Table 2.3 *Regime Characteristics Determine State Investment Behavior via State Capacity and Motivation to Intervene*

Regime type	Explanatory variables: Regime characteristics		Intervening variables: state capacity to intervene — SOE and SWF characteristics			Intervening variables: state motivation to intervene		Dependent variable
	Institutions that promote political competition	Institutions that reduce investment risk	SOE and SWF transparency	Public-private ownership: prevailing type of SOE	Prevailing type of SWF	Risks due to crowding-out effects	Risks due to economic liberalization	State investment behavior
NAR	None: no competition	None	Low	Public dominance: dominant state ownership, often unlisted	Savings	Low	Low	Mostly passive
SPAR	Modest: highly restricted competition (intraparty only)	Weak	Moderately low	Public-oriented: state ownership dominates for strategically important firms	Savings	Moderately low	Moderately low	Occasional displays of aggression
DPAR	Limited: restricted competition (intra- and interparty)	Moderate	Moderate	Public-private balance: hybrid SOEs	Savings	Potentially high	Potentially high	More frequent displays of aggression
Democracy	Effective: competitive	Strong	High	Private dominance: relatively few SOEs	Mostly specific purpose (macro-stability, foreign exchange, reserve, pension)	Low	Mostly passive	

level for these regimes. In SPARs, private business may gain opportunities to participate though the ruling party also forbids the existence of political opposition. Consequently, mounting an effective challenge to the ruling party is difficult for private business owners, especially when future business opportunities depend heavily on maintaining good relations with party leaders. DPARs present the best opportunity for private business to mount an effective and sustained challenge in the context of authoritarian regimes because DPARs permit political opposition even though political competition faces numerous restrictions.

Risks Due to Economic Liberalization
The risks to regime stability arising from crowding-out effects get magnified in the context of economic liberalization because of the expansion of opportunities available to private business. However, such risks to regime stability remain concentrated in authoritarian regimes. The risks to regime stability arising from economic liberalization stem from two sources – trade and finance.

Trade Liberalization's Risks. The implementation of trade liberalization in an effort to boost investment and, in turn, growth raises pressure to privatize SOEs and increases the resources available to private business owners. Pressures to privatize arise from the need to reduce distortions on prices and wages that are caused by large government-controlled sectors (e.g., supply and demand for labor and capital, elevated taxes, and crowding-out effects). While trade liberalization raises the economy's growth prospects, reducing the size of the government-controlled sector can generate negative political consequences for the ruling party's stability. Specifically, trade liberalization could strengthen asset owners who are not allied with the ruling party in authoritarian settings. Lowered trade barriers will benefit competitive firms that do not necessarily depend on government support and may be independent of the ruling party. Additionally, dislocations to workers will occur as the economy adjusts to greater openness, potentially contributing to discontent that non-ruling party affiliated asset owners could tap to build an opposition movement. Thus trade liberalization can enable private capital to leverage its power and threaten incumbent rulers most dramatically in the context of DPARs.

Financial Liberalization's Risks. Liberalizing financial policies to boost investment also generates pressures to privatize. Pressures to reduce the size of the government-controlled sector arise from the need to reduce moral hazard costs. These costs arise from a firm's ties to political leaders, conferring an implicit guarantee of a bailout should the firm run into trouble.[40] In good times, SOEs may attract disproportionately greater amounts of capital, thereby exacerbating the moral hazard problem, contributing to a harder crash landing when the economy contracts. Financial liberalization can magnify these costs by increasing the flow of portfolio capital that enters and exits the economy. To minimize these costs, the government must credibly commit to a hard budget constraint and be willing to allow politically linked firms to go bankrupt. This approach is normally not feasible or credible for political reasons, thereby raising pressures to privatize.

The risks to regime stability that may arise from reducing the size of the state sector mirror those that arise in relation to trade liberalization. As mentioned earlier, partial privatization of SOEs may be pursued for strategically important segments of the electorate to reduce these risks. However, the implementation of liberalizing financial reforms can generate three additional risks to regime stability above and beyond those that arise from trade liberalization, including (1) heightened exposure to an exogenous financial shock (or crisis), (2) an elevated threat of exit by capital owners, and (3) easier access to external finance for elite opponents. The primary political threat associated with these finance-related risks applies to authoritarian rather than democratic regimes because the major threat to most democracies is a change in the ruling party rather than regime change. Among authoritarian regimes, the risks are primarily concentrated in DPARs because they permit political opponents to compete in elections.

The heightened potential of a financial crisis emanating from outside the country was dramatically revealed to emerging markets during the 1990s. But even in the absence of a crisis, a further source of vulnerability arises from dependence on the global policy environment and the monetary policies of influential central banks such as the US Federal Reserve or the European Central Bank. Low-interest-rate environments can flood the global economy with liquidity, heightening the risks for emerging economies when the inevitable tightening occurs.[41] The stability of authoritarian regimes is particularly vulnerable,

[40] Chang (2000).   [41] Rodrik and Subramanian (2009).

although the magnitude of the threat depends on their level of integration with the global financial system. NARs tend to be the least integrated, but even for these regimes, which usually rely heavily on commodities sales, a sharp adjustment in the prices of commodities could have a dramatic impact on them. Brunei's experience in 1998 is a clear illustration of this phenomenon.[42]

With respect to the threat of exit by capital owners, regimes are confronted by varying degrees of vulnerability depending on the relative importance of mobile and immobile capital.[43] Authoritarian regimes will have more immobile capital because the regime controls more of the economy's major assets. NARs are the least vulnerable because they retain high levels of control over the economy, followed by SPARs. DPARs, which tend to have a greater mix of private and state ownership, are more vulnerable.

Finally, access to foreign capital primarily threatens authoritarian regimes, though DPARs more than NARs or SPARs. Because asset owners with control of substantial assets are more common to DPARs, they can pose a more serious threat to these regimes. This threat is magnified in the context of DPARs as compared with SPARs because the former permit opposition parties to run for election.

State Investment Behavior

For each regime type, I discuss the likelihood for states to engage in aggressive foreign investment behavior. Either SWFs or SOEs can engage in such behavior, but SWFs are likely to play an outsized role as a centralized agency that can effectively implement state policy directives across numerous SOEs. While savings SWFs are the most capable of initiating large ownership positions that can enable aggressive intervention in a target firm, not all savings SWFs will engage in such behavior. As discussed earlier, whether states engage in such aggressive behavior depends on the preexisting capacity *and* motivation to do so.

Narrow Authoritarian Regimes

State capacity to intervene in a foreign listed corporation is determined by the potential for public-private co-ownership, a sufficient level of

[42] Gunn (2001).   [43] Pepinsky (2009).

transparency and is aided by a SWF with the capacity to initiate large, long-term ownership stakes. In NARs, wholly state-owned firms will dominate and state sector transparency will be very low; together these two characteristics undermine the capacity for NARs to initiate large ownership positions in foreign listed firms. The desire for the NAR regime to remain opaque diminishes its willingness to take large foreign ownership positions that cross key disclosure thresholds. Additionally, the lack of transparency regarding the SOE initiating the investment reduces the willingness of foreign officials to permit a sizable ownership stake in a large corporation of importance to its national economy.

The motivation to intervene aggressively in the corporate sector arises from the need to address regime threats. This motivation could arise from an exogenous or holistic threat to the regime. But because political opposition is explicitly forbidden in NARs, a cohesive domestic resistance faces significant obstacles to organizing against the regime in the absence of an exogenous shock. This difficulty is heightened in NARs because the presence of private capital is diminished, thus denying resources to political challengers. While the potential for aggressive intervention exists due to the absence of effective checks on executive decision making, the lack of capacity coupled with the lack of political competition makes aggressive foreign interventions (via dominant ownership stakes in listed firms) unlikely.[44] Therefore, passive investments are expected to be more common.[45]

Single-Party Authoritarian Regimes

SPARs are more likely to meet the state capacity requirements for initiating state ownership positions in foreign listed firms. These regimes are likely to have firms that mix public and private ownership, thereby exhibiting the state's capacity to appease private investors. These regimes are also likely to rely on savings SWFs to administer the state's ownership positions in large firms, facilitating the state's capacity to implement its investment strategy. Finally, SPARs will have surpassed a minimum threshold of transparency for private investors to co-invest alongside the state and for its SOEs and SWFs to invest in

---

[44] In other words, the absence of institutional checks heightens the capacity for a ruler to initiate aggressive foreign interventions for personal reasons.
[45] It is worth noting that state agencies from NARs could make large investments in other types of foreign assets, such as real estate, private businesses, or bonds.

other countries with a comparably low transparency threshold (other authoritarian regimes).

With regard to the motivation to intervene in order to curb risks to regime stability, these primarily arise from an exogenous/holistic threat to the regime (e.g., a financial crisis) or from factional conflict within the ruling party (intraparty competition). Crowding-out effects may create heightened intraparty conflict if economic development and/or state ownership occur unevenly across the economy. Likewise, the elevated levels of state ownership in such regimes may produce economy-wide crowding-out effects, thereby contributing to a holistic regime threat and generating pressures to invest in foreign markets. These intraparty and holistic threats may be exacerbated by the career incentives of party members. If career prospects depend on growth in a local jurisdiction, then private capital may be encouraged to engage with global markets. When this is coupled with over-lending and over-borrowing policies that increase international trade and financial ties, deleterious economic and political consequences may emerge when foreign markets enter a downturn. To address these problems, party leaders will turn to SOEs and/or state investment agencies to intervene in the domestic market to address intraparty conflict. Incumbent rulers will also turn to SOEs and SWFs to intervene in foreign markets when they encounter an existential threat to their rule.[46] Thus state intervention will be aggressive in response to these threats but will otherwise be more passive.

Dominant-Party Authoritarian Regimes

Among authoritarian regimes, DPARs have a high capacity for intervening in foreign listed firms. DPARs are likely to have SOEs with a balanced mix of public and private ownership, thereby exhibiting the state's capacity to appease private investors. In addition, DPARs are likely to rely on savings SWFs to administer the state's ownership positions in numerous enterprises, which facilitates the implementation of a state-directed investment strategy. Finally, DPARs will have a higher level of state sector transparency than SPARs, a necessary precondition for private investors to co-invest alongside the state. Due to this greater transparency, DPARs are likely to face fewer obstacles when

[46] See Norris (2016).

their state-owned entities enter foreign markets, though they will likely have difficulties entering countries with a higher transparency threshold. Nevertheless, DPAR state-owned entities can potentially enter a larger set of countries than those from SPARs. Thus, in comparison with NARs and SPARs, DPARs possess the greatest capacity for state intervention in the corporate sector of foreign markets.

DPARs also possess a stronger motivation to intervene than SPARs and NARs. In addition to confronting the same exogenous/holistic regime threats and intraparty competition pressures as SPARs, ruling parties in DPARs must also contend with *interparty* competition. By permitting political opponents to compete in elections, elite challengers can gain a toehold with which to mount an organized resistance to incumbent rulers. Such resistance is likely to elicit a strong reaction from incumbent rulers in the form of corporate intervention. Private capital's strength and its capacity to mount an effective resistance to incumbent rulers will increase as economic development rises and crowding-out effects become more severe. Trade and financial liberalization can amplify the risks to regime stability as private capital gains access to more resources beyond the regime's control.

To respond to regime threats, DPARs will engage in more aggressive intervention tactics both at home and in foreign markets. At home, the ruling party will tighten its control of politically sensitive information and resources, which translates into increasing state ownership of the largest firms in strategically important sectors. However, pressures to reduce crowding-out effects will also yield reductions in the share of the economy controlled by SOEs.

DPARs will also encounter pressure to invest overseas in an effort to keep voter-investors happy. As investment opportunities dry up at home due to crowding-out effects, the state must go overseas to generate positive returns. This pressure is unique to DPARs (among authoritarian regimes) because citizens vote. It also heightens the pressure to strongly intervene both at home and overseas to ensure steady positive returns because the ruling party's legitimacy depends on economic performance in the absence of process legitimacy.

Due to this pressure to generate positive financial returns for voter-investors, it is often impossible to distinguish between political and market motivations driving state investment behavior. Higher investment returns are frequently a political objective in their own right.

Table 2.4 *Impact of DPAR Ruling Party Strength on State Investment Behavior*

Ruling party strength	SOE and SWF transparency	Public-private ownership: prevailing type of SOE	SWF type	State investment behavior
Weak	Lower	Stronger controls over strategically important firms; lower SOE share for overall economy	Savings	More aggressive
Strong	Higher	Weaker controls over strategically important firms; higher SOE share for overall economy	Savings	Less aggressive

After all, the surest way for an authoritarian leader to attract and retain popular support is to put money in citizens' pockets – especially in emerging economies, where the population frequently places a higher value on raising incomes than on democratic processes.

DPARs will therefore display variation both in relation to the other regime types and with regard to the varying strength of the ruling party. In other words, where DPARs fall within the DPAR range depends on the strength of the ruling party. When the ruling party is weak, I expect incumbent rulers to tighten their controls over information and resources vital to regime survival, as shown in Table 2.4.

In the context of economic liberalization, risks to regime stability are magnified because private capital can access funds beyond the reach of the regime. Private capital can also threaten to exit the economy, and a financial crisis could create an opportunity for political opponents of the regime. However, increases in state control as a reaction to the rising threat of private capital must be balanced against accompanying crowding-out effects that alienate private capital. To shore up popular support, incumbent rulers must also reduce the state's overall presence in the economy without compromising financial returns. This reduction requires state entities to engage in more aggressive foreign investment behavior. Aggressive foreign investments are important for improving returns for voter-investors and demonstrating continuing growth because the regime's legitimacy depends on economic performance. The weaker the ruling party, the more pressure it encounters to intervene aggressively in foreign markets.

Democracies

In democracies, state capacity to initiate large ownership positions in foreign listed firms is low. Although state sector transparency will be high, the state's control of corporate assets will be low, and a savings SWF with control over a large swath of the corporate sector will either be unlikely or encounter strong limits on taking large ownership positions.

Democracies also face a low motivation to intervene aggressively in the corporate sector because the main threat to incumbent leaders is the election of political opponents rather than regime collapse. Additionally, state ownership is largely circumscribed by owners of private capital because of their power to deny election victories to political representatives who do not comply with their preferences.

Extension: Coordination Capacity

The core theoretical framework developed above assumes that each regime type has an equivalent capacity to establish a SWF and that each state has an equivalent amount of surplus funds available to establish a SWF. Whether a state has access to sufficient surplus funds to establish a SWF, such as foreign exchange reserves or commodities sales, is beyond the scope of this book. However, if we take as given that states from the same type of regime have an equivalent amount of surplus funds, then they will display a varying propensity to establish a SWF. Take the governments of East Asia in the wake of the Asian financial crisis as an example. Countries across the region accumulated surplus foreign exchange reserves, but only a few of these countries established a foreign exchange reserve SWF or an alternate type of SWF to address macroeconomic instability. For example, Taiwan established a National Stabilization Fund, but the Philippines did not. Why? To account for this variation, I argue that we need to consider a regime's capacity to overcome coordination problems.

A regime plagued by fragmented interests incapable of overcoming their coordination problems will undermine the nation's capacity to address common goods issues. This is most clearly seen in the context of global trade or environmental agreements. In these international arenas, such coordination problems are often overcome by large powers capable of constructing a coalition, but this requires that such hegemons be willing to pay the accompanying costs. In the context of a domestic political arena, a single political jurisdiction capable of or willing to pay the costs of overcoming coordination problems may not exist.

In democracies with weak political parties, coordination problems can be especially acute.[47] Because of the lack of party-based discipline among political representatives, the political system can degenerate into cronyism. This occurs via rent seeking of state resources by particularistic interests, with political representatives acting on behalf of those interests – commonly owners of business groups.[48] The incapacity for coordination among political leaders in deciding the allocation of public finances for the economy's aggregate welfare hinders the creation of a SWF that could offer nontargeted benefits such as macroeconomic stabilization. Furthermore, privatizations, under the guise of boosting the economy's competitiveness, lead to the rapid sale of state assets to business owners as the key beneficiaries.

Authoritarian regimes are more disposed to centralized coordination by virtue of their centralized political structure. However, these regimes can also encounter coordination problems. For example, multiple agents (e.g., government ministries) may claim authority over a single SOE, creating a variety of agency costs (e.g., when they implement inconsistent policies or pass off the monitoring costs to another agent). Additional problems can arise when one set of SOEs reports to one principal (government agency), while another set of SOEs reports to a different principal. These overlapping arrangements diminish the state's capacity to exercise a uniform policy with regard to foreign state intervention. Consequently, state intervention will exhibit more heterogeneous behavior and may grant the SOE autonomy to pursue its own independent interests.

---

[47] Migdal (1988); Sidel (1999).   [48] Keefer and Vlaicu (2008).

3 | *Global Patterns*

I argue that the capacity and motivation for foreign state intervention in listed firms will vary by regime type. In this chapter, I focus exclusively on capacity indicators, including the scope of state ownership, the extent of state-sector transparency, and the prevalence of savings sovereign wealth funds (SWFs) among authoritarian regimes in comparison with democracies. I also examine whether the scope of state ownership and state-sector transparency vary across dominant-party authoritarian regimes (DPARs) in relation to the strength of the ruling party. Assessing foreign state ownership of listed firms requires detailed ownership data. Unfortunately, such data are not available at the global level, so I save an analysis of these patterns for the East Asia chapter (Chapter 4) and the country case studies (Chapters 5–7).

I begin with a discussion of how the variables of interest are measured and the sources of data used to construct them. In the second section, I examine whether authoritarian regimes display the expected patterns with regard to the capacity indicators mentioned earlier. The third section analyzes the responses of corporate ownership and state-sector transparency to changes in the structure of the political regime. In the fourth section, I examine state-sector patterns among DPARs in relation to the strength of the ruling party. The final section summarily concludes.

Data and Variables

The most comprehensive global measure for the prevalence of state-owned enterprises comes from the *Economic Freedom of the World* (Gwartney, Lawson, and Hall 2015). It provides an index of the prevalence of state-owned enterprises (SOEs) as a share of the economy (scaled from 0 to 10). Higher scores are given to countries in which state-owned enterprises are estimated to produce less of the country's output. As the estimated size and breadth of the SOE-sector increase, countries are assigned lower ratings. To provide a more intuitive interpretation of this variable, I invert this score so that a higher number corresponds to a larger SOE sector. This measure is useful not only for its comprehensive coverage but also for its holistic assessment of government intervention in the corporate sector, including regimes without publicly listed SOEs (and without stock markets). It therefore covers all regime types and represents a useful general assessment of the importance of SOEs to economies around the world. But this comprehensive coverage comes at the cost of precise measurement of state ownership stakes in listed firms. This is not surprising because compiling detailed ownership information is very time-consuming. Hence a data set that offers precise measures of state ownership will be examined for the subset of East Asian firms in Chapter 4. A second drawback is that annual data only begin in 2000; prior to this date, coverage occurs every five years, thereby precluding the use of longitudinal tests that assess changes from before the Asian financial crisis (and other developing-country crises around this time) to after. Summary statistics for this and the other dependent and explanatory variables are presented in Table 3.4 at the end of this chapter.

Transparency of the state corporate sector is not straightforward to measure because it encompasses both the political regime and the corporate sector. To measure transparency of each country's political regime, I use the Corruption Perception Index (CPI) score. The strength of this measure is its comprehensive coverage, which begins in 1995 for forty-eight countries and expands to 153 countries by 2015. A drawback, however, is that it focuses on corruption rather than transparency. While these concepts are related insofar as corruption is more likely when there is a lack of transparency, they are not perfect substitutes. The level of transparency can vary for a given level of corruption. For example, the case study on Brunei in Chapter 5 shows that this is a highly opaque political regime; however, its CPI score in 2013 was 60, which was nearly equal to that of Taiwan (61), a much more transparent regime. On average, it is likely that the CPI score is biased upward for countries that deserve a low transparency score, such as Brunei and other narrow authoritarian regimes (NARs), thus making it an imprecise indicator for NARs and single-party authoritarian regimes (SPARs).

Additional variables to be used to assess transparency of the state corporate sector include the extent of transparency in the corporate sector as well as SWF transparency. The extent of corporate transparency variable comes from the World Bank's Doing Business Database. The measure encompasses both listed and unlisted firms and offers comprehensive cross-sectional coverage; however, it only begins in 2014. Another drawback is that it measures transparency of all firms regardless of ownership. I also use Truman's SWF transparency measure. This focuses on SWFs specifically and is carefully constructed based on assessments across multiple dimensions of SWF governance. It offers the most accurate assessment of state-sector transparency, but it is not an ideal indicator because it focuses on SWFs rather than SOEs. Additionally, it is available for only two different points in time – 2007 and 2012. I use the latter time point because it covers more SWFs; the measure comes from Truman's SWF Scoreboard Index.[1]

Data for the identification and classification of SWFs come from International Monetary Fund (IMF) reports, including Kunzel et al. (2011) and Al-Hassan et al. (2013), and are supplemented with information from the Sovereign Wealth Fund Institute.[2]

With regard to the explanatory variables, I begin by identifying regimes along the continuum of regime types (authoritarian to democracy) based on the *ifhpol* variable, which comes from the Authoritarian Regimes Data Set (version 5.0). The *ifhpol* indicator combines the polity score (available from the Polity IV Project) with Freedom House scores to arrive at a score for the level of democracy (scaled 0–10). It provides coverage of a larger sample of countries than the polity variable alone. Full details of the construction of this variable are available in Hadenius et al. (2007). I follow their cutoff for the line between democracies and authoritarian regimes at 7.0, which is based on categorical measures of democracy by expert scholars in the field. I also update the variable to 2015 following the methods discussed in the Hadenius et al. codebook.

To distinguish between narrow, single-, and dominant-party authoritarian regimes (all of which have *ifhpol* scores below 7), I begin by identifying whether the regime possesses a legislature and whether the legislature has multiple parties. NARs are defined as lacking

---

[1] Bagnall and Truman (2013).
[2] Some SWFs can be classified under more than one category; these are assigned according to their dominant function. If this is not clear and they are classified as a savings fund along with other functions, then I categorize it as a savings fund because this category offers the greatest flexibility.

a legislature, SPARs possess a legislature but lack multiple parties, and DPARs possess both a legislature and multiple parties. The identification of whether an authoritarian regime possesses a legislature comes from the Cheibub, Gandhi, and Vreeland (2010) data set, as does the indicator for whether multiple parties are represented in the legislature with the *lparty* variable. Their data stop in 2008; I therefore update the variable to 2015 following the methods from Cheibub, Gandhi, and Vreeland's codebook.

To assess the strength of the ruling party in DPARs, I use a measure for the dominance of the largest political party in the legislature that comes from Hadenius et al. (2007) using the *partsz* variable. This measure counts the largest party's number of seats divided by the legislative assembly's total number of seats. I also update this variable to 2015 following the methods presented in the Hadenius et al. codebook.

Comparing Authoritarian Regime Types

Table 3.1 presents results for ordinary least squares regressions at five-year intervals to assess the strength of the relationship between each of the three authoritarian regime types in relation to democracy (which is omitted) and indicators for the SOE share of the economy as well as the CPI score. To provide symmetrical comparisons across time, I use five-year intervals because the SOE indicator is available only for 1990 and 1995. It is important to capture the change at these two points in time because considerable regime change occurred during the 1990s, as shown in Figure 1.2. At that time, numerous countries transitioned away from NARs or SPARs to either DPARs or democracy.

The contribution of SOEs to the national economy has been attributed to alternative explanations, as discussed in Chapter 1. I therefore incorporate appropriate controls, including log of gross domestic product (GDP) per capita, which is intended to account for the reduction in institutional voids associated with economic development and therefore the need for government intervention via SOEs. It is also regarded as influencing the level of corporate transparency – better institutional environments correspond to greater information availability. I also include a variable for whether a country has a common-law legal origin. La Porta et al. (2007) argue that common-law privileges market-enhancing outcomes over the state (as in civil law), and one would

Table 3.1 *SOE Share and CPI Score: Authoritarian Regime Types in Comparison with Democracies*

	SOE share						CPI score				
	1990	1995	2000	2005	2010	2015	1995	2000	2005	2010	2015
DPAR	-0.6	-0.4	1.7****	2.7***	1.1*	0.7	-1.2	-0.5	-0.57*	-0.8***	-0.75***
	(-0.8)	(-0.6)	(2.3)	(4.1)	(1.7)	(1.1)	(-1.2)	(-1.39)	(-1.8)	(3.1)	(-2.9)
SPAR	1.4**	2.9***	4.7***	5.6***	3.6*	5***	2.3***	-0.1	-1.1**	-1.3***	-1.8***
	(2.3)	(4.3)	(4.1)	(4.6)	(1.8)	(18.8)	(2.8)	(-0.3)	(-2.3)	(-2.6)	(-2.8)
NAR	2.6***	2.3**	3.9***	2	4.4***	3.4***	-0.05	0.13	-1.5***	-1.5***	-1.5***
	(3.1)	(2.1)	(3.1)	(1.4)	(4.87)	(3.1)	(-0.03)	(0.2)	(-3.6)	(-4.3)	(-4.1)
Log(GDP per capita)	-0.92***	-0.8***	-0.89***	-0.83***	-1***	-1***	2.6***	1.5***	1.2***	1.1***	1.1***
	(-4.23)	(-3.07)	(-3.4)	(-3.8)	(-5.18)	(-5.2)	(8)	(7.7)	(10)	(9.6)	(9.8)
Common law	-0.62	-1.4**	0.4	0.5	-0.27	0.6	1.4*	0.94***	0.68***	0.7***	0.52**
	(-1.26)	(-2.4)	(0.76)	(1)	(-0.58)	(1.1)	(1.8)	(2.8)	(2.6)	(3.08)	(2.13)
N	97	104	112	127	134	133	47	82	138	155	142
R^2	0.36	0.2	0.33	0.39	0.33	0.27	0.66	0.67	0.59	0.58	0.6

Note: Standard errors are robust and clustered by country; *t*-statistics are in parentheses. ***, **, and * indicates significance at the 0.01, 0.05, and 0.10 levels, respectively.

therefore expect a negative relationship between common law and SOEs.

Because the SOE share and CPI score indicators are not perfect measures for the underlying concepts of interest, we must remain modest when interpreting the results. Specifically, the indicators are unlikely to offer precise estimates for each concept but are nevertheless likely to offer useful assessments of cross-sectional variation and temporal trends. With the appropriate caveats in mind, we can proceed to an examination of the results.

Looking at the change over time for the SOE share, the DPAR variable indicates that these countries exhibit a statistically significant difference in the size of the state sector relative to democracies starting in 2000. This value peaks in 2005 and then declines over time. There are several explanations that could account for the observed patterns. First, the rise in the size of the state sector may be attributable primarily to regime transitions; countries formerly belonging to the SPAR or NAR categories shifted to the DPAR category. However, the data presented in the summary statistics indicate that the largest fraction of regime transitions occurred between 1990 and 1995. While it is possible that there is a considerable time lag between regime transitions and a rise in the size of the state sector, there are other explanations that might account for the sudden increase starting in 2000. For example, the onset of financial crises across the developing world in the middle to late 1990s may have contributed to stronger state controls in order for incumbent rulers to hang onto power, as articulated in Chapter 2. The evidence from NARs and SPARs is consistent with this explanation because the sizes of their coefficients also rise in 2000. A related observation is that the rise in the SOE share after 2000 coincides with efforts to promote liberalizing reforms in the wake of these crises by international organizations and demonstrates the gap that ensued between the rhetoric of complying with these reforms intended to reduce the state's role in the economy versus the outcomes. This is consistent with evidence from East Asia.[3] The theory predicts that the size of the state sector will decline for DPARs as the threat to incumbent rulers declines and the need to reduce crowding effects rises (coupled with stronger trade and financial liberalization). The decline in the size of the SOE share of the economy after 2005 is consistent with this interpretation.

[3] Walter (2008).

For example, Table 3.4 reports that the mean SOE share of DPARs declined from 6.02 in 2005 to 5 in 2015, while the standard deviation remained at around 3.3. Meanwhile, the mean SOE share for democracies increased modestly from 2.24 in 2005 to 2.63 in 2015, with the standard deviation increasing slightly from 2.34 to 2.72. Thus the decline in the SOE share is due to DPARs rather than an increase among democracies, although the gap between them remains considerable (the mean SOE share of DPARs is nearly twice as high as for democracies in 2015).

SPARs, by comparison, display consistently larger coefficients for SOE share in comparison with DPARs across the entire sample. The magnitude of the coefficient also peaks in 2005 but remains more than three times larger than the DPAR coefficient throughout the entire twenty-five years examined. It is clear that SPARs remain more resistant to liberalizing pressures than their DPAR counterparts.

Meanwhile, NARs also display larger coefficients than DPARs between 1990 and 2015, except for 2005 (when DPARs' SOE share peaked). In comparison with SPARs, the size of the coefficient is larger in 1990 and 2010 but otherwise smaller. Confidence in the relative sizes of the coefficients for NARs and SPARs is weakened both by the construction of the measure as mentioned earlier and by the small number of country observations for these regimes. Between 2000 and 2015, only two countries in the sample belong to the SPAR category (China and Iran), whereas only seven or eight countries were in the NAR category. It will therefore be helpful to examine SPARs and NARs in detail in Chapter 4 and in the case studies (China and Brunei, respectively; Chapter 5).

Turning to the CPI score results, DPARs exhibit statistically significant differences with democracies starting only in 2005. This is also true for the SPAR and NAR results, notwithstanding the SPAR result for 1995 with a coefficient with the opposite sign from expected (a positive sign rather than a negative sign; note, however, that there was only one SPAR country in the sample). Specifically, DPARs display a higher level of perceived corruption than democracies, with SPARs and NARs exhibiting perceived corruption levels around two times higher than DPARs in comparison with democracies. The results become stronger for the 2010 and 2015 time periods. The summary statistics for NARs and SPARs suggest that the results for 2005 onward are primarily due to the increase in the number of countries included in the sample; in 2000 there were only two SPARs and two NARs, whereas in 2005 there were seven SPARs and thirteen NARs. However, this explanation seems unlikely to account for DPARs because twenty-seven were included in the sample for 2000 (there were forty-two in 2005). An alternative explanation is that the perceived gap increased between leaders' official policies to implement liberalizing reforms and the reforms actually implemented. Evidence from the Malaysia and Singapore case studies is consistent with this view; specifically, leaders sought to reconcile the need to appeal to the masses (due to recurring elections) by growing the economy and reducing crowding-out effects while hanging onto power by preserving incumbent rulers' control over resources and information. The inherent conflict between these goals may have become more noticeable over time.

Although the indicators offer imprecise measures for the underlying concepts, there are four conclusions that deserve emphasis: (1) SOEs are not epiphenomenal, (2) SOEs have persisted among authoritarian regimes despite pressures associated with economic development and the global spread of liberalizing reforms, (3) SOE prevalence and CPI scores vary across types of authoritarian regimes, and (4) although DPARs, SPARs, and NARs share much in common in relation to democracies, there are important differences between DPARs relative to SPARs and NARs. Confidence about these generalizations will rise once more precise data are used in Chapter 4, in addition to the analytic narratives in the case-study chapters (Chapters 5–7).

Because the CPI score is an imperfect indicator for transparency of the state's involvement in the corporate sector, I also examine corporate transparency and SWF transparency measures. As shown in Table 3.2, corporate transparency is only significant with respect to NARs. There are a couple of different interpretations for this result. First, SOEs may dominate the corporate sector in NARs; hence corporate transparency more accurately reflects SOE transparency, which, in turn, mirrors the political arena. Second, family ownership is more common in DPARs and SPARs and therefore will be more similar to democracies.

Of all the transparency indicators, the SWF transparency measure accords most closely with theory. It is therefore reassuring that this indicator shows the lowest transparency for NARs and that DPARs have lower transparency than democracies. However, SWFs located in

Table 3.2 *Transparency and Savings SWF Patterns*

	Corporate transparency (OLS) 2015	SWF transparency (OLS) 2010	Savings SWF (logit) 2015
Democracy	–	–	–2.2**
			(–2.4)
DPAR	–0.2	–30***	–
	(–0.07)	(–2.85)	
SPAR	0.25	–0.6	–
	(0.23)	(–0.03)	
NAR	–2.1***	–58***	–
	(–3.04)	(–4.4)	
Log(GDP per capita)	1.03***	15.8**	0.99**
	(6.8)	(2.5)	(2.4)
Common law	0.29	7.4	1.1*
	(0.89)	(0.4)	(1.6)
Oil rents of GDP	–	–	0.04*
			(1.8)
N	155	24	90
R^2 or pseudo–R^2	0.28	0.55	0.36

Note: Standard errors are robust and clustered by country; *t*-statistics are in parentheses for the OLS tests. Z-values are in parentheses for the logit test. ***, **, and * indicate significance at the 0.01, 0,05, and 0.10 levels, respectively.

SPARs display transparency that is equivalent to that in democracies. What explains this unexpected result?

The SPAR result is due to the SWFs of China and Iran. While Iran has a savings SWF (the National Development Fund), China does not have one; instead, it has two foreign exchange reserve funds (the State Administration of Foreign Exchange and the China Investment Corporation) and a pension fund (the National Social Security Fund).

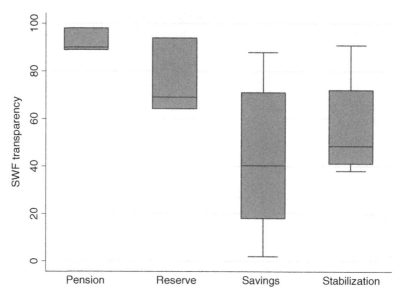

Figure 3.1 SWF transparency by type of SWF.

As mentioned in Chapter 1, it is important to distinguish between types of SWFs (savings, foreign exchange reserve, macro stability, and pension). Figure 3.1 displays SWF transparency by type of SWF, clearly illustrating that variation in SWF transparency is driven primarily by savings SWFs. Pensions funds are the most transparent (with a mean transparency of ninety out of a hundred), followed by foreign exchange reserve (with a mean transparency of sixty-seven out of a hundred), and then macro stability funds (with a mean transparency of forty-seven out of a hundred), with relatively low variation within each category. On average, savings SWFs are the least transparent (around forty out of a hundred), but with considerably greater variation than the other SWF types. Thus, because China lacks a savings SWF but has other types of SWFs, the SPAR measure in Table 3.2 displays an aberrantly high score. Indeed, Figure 3.1 illustrates the importance of focusing on savings SWFs when discussing how political regimes vary in their use of SWFs to implement investment strategies.

The last column of Table 3.2 also displays results for the prevalence of savings SWFs in democracies versus authoritarian regimes. Recall from Chapter 2 that savings SWFs are expected to be more common to authoritarian regimes regardless of the specific type. This is due, in part, to the need for a centralized agency that rulers can use to administer control over sprawling state-owned corporate assets. Because oil rents are widely noted as an important source of revenue for the establishment of a savings fund, I include a control for oil rents as a fraction of GDP.[4] The results nevertheless indicate that savings SWFs are less prevalent among democratic regimes. The summary statistics show that they are most common to NARs (75 percent of these regimes have one), then SPARs (28 percent), and then DPARs (18 percent) as compared with democracies (10 percent). Altogether the analyses presented thus far suggest that SWFs and SOEs exhibit characteristics of both prevalence and transparency that conform to one another. That is, SOEs and savings SWFs are most common to authoritarian regimes, reinforcing the need to examine them together and suggesting that they share common political determinants. Moreover, there are clear differences between DPARs relative to SPARs and NARs.

The Consequences of Regime Transitions

In addition to identifying whether indicators for the control of resources and information exhibit the expected patterns across regimes, I expect regime *change* to yield corresponding changes in the information and resources controlled by the incumbent rulers. More specifically, I expect that regime transitions that move a country toward democracy will display a subsequent decline in the SOE share of the economy and a corresponding increase in the CPI score.

As shown in Figure 1.2, most regime transitions occurred during the 1990s, which is before annual data for SOE share become available and also before most authoritarian regimes are included in the CPI database. Thus, to assess these claims in the context of the 1990s, it is necessary to examine five-year-interval data. The "Regime change" column in Table 3.3 indicates the type of regime transition that occurred between time $t - 1$ and time t. These correspond to five-year time intervals, so $t - 1$ would, for example, correspond to 1990, and time t would equal 1995. Along the top row, SOE share and CPI score changes are reported for time t to time $t + 1$, or 1995 to 2000.

---

[4] Megginson and Fotak (2015).

Table 3.3 *Long-Term Change in SOE Share and CPI Score Following Regime Change, 1990–2015 (5-Year Intervals)*

	SOE share 5-year change (t to $t + 1$)		CPI score 5-year change (t to $t + 1$)	
Regime change($t − 1$ to t)	Total observations	Mean	Total observations	Mean
A Toward democracy		Negative (or less positive) change expected		Positive (or less negative) change expected
NAR to SPAR	1	0	0	
NAR to DPAR	10	−0.6	8	1.6
NAR to Democracy	0		0	
SPAR to DPAR	7	−0.14	2	2
SPAR to Democracy	3	−0.67	1	0.1
DPAR to Democracy	21	−0.9	12	0.4
B Toward NAR		Positive (or less negative) change expected		Negative (or less positive) change expected
Democracy to DPAR	10	−0.7	9	0.19
Democracy to SPAR	0		0	
Democracy to NAR	0		0	
DPAR to SPAR	0		0	
DPAR to NAR	3	0.3	2	0.35
SPAR to NAR	0		0	

Panel A identifies regime changes that move in the direction of democracy (e.g., from NAR to DPAR) and are therefore expected to yield changes in SOE share that decline over time (or are less positive) relative to the equivalent regime transition in the opposite direction (e.g., DPAR to NAR), as indicated in panel B. The "Total observations" column indicates the total number of regime changes that occurred with SOE share change data available. For example, ten countries transitioned from NAR to DPAR, with an average decline in the SOE share for the subsequent five-year time period of 0.6. Overall, there were forty-two democracy-oriented regime transitions compared with thirteen NAR-oriented regime transitions for SOE share changes, but because the number of observations is usually small for each type of regime transition, it is not possible to draw confident conclusions about the magnitude of the changes, let alone make comparisons between them. Modest conclusions should therefore be drawn only with regard to the overall size of the change across all democracy-oriented regime transitions in comparison with NAR-oriented regime transitions. In this regard, the results match the expectations. Specifically, the five-year change to SOE share in panel A is consistently declining at a faster pace than for the regime transitions in panel B.

Turning to CPI score five-year change, there were twenty-three democracy-oriented regime transitions and eleven NAR-oriented regime transitions with CPI score change data available (recall that the CPI score only starts in 1995 for a smaller sample of countries, whereas a large number of regime transitions occurred between 1990 and 1995). Bearing in mind the aforementioned caveat about interpretation of the results with regard to a small number of observations, the results indicate that when a democracy-oriented regime transition occurred, the country's CPI score would increase in the subsequent five-year period at a faster pace than in a NAR-oriented regime transition. That the CPI score increased for panel B regime transitions suggests that exogenous forces have a smaller independent effect on the extent of change, such as the global diffusion of liberalizing reforms.

To complement the analysis of long-term changes, I also examine short-term changes with annual data. To assess the magnitude of short-term change that occurs in the wake of a regime transition, I focus on democracy-to-DPAR transitions or vice versa – the two regime transitions with the largest number of observations in the five-year data sample. For the annual data sample, there were twenty-four DPAR-to-democracy transitions with SOE share data for 2000 or later and twenty-one with CPI score data for 1995 or later; there were twenty-one democracy-to DPAR transitions for both SOE share and CPI score data. There are more observations for the annual data for two reasons: (1) some countries experienced two or more regime transitions within a five-year period, so the five-year data fail to capture this, and (2) data are available for CPI score and SOE share for annual time points prior to being included in the next five-year interval. Thus the annual data offer a more accurate presentation of the short-term changes due to a larger number of observations, whereas the five-year data bias toward regime transitions that are more stable and therefore present a more confident depiction of long-term trends.

Figure 3.2 displays impulse-response functions and the 5 percent error bands generated by Monte Carlo simulations for the speed with which either the SOE share or the CPI score changes immediately following a regime change.[5] Both these variables are measured on a 0–10 scale, allowing comparisons to be made easily. The panels reveal that the changes to SOE share (*dsoe*) and CPI score (*dcpiscore*) are far greater when regimes transition to DPAR from democracy than the reverse. Specifically, the first-year change in the SOE share following a regime transition from democracy to DPAR is about eight times higher than the reverse regime transition (0.039 versus 0.005); the first-year change in the CPI score is twenty times higher following a democracy-to-DPAR transition than a DPAR-to-democracy transition (0.02 versus 0.001). Theoretically, this is consistent with the institutional arrangements of these regimes; DPARs face fewer checks and balances than democracies and can therefore implement more dramatic changes.

With regard to the change in SOE share, the rapid increase for new DPARs is indicative of a greater reliance on SOEs in the long term compared with democracies, as observed in Table 3.3 (with a less negative decline in SOE share) and with regard to the regression results in Table 3.1. With regard to the change in CPI score, new DPAR regimes also display a far greater rise in CPI score than

---

[5] To calculate the impulse-response function with panel data, I use the *pvar2* estimation command first developed by Inessa Love (see Love and Zicchino 2006) and updated and revised by Ryan Decker (http://econweb.umd.edu/~dec ker/code.html). The revised version was first used by Fort et al. (2013).

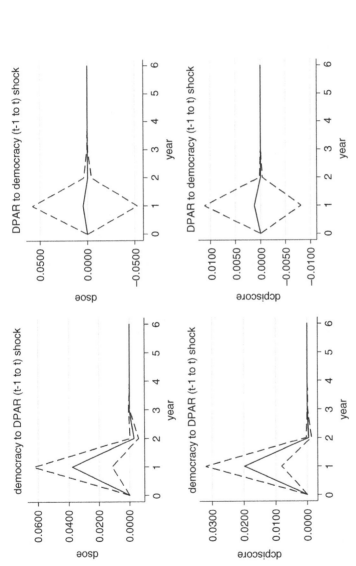

Figure 3.2 Short-term change: impulse responses for change in SOE share and CPI score following regime change from DPAR to democracy or vice versa with annual data. *Note:* Errors are 5 percent on each side generated by Monte-Carlo with 1,000 repetitions. *Sources:* CPI Score Annual Data: 1995–2015; SOE Share Annual Data: 2000–15.

new democracies, but this is not indicative of the longer-term patterns observed in Table 3.3 or the regression results in Table 3.1, where democracies display higher CPI scores. A possible explanation for this divergence between the short and long term is that weak democracies (e.g., the Philippines or Thailand) are more likely to experience a DPAR regime transition. For these weak democracies, corruption is already high; when a new DPAR regime takes power, anticorruption policies are quickly implemented to boost investment and promote growth. In the long run, however, anticorruption policies are more effective in democracies, although they may be slower at implementing them. The inverse of this logic may account for the large error bands for the SOE share and CPI score changes following a DPAR-to-democracy transition; weak democracies may be captured, via patronage politics, to the benefit of one group. As a result, this group may benefit from an increase in corruption and/or SOE share.

Strongly and Weakly Dominant Ruling Parties in DPARs

I now examine whether the strength of the ruling party in DPARs results in observable differences with regard to the control of resources and information, as manifested by the SOE share and CPI score. The theory predicts that weakly dominant ruling parties will exert stronger controls over information, resulting in lower transparency. The theory also predicts that weakly dominant ruling parties will exert more control over the largest firms in the corporate sector but create more opportunities for small and medium-sized enterprises. Thus the predictions for the overall SOE share are mixed.

Figures 3.3 and 3.4 display the results for CPI scores and SOE shares corresponding to whether the ruling party in a DPAR is strongly or weakly dominant for each five-year interval from 1995 to 2015. Ruling-party strength is determined by identifying the median proportion of seats held by the ruling party in all DPARs for a given year (using the *partsz* variable mentioned earlier) and then taking the average proportion of seats held by ruling parties that lie above or below the median. The CPI score results clearly match the predictions: DPARs with a strongly dominant ruling party have consistently higher CPI scores than DPARs with a weakly dominant ruling party. There is a sizable difference in the CPI scores in 1995,

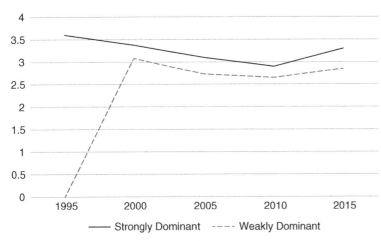

Figure 3.3 CPI scores and ruling-party dominance in DPARs, 1995–2015.

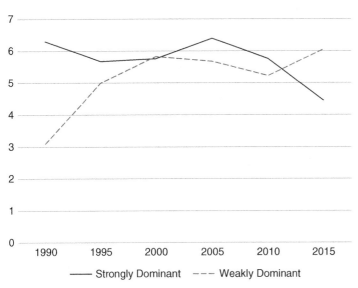

Figure 3.4 SOE shares and ruling-party dominance in DPARs, 1990–2015.

which may be due to the small number of observations at this time (there are only eleven total observations; in 2000 there are twenty-seven observations) and lingering patterns associated with the Soviet Union's sphere of influence.

Figure 3.4 displays far more mixed results with regard to SOE share, which matches the theoretical expectations that some combination of state ownership of the largest enterprises will be coupled with policies that cater to small and medium-sized enterprises (private capital). The overall trend during the 1990s is for weakly dominant ruling parties to increase their reliance on SOEs. There are two different interpretations for this. First, it may be attributable to regime change, with former NARs and SPARs with large state sectors transitioning to DPAR political systems. The summary statistics in Table 3.4 indicate that the number of DPARs increased from nineteen to thirty-five between 1990 and 1995 but remained constant at thirty-five in 2000, so this explanation cannot account for the increase between 1995 and 2000. A second, complementary explanation is that weakly dominant incumbent rulers of DPARs increased their reliance on SOEs in response to financial crises that swept across the developing world in the middle to late 1990s, and this trend persisted afterwards as a counterreaction to the global diffusion of liberalizing reforms that increased the power of private capital. The overall upward trend among weakly dominant ruling parties, compared with the overall downward trend for strongly dominant ruling parties, is consistent with this explanation. Further evidence for this explanation will be examined with more detailed ownership data in Chapter 4 and in the Malaysia and Singapore case studies (Chapters 6 and 7, respectively). In these two cases, Malaysia conforms more closely to the weakly dominant ruling-party pattern, whereas Singapore adheres more closely to the strongly dominant ruling-party pattern.

Conclusions

The results from the SOE share of the economy indicate that authoritarian regimes display a higher prevalence of SOEs in comparison with democracies. They also suggest that the SOE share is highest among SPARs and NARs, with DPARs sitting between them and democracies. The CPI score results display a similar pattern. Additional tests for corporate transparency indicate that NARs are more opaque than democracies and that SWFs from NARs are the least transparent, followed by those from DPARs, and their opacity is significantly greater than the transparency of SWFs located in democracies.

Finally, savings SWFs are more likely to be located in authoritarian regimes than in democracies, even after controlling for oil rents.

Turning to the long-term change in the SOE share and the CPI score following a regime change, the five-year indicators match the expected predictions. Specifically, when regimes move in a democratic direction, the SOE share declines and the CPI score increases (indicating less corruption/more transparency); likewise, when regimes move in an authoritarian direction, the opposite occurs. The short-term change, as displayed with the impulse-response functions, indicates that new DPARs that were formerly democracies exhibit dramatic increases in their SOE share and CPI score; new democracies that were formerly DPARs exhibit far more modest increases. These patterns are consistent with the institutional arrangements of these regimes – DPARs have fewer checks and balances, allowing significant changes to be implemented quickly.

Finally, the strength of the ruling party also displays patterns that vary across DPARs with regard to CPI scores and the SOE share of the economy. Specifically, DPARs with strongly dominant ruling parties possess consistently higher CPI scores, indicating lower corruption (and more transparency). Additionally, DPARs with strongly dominant ruling parties display a variable decline in the SOE share of the economy over time.

While the results are generally consistent with the argument presented in Chapter 2, the measures used are not perfect indicators for the underlying concepts. It is therefore necessary to examine more detailed indicators, which requires a narrowing of the sample to the East Asia region followed by contextualization for the observed patterns with case studies.

Table 3.4 *Summary Statistics*

SOE share		Democracy	DPAR	SPAR	NAR
1990	Obs.	55	19	16	12
	Mean	4.45	4.78	7.5	7.91
	SD	2.7	2.9	1.71	2.42
1995	Obs.	60	35	3	9
	Mean	4.73	5.37	9.3	7.2
	SD	3.12	3.25	1.15	2.63
2000	Obs.	70	35	2	7
	Mean	2.74	5.8	8	6.7
	SD	2.58	3.52	2.82	2.49
2005	Obs.	83	36	2	8
	Mean	2.24	6.02	8	4.5
	SD	2.31	3.3	2.82	3.11
2010	Obs.	83	46	2	7
	Mean	3.12	5.52	7	7.28
	SD	2.34	3.29	4.24	2.75
2015	Obs.	82	50	2	7
	Mean	2.9	5	9	6.28
	SD	2.63	3.21	1.41	2.62
Total	Mean	3.24	5.44	7.85	6.76
	SD	2.72	3.26	1.91	2.76

CPI score					
1995	Obs.	33	11	1	3
	Mean	3.64	2.1	2.16	1.43
	SD	3.13	3.01	–	2.47
2000	Obs.	52	27	2	2
	Mean	5.84	3.11	2.8	3.15
	SD	2.29	1.61	0.42	1.2
2005	Obs.	80	42	7	13
	Mean	5	2.91	2.72	3.9
	SD	2.37	1.33	0.65	1.78
2010	Obs.	85	54	9	14
	Mean	4.94	2.82	2.67	4.09
	SD	2.21	1.25	0.78	1.95
2015	Obs.	80	57	6	10
	Mean	5.35	3.17	2.97	4.79
	SD	1.95	1.49	1.12	1.67
Total	Mean	5.27	2.94	2.74	3.9
	SD	2.32	1.54	0.78	1.94

Table 3.4 (*cont.*)

		Democracy	DPAR	SPAR	NAR
Corporate transparency					
2015	Obs.	92	58	5	11
	Mean	4.78	3.67	3.8	3.6
	SD	2.19	2.13	3.03	1.62
SWF transparency					
2010	Obs.	10	7	2	6
	Mean	70.6	43.28	51	32.58
	SD	23.46	27.15	18.38	23.69
SWF savings					
2015	Obs.	99	59	7	12
	Mean	0.1	0.18	0.28	0.75
	SD	0.3	0.39	0.48	0.45

4 | *East Asia Patterns*

This chapter provides a descriptive overview of country-level patterns across East Asia before turning to the analytic narratives in the country case studies. I begin with an overview of the characteristics with regard to each state's *capacity* for public-private ownership. This entails identifying the balance between state and private ownership among a country's largest listed and unlisted firms. After identifying the countries with an abundance of listed firms with state and private co-ownership, I conduct a detailed investigation to identify states' precise ownership stakes.

The subsequent two sections further gauge each state's capacity for entering into public-private ownership arrangements, including the transparency of the state sector as well as an overview of sovereign wealth funds (SWFs). Transparency enables private investors and foreign policymakers to evaluate the investing firm's/state's proposal as well as its motivations in order to decide whether to permit the investment in the case of foreign policymakers or to engage in co-ownership in the case of private investors. The type of SWF determines the capacity for initiating large, long-term ownership positions that could lead to changes in the target firm, such as replacing executives, directors, initiating mergers or divestments, or altering firm strategy in some way (e.g., integrating it with the SWF's other businesses).

The final section identifies the extent of large foreign state ownership positions initiated by each states' state-owned enterprises (SOEs) and SWF(s). The evidence presented in this final section is suggestive that dominant-party authoritarian regimes (DPARs) may be more strongly *motivated* to intervene in the corporate sector than other regime types and indicates the need for closer investigation in the case-study chapters.

The Prevalence of State Ownership across East Asia

To identify the balance of public versus private ownership, I first examine the prevalence of listed versus unlisted SOEs for each country's largest firms. This offers a first cut at identifying the balance between public versus private ownership and allows me to narrow the subsequent analysis to countries and regimes for which a precise assessment of the state's holdings is obscured by layers of indirect ownership stakes – DPARs and democracies. It is immediately clear that public ownership dominates private ownership in single-party authoritarian regimes (SPARs), so I save a detailed examination of state ownership for the China case study in Chapter 5.

Next, I delve more deeply into identifying the prevalence of state ownership among the largest listed firms in DPARs and democracies. The sample used for this analysis consists of the 200 largest listed firms for each of nine economies in 1996 and 2008. First I identify precise ultimate ownership levels for different owners in this sample of firms. Then I present the relative importance of dominant and minority state ownership positions to assess the extent of states' direct controls over the corporate sector in comparison with nonstate owners. After this, I display regime versus industry variation in order to confirm that state ownership patterns are primarily related to regime type rather than industry. Finally, I turn to an analysis of the mechanisms – either political or market – that contribute to changes in state ownership over time.[1]

Listed versus Unlisted SOEs among a Country's Largest Firms

Table 4.1 lists countries by regime type, the date when their stock exchange was established, the number of companies listed on it for 1996 and 2008, and the proportion of listed firms that are SOEs. With regard to this last column, the data provided for DPARs and democracies are due to the analysis in the subsequent section. A strict focus on the prevalence of listed versus unlisted SOEs does not permit a precise estimate of state ownership.

Recall that the extent of state ownership is expected to vary with regard to regime type. Thus countries that transition from one regime type to another should exhibit corresponding changes to the prevalence of state ownership. Of the countries listed, three experienced regime change during the period under examination, including Indonesia,

---

[1] For an excellent overview of corporate ownership in Southeast Asia, see Samphantharak (2017).

Table 4.1 *East Asian States and Their Stock Market Characteristics*

Regime type (1996–2015)	Country	Year stock market established	Number of listed firms, 1996	Number of listed firms, 2008	Proportion of listed firms that are SOEs, 2008[a]
NAR	Brunei	NA	0	0	NA
	Myanmar (until 2012)	1996	2	2	100%
	North Korea	NA	0	0	NA
	Thailand (2006–7 and 2014–present)	1975	NA	NA	NA
SPAR	China	1990	524	1,604	70%[b]
	Laos	2011	0	0	NA
	Vietnam	2000	0	162	78%[c]
DPAR	Cambodia	2012	0	0	NA
	Indonesia (until 1999)	1977	253	NA	NA
	Malaysia	1964	621	972	39.7%
	Myanmar (since 2012)	NA	NA	NA	NA
	Singapore	1910	216	455	20.5%
Democracy	Indonesia (since 1999)	1977	NA	396	14%
	Japan	1878	1,749	2,374	6.3%
	South Korea	1956	760	1,789	6.9%
	Philippines	1965	216	244	5.2%
	Taiwan	1962	382	718	9.2%
	Thailand (1996–2006 and 2008–2014)	1975	454	525	12.8%

[a] See Table 4.2.

[b] Szamosszegi and Kyle (2011). Data are for 2004, at which time the state retained an average of more than two-thirds of the shares of listed SOEs.

[c] Hong and Biallas (2007).

Thailand, and Myanmar. Indonesia and Thailand have both experienced recent periods under military rule, despite longer periods as a democracy. Indonesia transitioned from a DPAR to a democracy in 1999, whereas Thailand transitioned from a democracy to a narrow authoritarian regime (NAR) and then back to a democracy between 2006 and 2007, followed by another transition back to a NAR in 2014. We may therefore see relatively higher levels of state ownership in these two countries compared with other democracies. Myanmar also experienced regime change, from a NAR to a DPAR in 2012. Because this is relatively recent, the magnitude of change to state ownership is unlikely to be large.

With regard to the establishment of a stock exchange, it is useful to begin by observing that they are almost nonexistent among the countries in the NAR category, including Brunei, Myanmar, and North Korea. Thailand's moment as a NAR from 2006 to 2007 was too brief to permit established corporate ownership patterns to reflect regime characteristics. Among the remaining NARs, the lack of listed firms is consistent with the expected controls that these regimes exert over their country's strategic resources.

There are three countries that fall into the single-party authoritarian regime (SPAR) category, including China, Vietnam, and Laos. The immediate difference between this group and the NAR group is that two of the SPAR countries, China and Vietnam, established stock markets prior to 2008, and they both have a large number of listed firms. Laos is a relative latecomer, having only established a stock market in 2011. As of 2016, it had five listed companies. With regard to China's and Vietnam's listed firms, state ownership dominates – for both countries, at least 70 percent of listed firms qualify as state owned.[2] While these firms tend to be among the largest for each country, there are many, sometimes large SOEs that remain unlisted. For Vietnam, only around 4 percent of SOEs are listed on the stock market.[3] Thousands of SOEs owned by China's local governments are not listed, as well as many of the largest SOEs owned by the central government.[4] This will be discussed in more detail in the China case study in Chapter 5.

---

[2] Szamosszegi and Kyle (2011); Hong and Biallis (2007).
[3] Kim, Nam, and Cuong (2010).   [4] Naughton and Tsai (2015).

Next is the DPAR category with Cambodia, Indonesia, Malaysia, and Singapore. As mentioned earlier, Myanmar only transitioned into this category in 2012. While Cambodia formally qualifies as a DPAR because it has held semicompetitive elections since 1993 and has a legislature, it bears characteristics more akin to a NAR. Cambodia's current prime minister, Hun Sen, is one of the world's longest-serving leaders, having been in power since 1998. He is a dictator who has assumed authoritarian control through violence, intimidation, and corruption, including a personal guard that reportedly has capabilities rivaling those of the country's regular army.[5] Reflecting his centralized control of power, the country established a stock market only in 2012, but with only two listed firms as of 2016.

Immediately after the 1997–98 Asian financial crisis, Indonesia transitioned to a democracy while its state-owned assets increased as many highly indebted banks, and the conglomerate groups they were part of, came under the management of a government-run restructuring agency. Many observers, however, expected state ownership to decline because these assets were to be reprivatized under Indonesia's IMF loans.[6] Because the private sector flourished in the economic recovery after 2002, it was easy to conclude that the state-owned sector was in relative decline. For example, Aspinall writes: "other critical sectors of capital ... have continued their relative decline in weight and influence. State-owned and military businesses have declined [as] large sectors of the economy that were once reserved for state-owned enterprises have been deregulated and the old state monopolies now find themselves competing with private firms in these sectors."[7] Nevertheless, the proportion of Indonesia's largest listed firms with a dominant share of state ownership grew after the Asian financial crisis. At the 10 percent cutoff, the state-owned share increased from 10 percent in 1996 to 14 percent in 2008.[8] One reason was the partial privatization of some formerly fully state-owned companies. Indonesia's privatization predates the financial crisis; the government established a mode of semiprivatization through listing a minority of shares, leaving itself as the dominant shareholder (typically with over 50 percent ownership). Before the crisis, however, only a few such privatizations occurred,

---

[5] Adams (2012); Marshall (2012); Thu (2013); Fuller (2014).
[6] Caprio et al. (2005).   [7] Aspinall (2013).
[8] Carney and Hamilton-Hart (2015).

starting with cement maker Semen Gresik in 1991, two telecommunications firms (Indosat and Telkom) in 1995, and a bank (Bank Nasional Indonesia) and a tin-mining company (Timah) in 1996.[9] After the crisis, there were both decreases in the government-owned shares of these listed SOEs and further semiprivatizations through listing. In 2008, the total number of listed SOEs with dominant state ownership was fourteen, while twenty-one had a minority state share. Meanwhile, there were 113 unlisted SOEs, though these tended to be smaller than their listed counterparts. Although the total number of SOEs has fallen over time, this largely reflects consolidation. A ministry official reports that the assets of SOEs increased by 40 percent over 1992–96 (and by 78 percent over 1992–97) versus a 170 percent increase over 1998–2004.[10]

For Malaysia and Singapore, the largest companies are normally listed on the stock market, including nearly all the largest SOEs. In the case of Malaysia, only two of its largest SOEs were not listed in 2008 – Felda Global Ventures (a plantation group) and Petronas (the national oil company). Felda was privatized in 2012. For Singapore, there are a handful of large SOEs that are not listed, including Mediacorp, PSA International, and Singapore Power; however, Singapore's Ministry of Finance has stated that the government prefers to list the companies it owns in order to subject them to market pressures and ensure profitability. Thus, for these DPAR countries, unlisted SOEs represent a small fraction of the state-owned corporate sector.

The final regime category is democracy. In the high-income democracies of Japan, South Korea, and Taiwan, unlisted SOEs may be important to specific sectors (often for economically necessary roles such as when there exists a natural monopoly) but contribute to a small and declining fraction of national gross domestic product (GDP). In Taiwan, for example, there were twenty-one SOEs as of 2005; nineteen were unlisted as of 2015.[11] In relation to the size of Taiwan's economy, SOEs contributed to less than 8 percent of GDP in 2005, which was on a declining trend since the 1980s; presumably their share of GDP has fallen further since. Korea had twenty-three SOEs as of 2008, with only six of them large enough to be considered

[9] Prasetiantono (2004, 141).   [10] Fitriningrum (2006).
[11] Pao, Wu, and Pan (2008). They exert the greatest impact on the telecommunications, electricity, petroleum, railway transportation, tobacco and wines, water supply, and shipbuilding industries.

for privatization.[12] In Japan, most of its large SOEs have already been privatized. The most recent privatizations were completed in the late 1990s and early 2000s, including Japan National Railway and Nippon Telegraph and Telephone.[13] In 2015, the privatizations of Japan Post Holdings Co. and its financial subsidiaries, Japan Post Insurance and Japan Post Bank, Japan's largest insurance company and bank, respectively, were completed. While privatization does not necessarily equate to the government completely divesting of its ownership stake, it does suggest that if the firms are among the largest 200 publicly listed firms, then they will be identified in the analysis below.

In the Philippines, the number of SOEs has undergone considerable change over time, corresponding to the country's changing political regimes.[14] Before World War II, when the Philippines was a democracy, there were three SOEs. This number increased to thirteen after the war, followed by sixty-five before Marcos took power in 1965 and changed the regime to a NAR in 1972. SOEs then spiked to 303 by 1984 and then fell to 225 in 1989, after the country had transitioned back to democracy in 1986. SOES continued to fall to 125 in 2004 before a slight increase to 128 in 2013.[15] However, the number of SOEs in the top 1,000 corporations has fallen from forty-eight in 1985 to ten in 2009.[16] Only three SOEs made it into the top 100 corporations in 2009, including the Land Bank of the Philippines (unlisted), the Development Bank of the Philippines (unlisted), and the Home Development Mutual Fund (unlisted). Among the country's largest firms, private ownership dominates via sprawling family-owned conglomerates.

In Indonesia and Thailand, regimes with recent histories of military/ authoritarian rule, SOEs continue to play an important role in the economy. In Indonesia, there were 141 SOEs in 2010. Sixteen SOEs (in which the government was the dominant owner) were listed on the stock exchange, and they represented 29.5 percent of total stock market capitalization (of 410 total listed firms).[17] The twelve largest SOEs accounted for more than 90 percent of total SOE assets.[18] Although

---

[12] Park (2009).   [13] Tamamura (2004).
[14] SOEs are referred to as *government-owned and controlled corporations* in the Philippines.
[15] Governance Commission for GOCCs (2016).   [16] Batalla (2012).
[17] Abubakar (2010).
[18] Astami et al. (2010). SOEs are major players in telecommunications, banking, cement, oil and gas, mining, and infrastructure.

many SOEs are not listed on the stock exchange, the largest SOEs that represent the dominant contribution of SOEs to the Indonesian economy are listed.[19]

In Thailand, there were sixty-three SOEs in 2002, six of which were listed on the stock exchange.[20] By 2010, the number of listed SOEs had increased to fifteen; they accounted for about 20 percent of total stock market capitalization.[21] However, several of the largest SOEs, by assets, were not listed either in 2002 or since then.[22] Following the transition to military rule in 2014, the new government has increased its control of SOEs, of which there were fifty-six.[23]

This survey of listed and unlisted SOEs indicates that unlisted SOEs are the most prevalent among NARs, followed by SPARs. China, a SPAR, has liberalized more than Vietnam, and many of the largest SOEs are publicly listed in order to raise money from private investors. However, the government almost always retains an ownership stake in excess of 50 percent (on average, state ownership is 70 percent). Thus it is clear that public ownership dominates private ownership for the largest firms in SPARs. Public ownership and private ownership seem to be more balanced for DPARs, and the balance is likely tilted toward private shareholders for democracies. But because it is difficult to identify the exact ownership stake for ultimate owners of listed firms, it is necessary to delve more deeply to uncover whether ownership patterns correspond to regime types for DPARs and democracies.

Ultimate Corporate Ownership in DPARs and Democracies

There are a couple challenges associated with accurately identifying a state's ownership position in relation to private investors for publicly listed firms. First, SWFs usually do not report the full extent of their corporate holdings, if any such holdings are even reported. For example, Temasek reports only major investments in which it has a direct

---

[19] Carney and Hamilton-Hart (2015). Also see the website of the Ministry of State-Owned Enterprises.

[20] Nikomborirak and Cheevasittiyanon (2006).

[21] SET News No. 150/2010, December 13, 2010.

[22] Nikomborirak and Cheevasittiyanon (2006). Detailed information about Thailand's SOEs is available from the State Enterprise Policy Office website: www.sepo.go.th/. SOEs operate primarily in service delivery, in particular, the energy, telecommunications, transportation, and financial sectors.

[23] *Wall Street Journal*, June 17, 2014.

ownership stake.[24] This is problematic for identifying the full extent of its corporate holdings because it has numerous unreported direct holdings as well as even more indirect ownership stakes. To obtain an accurate picture of state ownership, it is therefore necessary to identify each firm's shareholders and then work one's way up to the ultimate owner.

However, acquiring such detailed information about corporate ownership positions (the ultimate owners as compared with the immediate owners) is very time-consuming, making it impractical to do so for a large sample of firms and countries at the global level. It is more feasible for a regional grouping of countries. Claessens et al. assembled such a data set for nine East Asian economies in 1996 – just prior to the onset of the Asian financial crisis.[25] This is an opportune moment to assemble such a data set in order to evaluate what changes, if any, occurred in response to the newly recognized vulnerability that authoritarian leaders faced. But assessing such responses requires data at a point in time sufficiently distant from the crisis to have allowed new patterns to become established. Post-crisis data for 2008 were assembled for the same group of countries by Carney and Child.[26] Details on the compiling of the data set are provided in the Appendix 4A.1. The Carney-Child data set offers symmetrical coverage for nine economies, including Hong Kong, Indonesia, Japan, South Korea, Malaysia, the Philippines, Singapore, Taiwan, and Thailand. The data set is comprised of each economy's largest firms, drawn from the 200 largest by market capitalization.

The difficulty with tracing the ultimate owners of each country's largest listed corporations is amplified by the fact that most of the largest firms in the region are owned by families who frequently try to conceal their corporate holdings. Although the collection of data began with the 200 largest by market capitalization in 2008 (supplementing the previously collected data for 1996 by Claessens et al.),[27] it was possible to accurately identify ultimate owners and their positions for only a subset. Nevertheless, the number of firms with ultimate ownership identified is still large enough to make confident characterizations about the prevalence of different owners in each economy. For example, numerous qualitative accounts of the Philippines identify

---

[24]   See the Temasek Review Annual Reports.   [25]   Claessens et al. (2000).
[26]   Carney and Child (2013).   [27]   Claessens et al. (2000).

family-owned conglomerates as dominating the private sector.[28] Although this country has the fewest firms with ultimate owners accurately identified (114), the data for 2008 are consistent with this qualitative characterization. Likewise, the state is often regarded as a prominent owner of large corporations in Singapore, and the data from 1996 and 2008 match this expectation.[29]

In addition to quantifying just how important certain owners are to each country's largest listed firms, the data are also beneficial for confirming whether anecdotes correspond to more general patterns. For example, news stories suggested that states embarked on an increasing number of foreign ownership positions following the Asian financial crisis, often through a SWF. The data for 2008 reveal just how pervasive this is with regard to both which states and state entities are initiating these positions and which countries most frequently host these investments. In 1996, foreign state ownership was so small that it was not even identified as a distinct category. No mention of it is made in Claessens et al.[30]

Table 4.2 shows the relative importance of ultimate owners across the region in 1996 and 2008. Specifically, for each firm, each of its ultimate owners with a stake equal to or above 10 percent was identified. The total sample includes 1,296 firms in 2008 and 1,606 firms in 1996. Families are the most prevalent type of ultimate owner in 1996, followed by varying types of widely held ownership (e.g., shareholders, a widely held corporation, or a widely held financial company). State ownership is the least prevalent form of ownership in 1996, although it was most prevalent in Singapore and Malaysia (21.8 and 19.4 percent, respectively). Overall, the state was an ultimate owner of 9.2 percent of all firms in the 1996 sample.

By 2008, family ownership had generally declined, though it remained the most dominant form of ownership. Taiwan, Thailand, and Indonesia underwent the most pronounced shifts away from family ownership. By contrast, family ownership in the Philippines actually increased; Japan, South Korea, and Singapore also saw no decline in the dominance of family ownership. Meanwhile, state ownership increased. Overall, the state was an owner of more than twice as many firms in 2008 as in 1996 (19.6 percent); the prevalence of

---

[28] See, for example, McCoy (1993) and Sidel (1999).   [29] Low (1998).
[30] Claessens et al. (2000).

Table 4.2 *Relative Importance of Ultimate Owners across the Region,*
1996 and 2008

Ultimate corporate owners in East Asia, 1996 and 2008	Year	No. of firms	Family (%)	State (%)	Widely held (%)	Foreign state (%)
Hong Kong	1996	200	65.5	4	30.5	
	2008	158	60.6	28	10.7	0.6
Indonesia	1996	178	68.6	10.2	21.2	
	2008	132	57.3	14.1	20.8	7.8
Japan	1996	200	6.8	2.5	90.8	
	2008	136	9.6	6.3	83.1	1.1
Korea	1996	200	51.8	6.8	41.6	
	2008	159	54.5	6.9	37.6	0.9
Malaysia	1996	200	56.9	19.4	23.7	
	2008	154	51.5	39.7	6.2	2.6
Philippines	1996	120	42.1	3.6	54.4	
	2008	114	78.5	5.2	12.9	3.4
Singapore	1996	200	53.3	21.8	24.9	
	2008	131	60.2	20.5	13.9	5.3
Taiwan	1996	141	65.6	3	31.4	
	2008	163	13.8	9.2	77.1	0
Thailand	1996	167	56.5	7.5	36.1	
	2008	149	37.8	12.8	41	8.5
Total	1996	1,606	51.6	9.2	39.2	
	2008	1,296	46.1	16.2	34.3	3.4

Note: State ownership includes firms with a state agency/ministry controlling at least 10 percent of the voting stock. Data are for each country's 200 largest publicly listed firms at the end of 1996 and 2008. "Widely held" includes widely held financial institutions, widely held corporations, and individual shareholders.
Source: Carney and Child (2013).

domestic state ownership increased by 7 percent to a total of 16.2 percent, whereas the proportion of firms with foreign state ownership in 2008 came in at 3.4 percent. As the table shows, countries exhibited clear variance with regard to increases and decreases across each of the ownership categories, but one of the clear patterns to stand out is the continuing importance of the state to both Singapore and Malaysia.

In fact, focusing exclusively on the proportion of firms with state ownership within each of these two countries understates the importance of each of these countries' total state ownership positions because they are the two countries that most frequently engaged in foreign state ownership. In essence, the data clearly show that state ownership by these two DPARs remains robust in the wake of the Asian financial crisis.

Hong Kong also displays an increase in state ownership, but this is largely due to mainland Chinese companies becoming newly listed on the Hong Kong Stock Exchange. Hence this is not indicative of domestic political dynamics to which my theory speaks. But the importance of SOEs to Hong Kong illustrates the importance of the state as a shareholder to China's listed firms, which tend to be the country's largest.

The State as a Dominant or Minority Owner

Recall that among NARs and SPARs the state was either the sole or the dominant owner for almost all SOEs, indicating the regime's strong control over the corporate sector. I examine the extent of dominant and nondominant (or minority ownership with an ownership stake above the 10 percent threshold) state ownership for DPARs and democracies in Figure 4.1.

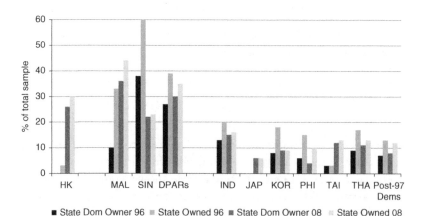

Figure 4.1 The state as a dominant and nondominant owner.

To clarify differences among countries with regard to their regime type, they have been grouped together into three categories. On the left is Hong Kong, which is an outlier because of its handover to China in 1997 and the subsequent surge in SOEs on its stock exchange. The small difference between firms with dominant and nondominant state ownership for 2008 is indicative of state ownership stakes for listed firms in Shanghai and Shenzhen. When the Chinese state holds an ownership stake, it is almost always a dominant stake.[31] In the middle are the two DPARs, Singapore and Malaysia. They clearly exhibit higher levels of state ownership than the post-1997 democracies. For both countries, the difference between nondominant and dominant state ownership changed dramatically after the Asian financial crisis – regimes in both countries move strongly toward dominant ownership even though it was for a smaller proportion of all firms in the case of Singapore.

Except for Thailand's brief period with a military regime in 2006, those countries positioned on the right side of the figure were all democracies in the wake of the 1997 crisis and up to 2008, and they all display relatively lower levels of state ownership, which is consistent with the global data. As a result, it is uncertain that the proportion of dominant versus nondominant state ownership is indicative of the regime's efforts at exerting greater control over strategically important parts of the corporate sector.

Overall, these patterns clearly indicate that the reliance on state ownership is more closely associated with regime type than with level of development or other explanations, which is consistent with the statistical tests presented in Chapter 3.

Regime versus Industry Patterns

When examining the relative level of state ownership across firms, one might consider whether state ownership is more closely associated with a particular industry rather than reflecting attributes associated with certain political regimes. For example, if some industries are of high importance to national security regardless of the political regime, then we should focus our attention on the particular attributes of that industry rather than on the impact of political arrangements. Data

---

[31] Wang (2014).

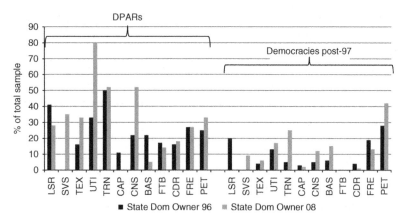

Figure 4.2 Regime versus industry state ownership patterns: DPARs and democracies post-1997.
Note: LSR = leisure; SVS = services; TEX = textiles; UTI = utilities; TRN = transportation; CAP = capital goods; CNS = construction; BAS = basic industry; FTB = food and tobacco; CDR = consumer durables; FRE = finance and real estate; PET = petroleum. Industry categories are based on those identified in Campbell (1996).

from the global sample are too coarse to permit a detailed comparison of country versus industry patterns. The data compiled here, however, do enable such a comparison. Figure 4.2 displays the prevalence of state ownership by both country and industry, with firms located in Singapore and Malaysia on the left and firms located in the remaining countries (except Hong Kong) on the right.

If industry were more important than political regime, then we should observe consistently high (or low) levels of state ownership for both groups of countries. There appear to be two industry candidates – petroleum (PET) and capital goods (CAP). That these are the only two industries to exhibit consistent levels of state ownership across the two regime categories is reassuring for the analysis of Chapter 3 because it suggests that politics matters more than industry. Although petroleum exhibits a level of state ownership independent of regime type according to this small sample of nine countries, the analysis from Chapter 3 controlled for oil rents as a fraction of GDP with a much larger sample. To the extent that oil rents as a fraction of GDP correlate with the propensity for state-owned oil companies (which seems highly plausible when we consider the prevalence of them across oil-rich monarchies), it is again reassuring that the results from the analysis in Chapter 3 indicate that political factors matter, conditional on the size of the petroleum sector. Hence the one industry that may exhibit ownership patterns that deviate from those driven by political factors is basic industry. But given that this is the only outlier, it is more likely that it is simply that – an outlier – rather than indicative of this industry being exceptional in some way (one might have expected that with petroleum instead).

Data from Hong Kong also indicate that Chinese SOEs from all industries have been listed on the stock exchange following the handover in 1997 (there were no firms with dominant state ownership in 1996). It is likely that the demand for capital by some Chinese SOEs has led to a greater push to list in Hong Kong, such as capital-intensive firms. But given Hong Kong's autonomous status, we should look to the mainland to discern the role of the regime relative to industry. In this regard, the evidence clearly indicates that the state is a dominant owner of large firms across all industries, notwithstanding the greater importance of certain industries to China's rapid development.[32]

How State Ownership Changed

Changes to the prevalence of state ownership among each country's largest listed firms may be due to politics or changing market valuations. Because state ownership of the largest SOEs is of high importance to political rulers of DPARs, I expect political mechanisms to play a bigger role in accounting for changes to state ownership in comparison with democracies. There are four main political mechanisms. The first political mechanism concerns the state purchasing ownership stakes in already publicly listed firms that are not owned by the state. This is complemented by the state selling stakes in listed firms to private owners. Third, mergers between a state-owned company and other non-state-owned firms could occur. The fourth political mechanism regards partial privatization of newly listed SOEs. While it is possible that politics may have little to do with individual decisions for each of these mechanisms, I expect political mechanisms to be more common in DPARs than in democracies, on average. But to assess the

---

[32] Ibid.

Table 4.3 *State Ownership Changes: Distinguishing between Political and Market Mechanisms*

	Political mechanisms				Market mechanisms	
	State buys stakes in non-SOE firms (% of total 1996 firms)	State sells stakes in SOEs (% of total 1996 firms)	Newly listed SOEs in 2008 (% of total 2008 firms)	Mergers and acquisitions the state (% of total 1996 firms)	Market valuation rises (% of total 2008 firms)	Market valuation falls (% of total 1996 firms)
DPARs	11	2.8	8.7	2.8	17.9	6
Post-1997 democracies	1.5	0.6	3.4	0.16	3.5	0.58

Note: See Carney and Child (2013) for details regarding these ownership changes.

importance of market mechanisms accounting for changes to the pre-valence of SOEs in the sample, I report the number of SOEs entering or leaving the sample between 1996 and 2008 simply due to changing market valuations.

The data displayed in Table 4.3 reveal that the most important con-tributor to the rise in SOEs in DPARs is the acquisition of formerly non-state-owned firms (11 percent). For post-1997 democracies, there was a small increase of only 1.5 percent. The ratio of state acquisitions to sell-offs is considerably higher for DPARs (11/2.8 = 3.9) than for post-1997 democracies (1.5/0.6 = 2.5), indicating the greater activism of the state in DPARs. Meanwhile, newly listed state-owned firms comprised 8.7 per-cent of the sample firms in DPARs versus 3.4 percent in post-1997 democracies. Examination of the initial listing dates for SOEs indicates that they mainly occurred prior to 2003 for both types of regimes. That a larger fraction of them remain under state control in DPARs indicates an interest by the state to retain an ownership position compared with democracies, where partial privatization is normally a first step toward full privatization, as will be seen more clearly in the Taiwan case study. With regard to the final political mechanism, mergers and acquisitions of SOEs were far more common in DPARs, totaling 2.8 percent of all 1996 firms versus only 0.16 percent for post-1997 democracies. This indicates that DPARs have exercised a greater interest in centralizing ownership and control of the corporate sector.

With regard to the market mechanisms for DPARs, 17.9 percent of all 2008 firms were SOEs that rose into the top 200, whereas 6 percent of 1996 firms fell out of the top 200. For post-1997 democracies, 3.5 percent of all 2008 firms were SOEs that entered the top 200, whereas 0.58 percent of 1996 SOEs fell out of the top 200. Thus both political and market mechanisms have played a more important role in contributing to the rise of SOEs in DPARs versus democracies. One interpretation for the rise of SOEs into the top 200 for DPARs is that state ownership may be perceived as conferring greater benefits after the crisis than before, which is very likely the case for Malaysia (see the case study in Chapter 6).

Summary

Overall, political regimes display the expected patterns with regard to state ownership of the largest corporations. NARs tend to retain absolute control over the country's SOEs; SPARs also retain dominant ownership of the largest SOEs, although they are likely to welcome minority ownership by private investors; DPARs engage in public-private co-ownership but with the state likely to retain a dominant stake in select firms; and democracies tend to have relatively few SOEs, notwithstanding the vestiges of military rule that have contributed to an elevated SOE presence for some countries (Thailand and Indonesia). Additionally, DPARs exhibit a greater propensity for political, rather than market, mechanisms to contribute to changes in state ownership of the largest listed firms in comparison with democracies.

State-Sector Transparency

Ascertaining the transparency of SOEs is not straightforward. A first indicator is the prevalence of listed SOEs, as presented in Table 4.1, because listing SOEs on a stock exchange requires that they reveal sensitive financial information in order to attract private investment. However, it is also necessary to consider measures for government transparency more generally, corporate governance indicators for listed firms, and the transparency of the SWF that may administer corporate ownership positions on behalf of the state. Government measures that have an impact on SOEs include fiscal allocations, penalties for revealing information about government spending, and various methods for directing resources to select groups often as a form of patronage. The extent of transparency regarding public procurement can be of particular importance because this often serves as a means of distributing patronage, and SOEs often play a role both in bidding for government contracts and in the distribution process. After winning a tender, an SOE may subcontract the project to numerous other firms that are selectively chosen for political reasons. All these political measures that reduce government transparency are unlikely to be reflected in corporate governance measures. Thus it is necessary to consider the transparency of the wider political environment in which the SOE operates before considering corporate governance more specifically.

Figure 4.3 presents Corruption Perception Index (CPI) scores for countries with well-established stock markets in order to compare them to their respective corporate governance scores in Figure 4.4. Several countries are excluded from these figures due to the absence

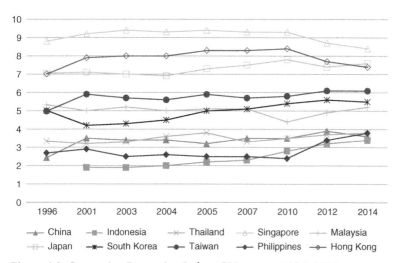

Figure 4.3 Corruption Perception Index (CPI) scores, 1996–2014.
Source: Transparency International; scores since 2012 are adjusted to a 0–10 scale.

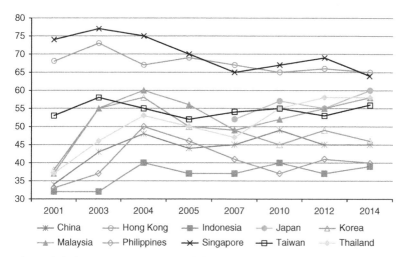

Figure 4.4 Corporate governance (CG) scores, 2001–14.
Note: Scores for 2001, 2003, and 2004 were rescaled to match those of later years. A more rigorous scoring methodology was introduced in 2004.
Source: CG Watch Reports, various years.

or very brief histories with a stock exchange, which prevents a comparison with their corporate governance scores. The excluded countries include three NARs (Brunei, North Korea, and Myanmar), two SPARs (Laos and Vietnam), and a DPAR (Cambodia). Although these countries either have zero or very few listed companies, thus enabling the government to hide SOEs' financial information, their CPI scores are not necessarily the lowest among all East Asian countries. For example, Brunei's CPI score in 2012 was 5.5, which is comparable with that of South Korea. Because Brunei's SOEs are wholly owned by the government and do not release financial information, the CPI score is clearly an imperfect indicator for SOE transparency. See the Brunei case study in the Chapter 5 for more details about Brunei's opacity. In 2014, North Korea's CPI score was 0.8, Myanmar's was 2.1, Laos' was 2.5, Vietnam's was 2.6, and Cambodia's was 2.1.

Turning to a comparison of the CPI scores in Figure 4.3 with the corporate governance scores in Figure 4.4, there are some notable points worth highlighting. First, CPI scores tend to be more stable over time. This is not entirely surprising because corporate governance is subject to regulation and enforcement by the government and is often directed at privately owned firms. Second, there is a general correspondence between CPI scores and CG scores. For example, Indonesia and the Philippines consistently remain at the bottom, while Singapore and Hong Kong are consistently at the top. Surprisingly, however, Korea, Taiwan, and Japan have tended to remain closer to the middle of the pack. This is probably more a reflection of the importance of strong corporate governance regulations for Singapore and Hong Kong, with economies that are heavily tied to the competitiveness of their financial services sector. But it is important to note that these aggregate scores obscure underlying opacity. Close examination of Singapore's political and corporate governance practices in Chapter 7 will reveal that critical features, tied to the mechanisms by which the ruling party co-opts elites, remain nontransparent. Third, there are some differences between countries' CPI and CG scores. For example, South Korea's CPI score is relatively better than its CG score; a speculative answer is that the chaebols are extremely powerful and prefer more opacity than the government can force them to reveal. Japan's CPI score in relation to its CG score displays a similar, though less sizable, discrepancy. By contrast, Thailand's CG score is relatively higher than its CPI score; this may reflect the heavy reliance on patronage by the government via unlisted SOEs.

A final difference between CPI and CG scores is that the former starts in 1996, whereas the latter only begins in 2001, after the Asian financial crisis. It was only after this crisis that corporate governance became widely recognized as a critical issue to the health of national economies. Table 4.4 identifies countries that implemented CG codes before and after 1997. Only Hong Kong had a CG code prior to the crisis. The rules, however, were fairly minimal, as indicated by the absence of requirements for independent directors or audit committees, mirroring the rest of the region. While these indicators are not specifically targeting corporate transparency, they do offer a reasonable indication for the seriousness regarding disclosures of corporate information as well as ensuring the credibility of that information. Following the crisis, the table shows that every country except Japan and China published at least two CG codes. Likewise, nearly every country requires independent directors and audit committees. While these region-wide improvements indicate a greater commitment to corporate transparency, there remains considerable variation, as seen in Figure 4.4.

Overall, the CPI indicators generally match the CG scores, though there are some notable differences. These differences point to the importance of looking more carefully into the political arrangements of each country to uncover how *strategic opacity* may be beneficial to a regime. For example, even though the CPI and CG indicators may both display high scores, the Singapore case will show that many aspects of government decision making remain shrouded from public scrutiny (e.g., via the state's monopolistic control over the media, the obstruction and intimidation of political opponents, and appointments to top executive and director positions). In addition to the transparency of the broader political environment and the more narrowly focused CG indicators, it is also important to consider the propensity for regimes to list SOEs in the first place because this forces the disclosure of sensitive financial information. Finally, we should also consider the transparency of the SWFs that may administer corporate ownership positions on behalf of the state. As presented in the next section (Table 4.5), SWF transparency scores generally correspond to the regime in which the SWF is located; specifically, SWF transparency is lowest for NARs (the Brunei Investment Agency) and highest for democracies (the Korea Investment Corporation). SWFs from SPARs

Table 4.4 *Changes in Corporate Governance before and after the Asian Financial Crisis (AFC)*

	Corporate governance code?		Independent directors required?		Audit committees required?	
	Before AFC	After AFC	Before AFC	After AFC	Before AFC	After AFC
China	No	2002	No	Yes	No	Yes
Hong Kong	1993	2004/2012	No	Yes	No	Yes
Indonesia	No	2001/2006	No	Yes	No	Yes
Japan	No	2015	No	Yes (as of 2015)	No	No (very few)
Korea	No	1999/2003	No	Yes	No	Yes (large firms)
Malaysia	No	2000/2007/2012	No	Yes	No	Yes
Philippines	No	2002/2009	No	Yes	No	Yes
Singapore	No	2001/2005/2012	No	Yes	No	Yes
Taiwan	No	2002/2011	No	Yes	No	Yes
Thailand	No	2002/2006/2012	No	Yes	No	Yes

Source: Allen (2014).

and DPARs are generally in the middle but with considerable variability depending on the specific fund. It is noteworthy, for example, that Temasek and Khazanah display high transparency scores, which should ease their capacity to invest in foreign markets.

Sovereign Wealth Funds

Table 4.5 categorizes the region's major SWFs by regime type, with the primary purpose of each fund identified on the right side of the table. There are three main funding sources for SWFs in the region, including oil, fiscal surpluses, and foreign exchange reserves (1Malaysia Development Berhad [1MDB] is an exception because its funding comes from sovereign debt). Fiscal surpluses include funds allocated from the government's budget, capital derived from SOE share sales, or funds allocated by other government-affiliated organizations (e.g., banks, government-supervised pension funds).

As discussed in Chapter 1, savings SWFs possess the greatest freedom to pursue large, strategic equity holdings. Countries with savings SWFs include Brunei, Vietnam, Indonesia, Malaysia, and Singapore. Although Vietnam's and Indonesia's funds engage in savings, they have so few assets that they are not influential investors outside their own country (as of 2015, they had total assets of US$3 billion and US$1.3 billion, respectively). 1MDB is also a savings SWF with the capacity to initiate large ownership positions; however, its unique status has led it to engage in investments that are not typical of other savings funds. But 1MDB also highlights the potential for savings SWFs to engage in a wide range of investment behaviors. I save a discussion of 1MDB for Chapter 6. Thus I turn now to the funds most capable of initiating sizable long-term corporate ownership positions. They include the Brunei Investment Agency, Khazanah, and Temasek.

A noteworthy feature of some of these savings funds is the dual or even multiple purposes they fulfill. Brunei's BIA fulfills all four purposes, though it is primarily a savings fund, whereas Malaysia's Khazanah serves dual purposes, though it is primarily a savings fund. By contrast, none of the other funds aside from Indonesia's serves more than one purpose. That these funds serve multiple purposes is indicative of the relatively greater fungibility of resources for savings SWFs.

Of the three savings funds with the greatest potential to initiate large ownership stakes and engage in activist intervention in target firms –

Table 4.5 *East Asian Sovereign Wealth Funds (SWFs)*

Country	Fund name	Year founded	Funding source	SWF assets 1996 (billion US$)	SWF assets 2008 (billion US$)	SWF assets 2015 (billion US$)	Truman score, 2012 (out of 100)	Linaburg-Maduell score, 2015 (out of 10)	Purpose: macro stability	Purpose: saving	Purpose: pension reserve	Purpose: reserve investment
NAR												
Brunei	Brunei Investment Agency	1983	Oil	15	30	39	21	1	X[a]	X[b]	X[c]	X[d]
SPARs												
China	National Social Security Fund	2000	Fiscal surpluses	–	82	247	77[e]	5			X	
China	China Investment Corporation	2007	FX reserves	–	200	650	64	8				X
China	State Administration of Foreign Exchange	1997	FX reserves	–	490	567	–	5				X
Vietnam	State Capital Investment Corporation	2006	Fiscal surpluses	–	0.5	3	–	4		X		
DPARs												
Malaysia	Khazanah Nasional	1993	Fiscal surpluses	3	19	39.3	59	9	X[f]	X[g]		
Malaysia	1MDB	2009	Debt	–	–	13.8	–	–		X		
Singapore	Temasek	1974	Fiscal surpluses	75	86	160	76	10		X		
Singapore	Government Investment Corporation	1981	FX reserves	110	220	320	66	6				X
Democracy												
Taiwan	National Stabilization Fund	2000	Fiscal surpluses	–	15	16.6	–	–	X[h]			

Indonesia	Government Investment Unit	2006	Fiscal surpluses	–	0.30	1.3	–	–	X^i	X^j	
South Korea	Korea Investment Corporation	2005	FX reserves	–	30	85	69	9	X^i		X^k
Hong Kong	Hong Kong Monetary Authority Investment Portfolio (Exchange Fund)	1993	FX reserves	69.4	202.8	359	70	8			X

[a] World Bank (2008).

[b] Kunzel et al. (2011).

[c] BIA manages funds from the Worker's Provident Fund.

[d] www.sovereignwealthfundsnews.com/bruneiinvestmentagency.php (accessed November 14, 2015).

[e] The score is for 2008 (Truman, 2011).

[f] Mokhtar (2004); www.khazanah.com/docs/speech20041004-KLBCKL.pdf (accessed November 14, 2015).

[g] Petrova et al. (2011).

[h] Taiwan Info. 2000. Stabilization fund to protect financial markets, January 28.

[i] www.swfinstitute.org/swfs/government-investment-unit/ (accessed November 14, 2015).

[j] www.swfinstitute.org/swfs/government-investment-unit/ (accessed November 14, 2015).

[k] Lunzel et al. (2010).

Sources: Sovereign Wealth Fund data: SWF Institute and Sauvant, Sachs, and Jongbloed (2012). Truman scores come from Bagnall and Truman (2013).

the BIA, Khazanah, and Temasek – only the latter two regularly engage in such actions. For example, Dewenter, Han, and Malatesta examine the prevalence of three types of SWF activism – monitoring, network transactions, and government actions.[33] In a sample of nineteen SWFs with 227 transactions occurring between 1987 and 2008, they found that Temasek displayed a significantly higher propensity to engage in network transactions, which include (1) the target firm signing a major business deal (i.e., large enough to be reported in the press) with another firm that is partially or wholly owned by the SWF, (2) the SWF taking an equity interest in another firm that is wholly or partially owned by the target firm, and (3) the target firm taking an equity interest in a firm that is partially owned by the same SWF.[34] In another study by Bernardo Bortolotti of the Sovereign Investment Laboratory, Temasek and Khazanah were identified as the only two SWFs (in a sample of nineteen SWFs) that could be regarded as "active" SWFs based on their inclination to have a presence on a target firm's board of directors as well as the independence of the SWFs' management.[35] The next section on foreign state ownership will add further evidence to the activist inclinations of Temasek and Khazanah by revealing that they were the only two funds in the region to maintain sizable ownership stakes in foreign listed firms as of 2008. The BIA, by contrast, is a distinctly passive investor, with most of its investments administered by third-party investment managers who take small stakes in target firms, thereby enabling the BIA to hide its investment activities. This is in keeping with the importance the regime attaches to secrecy, as reflected in the BIA's low transparency score (21 for the Truman score in 2012; the next lowest on the list is Khazanah at 59).

There are two other SWFs that draw on fiscal surpluses as their funding source, including Taiwan's National Stabilization Fund and China's National Social Security Fund. The former is a macro-stability fund established in 2000 with the purpose of dampening the effect of exogenous shocks to Taiwan's stock market. Two events were instrumental to its creation, including the Asian financial crisis and China's military posturing ahead of Taiwan's 1996 presidential election. When intervention is perceived as necessary, the Stabilization Fund can

---

[33] Dewenter, Han, and Malatesta (2010).

[34] These network transactions were also found to yield significantly higher returns in cross-border investments for Temasek, but not for other SWFs.

[35] Bortolotti (2014).

borrow up to US$6.4 billion from local financial institutions to purchase short-term holdings that must be returned immediately following the stabilization intervention. Thus rules governing the fund's activities strictly prevent it from exercising influence in target companies beyond propping up their stock price.

The other fiscally funded SWF is China's National Social Security Fund (NSSF), which is the only pension SWF on the list. It was set up in 2000 to address China's aging population. It is the most transparent fund in the region based on its Truman score (77), which is typical of pension funds (as seen in Chapter 3), even though its score is at the low end for this type of fund. Because safety and the preservation of capital are highly important to the fund's purpose, it follows a passive, diversified investment strategy. It is primarily focused on investments in China, with overseas equities accounting for only 8 percent of its total assets in 2014 through small stakes managed by third-party institutional investors.[36] Due to the importance attached to preserving and growing its capital to service future pension obligations, it is structured to be run with greater independence from political influence than China's two other SWFs.[37]

Although savings funds permit the greatest freedom for implementing a variety of investment strategies, including large, long-term ownership positions, the largest funds are those which manage foreign exchange reserves. Due to their responsibility for managing the country's foreign exchange reserves, foreign exchange reserve funds place a greater emphasis on safety and liquidity in their investments; this incentivizes them to take smaller equity positions. China's State Administration of Foreign Exchange (SAFE) and the China Investment Corporation (CIC) are the two largest foreign exchange reserve funds on the list as of 2015. Since CIC's creation in 2007, SAFE has endeavored to improve its returns by placing an increasing share of its capital in nontraditional central bank reserve assets, such as equities and private equity funds. SAFE's worry is that if the CIC demonstrates that it is more capable of managing foreign exchange reserves, then more assets may be transferred from SAFE to CIC.[38] Nevertheless,

---

[36] Leckie and Pan (2007) report that these include Northern Trust and Citibank, with Goldman Sachs and BNP-Paribas to join them. On its investment allocation, see www.ssf.gov.cn/Eng_Introduction/201206/t20120620_5603 .html (accessed March 14, 2016).
[37] Norris (2016).   [38] Hu (2010).

SAFE has refrained from taking large ownership stakes in foreign firms, favoring a passive investment approach that preserves its focus on safety and liquidity. For example, *The Economist* reported that SAFE held stakes in sixty-three of the Financial Times Stock Exchange (FTSE) 100 Index's constituent firms in 2011, with holdings varying in size from 0.18 percent in the Royal Bank of Scotland to 1.63 percent in ARM Holdings, a technology firm.[39] This investment strategy saved it from the considerable losses incurred by the CIC during the 2008 global financial crisis.

The CIC was established with US$200 billion in China's foreign exchange holdings in order to diversify how they are invested. CIC has three subsidiaries, including CIC International, CIC Capital, and Central Huijin Investment. The overseas investment and management activities of CIC are undertaken by CIC International and CIC Capital. CIC International was established in 2011 and manages most of CIC's overseas investments, including equities, bonds, real estate, and alternative investments. In an effort to enhance its returns, CIC International (and CIC prior to 2011) has been willing to take larger ownership positions than SAFE, but they have remained below the 10 percent ownership level; accordingly, it does not generally seek representation on firms' boards of directors or engage in other activist tactics, and in 2012, approximately 64 percent of its assets were managed by external managers as part of its effort to improve its investment returns following its poor performance during the 2008 crisis.[40] CIC Capital was established in 2015 to engage in direct investments, including infrastructure and agriculture, as well as to enhance investment in long-term assets. Central Huijin is the controlling stakeholder of the big four state-owned banks,[41] in addition to holding ownership stakes in numerous other Chinese financial institutions. It was created in 2003 to write off bad loans/assets of state-owned banks and later became a unit of the CIC when the Ministry of Finance injected its equity stake in Central Huijin into CIC as part of its initial capital contribution.

The next-largest foreign exchange reserve fund is Hong Kong's Exchange Fund, followed by Singapore's GIC, and then the Korea

---

[39] *The Economist*, March 14, 2011.
[40] Chuen and Gregoriou (2014, 319–22); Bortolotti (2014).
[41] These include the Industrial and Commercial Bank of China, the Agricultural Bank of China, the Bank of China, and the China Construction Bank.

Investment Corporation (KIC). Each of these funds also engages in equities investments, though in a way that ensures the safety and liquidity appropriate to foreign exchange reserve management. For example, Hong Kong's Exchange Fund intervened with more sizable holdings in its stock market following the Asian financial crisis in order to stabilize it, but these were short-term positions that did not lead the fund to influence the management of target firms. It continues to invest in domestic and foreign equities with small positions, and it does not seek to influence management of target companies. It adheres to the principles of preserving capital and investing in safe, liquid assets; thus it follows a conservative portfolio strategy including 73 percent bonds and 27 percent equities. In contrast to Hong Kong's Exchange Fund, Singapore's GIC is the most aggressive exchange fund in the region with a bond-equity portfolio of 35:65 as of 2013. Despite the greater allocation to equities, the GIC has continued to follow a passive invest- ment approach, with ownership stakes normally remaining below 5 percent. Accordingly, it does not maintain a presence on the boards of the firms in which it invests or engage in other forms of shareholder activism. The KIC sits between Hong Kong's Exchange Fund and Singapore's GIC, with 43.8 percent in public equities, 46.7 percent in bonds and similar instruments, and 9.5 percent in alternative assets such as private equity, real estate, and hedge funds.[42] Like these other exchange funds, it also employs a passive strategy with its equities investments that avoids taking large stakes in any individual firm.

While China does not officially have a savings SWF, its equivalent is the State-Owned Assets Supervision and Administration Commission (SASAC). It is responsible for managing the country's largest SOEs on behalf of the State Council. Vietnam's SCIC resembles SASAC with regard to its mandate of privatizing and managing large numbers of SOEs.[43] However, SASAC is not formally considered a SWF because it does not engage in new investments outside the companies in which it holds ownership stakes. Because of its importance to administering the state's ownership of China's largest SOEs, I discuss it in some depth in Chapter 5.

Overall, savings funds are found predominantly among the author- itarian regimes in the region; Indonesia's tiny SWF is the only savings

---

[42] See www.kic.go.kr/en/ki/ki030201.jsp (accessed March 15, 2016).
[43] Nguyen et al. (2012).

fund located in a democracy. Additionally, the savings SWFs of
Temasek and Khazanah display the greatest propensity for initiating
large ownership positions. The other SWFs do not engage in comparably large investment stakes, focusing instead on small ownership
positions that privilege passive investment behavior.

Foreign State Ownership

Figure 4.5 displays foreign state ownership positions by country of
origin. The data identify state acquisitions that exceed a 5 percent
equity ownership in one of the 200 largest listed firms in each of nine
East Asian economies. Given the strict restrictions on foreign investors in China, it would not be sensible to compare it with the other
East Asian economies.[44] As mentioned earlier, it is noteworthy that
no ownership positions were identified as being held by a foreign state
in the Claessens et al. data set for 1996. Foreign state ownership only

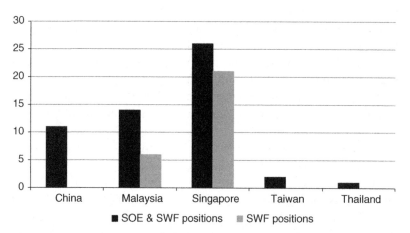

Figure 4.5 Foreign state ownership positions by country of origin, 2008.
Note: Sample includes the 200 largest firms by market capitalization for nine
East Asian countries. The *y*-axis indicates the nominal number of ownership
positions.
Source: Carney and Child (2013).

---

[44] China only permitted foreign investors to buy shares on the Shanghai and
Shenzhen stock exchanges starting in 2002 through its Qualified Foreign
Institutional Investor Program. However, the combined quota that could be
purchased was capped at US$20.7 billion as of April 2011.

appears in the wake of the Asian financial crisis. A number of countries from outside East Asia are identified as holding a small number of ownership positions. I restrict the reporting of foreign state ownership to the countries located in the East Asia region both because they are of intrinsic interest to this study and because they hold the largest number of ownership stakes. After taking these data reporting considerations into account, three East Asian countries stand out for their high levels of foreign ownership, including Singapore, followed by Malaysia, and then China. The governments of Taiwan and Thailand also have a small number of ownership positions. Interestingly, the data reveal that only the SWFs of Singapore (Temasek) and Malaysia (Khazanah) have ownership stakes large enough to permit their identification and to therefore potentially wield influence over the management of the target company. This observation is less surprising when we consider that savings SWFs are the most predisposed to taking large equity positions. But, in this regard, we might expect the BIA to be more prominent; however, the BIA's desire for secrecy can account for its absence from this list. This will be discussed further in Chapter 5. China's comparatively small presence may also be surprising, especially in relation to the size of its economy, but consider that it does not have a savings SWF (SASAC is the equivalent, which will be discussed in Chapter 5). China's overseas holdings are primarily due to SOEs with ownership stakes in Taiwanese or Singaporean firms; Chinese firms listed in Hong Kong and Singapore are excluded.

Figure 4.6 shows foreign state ownership positions by host country in 2008. Indonesia, Thailand, and Singapore have the highest numbers, respectively. Likewise, SWF ownership is highest for Thailand and Indonesia due to investments by Temasek and Khazanah. In Chapter 7, I engage in a structured comparison of their entry into the Indonesian banking and telecommunications sectors to evaluate differences in how they enter into and manage investments in foreign listed firms.

The most important point to take away from Figure 4.6 is that Khazanah and Temasek have initiated large ownership positions in the biggest firms located in every country in the sample except for Taiwan. Foreign officials and private investors must have been satisfied with the information provided by Temasek and Khazanah (and their affiliated firms) regarding the purpose of the investment. This is notable because most of these countries are democracies.

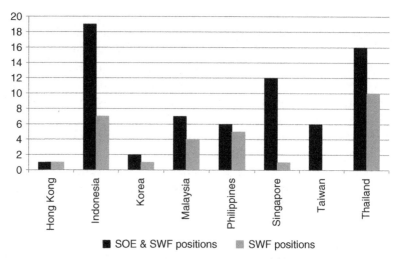

Figure 4.6 Foreign state ownership positions by host country, 2008.
Note: Sample includes the 200 largest firms by market capitalization for nine East Asian countries (China is excluded). The *y*-axis indicates the nominal number of ownership positions.
Source: Carney and Child (2013).

Conclusions

This chapter provides evidence for the *capacity* of different regimes to engage in public-private co-ownership, as well as indicators that reflect a stronger *motivation* on the part of some regimes to aggressively intervene in foreign listed firms. The indicators for state capacity to engage in public-private co-ownership include the prevalence of listed SOEs, state-sector transparency, and the type of SWF. The evidence from East Asia shows that NARs do not list their SOEs, while democracies have very few SOEs. In between, SPARs and DPARs host a large number of listed SOEs with state ownership dominating in the former; for DPARs, state ownership dominates for selected SOEs but is usually at a lower level than for equivalent firms in SPARs.

A first useful indicator for state-sector transparency is whether the regime publicly lists its SOEs. The evidence for East Asia indicates that NARs do not list them, thus denying the disclosure of important information from public scrutiny. For SPARs, DPARs, and democracies, indicators for state-sector transparency are not clear-cut. This is due to the fact that the state can engage in a wide range of activities that are not captured by the Corruption Perception Index or by corporate governance scores. It is probably best to view these indicators as a first approximation for the extent of state-sector transparency, requiring further investigation to identify the precise mechanisms by which regimes hide strategically important activities to sustain their rule, especially in the case of authoritarian regimes. In this regard, SWF transparency (especially savings SWFs) may offer helpful guidance because they often administer the state's corporate ownership positions. The evidence indicates a general correspondence between the type of regime and the level of SWF transparency, ascending from NAR up to democracy.

With regard to the types of SWFs located in particular regimes, the evidence shows that savings SWFs are located primarily in authoritarian regimes – Singapore, Malaysia, Brunei, and Vietnam. The savings SWFs of Singapore and Malaysia display the most activist investment behavior. Interestingly, China does not have a savings SWF; its equivalent is SASAC. Recent debates occurred about transforming it into a Temasek-like organization, though this initiative ultimately failed.[45] But given its importance to managing China's SOEs, I discuss it in Chapter 5. With regard to other types of SWFs – macro-stability, foreign exchange reserve, and pension – the evidence indicates that these do not initiate large ownership stakes in foreign firms.

Finally, the extent of large state ownership positions in foreign companies indicates that DPARs have a greater capacity to aggressively intervene in target firms. Specifically, the SOEs and SWFs of Singapore and Malaysia, Temasek and Khazanah, have entered into more large ownership positions of foreign listed firms than SOEs and SWFs from any other country in the region. This is remarkable when considering the size of their economies in relation to China's or to other large economies in the region (e.g., Japan and South Korea). But these patterns require explaining. That is, what are the causal reasons for Singapore and Malaysia to initiate so many large foreign ownership positions in the region's biggest companies in comparison with other states? To answer this question, I now turn to the country case studies.

---

[45] Naughton (2016).

APPENDIX 4A.1

Construction of the Corporate Ownership Data Set

In order to obtain accurate information about ultimate owners and thus compare the relative importance of state-owned to non-state-owned firms, it is necessary to restrict the focus to publicly listed firms. The sample is comprised of firms that are among each country's 200 largest publicly listed corporations by market capitalization in each year. Firms from the following nine countries were included in the sample: Hong Kong, Japan, Indonesia, South Korea, Malaysia, the Philippines, Singapore, Taiwan, and Thailand. The data set used for this study ultimately includes 1,606 publicly traded firms in 1996 and 1,296 publicly traded firms in 2008. The year 2008 is selected as the second time point because enough time would have elapsed for the immediate response to the 1997 crisis to have faded and new patterns to have consolidated their positions in order to test whether a durable transition to state ownership was underway.

As the starting point for collecting ownership data, the names of the largest 200 publicly traded firms (in terms of market capitalization) from each country's stock exchange are identified for the end of the calendar year 2008. The names for the 200 largest firms for each country in 1996 come from the Claessens et al. data set.[46] The approach for identifying ultimate owners in 2008 mirrors that of Claessens et al. so as to ensure methodologic consistency.

For each of the firms for the 2008 sample, identification of all shareholders owning more than 5 percent of the company's shares came from Thomson Reuter's Worldscope database. Where this information was not available through Worldscope, Bureau van Dijk's OSIRIS database was used or Gale's *Major Companies of Asia and Australasia 2008* handbook. Often the corporations in the data set are owned in turn by other companies. In order to trace ultimate ownership, the ownership structure of these intermediate shareholding companies had to be uncovered as well. Wherever

---

[46] Claessens et al. (2000) explain that their data set always covers the largest 100 firms in terms of market capitalization and is then supplemented with data for additional firms depending on the availability of the data. Hence the paper's analysis of the top 200 firms by country is a useful reflection of each country's largest firms in order to draw comparisons with a country's 200 largest firms in 2008.

these shareholding companies are publicly traded corporations them-selves, the above-mentioned exercise was repeated using the Worldscope and OSIRIS databases to identify their ownership. Where these companies have not been publicly traded, the process has been more arduous.

The intermediate non-publicly traded firms present in the ownership data are state owned, family owned, employee owned, or subsidiaries of public or other nonpublic corporations. To resolve the ownership structure of these non-publicly traded firms, the first resort has been to turn to the annual reports of the downstream publicly traded firm whose ownership is ultimately trying to be revealed. Often, through careful reading of this report, the ultimate owner of the intermediate firm may disclose this information. When the annual report has not been helpful in this regard, the website of the non-publicly traded firm sometimes discloses this information. Next, various stock exchange filings indicating the transfer of share ownership are used to identify ultimate owners. As a last resort, where none of the preceding has been informative, business reports and newspaper articles revealing the non-publicly traded company's owner, either explicitly or in passing, are used. These latter resources have been retrieved primarily through the LexisNexis and Alacra Store databases, as well as *Bloomberg Businessweek* online.

As a basis for inclusion in the data set, it is a requirement that all shareholders above a given ownership threshold can be traced, pro-vided that their shares are held in blocks sizable enough to be reported (typically around 5 percent). Some firms are included that are excep-tions to this rule in either of two ways. The first is if there exists an owner whose identity cannot be traced, but detailed information on a larger owner who claims more than 50 percent of the company's stock is available. The second is if there exists share blocks whose owners cannot be traced due to their being held via a nominee or trust account but whose sum total is less than the proportion of shares held by a revealed owner whose identity is traceable. In either of these cases, the largest shareholder can still be identified. Conversely, a company is excluded from the data set if shares held in trust (or through a nominee account) amount to a greater proportion of out-standing shares than that which the largest revealed shareholder can be shown to control. A company is also excluded from the data set if there exists a significant shareholder whose identity is not discernible due to a lack of information about the intermediate non-publicly traded firm through which these shares are owned.

It is recognized that a bias is likely introduced by excluding firms whose largest owners hold shares through trust accounts, nominee accounts, or holding companies whose ownership structure is not discernible. In putting together their earlier data set, Claessens et al. (2000) report the same problem regarding nominee accounts. By determining the group affiliation of the problematic firms, they conclude the direction of their bias is against uncovering family ownership.[47] Through the reading of annual reports and stock exchange filings, most nominee account holders have also been found to be an individual or family where the information has been revealed. Hence the direction of this bias is likely to be the same as that concluded by Claessens et al. – away from family ownership. Moreover, this is consistent with the stronger incentives for families and individuals to hide their control of a company through the use of trusts, nominee accounts, and shell holding companies. A related bias is introduced through the selection criterion used more generally. Widely held corporations are most easily identifiable, whereas corporations that have outstanding share blocks greater than the ownership threshold immediately lend themselves to the possibility of exclusion noted earlier. Taken together, these biases suggest that the reported incidence of widely held corporations is likely overstated, with the incidence of family ownership being understated. The incidence of state ownership is likely to be the most accurate.

---

[47] Companies that belong to the same business group are not treated or counted differently from firms that do not belong to a group when determining the relative ownership levels.

5 | Narrow Authoritarian Regime: Brunei; Single Party Authoritarian Regime: China; From Single Party Authoritarian Regime to Democracy: Taiwan

This chapter provides analytic narratives linking political regime characteristics to state-sector arrangements across three regime types – narrow authoritarian regimes (NARs), single-party authoritarian regimes (SPAR), and democracies. In NARs and democracies, the capacity for state intervention in foreign corporations is expected to be low; SPARs, however, are expected to have greater state capacity to intervene. Satisfying this necessary first condition opens up the possibility for these regimes to aggressively intervene if there exists a sufficient motivation – a threat to the incumbent rulers' hold on power.

I begin with the case of Brunei, which has persisted as a NAR into the contemporary period despite an economic crisis that threatened regime survival in 1998. In the wake of the crisis, state-owned enterprise (SOE) and sovereign wealth fund (SWF) characteristics persisted as before because regime characteristics did not change. Consequently, the state has consistently adhered to a passive investment strategy.

I next turn to the case of China, a SPAR that has successfully maintained regime stability while increasing trade and capital flows, contributing to the rise of private capital. China displays the necessary capacity characteristics to intervene in foreign listed firms. Public-private co-ownership is prevalent, though the state is nearly always the dominant partner among the largest firms. Thousands of firms are listed on its stock markets, illustrating that transparency meets a minimum threshold to attract private investors. Although transparency of the state sector remains relatively lower in comparison with dominant-party authoritarian regimes (DPARs) or democracies, it is sufficient for its SOEs to take large ownership positions in countries with comparably weak transparency requirements (other authoritarian regimes). Meeting the necessary capacity conditions to intervene, the Chinese state can act on its motivation to aggressively intervene in foreign firms, which is the need to grow the economy – up to the present, this has primarily involved meeting the demand for energy. Not meeting this demand would jeopardize the Chinese Communist Party's hold on power.

The third case is Taiwan – a country that underwent major regime change from SPAR to democracy during the 1980s and 1990s as trade and capital flows increased. Taiwan's regime transition illuminates how changing political characteristics contribute to the state's changing state-sector arrangements. The transition also illuminates the political dynamics contributing to these changes – the incumbent rulers who rely on large SOEs versus political challengers who garner support from private capital, especially small and medium-sized enterprises. The ascendance of private capital exercised through Taiwan's democratic political arrangements curtails both the *capacity* and the *motivation* for the state to engage in aggressive foreign investment behavior.

Narrow Authoritarian Regime: Brunei

In NARs, political competition is largely forbidden, and there are no effective institutional constraints on the executive that would reduce investment risk for private capital. Consequently, political rulers in NARs maintain tight control over the information and resources necessary to secure regime stability. One manifestation of these controls occurs via wholly state-owned enterprises that dominate the corporate sector. Such enterprises allow the political rulers to maintain control over the economy and its rents, as well as deny opportunities and resources to potential political opponents.

Additionally, these regimes maintain tight controls on the flow of information so as to hide from public scrutiny how state resources are used. These arrangements are compatible with unlisted SOEs, a highly opaque SWF, in addition to other political mechanisms to deny information to potential rivals, such as state ownership of the press and a nonindependent judiciary. Retaining maximum flexibility over the use of state funds is more compatible with savings SWFs versus other types of SWFs. The desire for opacity prevents these funds from taking large foreign equity positions; instead, they will tend toward a passive investment strategy that relies primarily on small equity stakes. Altogether NARs will lack the capacity to engage in aggressive foreign investments.

Brunei is a useful case to examine because it is in the same region as Malaysia and Singapore, and it shares common British colonial histories with them. It also shares ethnic, religious, and linguistic similarities with Malaysia, which allow for structured comparisons that can rule out alternative explanations. At the same time, its small population and abundant hydrocarbon wealth make it similar to resource-abundant Middle Eastern countries that have also adopted savings SWFs. This allows insights drawn from Brunei to be potentially applied to this larger set of countries. Finally, Brunei's regime also faced a serious threat in the wake of the Asian financial crisis, offering the opportunity to assess its response to economic liberalization's pressures in comparison with that of the other crisis-afflicted regimes in the region.

Precrisis Regime Structure and Capacity to Intervene

Brunei is a hereditary monarchy that lacks political competition and effective institutions to reduce investment risk. The current sultan's father, Omar Ali Saifuddien, ascended the throne in 1950 and resisted British proposals to merge Brunei with Sarawak and British North Borneo (Sabah) in order to retain independence and control over its oil fields. Oil was discovered in 1929. Brunei obtained internal self-rule under British protection with a 1959 constitution. In 1962, an election was held for a Legislative Council, which led to the Parti Rakyat Brunei (PRB, the Brunei People's Party) winning by a significant margin. But when it was prevented from forming a government, an armed rebellion ensued. This was suppressed by the British army, and a state of emergency was subsequently declared, enabling the monarchy to retain power ever since. In October 1967, the current sultan, Hassanal Bolkiah, succeeded his father. After Brunei gained independence on January 1, 1984, it became a constitutional monarchy with the sultan wielding full and uncontested control. For example, the sultan currently holds the offices of prime minister, minister of finance, minister of defense, and minister of foreign affairs and trade.

Reflecting the monarchy's monopoly on the political arena, the regime's major resources and information are fully controlled by it. For example, the regime has exercised dominant control over the hydrocarbons industry, including oil and liquefied natural gas, which contributes to 70 percent of the country's gross domestic product

(GNP).[1] Due to the monarchy's political and economic dominance, private capital has remained very weak. Seventy percent of those employed in the private sector are foreigners who are issued work permits for periods of two years or less. This allows the government to regulate the immigration of foreign labor out of concern that it might disrupt Brunei's society. Unlike Malaysia, where government patronage led to the emergence of a class of Malay entrepreneurs, a genuine Brunei Malay business class has remained embryonic, with well-educated Brueians going to work for the government.

Information is also strictly controlled by the state. This has been in place since the government imposed martial law in the country after the Brunei Revolt of 1962. Reporters Without Borders reports that there is "virtually no criticism of the government." The privately owned press, Brunei Press Sdn Bhd, publisher of the *Borneo Bulletin*, is controlled by the sultan's family. There is no stock market, so financial information about the economy's largest firms, owned by the sultan and his family, are not disclosed. Additionally, the royal family's economic activities inside Brunei are not reflected in the national accounts and fall outside the scope of the surveys conducted by the government's Economic Planning Unit. This separation extends to the provision of separate electricity supplies and telecommunications, among other services.[2]

Brunei's SWF, the Brunei Investment Agency (BIA), is a savings SWF established in 1983 when the sultanate took over investment activities from British crown agents. BIA invests the government's General Reserve Fund, which is funded with proceeds from the sale of hydrocarbons. Although the BIA is a government entity located in the Ministry of Finance, the line between its finances and those of the royal family remains indistinct, making its investments difficult to track. This opacity combined with the separation of the family economy from the Brunei economy has made a large fraction of Brunei's finances, including its corporate sector, closed to public scrutiny.

With regard to the BIA's foreign investment activities, the managing director of the BIA in 1991, Rahman Karim, stated that the agency handled only 40 percent of the Sultanate's reserves, which he estimated at US$27 billion.[3] The remainder, he indicated, was divided among

---

[1] Economist Intelligence Unit Country Report (2014).
[2] Australian High Commission (1994, 24–25).
[3] Hewison et al. (1993, 109–32); Gunn (2001, 78–86).

eight foreign banking and investment institutions, with 50 to 60 percent placed in bonds and the remainder in equity. It is estimated that BIA assets had risen to US$60 billion prior to the Asian financial crisis.

The 1998 Crisis

Without the capacity for private investment to mount an effective challenge, the incumbent rulers could withstand the crisis intact. Threats to the monarchy's reign arrived through the collapse of its largest conglomerate, Amedeo, in 1998. The collapse was triggered by the Asian financial crisis and the plunging price of crude oil and liquefied natural gas, which had fallen by 37 and 25 percent, respectively, over the previous year.[4] Amedeo was founded about four years earlier by the Sultan's younger brother, Prince Jefri Bolkiah, who was the Finance Minister and head of the BIA. Amedeo was estimated to have accumulated debts of around US$16 billion, in addition to US$14.8 billion that Jefri was personally accused of squandering, thus depleting BIA assets by the same amount.[5] Amedeo's demise resulted in the immediate repatriation of 20,000 foreign workers, equivalent to nearly 20 percent of the workforce, causing havoc in Brunei's retail sector. Additionally, private construction companies that worked with Amedeo faced bankruptcies, a significant rise in unemployment ensued, and tensions between fundamentalist and liberal Muslims increased.

Amedeo's collapse led to a crisis of regime legitimacy. In response, the Sultan brought a lawsuit against Jefri, accusing him of stealing and misusing more than US$28.8 billion in state funds.[6] For example, the vast majority of Amedeo's projects were for the prince and his family, including numerous multimillion-dollar projects such as the prince's private office, the now-abandoned private mosque in Jefri's office grounds, and the Jerudong Hotel. In addition to the lavish projects just mentioned, Jefri reportedly also spent US$2 billion over a ten-year period on 2,000 cars, seventeen airplanes, including a private Airbus A310, several yachts, quantities of jewelry, and more than a dozen homes.[7] Only about 10 percent of the total funds (US$4.4 billion)

---

[4] *The Nation*, July 16, 1998.   [5] *Wall Street Journal*, September 25, 2009.
[6] Civil Suit No. 31 of February 21, 2000, filed in the High Court of Brunei Darussalam
[7] Ford (2000).

injected into Amedeo from the BIA and other sources were spent on infrastructure improvements.[8] Jefri's overseas assets mirrored his Bruneian investments with their lavish price tags, including the British jeweler Asprey, the New York Palace Hotel, Hotel Bel-Air in Los Angeles, and Plaza Athénée in Paris.[9]

After Brunei's High Court ruled against Jefri, the case was referred to the Privy Council in London, the highest court of review for Brunei. In the end, an out-of-court settlement was reached in which Jefri would return all funds taken from the BIA. The private settlement was the most preferred solution for the Sultan because it maintained the privacy of the royal family's wealth and privileges while placing blame on Jefri individually.

The Continuation of Precrisis Arrangements

Despite the severe economic and political crisis, little meaningful change occurred in the control of state information and resources, reflecting the continuation of precrisis regime characteristics. Only superficial political reforms were implemented to stem popular anger. For example, the sultan reconvened the Legislative Council in 2004, which had been suspended for two decades. Its remit, however, was restricted to advising the sultan. The sultan also introduced a constitutional amendment providing for a third of the Legislative Council to be directly elected, although this was never implemented. In 2005, the council gained five indirectly elected members to represent village councils. They meet for a few days each year to hear presentations on the government budget and some policy issues.

In 2005, the registration of the Parti Pernbangunan (PP, the National Development Party) suggested some potential further opening up of the political process. The leader of the PP is also the former leader of the PRB, which won the 1962 Legislative Council election. However, Brunei's two other political parties were deregistered in 2007: the People's Awareness Party, for internal leadership squabbles, and the National Solidarity Party, for failing to disclose its accounts. As a result, the PP is the only legal political party, although it has never achieved electoral representation.

---

[8] Gunn (2008). These included a power station, a communications tower, and an international school.
[9] Kay (2009).

In addition to the lack of political competition or effective institutions that could reduce investment risk, the regime's stranglehold on information and resources continued. For example, investigative journalism and criticism of the government remain circumscribed by media controls and censorship. The press, including Internet sites published from Brunei, is subject to strict government censorship. In 2001, the government issued restrictive new laws giving it the right to close newspapers and ban foreign publications that it deemed detrimental to public morality or domestic security. Coverage of the government's activities and the royal family remains uncritical. Additionally, the government television network remained the sole television operator until 1999, when Brunei's first commercial cable television channel, Kristal, began broadcasting. In March 2004, the government arrested three Bruneians under the Internal Security Act for publishing information deemed subversive on the Internet.[10]

The BIA has also remained highly opaque. Since the scandal, for example, the sultan has remained the finance minister and therefore retains direct authority over the BIA. The secrecy governing the BIA's investments and the lack of a clear line between the state's and the sultan's personal funds have persisted. The BIA's founding legislation continues to make it one of a small group of SWFs (including the Kuwait Investment Authority and Oman's SWFs) whose officers have an explicit legal obligation to keep their activities secret. It has therefore maintained a mostly passive investment strategy so as to avoid the attention that it would attract from taking large ownership stakes. It is not a member of the International Forum of Sovereign Wealth Funds, and it has resisted moves toward greater transparency, arguing that news of its investments might move the markets.[11]

Likewise, Brunei's largest corporations remain firmly in the hands of the monarchy, and a stock exchange has still not been created which would require disclosures to shareholders. For example, a new national oil company, PetroleumBRUNEI, was established as a "private limited company" in January 2002; it supersedes the former Brunei Oil and Gas Board and the Petroleum Unit. It is wholly owned by the government and no information about its finances is provided on its website.

---

[10] They were released in July 2006 as part of tentative moves toward political reform.

[11] This is the same justification given for Singapore GIC's opacity.

The declared motivation for creating this company was to more closely match the business practices of Malaysia's highly successful national oil company, Petronas, but it also enables the regime to lessen its dependence on foreign oil companies (Shell) in exploration and refining. And despite the economic crisis resulting from Amedeo's bankruptcy, no major initiatives were launched to improve firms' corporate governance rules, accounting standards, or information dissemination, as occurred for other countries in the region.

For years after the crisis, Brunei's lack of transparency even extended to basic information about the monetary and fiscal components of the economy. For example, it did not have a central bank until 2011, and for many years it lacked published economic data that would meet IMF requirements. In its 2005 evaluation of Brunei's economy, for example, the IMF concluded, "Directors saw scope to enhance fiscal transparency, noting that the limited availability of information continued to hamper fiscal policy analysis."[12] The World Trade Organization (WTO) echoed these complaints with regard to Brunei's corporate sector, citing the BIA and another government-owned firm, Semaun Holdings, by name.[13]

Conclusion

In the Brunei case, the financial crisis produced little meaningful change. Both before and after Amedeo's collapse, the political regime permitted neither political competition nor effective institutions to reduce investment risk. These regime characteristics led to the regime's monopolized control over vital resources and information. For example, the corporate sector has remained dominated by companies linked to the regime and dependent on its oil wealth. Private capital has wielded minimal influence, depriving it of opportunities to leverage access to international capital markets or to magnify economic instability through a rapid exit. Brunei's single SWF, the Brunei Investment Agency, continues to permit state funds to be intermingled with the sultan's personal funds and is under the sultan's total control. Finally, foreign investments by the BIA have remained passive both before and

[12] International Monetary Fund (2005).
[13] Semaun Holdings is a wholly owned private company created by the government in 1994 to promote industrial and commercial development (Gunn 2008).

after the crisis, with investment managers purchasing small stakes that enable the BIA to shield its investments from public scrutiny (by remaining below official disclosure thresholds). In summary, Brunei illustrates how political rulers in a NAR uphold opacity over the state sector in order to maintain their control of information and resources, yielding a passive investment strategy in foreign listed firms. Economic globalization has had little impact on these arrangements because private capital remains embryonic and cannot mount a credible, sustained threat to the regime.

Single-Party Authoritarian Regime: China

In a SPAR, the political system increases access to the resources and information deemed vital to preserving regime stability relative to a NAR. This is accomplished with the institutionalization of the ruling elite via a political party coupled with the establishment of a legislature that expands access to and regularizes decisions governing the distribution of state resources. These institutional arrangements yield a greater capacity for public-private ownership than in NARs, though public ownership will dominate private ownership. Accordingly, SOEs with dominant state ownership are likely to be established in these regimes. I also expect SPARs to establish a savings SWF because these are best suited for large, long-term ownership stakes that can centralize the control of sprawling state-sector assets. State-sector transparency (SWFs and SOEs) is expected to be higher than in NARs because political leaders must maintain greater accountability to a wider cross section of elites. Altogether these arrangements yield a greater capacity for aggressive state intervention, especially in regimes with comparable transparency requirements (other authoritarian regimes). The motivation to intervene in foreign markets will be driven primarily by an existential threat to the regime's survival; otherwise, it will be relatively passive. Specifically, ruling parties in SPARs are concerned primarily with exogenous/holistic regime threats but must also consider intra-party factional politics that could undermine regime stability.

Regime Characteristics

Two institutional features distinguish China's political regime from Brunei's – its ruling party and its legislature. Together these expand access to state information and resources. In China, the Chinese Communist Party (CCP) has implemented an "incentivized hierarchy" model in which political officials' core incentive is promotion.[14] The mechanism by which CCP officials vie for promotion resembles that of a rank-ordered tournament in which participants are given a ranking relative to others rather than being assessed based on absolute performance criteria.[15] The ranking primarily depends on the capacity of an official to meet (and preferably exceed) specific growth (and other) targets for his or her political jurisdiction.[16] As officials ascend the ranks of the party hierarchy, they gain greater control over state resources and information. The competition for promotion into senior positions generates considerable intraparty competition, which is the only form of political competition permitted. Through this institutionalized party system, the CCP widens access to state resources and information to a wide swath of loyal party members.

The second difference is China's legislature, the National People's Congress (NPC), which has nearly 3,000 members. The NPC meets only once per year in March for a period of two or three weeks. The NPC Standing Committee, which has effectively the same powers as the NPC itself, carries on the work of the NPC throughout the year with its approximately 170 members.[17] The NPC is widely regarded as wielding a "rubber stamp" for policy decisions already made either in the State Council or high-level CCP bodies.[18] NPC deputies are chosen every five years via a multitiered representative electoral system. Delegates are elected by the provincial people's assemblies, members of which, in turn, are elected by lower-level assemblies, and so on through a series of tiers to the local people's assemblies, which are directly elected by the electorate. Due, in part, to the multilayered selection process, certain groups are overrepresented – recently, CEOs/businesspeople.[19] About one-sixth of NPC deputies were CEOs or leaders of companies in the 11th NPC (2008–13).

The NPC itself does not invite public input; however, its existence does create opportunities for private capital to influence policy and to reap benefits not otherwise available. This occurs in two ways:

---

[14] Li and Zhou (2005); Naughton (2008); Carney (2012).
[15] Lazear and Rosen (1981).   [16] Chen, Li, and Zhou (2005).
[17] Certain laws and appointments require the approval of the full plenary session (Jiang 2003).
[18] Tanner (1999).   [19] Dickson (2008); Kennedy (2008); Truex (2016).

lobbying and NPC membership. Deng and Kennedy find that large companies and business associations can have a substantial effect on Chinese public policy via lobbying.[20] National policy decisions typically involve multiple actors over an extended period of time.[21] Rather than achieving their aims through *guanxi*, Deng and Kennedy find that business associations exert influence by, among other things, providing information to deputies and strengthening their public standing. To be effective in their lobbying efforts, companies and associations will hire former officials who are more valued for their knowledge about the inner workings of the political system rather than their relationships with specific individuals in office. One such form of specialized knowledge regards the opinions and motions process. Motions are short policy proposals, often calling for a new piece of legislation, that require the signatures of thirty or more deputies. Individual deputies may also file shorter, less developed formal opinions. These proposals are then submitted to different NPC working committees and can eventually become bills, or they may be incorporated into policies in more informal means by various ministries and agencies. This policy-making process obviates the reliance on self-enforcing agreements because the authority of the state stands behind them (in Vietnam, by comparison, Jensen et al. report that self-enforcement is common).[22]

A second means by which the NPC enables private industry to gain access to resources occurs through CEO membership. Truex finds that affiliated firms of Chinese CEOs benefit from CEO membership on the NPC due to positive external perceptions and the "reputation boost" of the position; to a lesser extent, CEOs benefit from their policy influence. CEO membership on the NPC also improves access to information about likely changes to national policy.[23] Draft laws usually circulate between the NPC, the State Council, and relevant government ministries for months before they are made public, granting NPC companies time to adjust their management and business practices.

In comparison to Brunei, which lacks a ruling party and a legislature, China's CCP and NPC create opportunities for private capital to expand access to state-administered resources and information. But this expanded access remains limited in comparison with democracies, such as Taiwan, and even DPARs, such as Singapore or Malaysia.

---

[20] Deng and Kennedy (2010).   [21] Judd (2008).   [22] Jensen et al. (2014).
[23] Truex (2016).

State-Owned Assets Supervision and Administration Commission

As discussed in Chapter 4, China hosts several SWFs, including the China Investment Corporation (CIC), State Administration of Foreign Exchange (SAFE), and the National Social Security Fund (NSSF). However, none of these normally takes large, long-term equity holdings that would permit aggressive intervention in a target firm. China's equivalent organization to the savings SWFs of Singapore (Temasek), Malaysia (Khazanah), and Brunei (BIA) is SASAC.

SASAC is more similar to Temasek and Khazanah than the BIA because its funds do not originate from commodities sales. There are some important differences, however. First, SASAC did not receive any funds from its firms (e.g., dividends) until 2007 when a minimal amount was collected (RMB14 billion). This rose to RMB97 billion by 2012, still well under 10 percent of the central SASAC firms' profits and very low compared with Singapore and Malaysia, where industrial firms typically pay dividends greater than 25 percent of their earnings.[24] Second, SASAC does not exercise the same degree of control rights over its firms, such as appointments of top executives. Third, in some cases the SOEs have equal standing to SASAC in the state's institutional hierarchy (e.g., national oil companies and the CEOs of many SOEs). Hence it cannot act independently of the firms in which it maintains ownership rights; often, it is incapable of forcing firms to implement desired reforms. These overlapping authority structures create significant coordination problems that have prevented SASAC from evolving into a more centralized asset-management agency, like Temasek,[25] and enable it to more effectively implement corporate governance reforms that would diminish state control to the benefit of private capital. But the fundamental reason for the preservation of these arrangements is that the CCP leadership has chosen not to change them because they uphold the prioritization of policy goals over pure commercial gains, to be discussed further later.

SASAC was established in 2003 following a series of market-oriented reforms and corporate restructuring to China's state sector.[26]

---

[24] Lardy and Subramanian (2012, 72).   [25] Shih (2008).

[26] Central Huijin was also established in 2003. It owns majority stakes in the big four Chinese banks. These include Bank of China, Industrial and Commercial Bank of China, China Construction Bank, and the Agricultural Bank of China.

Its creation marked the end of dramatic state-sector downsizing in order to restore profitability and a new emphasis on state-sector stability. An important impetus to its creation was China's accession to the WTO in 2001, which served as a powerful lever to push forward structural reforms and to facilitate its transition to a full market economy in the face of internal resistance.[27] SASAC was established as an "ownership agency," with two primary goals: improve corporate governance and restructure SOEs so that they would be more concentrated in sectors in which they had some comparative advantage and for which an economic justification for continued state ownership existed. SASAC was initially granted ownership rights over 196 nonfinancial state firms; due to consolidation of state assets, this fell to 103 by 2016. To get a sense of its size in comparison with other savings SWFs, forty-five corporations on the Global Fortune 500 list for 2012 were owned by SASAC, with combined assets worth US$4.5 trillion, which was more than five times larger than the largest SWF at the time (Norway's SWF).

While the overall state sector shrank since SASAC's inception, central SASAC firms have grown in both the number of workers and the total value of assets, magnifying the CCP's centralized control over state-sector resources and information.[28] Between 2002 and 2010, its share of employment for all state-run industry increased from 24 to 43 percent, and its share of capital stock increased from 48.3 to 61 percent. The concentration of corporate assets has been accompanied by a reduction in the state's control over small and medium-sized firms – a manifestation of China's "grab the big, release the small" reform policy initiated in 1997.

The SASAC system can be seen as a gigantic pyramid. SASAC sits at the top with a relatively small number of companies directly beneath it – 103 as of 2016. Each of these top-level companies, in turn, sits at the top of a pyramid with ownership and control over many subsidiaries – in 2010, the total number of companies under SASAC's ownership was a remarkable 23,738.[29]

The broader corporate sector mirrors this structure – it can be viewed as having three tiers.[30] The top-tier companies are the central SASAC firms – China's "national champions." These are the companies that

---

[27] Leng (2009). [28] Naughton (2015).
[29] 2011 Yearbook; Naughton (2015). [30] Pearson (2015).

the government considers the most strategic due to their support of many ancillary industries. They include companies that provide a stable supply of energy, power, transport and communication services, and industrial materials. Due to their focus on the provision of basic inputs to the broader economy, SASAC firms are neither the most technologically dynamic firms, nor are they major contributors to China's export economy. For example, all central SASAC firms in 2006 provided only 3.6 percent of China's total exports[31] versus more than 60 percent provided by foreign-invested firms. In high-tech sectors, the difference is even more pronounced. Only a tiny number of central SASAC firms produced any high-tech exports; by comparison, foreign invested enterprises produced 87 percent in 2007.[32] China's technologically most dynamic firms, such as Huawei and Hai'er, are typically not SASAC firms or subsidiaries but rather hybrid firms with some local government participation alongside substantial private ownership.

Moving down from SASAC and the top-tier firms are the middle-tier firms, over which the state asserts less central oversight. Firms from the automobile industry are this category, as well as large pharmaceuticals, chemicals, steel, telecommunications equipment, heavy industrial machinery, and, more recently, biotechnology and alternative energy manufacturing. Local SASACs and their SOEs also fit into this category.

The bottom tier is where the vast majority of Chinese businesses are located – such as medium-sized and small manufacturing, personal services, and retail firms. This category includes a large fraction of China's export-oriented manufacturing firms, as well as small-scale firms for the domestic Chinese market that are not "strategic," such as coal mining.[33]

Market Reforms within the Cage of State Ownership

With its establishment in 2003, SASAC sought to introduce basic corporate governance reforms to top-level firms, including (1) transforming them into 100 percent listed entities such that all their assets would be incorporated into the listed company and (2) introducing functioning boards of directors with outside, independent directors.

[31] Naughton (2015).   [32] Pearson (2015).   [33] Ibid.

However, this transformation process has proceeded at a painfully slow pace, especially after the global financial crisis of 2008–9, which shook the Chinese leadership's confidence in market solutions and increased their reliance on a state sector that could deliver quick economic responses. By the end of 2008, only twenty SASAC top-level firms (of 142) could be considered "100 percent listed," while twenty-four were carrying out "experiments" in which independent directors make up half or more of the board of directors.[34] Looking at the larger state sector beyond central SASAC firms alone, only 50 percent of state-owned firms were publicly listed by 2013; the state still retained control of 75.4 percent of the equity of all state-owned firms, leaving little room for minority investors.[35]

Difficulties with implementing corporate governance reforms are due to three related roadblocks: (1) institutional legacies that preserve the status quo, (2) SASAC's lack of appointment powers, and most fundamentally (3) political leaders who favor the preservation of state control in order to pursue CCP policies above commercial interests.

Institutional Legacies

While the top-level SASAC firms have dramatically improved their operations and performance since the 1990s, most have successfully resisted adhering to SASAC reforms. The top-level firms have sought to preserve their privileged position with near monopolies. Because the top-level firms originate from line ministries, they are embedded in strong networks of cooperating bureaucrats and officials, and many have long-standing links to top CCP officials.[36] As a result, the largest SOEs are the most tied to powerful interest groups, the least transparent, and the most resistant to reforms.

These conflicting interests between SASAC and the top-level firms have resulted in the withholding of resources to SASAC by the companies it "owns" despite the implementation of corporatization reforms. A typical corporatization process involves listing the strongest performing factory or group of factories in a larger, state-owned group company.[37] The group company is often the top-level company of the group. It will typically retain control of 40 to 50 percent of the

---

[34] Naughton (2015).   [35] Rutkowski (2014).
[36] In some cases, they have links to specific families (Naughton 2015).
[37] Keister (1998, 2000); Guthrie et al. (2007).

shares, with 20 to 30 percent designated for institutional shareholders (often state affiliated); the remaining 30 percent of shares will be for the public as free-floating shares. As the residual claimant on firm profits, group companies operate with enormous discretion – they can move funds upward and effectively quarantine them, as well as redistribute them among firms in the group, depriving SASAC and minority share-holders of claims on firm profits. Not until mid-2007 could SASAC even have a legal claim on SASAC firms' profits.[38] This entrenched power of top-level firms vis-à-vis SASAC has enabled them to resist "excessive" corporatization reforms.

Lack of Appointment Powers

A second important limitation SASAC faces with achieving its objectives is the lack of power to appoint the most important managers of the companies it "owns." Instead, the party has the final say about all key personnel matters.[39] Of greatest importance is the Communist Central Committee Organization Bureau, which decides the top manager and chairman of the board appointments for the fifty-three largest SASAC enterprises due to their influence over the allocation of resources and patronage.[40] These firms rank as vice-ministries in the Chinese bureaucratic system, and the CEO as an individual will sometimes have full ministerial rank (an equivalent rank to SASAC). This appointments procedure is facilitated by the government's controlling share of greater than 51 percent of the total equity outstanding for nearly all SOEs, which makes other shareholders irrelevant to the selection process.

Moreover, the CCP has implemented an "incentivized hierarchy" system that presents officials with the prospect of a stable and predictable long-term career contingent on their loyalty to the party.[41] As a result, managers of state firms have very strong incentives to subordinate the interests of the individual firm to national interests, and SASAC's role becomes subordinate to the preferences of CCP leaders.

While the lack of appointment powers reduces the authority of SASAC over top-level firms, this resembles the procedure used by Singapore's People's Action Party (PAP) until the mid-1990s when

---

[38] This is due to efforts starting in 1994 to strengthen the financial position of state firms and build support for further reforms by abolishing the requirement that state firms remit after-tax profits to the government.

[39] Chan (2009).   [40] McNally (2002).   [41] Naughton (2008).

Temasek was finally granted authority over appointments. Prior to this time, Temasek did not face comparable problems. The more fundamental issue therefore regards the divergence of SASAC interests from those of CCP leaders.

Preferences of CCP Leaders

Despite corporatization, SOEs continue to underperform on a commercial basis. For example, the return on assets (ROA) of listed SOEs have fallen from around 7 percent in 2006 to 5.4 percent in 2013, approaching the ROA of unlisted SOEs – 3.8 percent in 2013 (this has remained fairly steady since 2006).[42] However, it is unclear whether the declining performance of listed SOEs is due to the changing global or national economic environment (e.g., the global financial crisis of 2008–9 and China's reaction to it) or because less profitable segments of state business groups have been corporatized. In either case, it has led to recent calls for a "Temasek model": improve the management of state firms by packaging them into listed entities managed by professional financial management companies with the explicit aim of maximizing asset value.[43] Temasek has been committed to selling underperforming state-owned assets and investing in private or foreign companies to improve the performance of its portfolio. Of the thirty-five state-owned companies in Temasek's portfolio at inception, only eleven firms remain. The rest were divested or liquidated. Today only 30 percent of Temasek's portfolio is exposed to Singapore.

However, the initiative to prioritize SOEs' financial performance was undermined by President Xi Jinping after the Third Plenum in 2013 when he insisted that SOEs retain a "dominant role" in many key sectors, thereby requiring the preservation of SASAC's existing arrangements.[44] This would also ensure that CCP leaders could call on SOEs to pursue the party's shifting policy priorities ahead of their own commercial interests.

For decades, CCP leaders justified state ownership on the grounds that it offered stability. In the 1990s, when few state firms were profitable, economic reform, including corporatization, was prioritized. Corporatization occurred slowly, however, because public ownership provided a way to buffer workers from unemployment and the lack of a social safety net during a period of rapid change. But now that social

---

[42] Rutkowski (2014).   [43] Naughton (2016).   [44] Ibid.

welfare institutions are being put in place[45] and the profitability of SOEs has been restored, priorities have shifted. Political leaders are now placing more emphasis on various forms of security – economic, resource, and national defense – as a justification for state firms. State control of telecommunications, petroleum, and most of the other basic industries to which top-level SASAC firms belong meet these criteria.

China's state-sector pyramids enable the state to protect and extend its influence via an opaque governance system at the top, while minority shareholders provide the bulk of financing for lower-tier subsidiaries. These corporate ownership arrangements complement and are reinforced by the CCP's "incentivized hierarchy" that preserves party loyalty. These arrangements, which privilege insiders at the expense of outsiders, present numerous challenges related to strengthening corporate governance and improving the transparency and accountability of the corporate sector.

Corporate Governance and Transparency Challenges

The creation of central SASAC was an important part of the effort to improve corporate governance and with it corporate transparency throughout China's state-enterprise system. While opacity remains prevalent at the higher echelons of the corporate hierarchy, this initiative was more successfully implemented for the hundreds of smaller firms at the bottom of the pyramid because they were restructured into market-oriented corporations and listed on China's stock markets. Yet even the smaller firms that have made the biggest strides in improving their accountability to outside investors remain mired in challenges that preserve their inferior corporate governance standards vis-à-vis their counterparts in Singapore and Malaysia. One important reason for China's weaker investor protections relative to these DPARs is that China does not hold regular elections, so a direct link between SOE performance and voters/investors is absent. In DPARs, the ruling party must retain the support of voters whose savings are heavily invested in listed SOEs by ensuring that SOEs perform well.

The disconnect between firm performance and voters/investors gets reflected in a variety of corporate governance dimensions that contribute to relatively worse disclosures about corporate performance in

---

[45] Frazier (2015).

comparison with Singapore or Malaysia. These dimensions include the large number of SOEs without public listings, the expropriation of minority shareholders via state-owned groups, the lack of incentive-based compensation, the ineffectiveness of bank monitoring of managers, weak legal protections for investors, weak institutional investors, and the absence of a managerial labor market.

First, publicly listed SOEs must adhere to a stock exchange's corporate governance rules and regulations to be listed, including the regular disclosure of corporate information. But because only 50 percent of state-owned firms were publicly listed by 2013, a large number of SOEs remain relatively opaque. Additionally, many top-level SASAC firms remain unlisted, and those group companies with listed firms often retain unlisted companies too. The high proportion of unlisted SOEs coupled with top-level SASAC firms that own both listed and unlisted subsidiaries undercuts the transparency-enhancing reforms that occur among the listed firms because their profits can be redistributed to the unlisted group firms. In Malaysia and Singapore, nearly all large SOEs are listed, forcing adherence to the corporate governance codes and reducing the opportunities for tunneling or redistribution of funds.

Related to this is the second issue – Chinese SOEs' pyramidal ownership structure. Because Chinese SOEs often belong to state-owned business groups, the state has the capacity to expropriate wealth from minority shareholders via *tunneling*.[46] Evidence indicates that this is not uncommon.[47] These issues could theoretically arise in Singapore and Malaysia, though the scope of the problem is not as great because such expansive state-owned groups do not exist and nearly all large SOEs are listed.

Third, Chinese SOEs lack incentive-based compensation contracts that reward good managerial performance with financial gains such as stocks, options, raises, and bonuses. Although the China Securities Regulatory Commission encourages the use of incentive-based pay, such compensation arrangements remain ineffective for two reasons.[48]

---

[46] Using the 20 percent share ownership threshold employed by La Porta et al. (1999) to identify the existence of controlling shareholders means that most listed firms have at least one controlling owner. With this control, an owner can expropriate from minority shareholders via outright theft and fraud or through more subtle means such as intercorporate loans, loan guarantees for related companies, favorable transfer pricing for related companies, and the dilution of new shares.

[47] Liu and Lu (2007); Peng et al. (2011).   [48] Jiang and Kim (2015).

First, because managers of SOEs are civil service employees, their salary is capped at a certain multiple of average workers' pay to preserve social harmony within the firm. Second, the primary incentive for SOE managers is to be promoted to a high-level government position, thereby undermining the need for incentive-based compensation.[49] Hence a relation between managerial compensation and firm performance in SOEs has not been found.[50] Temasek and Khazanah have long had effective performance-based compensation arrangements, strongly aligning the incentives of managers with the firm's financial performance.

Fourth, bank monitoring of managers is ineffective in China, although this can often be an effective governance tool in the context of concentrated ownership.[51] This is ineffective in China because both banks and the firms to which they primarily lend are state owned. For example, Qian and Yeung find that banks continue to lend to firms even when firms' controlling shareholders are known to be tunneling from their minority shareholders.[52] Hence these authors argue that for capital markets to develop in a way that effectively permits the reduction of agency costs (and associated expropriation of minority shareholders coupled with the lack of transparency about firm finances), the banking system needs to become more effective at disciplining borrowers. In Singapore, only one of the city-state's big four banks is state owned (DBS). In Malaysia, banks are predominantly state owned, but there are stronger protections for investors in place that prevent a comparable level of expropriation.

In the absence of effective disciplining arrangements within SOEs or state-owned groups, a strong legal system can help to compensate. But despite the issuance of numerous company laws and securities regulations, China's legal system remains ineffective at protecting investors.[53] When the quality of China's legal system is compared with that of forty-nine other countries around the globe,[54] Allen et al. find that it falls below the average and that enforcement in particular is significantly below average.[55] Kato and Long likewise contend that China

---

[49] Firth et al. (2006, 2007); Chen et al. (2010).
[50] Firth et al. (2006); Kato and Long (2006); Conyon and He (2011).
[51] Fama (1985); Sharpe (1990); Diamond (1984, 1991).
[52] Qian and Yeung (2015).
[53] Allen et al (2005); Pistor and Xu (2005); Liu (2006); Zou et al. (2008).
[54] As compiled by La Porta et al. (1998).   [55] Allen et al. (2005).

has neither a comprehensive set of legal rules necessary to protect minority shareholders nor the capacity to enforce existing laws.[56] However, the Chinese government recognizes that its laws and enforcement are weak and has begun taking steps to improve them.[57]

Powerful institutional investors could compensate for a weak legal system. As large long-term shareholders of firms, institutional investors may engage in shareholder activism or monitoring.[58] In China, however, institutional investors are neither large shareholders at the firm level in comparison with controlling owners (families or the state), nor do they have long-run horizons.[59] The capacity for institutional investors to exert influence over firms in other countries arises when the firm's ownership is diffuse, but diffuse ownership does not exist in China. Moreover, the evidence indicates that the turnover rate of institutional investors is very high.[60] Hence institutional investors lack the incentive to monitor and intervene in firms in which they own shares for the short term. In Malaysia, by comparison, two of the most important "owners" of listed companies are institutional investors – the Employees Provident Fund and the National Equity Fund (PNB). The equivalent institutional investor in Singapore is the Central Provident Fund, which is a powerful, long-term investor in domestic firms.

Another external mechanism by which to reduce governance problems is via an active managerial labor market. The potential to be hired by another firm can incentivize managers to improve their reputation by demonstrating a commitment to act in the best interests of shareholders and thereby minimize agency costs.[61] In China, however, an active market for managers does not exist for SOEs. SOEs are prevented from competing among themselves because an Organization Department maintains an exhaustive list of government employees at the central, provincial, municipal, and county levels, and it decides all the state's important personnel assignments, including SOEs managers.[62] This may change as SOEs become increasingly focused on profits; SASAC, for example, has started to increase its activity in recruiting top managers.[63] In Singapore, by comparison, professional managers

---

[56] Kato and Long (2006).   [57] Jiang and Kim (2015).
[58] Gillan and Starks (1998).   [59] Chen et al. (2007).
[60] Jiang and Kim (2015).
[61] Fama and Jensen (1983); Jensen and Meckling (1976).
[62] Kato and Long (2006).   [63] Jiang and Kim (2015).

are actively recruited for top roles in SOEs. In Malaysia, Khazanah has also implemented performance metrics for managers of SOEs, and an active managerial labor market has emerged.

In summary, China's corporate governance reforms are the result of a dual-track process that roughly mirrors broader efforts to shift the economy in a market-oriented direction while preserving CCP control over the country's vital resources and information. Dominant state ownership permits political priorities to be placed above profit maximization and state interests above investors' rights. In the absence of a strong tie between CCP priorities and voter/investor interests, as exists for Singapore and Malaysia, corporate transparency is likely to remain relatively lower.

Foreign Investment Behavior

An objective and valid comparison can be made between Singapore and Malaysia versus China in terms of their investment behaviors in foreign listed firms by analyzing their ownership positions for the same sample of firms. Evidence for this is presented in Figures 4.5 and 4.6. It shows that Chinese state entities have far fewer ownership positions in large listed East Asian firms than state entities from Singapore or Malaysia. When we compare the number of these positions in relation to the size of their economies, the difference is profound.

Central SASAC SOEs are the main actors responsible for China's outward foreign direct investment (OFDI). OFDI covers all foreign investments, including those in both listed and unlisted assets. But even with this inflated value, China's OFDI remains a small fraction of total SASAC firms' assets, especially in comparison with Temasek and Khazanah. For example, around 70 percent of Temasek's assets have been invested overseas since 2008, whereas Khazanah's foreign investments reached 41 percent of its total assets in 2015. When we consider that central SASAC assets were greater than US$4.5 trillion in 2012 and that the cumulative total of China's outbound mergers and acquisitions between 2004 and 2012 were around US$247 billion (see Figure 5.1), this equates to less than 6 percent of total SASAC assets. But this is a significant overestimate because the US$4.5 trillion amount is based only on Chinese firms on the Fortune Global 500 list and therefore ignores most of the companies owned both directly and indirectly by SASAC.

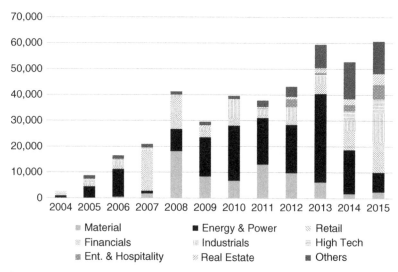

Figure 5.1 Completed outbound Chinese cross-border merger and acquisition (M&A) transactions by industry of target (aggregate value, US$ million). *Source:* Bloomberg, Thomson, Rhodium Group; includes disclosed value of all completed M&A transactions by ultimately Chinese-owned firms.

However, one might argue that SASAC firms' lack of foreign investment is due to the low level of domestic economic development, making a comparison with Singapore and Malaysia problematic because the crowding-out effects are not yet as severe. In this regard, it is useful to evaluate the nature of central SASAC firms' foreign investment behavior independently of its foreign investment intensity. The theory tells us that SPARs will engage in activist interventions when the regime faces a threat to its survival. But once this threat subsides, more passive investment behavior will ensue. This is precisely what is observed.

CCP legitimacy depends on growth and stability, and this, in turn, depends on an adequate supply of energy resources to fuel industrialization. For decades this has meant an adequate supply of oil. Thus we should observe more activist state intervention in the oil sector specifically but more passive investment behavior for other sectors. Likewise, once energy supplies meet or exceed expected demand, we should observe national oil companies operating with greater discretion – pursuing commercial priorities in place of national policy goals and reducing their activist behavior.

Consistent with this expectation, numerous studies have found that the main motives of China's OFDI involve securing supplies of natural resources – mineral resources and fuel – to support the country's long-term economic development.[64] "In the post-Mao era, China's central leadership sees economic growth as a life and death matter for the regime."[65] Ensuring that Chinese oil companies could secure adequate energy supplies has been vitally important to this end.[66]

China has three major national oil companies – China National Petroleum Corporation (CNPC), China National Offshore Oil Corporation (CNOOC), and Sinopec. These companies have been the country's most active overseas investors since the early 1980s, and they have continued to dominate China's OFDI into the contemporary period. Since 2000, China's national oil companies have expanded their overseas oil equity production from a mere 0.15 million barrels per day to a staggering 1.6 million barrels per day by the end of 2013. Figure 5.1 illustrates the persistent appetite for energy and material assets since 2004, except for a shift to financials in 2007–8 and the move toward nonresource sectors in 2014–5. These investments have bolstered China's importance in the global petroleum industry, making it the world's second-largest oil consumer, largest oil importer, and fastest-growing overseas petroleum investor.[67]

Both CNPC and Sinopec are bureaucratically ranked at the ministry level, the same as SASAC, while CNOOC, for historical reasons, has the lower status of a general bureau (just below the rank of vice-ministry). The CEOs all hold the rank of vice-minister.[68] Because it is in the interests of the CCP that the major oil companies are commercially successful and that they are able to secure adequate energy supplies, it is common for oil companies' commercial interests to align with government foreign and trade policies.[69] For example, the Chinese government has for many decades cultivated relationships with developing countries in Africa and the Middle East (where a large fraction of the world's authoritarian regimes are located), yielding benefits to China's oil majors. These countries are suitable targets for Chinese acquisitions not only because of their appetite for foreign

---

[64] Buckley et al. (2007); Cheung and Qian (2009); Cheung et al. (2012); Kolstad and Wiig (2012); Liu et al. (2005); Tolentino (2010); Wei and Alon (2010); Hanemann and Gao (2016).
[65] Xu (2011).   [66] Downs (2010).   [67] Khaitan (2014).   [68] Liao (2015).
[69] Jiang and Sinton (2011).

investment but also because their transparency requirements are comparable to those of China. Chinese oil companies can successfully enlist the diplomatic support of the Chinese government in initiating and closing deals.[70]

National oil companies have gained strong support from the central government in signing long-term supply deals, building transnational pipelines, and completing acquisitions of foreign firms since the Going Abroad (or Going Out) policy was introduced in 1999. Two state-owned banks – the China Development Bank (CDB) and the China Export-Import Bank – have played an instrumental role in funding many of these foreign investments.[71] For example, in September 2010, both CNPC and Sinopec formed strategic alliances with the CDB; it subsequently agreed to provide US$30 billion in loans to CNPC at low rates over the next five years to support CNPC's expansion abroad. This was on top of US$44 billion in loans that CDB provided to resource-rich countries in 2009, with China's national oil companies as the indirect beneficiaries of these loans as they received long-term oil and gas supplies at the same time. Some observers have suggested that China's national oil companies, flush with cash, have been paying a premium for assets, freezing other bidders out. One report, for instance, concluded that in 2009 the total premium paid by the Chinese companies increased to 40 percent above the base valuation of acquired assets.[72] With the financial support of Chinese banks and, in some cases, the direct involvement of the Chinese government in finalizing the deals, national oil companies diversified their investments out of Africa and the Middle East with new projects in Venezuela, Brazil, Ecuador, Kazakhstan, and Turkmenistan.[73]

Nevertheless, debate has emerged regarding the motivation for the international expansion of the Chinese oil majors in recent years. Oil majors have a strong business interest to expand internationally because overseas operations are more profitable and free from government interference than those within China.[74] This has contributed to the small fraction of oil produced overseas that makes it back to China – only 10 to 20 percent.[75] Many analysts therefore argue that this has enabled China's oil majors to manipulate the government to

[70] Ibid.   [71] Ibid.   [72] Wood Mackenzie (2010).
[73] Jiang and Sinton (2011).   [74] Ibid.
[75] Lieberthal and Herberg (2006); Houser (2008).

adopt policies preferable to their commercial interests.[76] A number of factors are pointed to as amplifying oil majors' lobbying power relative to the government agencies tasked with overseeing them, including their long lineage associated with the government ministries, the large size of the companies in the oil industry, the strategic importance of oil as a "pillar" industry, and the company leaders' high ranks within the CCP.[77] However, these features have not changed since the 1980s or 1990s. The crucial change that has occurred is the demand for energy supplies by the CCP leadership. Only once petroleum supply requirements are met will CCP leaders permit the national oil companies to pursue their commercial interests.

This is reflected in the national oil companies adopting a major adjustment in their investment behavior. They have increasingly sought minority, passive ownership stakes in strategic "learning" assets, which contrasts with their historical practice of paying above-market prices to own controlling equity stakes in projects to lock in supply.[78] Examination of national oil companies' overseas acquisitions exhibit a clear shift toward smaller ownership stakes.[79] The average ownership stake for the thirty-seven acquisitions completed between January 2002 and December 2010 was 57.6 percent. Between January 2011 and December 2013, forty-three more acquisitions were completed, with an average ownership stake of 40.2 percent. It should be noted that because these acquisitions encompass both small and large companies (mostly the former), they are not comparable with those identified in Chapter 4, which involved ownership positions exclusively in East Asia's largest corporations. Thus we must restrict the focus to changes in the ownership trend over time. In this regard, Chinese petroleum investments not only have become smaller but also have shifted away from a handful of developing countries with authoritarian regimes – especially Sudan (NAR until 2010, then DPAR), Angola (SPAR until 1992, then DPAR), Venezuela (DPAR), and Kazakhstan (DPAR) – to more diverse destinations, including the United States and Canada (democracies). National oil company investments in countries with higher transparency requirements have frequently run into roadblocks, forcing them to accept smaller positions or to forgo investments altogether. For example, CNOOC's attempt to acquire US oil company

---

[76] Andrew-Speed (2004); Cunningham (2007); Downs (2010).
[77] Jiang and Ding (2014).   [78] Khaitan (2014).   [79] Jiang and Ding (2014).

Unocal was blocked by the US government in 2005.[80] This failure was due to the competing bidder, Chevron, creating enough political uncertainty about CNOOC's independence from political influence despite CNOOC's effort to portray itself as operating purely based on market principles. This characterization was undermined when it was discovered that US$7 billion of the US$18.5 billion all-cash offer was financed by a loan from CNOOC's parent – the top-level SASAC firm, which is simultaneously the controlling shareholder.[81]

Having learned some important lessons, CNOOC successfully won approval from Canadian authorities to complete a US$15.1 billion acquisition of Nexen in 2012. However, this deal is best seen as an anomaly. Prime Minister Stephen Harper said in a statement that the deal's approval should not be seen as the "beginning" of a trend but rather as the "end of a trend."[82]

With China's two other national oil companies, the nonlisted parent company usually takes the lead in international transactions, bringing in the listed subsidiary when it is convenient. CNPC, the top-level parent of Petrochina, has significant investments in Sudan and Kazakhstan; China Petrochemical Corporation, top-level parent of Sinopec, teamed up with CNPC to buy assets in Ecuador. In these cases, the parent firms use their lack of transparency to shield the listed company from the appearance of involvement so that it will avoid being the target of shareholder activism.[83] This lack of transparency is possible when initiating large investments in other authoritarian regimes.

In summary, China's OFDI is small in relation to total assets owned by SASAC, especially when OFDI is restricted to investments in foreign listed firms. Depending on the political regime of the country in which the target firm is located, Chinese SOEs are more likely to initiate a large or minority ownership stake. In countries with lower transparency requirements, as with authoritarian regimes, large ownership stakes are common; for advanced democracies, smaller stakes are more prevalent.[84] And as China has satisfied its energy demands, its SOEs have shifted their investments toward smaller stakes in advanced democracies where they are placing greater emphasis on services-oriented industries to promote China's continued growth.

[80] CNOOC's Bid for Unocal (2005). [81] Naughton (2015).
[82] Vieira (2012). [83] Sudan Divestment Task Force (2007).
[84] Coates (2015); Economist (2013).

Conclusion

China is a SPAR that has successfully maintained regime stability despite rising pressures associated with rapid development in addition to rising trade and capital flows. The ruling party and the legislature have granted access to state resources to a wider set of elites than in Brunei, including private capital. Meanwhile, the CCP's power is sustained via its control of SOEs that dominate the basic industries that the rest of the economy depends on, thereby granting opportunities to private capital without sacrificing political control. This has contributed to a greater capacity for hybrid public-private ownership. Transparency remains poor for the upper echelons of the state sector where the elite wield greatest influence. Lower tiers have more fully implemented transparency-enhancing reforms, though a variety of corporate governance challenges persist that prevent them from achieving comparable investor protections to those found in Singapore and Malaysia. Foreign investment has also remained inconsequential across nearly all sectors except for petroleum, where the government's motivation to intervene has been high. Because growth is a "life or death" issue for the CCP, and petroleum supplies have been vital to this, China's three major oil companies have historically engaged in aggressive foreign acquisitions in other authoritarian regimes with comparably low transparency requirements. The target firms were subsequently merged into the acquiring company, personnel changed, and their sales and distribution diverted to new customers. But now that petroleum supplies are sufficient and this threat to the ruling party has subsided, aggressive foreign interventions are being replaced by minority positions in services-oriented firms in more advanced economies. While the CCP has successfully held on to power, the Taiwan case demonstrates that as the power of private capital grows, regime transition could occur, contributing to the decline of the state sector.

From SPAR to Democracy: Taiwan

In a democracy, I expect SOEs to be relatively unimportant to the corporate sector, notwithstanding SOEs that serve economically useful functions such as natural monopolies or projects that private capital would be unwilling or unable to fund. I also expect state-sector transparency to be relatively better than that found in other regimes because the leaders are held accountable to constituents and the possibility of monopolized control of information and resources is diminished by formal institutional arrangements (i.e., checks and balances). If a SWF is established, its remit will be restricted to a specific purpose due to the need to maintain accountability to voters/taxpayers, making savings SWFs less likely. Finally, I expect the SWF to engage in more passive investment behavior. Aggressive corporate intervention involving the state taking on a majority ownership stake would run counter to the interests of private capital of keeping state involvement in the marketplace at a minimum.

Taiwan is useful to assess these hypothesized relationships not only as a democratic regime but also for how state intervention changed as the regime transitioned from a SPAR to a democracy. As a SPAR, Taiwan's state-sector arrangements display strong similarities to those exhibited by contemporary China. Resource scarcity coupled with vulnerability to invasion by mainland China led the Kuomintang (KMT) to pursue growth as a means by which to secure the nation's survival. SOEs and the KMT's party-owned firms dominated the largest enterprises, supplying inputs to multitudes of small downstream family-owned firms. While SOEs were important, they did not dominate the economy as completely as in Brunei.

As political reforms were implemented, allowing opposition parties to compete in national elections, privatization ensued. Taiwan's moment as a DPAR, from 1987 to 1996, witnessed the rise of mixed public-private SOEs, and private capital made important inroads into the policymaking arena. The rise of private capital and a concomitant decline in SOEs continued as the regime transitioned to a democracy. Likewise, state-sector transparency improved at each stage. Through the transition, the interests of private capital gained strength, yielding a reduction in the state's crowding-out effects. Private capital's influence was magnified by liberalizing reforms with respect to trade and capital (especially with the United States).

Taiwan also serves as a useful case for illustrating the conditions necessary for a SWF to be established in the context of a democracy – strong political parties. When parties are weak in comparison with individual politicians, coordination capacity is reduced. The Philippines offers a useful contrasting case in this regard.

Evolving Regime Attributes

From 1945 until 1987, Taiwan was a SPAR ruled by the KMT, with opposition parties legally banned. Following the lifting of martial law in 1987, the first competitive elections for the National Assembly and the Legislative Yuan were held in 1991 and 1992, respectively. These were followed by the first direct election for president in 1996, which is commonly regarded as the starting point for Taiwanese democracy.[85] Prior to this, Taiwan resembled a DPAR. In 2000, the Democratic Progressive Party (DPP) candidate won the presidential election, and in 2001, the DPP gained a majority in the Legislative Yuan.[86] Since 1996, five presidential elections have been held, and since 1992, seven elections to the Legislative Yuan. With control of the two branches of government alternating between the two dominant parties – the KMT and the DPP – Taiwan appears to have successfully transitioned to a consolidated democracy.

In the KMT single-party era, local factions constituted the basic building blocks of Taiwanese politics. Factions were comprised of members of the same family or kinship group as well as others via personal relationships.[87] The KMT built clientelist relationships with factions through the regular delivery of patronage in exchange for support in local elections.[88]

These local-level clientelist networks were complemented by national-level controls in which the KMT led the economic bureaucracy in implementing a model of state-led development. This included maintaining tight controls over the financial sector, major industrial conglomerates, and landed property. Because there was no effective separation between the party and the state, the KMT's monopoly over vital economic resources granted it tremendous financial leverage. Through its monopoly on basic inputs such as steel, petrochemicals, and heavy machines, the KMT could exert control over "subservient downstream firms" that competed for contracts with public enterprises.[89] Because they could be replaced, private firms were discouraged from forming

---

[85] Jacobs (2012); McAllister (2016).
[86] The National Assembly was frozen in 2000.   [87] Fell (2012).
[88] Political office granted access to local monopoly and oligopoly rights and "money machines" such as the credit departments of the fishermen's associations, the water conservancy associations, and the farmer's associations. See Fell (2012).
[89] Chu (1994, 134).

alliances that could challenge KMT supremacy. Additionally, important business leaders were kept under control through the hierarchical system of industrial associations in which membership was mandatory.

Democratization challenged existing arrangements at both the local and national levels. At the local level, factions could form alliances with opposing political parties and expand their network, while the business community could also band together and challenge the KMT's political and economic dominance. To maintain the support of the business community, the KMT moved to the awarding of public procurement projects such as real estate development and construction projects. Nevertheless, numerous private enterprises began to prosper once freed of the KMT's economic straitjacket. Strategic relationships formed between actors of the business community and politicians in different parties, and businesspeople often sought political office themselves.

While local factions were now free to forge political ties to opposition parties, none of these parties had the financial means to sustain the factions in the way the KMT could. Instead, the DPP's political heavyweights would support local politicians by visiting them in their home districts, thus boosting their image. In this way, one can see the early manifestation of party identification playing an influential role in the election of local politicians. Because the DPP did not have a reputation for engaging in corruption and stealing from the national budget for local interests, voters who favored a clean government would opt for DPP candidates. Although corruption and questionable deals did occur among DPP politicians, they were not perceived to be as systematic as with the KMT.

Because the delivery of patronage to local factions was tied to an individual representative's reputation, party discipline was low and coordination difficult for the KMT in particular. The KMT attempted to boost its image among the general public by eliminating the most delegitimating practice associated with its clientelist practices – vote buying. This marked the beginning of piecemeal efforts by the KMT to appear to address corruption without addressing the root cause that would otherwise undermine its electoral strength. Despite the KMT pushing through political reforms in the 1990s, it was unable to reverse its decline. The party was dogged by constant corruption scandals and ties to organized criminal networks, or "black gold."[90]

[90] Göbel (2004).

In 2000, the DPP won the presidential election, followed by the Legislative Yuan in 2001, significantly raising the fight against corruption and "black gold." These efforts will be discussed further in the subsection on corporate transparency. As part of its efforts to break up or weaken the KMT's control over the economy and its vital resources, the new DPP administration also replaced key personnel in SOEs and banks as well as in the bureaucracy. Additionally, the large party- and state-owned enterprises were weakened as economic liberalization subjected them to competition with private enterprises that emerged without political protection. One direct result was that many of these politically protected firms started to incur severe losses. This, in part, contributed to calls for privatization, which will be discussed further in the next subsection.

Over time, parties became differentiated from one another not simply on the basis of their effectiveness at delivering patronage but also on the basis of issues. This contributed to increasingly strong bonds between voters and parties, enhancing the relative importance of party reputation in relation to an individual politician's reputation.

A series of indicators used by Mainwaring and Scully's definition of party institutionalization confirm that Taiwan's two main parties have become stable and entrenched features of the island's political system. The indicators include electoral volatility, the degree of party fragmentation, the scope of party identification, and party cohesiveness.[91] *Electoral volatility* refers to the turnover of seats each election for each party. This indicator has declined as the number of competing parties has fallen from four (1996) to three (2000 and 2001) to two (2004, 2008, and 2012), indicating that volatility is due to electoral swings between the two leading parties. Only in the legislative election of 2001 was one of the two leading parties (the KMT) relegated to the third-party position. *Party system fragmentation* looks at the number of relevant parties and their relative size with regard to winning votes. This indicator also shows that the KMT and the DPP have emerged as the two main parties, with other parties capturing declining fractions of the total vote share over time. The *scope of party identification* by Taiwanese voters has increased incrementally since the early 1990s and has ultimately converged on the two leading parties – the KMT

[91] Cheng and Hsu (2015).

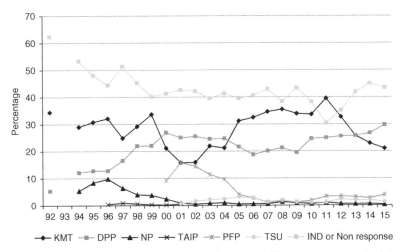

Figure 5.2 Changes in the party identification of Taiwanese as tracked in surveys by the Election Study Center, National Chengchi University (1992–2015).
Note: KMT = Kuomintang; DPP = Democratic Progressive Party; NP = New Party; TAIP = Taiwan Independence Party; PFP = People First Party; TSU = Taiwan Solidarity Union; IND = Independent.

and the DPP. Figure 5.2 shows the consistent increase in party identification over time, with voters identifying with either the DPP or KMT. The rising level of party identification can also be observed by the decline in those who report that they are independent or gave no response (except for the recent upturn from 2012). Moreover, the figure also shows that there were more numerous parties at the earlier stages of Taiwan's democratic period when party identification was weaker, but this has since evolved into two dominant parties. The figure confirms that the KMT and DPP have developed identifiable and stable policy reputations. Moreover, McAllister reports that the level of party identification is higher among younger voters who have grown up with Taiwan's new democratic arrangements than among older voters, which is a healthy sign for the future of Taiwanese democracy.[92] Finally, the *cohesion and internal party discipline* of the KMT and DPP have become quite considerable. Cheng and Hsu report that

[92] McAllister (2016).

Party headquarters for the KMT and the DPP draft platforms, conduct surveys, manage candidate selection for national and local elections and select their own leadership according to codified procedures, and chart strategies for legislative battles. Party switching and the creation of new parties are not common. The two parties have grassroots organizations in society as well as card-carrying rank-and-file members. The two leading parties can and do nurture the reputation of their labels and political brand names. A party label is not simply a flag of convenience for candidates. There are factions, but party headquarters are typically able to determine party candidates and have been able to discipline the members who deviate from the important party line.[93]

The dominance of these two political parties has led to heated contests to appeal to the strategically important median voter in order to surpass the majority threshold necessary to control the legislature and win presidential elections.[94] This has contributed to a strong coordination capacity, yielding the establishment of public goods such as a SWF, to be discussed further below via comparison with the Philippines.

Precrisis State Intervention

Prior to 1945, Taiwan was a Japanese colony for fifty years. Following the war, the KMT expropriated all Japanese-owned industrial assets and turned them into either state- or KMT-owned enterprises. Both types of enterprises were located in protected and strategic sectors of the economy, and both benefited from monopoly government contracts and special privileges over private capital.[95]

In the early 1950s, SOEs accounted for 56 percent of Taiwan's industrial output,[96] making it one of the largest public enterprise sectors outside the communist block and sub-Saharan Africa.[97] State-owned enterprises dominated the economy through their control over the supply of inputs that would go to tens of thousands of small and medium-sized firms.[98] The initiative to privatize Taiwanese SOEs arose soon after opposition parties were permitted in 1987. The DPP pushed

---

[93] Cheng and Hsu (2015, 118).

[94] Seventy-three of 113 seats are elected via majoritarian constituencies, which incentivized parties to appeal to the median voter. Thirty-four seats are elected via proportional-representation constituencies. Six seats are designated for aboriginal populations.

[95] Fields (1998, 5–7); Kuo (2000, 12).   [96] Amsden (1979).

[97] Wade (1990, 176).   [98] Hamilton (1997).

for privatization both because SMEs were a core support group and as part of its effort to reduce the inordinate financial advantages that SOEs conferred to the KMT. The KMT resisted privatization because state- and party-owned firms could be used to fund the salaries, pensions, and other benefits for full-time party employees. They could also be used to fund increasingly costly political campaigns that were "highly personal and outrageously expensive"[99] – even more costly than in either Japan or Korea. SOEs and party-owned firms could also be used to deliver patronage, such as lucrative construction and other types of contracts (e.g., natural gas delivery) to local party bosses. But, over time, the increasingly competitive party dynamics enabled the Legislative Yuan to curtail the use of government funds to purchase land for public construction projects, especially as SOEs became an increasingly costly drain on public finances.

Privatization gained additional popular support following the publication of a book coauthored by Professor Chen Shih-meng of the National Taiwan University titled, *Disintegrating KMT-State Capitalism*, that revealed the numerous secretive linkages between SOEs and KMT enterprises and accused the KMT regime of stealing enormous wealth from the state.[100] Negotiations for membership in the WTO added further pressure to privatize, especially because of Taiwan's high level of dependence on trade.[101] Economic liberalization subjected SOEs to the disciplining power of market forces. These pressures were amplified by Taiwan's desperate effort to join international organizations in order to gain recognition as a sovereign state independent of the People's Republic of China (PRC), forcing it to comply with international demands to liberalize the economy.

Political consensus to privatize was ultimately reached among all parties and became a priority task for the government in 1996, the year of the first presidential election.[102] The KMT recognized the need to be perceived as a prudent steward of the economy and to combat the negative perceptions of corruption attached to it. By 2005, thirty-nine SOEs had been privatized, with the government retaining ownership of nineteen companies.[103] The privatization of state banks, manufacturing

---

[99] Fields (1998).   [100] Chen et al. (1991).   [101] McBeath (1997).
[102] Wang (2005).
[103] The most commonly used privatization method was the sale of shares to the public through the stock market (twenty firms by 2005), followed by asset sales (twelve), then as equity contribution (as in the context of a merger or through

firms, and other firms engaged in international competition occurred the most quickly, whereas the privatization of SOEs enjoying monopolies, such as energy and public utilities, has occurred far more slowly.[104]

Coordination Capacity in the Creation of SWFs: Taiwan and the Philippines Compared

Taiwan did not succumb to the Asian financial crisis due to its strong macroeconomic fundamentals, including negligible foreign debt, a current account surplus, abundant foreign exchange reserves, and a floating exchange rate system.[105] Because its economy is dominated by small business, the buildup of large short-term dollar-denominated debt also did not occur as in other crisis-afflicted countries. But due to contagion effects, the combined exchange rate and stock market index for Taiwan dropped by 35.4 percent between June 30, 1997, and June 30, 1998, a significant decline but far more modest than in Indonesia (122.1 percent), Malaysia (96.7 percent), Korea (95.3 percent), Thailand (88 percent), or the Philippines (78.2 percent).[106] Although the impact of the crisis was far less severe than in neighboring countries, Taiwan nevertheless launched a SWF, the National Stabilization Fund (NSF), in January 2000 with the specific purpose of stabilizing financial markets.

The NSF was established by passage of a statute by the Legislative Yuan, with members of both the KMT and the DPP supporting its creation. It was endowed with total assets of US$16.1 billion and was timed to start operations ahead of the March 2000 presidential election. Resources for the fund came from the government-supervised labor pension, labor insurance and public pension funds, postal savings deposits, and the treasury. These resources could be used as collateral to borrow up to a maximum of US$6.4 billion from local financial institutions, which had to be returned immediately following a stabilizing intervention.

The establishment of the stabilization fund was initiated by KMT President Lee Teng-hui in June 1999 in anticipation of large flows of capital into the stock market following Taiwan's accession to the

the formation of a joint venture through contributions in kind) (four), and then employee buy-outs (three). See Pao, Wu, and Pan (2008).
[104] Wang (2005).   [105] Chen (2000).   [106] Ibid.

WTO, which occurred on January 1, 2002. Following its creation in January 2000, Taiwan's NSF was used to prop up the stock market in March 2000 ahead of the presidential election on March 18.[107] Calls for independence from China by DPP candidate Chen Shui-bian contributed to market nervousness over the prospect of an invasion by the PRC.[108] However, the impetus for a stabilizing fund also followed from two successful interventions in the previous four years. In 1996, the government disbursed US$6.5 billion to stabilize the stock market when panic among investors was triggered by aggressive military posturing from Beijing.[109] Similar action was taken in 1997 when the stock market was shaken by Asia's financial contagion. That such a fund was supported by members of both parties in the Legislative Yuan suggests a growing importance attached to each party's reputation as an effective steward of the economy and the parties' capacity to overcome coordination problems.

Coordination Problems in the Philippines

In the Philippines, such coordination problems have prevented the establishment of a SWF despite declines in the exchange rate and stock market index that were more than twice those of Taiwan's. Powerful local families form the building blocks of electoral competition and politics in the Philippines. Such familial coalitions have "a unique capacity to create an informal political team that assigns specialized roles to its members, thereby maximizing condition and influence."[110] Kinship networks act to ensure that elected representatives deliver patronage and clientelist goods from the government, enhancing the consolidation of their wealth and influence.

Congress acts as the nexus for these national-local clientelist exchanges. Because representatives are tied to local family networks rather than to a national political party, individual representatives commonly engage in party switching in order to maximize the delivery of resources to their local support coalition, contributing to the formation of short-lived dominant parties. Public opinion surveys have consistently shown that citizens do not vote for representatives on the basis of party reputation; for example, a survey conducted by Pulse Asia in March 2010 found that 91 percent of respondents did not identify with

[107] CBC News, March 16, 2000.   [108] Ibid.
[109] Taiwan Info, January 8, 2000.   [110] McCoy (1993, 10).

any political party. Teehankee also reports that since 1987, an average of 33.5 percent of all lower house representatives elected to Congress switched parties,[111] with 60.2 percent of these party switchers jumping into the party of the sitting president in order to magnify their access to national resources.

The political clan also makes it possible to exercise influence beyond the term limits of a single politician through intergenerational clientelist bonds.[112] The construction of "political dynasties" has occurred by members of the same clan occupying numerous local positions who continuously succeed each other in these positions. To maximize access to government resources, families will also seek to capture the most potent combination of local political offices, such as holding the congressional district seat together with the gubernatorial seat or a big city mayoralty seat.[113] As of 2010, for example, the Philippine Congress had the highest percentage of elected dynastic legislators in the world at 68 percent, followed by Mexico at 40 percent, Japan at 33 percent, and Argentina at 10 percent. The US Congress had only 6 percent.[114] Around 160 of these political clans have had two or more members who have served in Congress, and they account for more than 400 of the 2,407 men and women who have been elected to the Philippines national legislature since 1907.[115]

Many therefore regard the legislature as being controlled by elite families with considerable influence over almost all aspects of state function.[116] The public service, for example, is widely known to provide opportunities for plunder to families in power since the Spanish period,[117] and corruption is regarded as the most problematic factor for doing business in the country (the Philippines is ranked 141 of 144 countries for the ease of starting a business according to the *Global Competitiveness Report*).[118] Due to the focus on the provision of particularistic goods, there is an underprovision of public goods and services. For example, the provision of infrastructure, as well as health and primary education, is among the lowest in the region according to the *Global Competitiveness Report*. Instead, these tend to be privately provided. When agreement is reached on national projects, it is often due to the government's capacity to deliver particularistic goods for

[111] Teehankee (2013).   [112] Muno (2010).   [113] De Dios (2007).
[114] Mendoza et al. (2012).   [115] Teehankee (2013).
[116] McCoy (1993, 433); Kondo (2014).   [117] World Bank (2000).
[118] Schwab (2014–15).

local interests. For example, the Countrywide Development Fund (CDF) was created in 1990 as a means by which to deliver projects to all congressional districts and the local constituencies of senators. In 2000, the CDF was replaced by the Priority Development Assistance Fund, which served the same purpose.[119] As a result, Philippine infrastructure is ranked at 104 of 139 countries in the *Global Competitiveness Report*.[120] The capture of national government by local interests is also cited as a major reason for the failure of land reform.[121]

Taiwan's Post-1997 State Intervention

Despite the importance of large SOEs to strategically important segments of the economy, family-owned firms have otherwise dominated the marketplace. For example, in 1983, eighty-seven of Taiwan's ninety-seven business groups were owned by families.[122] This pattern has persisted into the post–Asian financial crisis period. In 2006, sixty-two of the top 100 Taiwanese business groups were family owned, and the total revenue of these sixty-two groups constituted 89.1 percent of Taiwan's gross national product (GNP). Additionally, Yeh et al. found that around 76 percent of the major listed companies in the Taiwan Exchange market were family owned.[123] Figure 5.3 displays the proportion of firms by industry that are state owned in 1996 and 2008, revealing a pattern consistent with these studies – SOEs constitute a very small fraction of Taiwan's largest listed firms.

Table 5.1 reports the breakdown into political and market mechanisms that accounts for the changes to the prevalence of SOEs among Taiwan's largest listed enterprises between 1996 and 2008. The second column displays a significantly higher proportion of SOEs being sold between 1996 and 2008 in comparison with either DPARs or post-1997 democracies; likewise, the first column indicates that the state bought no significant stakes in large listed firms over this time period. Newly listed SOEs were positive due to the government's ongoing privatization program, but no mergers and acquisitions (M&As)

---

[119] Nograles and Lagman (2008).   [120] Schwab (2010).
[121] Abinales and Amorozo (2005); You (2015).   [122] Hamilton (1997, 148).
[123] Yeh et al. (2001).

Table 5.1 *State Ownership Changes: Distinguishing between Political and Market Mechanisms*

	Political mechanisms				Market mechanisms	
	State buys stakes in non-SOE firms (% of total 1996 firms)	State sells stakes in SOEs (% of total 1996 firms)	Newly listed SOEs in 2008 (% of total 2008 firms)	M&As by the state (% of total 1996 firms)	Market valuation of SOEs rises (% of total 2008 firms)	Market valuation of SOEs falls (% of total 1996 firms)
Taiwan	0	4.2	1.8	0	3.6	0
DPARs	11	2.8	8.7	2.8	17.9	6
Post-1997 democracies	1.5	0.6	3.4	0.16	3.5	0.58

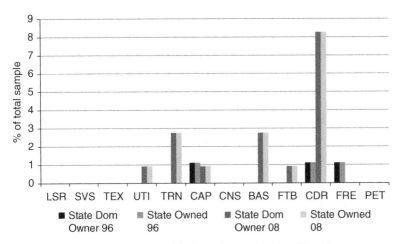

Figure 5.3 Taiwan state ownership by industry, 1996 and 2008.
Note: LSR = leisure; SVS = services; TEX = textiles; UTI = utilities; TRN = transportation; CAP = capital goods; CNS = construction; BAS = basic industry; FTB = food and tobacco; CDR = consumer durables; FRE = finance and real estate; PET = petroleum. Industry categories are based on those identified in Campbell (1996). *State Dom Owner 96* and *State Dom Owner 08* indicate firms for which the state was the dominant owner for each year. *State Owned 96* and *State Owned 08* indicate firms for which the state was a minority or dominant owner for each year.

were registered. Overall, the political mechanisms are consistent with the dominance of family-owned firms in the economy alongside a modest, and declining, role for the state.

State-Sector Transparency

SWF Transparency

To ensure accountability and transparency, the law that created Taiwan's NSF stipulated that its management committee would include individuals from a range of backgrounds and organizations, including the governor of the Central Bank of China; the minister of finance; the minister of transportation and communications; the director general of budget, accounting, and statistics; the chairman of the Council of Labor Affairs; the director general of the Central Personnel Administration; and a panel of scholars and experts recommended by the legislative caucuses.[124] The chair would be the vice premier, and the Legislative Yuan would act as the monitor of the fund. A quarterly report would make public the account balance and detail the fund's operations.

Corporate Transparency

Since the Asian financial crisis, corporate governance in Taiwan has generally remained in the middle of the pack among the Asian countries included in the CG Watch reports. This ranking largely reflects the interests of family business owners who seek to preserve their control against the competing interests of institutional investors who favor stronger protections for outside shareholders. But because pension funds and other institutional investors remain relatively small, family owners largely get what they want.

As is typical in other countries in which family ownership is the dominant type of corporate ownership, family control of firms affiliated with a business group has been exercised through a pyramid structure or a cross-holding pattern.[125] But Taiwanese firms more frequently turn to externally associated investment companies to acquire shares within a target firm in order to hide their activities.[126] In some cases, even philanthropic organizations such as hospitals, foundations, and universities are used. The use of such nonprofit organizations offers an effective tool by which to hide ownership information from the public. Opacity is further heightened by the fact that the Securities and Futures Bureau in Taiwan only requires family board members within two degrees of kinship to be disclosed; distant family members sitting on boards of directors or on external associated investment companies are therefore difficult to trace. As a result, the identification of corporate ownership through listed companies and publicly available information can underestimate the true extent of family control.

The desire for opacity has meant that until the late 1990s, there remained an absence of effective audit committees in publicly listed companies and very low levels of institutional ownership.[127] Corporate transparency therefore remained low. The persistence of these

---

[124] Taiwan Info, January 28, 2000.
[125] Hamilton (1997); Whitley (1999); Chang (2006).   [126] Yeh et al. (2001).
[127] Ibid.

arrangements has slowed efforts to strengthen rights for outside share-holders, including efforts to improve transparency among listed firms following the Asian financial crisis.

Because of the dominance of family ownership, the state has not exerted a significant independent influence on listed firms' corporate governance and transparency. To ascertain the extent of transparency for the state sector, it is useful to examine state-business interactions, as in the context of public procurement.

As mentioned earlier, the KMT had relied on patron-client networks to distribute patronage before the transition of power to the DPP in 2000. Through the KMT's party- or state-owned enterprises, patronage was distributed to local factions, which, in turn, would distribute it to their followers or voters. Initial democratization led to an environment in which politicians depended on the support of local business (and factions), which, in turn, counted on the KMT granting them privileged access to government resources. However, the first electoral victory of the opposition party, the DPP, enabled anticorruption and transparency-enhancing measures to be implemented.

On coming to power in 2000, the DPP administration fought corruption not only to deliver on its campaign promises – a major reason for its victory[128] – but also, more importantly, to weaken the existing apparatus that benefited the KMT. For the DPP, fighting corruption and changing the rules of the game were not only campaign promises but also necessary for its political survival.[129] But because the KMT, the business sector, local factions, and vote brokers were so interwoven with each other, the DPP could not simply take the KMT's place. Indeed, the KMT retained a significant power base in the legislature, in the bureaucracy, and in local governments.

Anticorruption and Transparency Laws

Within two months of taking office in 2000, the DPP administration drafted a comprehensive and ambitious Program for Sweeping Away Organized Crime and Corruption. It included revisions to existing

---

[128] Fell (2002).
[129] Göbel (2004). Although individual DPP politicians were not immune to engaging in corrupt practices, the difference compared with the KMT was that these were acts of individual wrongdoing and not part of a machine that held the regime in place.

laws, the drafting of new laws, curtailing access to government funds, and strengthening enforcement.[130]

A series of existing laws was updated to prevent organized criminals from running for political office, forbid civil servants from accepting gifts or donations, and impose penalties for repeat offenses. Additionally, the assets of government officials and their immediate relatives would be made more transparent, financial institutions would be required to report large money movements and establish a bank account database, and authorities could presume corruption where an official's wealth exceeded his or her income level and confiscate funds the official could not account for.

Three new "Sunshine Laws" were also implemented between 2001 and 2008 that (1) forbade public officials from using their positions for private gain, (2) forbade "quid pro quo exchanges," set ceilings for donations to political parties, and limited the sum of anonymous donations that could be accepted, and (3) required lobbyists to apply for a lobbying permit with the Ministry of Interior and make their lobbying activities public.

The DPP administration also implemented new measures to regulate access to government funds, including the cessation of legislators being able to "recommend" the financing of small-scale construction projects to the directorate general of budget, accounting, and statistics. This common practice from the KMT era to maintain its local clientelist networks was ended by the DPP amid great protest.[131]

Enforcement

Anticorruption enforcement has tended to display swings that correspond to whether the DPP or KMT is in office. For example, the number of people charged with corruption increased steeply after the DPP won the presidency in 2000. Following the DPP's victory in the 2004 presidential election, the number of people involved in lawsuits filed with local prosecutors also saw a sharp and sustained increase. When the KMT took office in 2008, these activities quickly declined.[132] However, this pattern changed in 2011. Following a first abortive effort at creating a centralized anti-corruption task force in 2000, the

---

[130] Ibid.   [131] Ibid.

[132] These swings in anticorruption lawsuits are also reflected in the total sums involved, as well as the number of guilty verdicts in asset declaration lawsuits.

Agency Against Corruption (AAC) was established in 2011 by a KMT-led government. While the KMT had previously obstructed many of the DPP's anti-corruption measures, it implemented the AAC to counter its historically low popularity in the wake of a corruption scandal involving three High Court judges who accepted bribes in return for clearing a former KMT legislator of corruption charges.[133] The result has been to force the KMT to adopt increasing intolerance of corruption in order to win reelection because its reputation increasingly affects individual politicians' chances.

Conclusions

Taiwan displays state intervention outcomes that have evolved over time as the regime transitioned from a SPAR to a consolidated democracy. During its SPAR period, KMT rule was sustained through its party-owned enterprises in addition to its control of large SOEs that supplied key inputs for thousands of privately owned small and medium-sized enterprises, mirroring contemporary China's arrangements. Taiwan's rapid development gave rise to increasingly powerful private business owners that successfully pressed for the withdrawal of the state. Increasing economic liberalization pushed SOEs into the red, forcing the state to sell them off. This, coupled with growing anger over government opacity and corruption, contributed to regime transition and the privatization of the state sector.

As democratization reforms ensued, state- and party-owned enterprises retreated. Additionally, state-sector transparency improved as policymakers became more directly accountable to the electorate. The opposition party, the DPP, was instrumental in pushing for transparency reforms, eventually forcing the KMT to embrace them. For example, support from both the KMT and the DPP led to measures that would ensure the NSF's transparency with quarterly reports and accountability to the public via oversight by the Legislative Yuan. Taiwan's NSF also engaged in passive investments that would not contravene the interests of private capital. Its purpose is simply to prop up shares during times of heightened uncertainty arising from political or economic risks; hence it takes temporary minority ownership stakes. Due to the decline of SOEs and the limits on the NSF,

---

[133] Chao (2010).

Taiwan's state sector does not initiate substantial investments in foreign firms.

Finally, the Taiwan case illustrates the importance of coordinating capacity to the establishment of a SWF. The primary difference between Taiwan and the Philippines regards the importance of individual versus party reputation for candidates running for public office. Stronger party identification enhances the need for candidates to abide by a party platform that is designed to appeal to the median voter. A critical part of this involves the party establishing and maintaining a credible commitment to the economy's performance via stable growth. Because party reputation supersedes an individual representative's reputation, greater emphasis is placed on the provision of public goods in place of patronage diverted to particularistic interests. The greater emphasis on public-oriented goods is also likely to give rise to a SWF with a specific purpose, and in Taiwan we observe the creation of the NSF.

Chapter Conclusions

The cases presented in this chapter yield four insights into the relationship between political regimes and state intervention in the corporate sector that merit highlighting: (1) the cases corresponding to NAR, SPAR, and democracy types display political regime–state-sector arrangements that *complement* one another in ways that clearly differentiate the regimes from each other, (2) the Taiwan case demonstrates how *change* occurs, with state-sector arrangements and political regime characteristics co-evolving together, (3) *coordination problems* can impede the establishment of a SWF, and (4) only China, the SPAR, displayed the *capacity* and *motivation* to initiate large investments in foreign firms located primarily in other, equally opaque authoritarian regimes.

The cases demonstrated that controls over information and resources critical to sustaining regime stability become progressively more relaxed as we move from a NAR to a SPAR and then to a democracy. State-sector arrangements manifest how these controls are implemented in practice: wholly state-owned firms dominate in a NAR, a mixture of state-owned and private firms exists in a SPAR, and private ownership dominates in a democracy. Likewise, transparency improves as state ownership declines and regimes move toward democracy. Consequently, we can expect DPAR arrangements to stand between SPARs and democracies.

But the important question arises as to how change occurs. In this regard, the Taiwan case is illuminating. Opportunities for private capital were hindered by the overreach of the state sector. Rising trade and capital flows exposed and amplified the poor performance of SOEs, ultimately forcing them to liquidate or privatize, thereby depriving the incumbent rulers of vital resources. These same liberalizing policies expanded access to resources for private capital, boosting their support of political opponents to the incumbent regime. While the market pushed the country in the direction of greater openness, incumbent rulers resisted via the preservation of opacity and corruption that enabled the diversion of resources to favored groups. But political opponents mobilized popular support against this arrangement and ultimately prevailed in forcing politicians to become accountable to voters and taxpayers, who increasingly favored private capital via democratic reforms. As a result, the state sector retreated and transparency improved. While the Taiwan case illustrates how change from a SPAR toward a democracy can occur, the Singapore and Malaysia cases will show how a DPAR regime can preserve authoritarian rule with state-sector arrangements that fall between a SPAR and a democracy.

Third, there is the question about the conditions that enable the establishment of a SWF in the first place. The China case indicates that the capacity to overcome coordination problems may be especially important in this regard. Institutional legacies associated with the allocation of state resources to line ministries were difficult to displace with the creation of SASAC. Additionally, the varying ranks of SOEs and their managers in China's party hierarchy complicated SASAC's mission to implement corporate governance and restructuring reforms. As a result, SASAC has been denied two of the fundamental rights afforded "ownership" that other SWFs possess: the power to appoint managers and collect dividends (and thereby make independent investment decisions). SASAC is therefore denied the distinction of being a SWF like Temasek or Khazanah.

In the context of a democracy, powerful fragmented business owners can create coordination problems that undercut the capacity for the government to establish public goods, such as a SWF. In the Philippines, business owners of large conglomerates are very powerful and ensure that politicians get elected to government who will faithfully represent their specific interests above those of a political party. In Taiwan, by contrast, private businesses are much smaller; family owners tend to be far less powerful. As a result, the reputation of a political party is far more important than that of an individual politician. Through their capacity to overcome collective action and coordination problems, strong political parties can implement public policies that serve the public good, such as a SWF.

Finally, China was the only case with state entities that initiated large ownership stakes in foreign firms. This accords with the theoretical expectations. As a SPAR, China demonstrated the capacity for public-private co-ownership that would assuage private investors about co-investing with the Chinese state. China also has sufficient transparency to allow private investors to properly value the risk of co-investing with a state entity and to allow foreign officials to determine whether to permit Chinese state investments in their markets. Additionally, China has the motivation to engage in aggressive foreign acquisitions. Satisfying energy demands is a "life or death" issue for the Chinese Communist Party. But China's foreign investments, in relation to the state sector's total investments, are tiny compared with those of two other authoritarian regimes – Singapore and Malaysia.

6 | Dominant Party Authoritarian Regime with a Weakly Dominant Ruling Party: Malaysia

Dpars in Comparative Perspective

This chapter and the next present analytic narratives of dominant-party authoritarian regimes (Dpars). These regimes are expected to display a greater *capacity* for aggressive foreign state intervention in listed firms as well as greater *motivation* to intervene in comparison with all other regime types. In Chapter 5, the narrow authoritarian regime (NAR) case (Brunei) displayed a low capacity for aggressive foreign state intervention; the state sector's low transparency coupled with the state's dominance over private investors make it unsuited to taking large positions in foreign listed firms. Instead, passive investments are the primary method by which its sovereign wealth fund (SWF) invests overseas.

The democracy case (Taiwan) also displayed a low capacity for aggressive foreign state intervention. The state sector has simply been overwhelmed by private capital, thus denying it of opportunities to make profitable investments that could otherwise go to private business. State investments occur only in the service of private capital, such as stabilizing financial markets via small, short-term equities purchases via the National Stabilization Fund.

The single-party authoritarian regime (SPAR) case (China) displayed both the capacity and motivation to aggressively intervene in foreign listed firms. Many of China's largest firms are listed on a stock market, introducing the minimum level of transparency necessary to appease foreign policymakers and demonstrating the capacity to meet private investor obligations. Although state ownership dominates and transparency remains relatively low for the largest firms (the oil majors), they are adequate for initiating aggressive investments in foreign markets with comparably low transparency requirements. China's motivation for aggressive intervention stems from its need for energy supplies in order to meet economic growth objectives to sustain the Chinese

Communist Party's (CCP's) rule. Thus China's aggressive foreign investments have been restricted to firms in the oil and gas sector located in authoritarian regimes with relatively high opacity.

Both the DPAR cases examined in this and the next chapter exhibit a greater capacity to aggressively intervene in foreign listed firms in comparison with the other regime types. The largest firms have more balanced public-private co-ownership with greater transparency levels, thus demonstrating a stronger commitment to meeting private investors' needs as well as the ability to meet the transparency requirements of regulators from a larger set of countries. Both Singapore and Malaysia have well-established stock markets with a large number of listed companies. Additionally, both countries have large, economically significant savings SWFs that offer a centralized platform for coordinating foreign investments.

But, as argued in Chapter 2, state capacity to intervene is insufficient for aggressive intervention. States must also possess a strong motivation. The key motivation arises from threats to the ruling party's hold on power, with private capital playing a pivotal role. In this regard, Singapore and Malaysia also share important similarities. Both countries have sustained a high level of growth, with private capital's calls for the state to reduce its crowding-out effects rising over time. Additionally, both countries were early adopters of liberalizing trade and financial reforms, potentially amplifying private capital's influence. These dual pressures can result in meaningful influence for political challengers as compared with other authoritarian regimes because DPARs hold regular, semicompetitive multiparty elections. A ruling party that is weakly (strongly) dominant in relation to political opponents will engage in more (less) aggressive state intervention in the corporate sector – both at home and in foreign markets.

The Malaysia case is an illustration of a DPAR with a weakly dominant ruling party; the Singapore case corresponds to a DPAR with a strongly dominant ruling party. Malaysia's ruling party became weakly dominant following the 1997 crisis and has faced a growing threat from political opponents ever since, whereas Singapore's ruling party has remained strongly dominant. I argue that these persistent differences in the strength of each regime's ruling party is the primary reason for the enduring differences in their levels of state intervention in the corporate sector since the Asian financial crisis. However, the logical extension of the argument naturally leads us to expect varying levels of intervention over time depending on the relative strength of the ruling party following each election. I now turn to an examination of the Malaysia case to assess these claims.

Malaysia's Varying Political–State-Sector Characteristics

Since the 1974 election, Malaysia has been dominated by a single major political coalition – Barisan Nasional (BN).[1] BN is dominated by one political party, the United Malays National Organization (UMNO), which coordinates with about a dozen smaller ethnic and regional parties. Cooperation in the division of the electoral map before elections has allowed these parties to maintain continuing dominance over Malaysian politics. BN's continuing dominance has been based on state-led discriminatory and redistributive policies that benefit Bumiputeras primarily at the expense of the Chinese and Indian communities. This state-led program was entrenched following the "New Economic Policy" in 1971 that instituted, among other measures, mechanisms designed to place 30 percent of the ownership of the corporate sector into the hands of Muslim Malays. During the 1980s and 1990s, this was accomplished with discriminatory privatization policies that favored a Bumiputera business elite, resulting in crony-based political intervention in the corporate sector. But following the Asian financial crisis, the state reasserted its control because the ruling party coalition was significantly weakened. These controls were amplified in the wake of the 2008 election when the ruling party coalition experienced its worst result since independence. Figure 6.1 displays the BN's vote and seat share since its first election in 1974.

The chapter proceeds in three parts corresponding to three distinct episodes when the ruling party coalition became relatively weaker or stronger in the context of enduring weakness following the Asian financial crisis. Table 6.1 summarizes the theoretical expectations and corresponding case evidence for each episode.

Part A of the table examines the time period immediately following the Asian financial crisis, from 1997 to 2003. The crisis dramatically revealed the dangers to regime stability arising from economic liberalization. The strongest opposition party in Malaysia's history, the

---

[1] Prior to 1973, Barisan Nasional was known as the Alliance. UMNO has remained the dominant party in both of these ruling party coalitions.

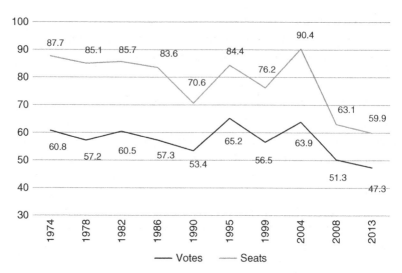

Figure 6.1 Barisan Nasional's vote and seat share, 1974–2013.

Barisan Alternatif, rapidly formed and challenged the incumbent rulers. This culminated in a significant decline for the BN's parliamentary seat share in 1999, as well as the loss of two states. To reclaim the ruling coalition's standing, Mahathir aggressively asserted greater state control over corporate assets as well as the availability of politically sensitive information.

Part B in the table focuses on the period when the ruling coalition's strength improved following the 2004 election – 2004–7. The BN's overwhelming victory enabled its leaders to implement major reforms with regard to the state's newly acquired corporate assets. One manifestation of this new approach was the GLC Transformation Program, which greatly improved the transparency and accountability of the corporate sector; at the same time, the government's aggressive corporate interventions were moderated.

Part C of the table focuses on the BN's weakly dominant rule from 2008 to 2015 when its vote share declined to its lowest point in history. The BN's political weakness generated pressures to reduce the crowding-out effects of the greatly enlarged state sector via a major foreign investment initiative. At the same time, state-sector transparency declined as state controls over strategically important sectors of the economy became more aggressive in an effort to direct patronage to key constituent groups.

One point of clarification regarding terminology is necessary for the discussion in this chapter. In Malaysia, *government-linked company* (GLC) is the conventional term used to refer to state-owned enterprises (SOEs). Likewise, the term *government-linked investment company* (GLIC) is used for state agencies that administer the state's ownership stakes in GLCs. There are numerous GLICs, including Khazanah, the Employees Provident Fund (EPF), and others. To preserve consistency with the Malaysian literature, I use the GLC and GLIC terminology.

Table 6.1 *Theoretical Expectations and Summary of Case Evidence*

Theoretical expectations	Case evidence	Case evidence
Relatively weaker ruling party	Part A: 1997–2003	Part C: 2008–15
Transparency: lower	Foreign investors exit and do not return until corporate transparency improves and corruption is reduced	Perceptions of corruption worsen amid the use of opaque public tenders for large projects
State ownership: higher for large firms; less crowding-out	Many large firms acquired by the government; the reduction of crowding-out was not prioritized	GLCs grow in size while purchases by 1MDB and other GLICs increased; infrastructure contracts go to Bumiputera small and medium-sized enterprises via GLCs.
SWF: savings	Bigger role for Khazanah	1MDB established in 2009

Table 6.1 (*cont.*)

Theoretical expectations	Case evidence	Case evidence
Investment behavior: more aggressive	Khazanah and other GLICs aggressively intervene in domestic market	Aggressive expansion by Khazanah-owned firms into foreign markets
Relatively stronger ruling party	**Part B: 2004–7**	
Transparency: higher	Improvements to corporate and SWF transparency via the GLC Transformation Program	
State ownership: lower for large firms; more crowding out	State acquisitions stop; assistance to small and medium-sized enterprises fails, creating opportunities for GLCs to fill voids.	
SWF: savings	Khazanah remains the preferred agency for administering state ownership	
Investment behavior: less aggressive	State intervention is relatively less aggressive than in the other two time periods	

Part A. Relatively Weaker Ruling Party: 1997–2003

Malaysia's privatization program from the mid-1980s to the 1990s multiplied political leaders' crony ties, culminating in a major threat to Malaysia's incumbent regime following the onset of the Asian financial crisis. These crony ties magnified the capacity for elites to challenge the regime by expanding the resources at their disposal. Until 1998, the ruling party coalition faced an opposition that was fragmented and weak. Political party opposition solidified at the height of the Asian financial crisis when Mahathir sacked Anwar as finance minister and deputy prime minister.[2] What began as an intraparty dispute spilled over into the formation of an alliance of opposition parties, the Barisan Alternatif (Alternative Front), ahead of the 1999 elections. Mahathir took decisive action with aggressive state intervention. Khazanah, previously a passive investor, suddenly became a highly aggressive instrument of state power. In the 1999 election, for the first time since BN's formation in 1973, UMNO won fewer votes than its coalition partners combined, decisively shaking its legitimacy. The regime renewed its aggressive interventions into the corporate sector by renationalizing previously privatized firms and placing them under the prime minister's control. All throughout this episode, transparency suffered as government critics were silenced and questionable corporate transactions were shrouded from public scrutiny.

Aggressive State Intervention

The rapid growth of Bumiputera-owned firms emerged after the introduction of the New Economic Policy (NEP) in 1970, which sought to provide ethnic Malays with a larger share of the economy through the aim of 30 percent equity ownership, much of which was then owned by foreign enterprises.[3] Privatization initiated at both the federal and state levels since the 1980s was seen as a solution to the inefficiency and wastage that rapidly accumulated alongside the rapid growth of the public sector under the NEP. Privatization was also intended to promote a new class of Bumiputera entrepreneurs and business owners. But the absence of an independent, accountable monitoring body to ensure transparency and proper implementation of the privatization policy expanded opportunities for political involvement in business, leading to numerous allegations of nepotism and cronyism.[4] In the late 1980s and early 1990s, there was a marked increase in the number of corporate dealings that involved fraud, bribery, asset stripping, favoritism, and misuse of power.[5] A key figure in the implementation of the privatization agenda was Daim Zainuddin.

---

[2] Anwar was held responsible for a number of unproductive megaprojects and refused to subsidize the troubled UMNO-affiliated Renong Group, as well as the shipping company owned by Mirzan Mahathir, the prime minister's son (Gomez 2004). There are even indications that Anwar and his supporters tried to overthrow Mahathir, his former mentor, as party leader at the UMNO general assembly in June 1998 (Khoo 2003).
[3] Gomez and Jomo (1999).   [4] Jayasankaran (2003).
[5] Gomez and Jomo (1999).

When the Asian financial crisis struck, the incumbent rulers embarked on a renationalization initiative to save select firms from bankruptcy. A range of state-run entities under the control of the prime minister (Mahathir) and the minister of finance (Daim Zainuddin) were called on to participate, including Khazanah, Petronas (the national oil company), Bank Negara (Malaysia's central bank), the Minister of Finance, Inc., the Employees Provident Fund (EPF), the Civil Servants Pension Fund (KWAP), and the National Equity Fund (PNB). As others have documented, corporate rescues were implemented in a highly politicized manner initially designed to benefit allies of Daim and Mahathir over Anwar.[6] Later, Daim would fall out of favor with Mahathir, and his cronies lost their businesses as well.

The first of these funds called on to react to the crisis in early September 1997 was Khazanah – Malaysia's savings SWF.[7] Khazanah was created in 1993 in response to the Ministry of Finance–led initiative to restructure nonfinancial public enterprises. Khazanah's initial endowment came from the privatization of these companies. Until the Asian financial crisis, Khazanah was primarily a passive investor.[8] But when the crisis struck, Mahathir quickly turned to Khazanah to assume a new, highly activist role that benefited select cronies under the guise of rescuing the economy. This occurred in three ways. First, Khazanah directly injected capital into ailing firms in exchange for equity, a move that has been widely interpreted as bailouts to politically connected business figures.[9] Second, loans were made to Danaharta, an asset management company established by the government in 1998 to isolate poor-quality debt and remove it from the books of financial institutions. Danaharta borrowed a total of RM1.3 billion from both Khazanah and the EPF.[10] Third, Khazanah issued RM3 billion worth of bonds as part of its contribution to a special fund set up to support the stock market. The fund was used to

---

[6] See, for example, Johnson and Mitton (2003).

[7] That Khazanah was the first fund called on reflected the unilateral power of the prime minister to dictate how its resources were used. This power was further amplified when Mahathir later assumed the position of both finance minister and prime minister (following Daim's exit in 2001), a practice upheld by both Abdullah and Najib.

[8] *Malaysian Business*, January 16, 2004; Lord (2004).

[9] Jomo (1998); *Business Times*, September 19, 1998; *Business Times Singapore*, July 19, 2001; *Malaysian Business*, January 16, 2004.

[10] *Business Times*, August 27, 2003.

"buy shares from Malaysians at a premium while those sold by foreign-ers [were] purchased at market value."[11] Khazanah also bought stocks directly in order to prop up the index.[12]

Other GLICs were called on to make unprecedented interventions as well, often raising concerns due to the opacity surrounding their actions. For example, the EPF, which manages the compulsory retire-ment savings plan for all private-sector workers, increased its alloca-tion to equities from 15.6 to 21.1 percent between 1996 and 2000.[13] Concerns about political influence over the use of EPF funds mounted between 1997 and 1999 as the EPF loaned RM31 billion to seventy-one Malaysian companies to compensate for the lack of bank lending.[14] Bank Negara and Petronas also played a vital role in rescuing firms via dubious, nontransparent transactions.[15]

These opaque interventions fueled negative investor perceptions, which were worsened by the growing alienation of working people whose life savings were locked into a state fund that appeared to be used to socialize the losses of UMNO cronies. Results of the 1999 general election and the December 2000 by-election reflected a sus-tained alienation of traditional UMNO supporters. To revive support from its Bumiputera electoral base, the regime purchased shares so as to benefit Malays over non-Malays; the PNB's Malay-only investment funds played a central role in this effort. The PNB is under the jurisdic-tion of the Bumiputera Investment Foundation (Yayasan Pelaburan Bumiputera [YPB]), which is chaired by the prime minister. It was established by the government in 1978 to increase Malay ownership in the corporate sector by purchasing shares of publicly held companies and keeping them in trust for Malays. When the Asian financial crisis struck, it was the largest investment body in Malaysia with around seven million investors and held equity stakes in more than 200 com-panies that were listed on the Kuala Lumpur Stock Exchange (KLSE) through its unit trusts as of March 1, 2000.[16] It also had an ownership

[11] *Business Times*, September 5, 1997.
[12] *Asian Wall Street Journal*, September 22, 1997.
[13] Freeman and Than (2002, 65–66).   [14] Ibid.
[15] On Bank Negara, see Gomez and Jomo (1999, 50); Mahani (2002, 150); and Pepinsky (2009). On Petronas, see Pepinsky (2009, 137–38); Varkkey (2015).
[16] Unit trusts managed by PNB that are only for Bumiputera Malaysians include Amanah Saham Nasional (ASN) since 1981, ASN 2 since 1999, ASN 3 Imbang since 2001, Amanah Saham Bumiputera (ASB) since 1990, ASB 2 since 2014,

stake of more than 50 percent in twenty-two companies, comprising nearly 10 percent of total market capitalization.

Evidence for the preferential treatment awarded Malay investors comes from the returns for the two largest Bumiputera-only unit trusts, ASN and ASB, which averaged about 15 percent annually over the previous fifteen years.[17] Although the country's gross domestic product (GDP) contracted by more than 8 percent in 1997, ASB's return was still 11.5 percent, down from 13.25 percent for the previous year; ASN's 1997 return was 10.5 percent, down from 13.75 percent for 1996. Also, Tabung Haji, which was established in 1963 to help Muslims save for the pilgrimage to Mecca, declared a 9.5 percent return in 1997, which was identical to 1996.[18] By contrast, the EPF, which is for all Malaysians and which opposition parties and nongovernment organizations (NGOs) complained about being used to bail out cronies, had a dividend of only 6.7 percent for 1997. In reaction to these divergent returns, DAP leader Lim Kit Siang criticized the government for playing favorites with its unit trust schemes.[19]

As discussed in Chapter 2, this link between the government and voter-investors is an important tie that motivates higher returns not only for the savings funds mentioned here but also for the GLCs and GLICs that own them. Khazanah, as the lead GLIC for reforming GLCs, will play an increasingly activist role in pushing GLCs to improve performance.

Surveying the Transition to State Ownership

Although a variety of GLICs intervened following the onset of the crisis, Bank Negara played a central role in orchestrating the rescue

Amanah Saham Didik since 2001, Amanah Saham Gemilang since 2003. Other unit trusts include Amanah Saham Wawasan 2020 since 1996 with a quota of 51 percent for Bumiputeras and 49 percent for non-Bumiputeras, Amanah Saham Malaysia since 2000 for all Malaysians, Amanah Saham Pendidikan since 2003 for all Malaysians, Amanah Saham Kesihatan since 2003 for all Malaysians, Amanah Saham Persaraan since 2003 for all Malaysians, and Amanah Saham 1Malaysia since 2009, with 50 percent for Bumiputera, 30 percent Chinese, 15 percent Indian, and 5 percent others.

[17] *Business Times (Malaysia)*, September 8, 1997.
[18] Tabung Haji managed around RM7 billion in 1998; Rahman and Ahmed (2000).
[19] Lim (1998). While this rate was significantly lower than the Malay-targeted funds, it was consistent with a longer-term pattern of comparatively lower returns – since 1980, the EPF had an average dividend rate of 8.1 percent, and 7.7 percent for 1996.

of selected firms through three organizations established in the fall of 1998 – Danamodal, Danaharta, and the Corporate Debt Restructuring Committee (CDRC). Danamodal handled capital injections into banks. Danaharta was set up to purchase bad loans and recover the funds provided to banks by adding value to nonperforming loans and properties used as collateral. The CDRC was designed to act as a mediator between corporate borrowers – the CDRC involved senior officials of the government and the central bank and functioned more like a national policy committee.

By August 2002, when CDRC operations officially ended, it had successfully resolved forty-seven cases with debts valued at RM43.9 billion, or 14 percent of Malaysia's GDP, held by the country's fifty major companies, on condition that they undergo restructuring.[20] The ten banks that received public funds reshuffled top management under the guidance of Danamodal, with seven having made full repayment by the middle of 2002.[21] Nearly all these firms remained under the ownership of the state following their restructuring exercises. Danamodal closed its core operations in late 2003; Danaharta ceased operations in 2005.

How pervasive was the transition to state ownership? In which industries did the state have the biggest presence? And how important were alternative mechanisms in contributing to the state's new corporate ownership role? To answer these questions, I examine a sample of the largest 200 firms by market capitalization at the end of 2008.[22] GLCs tend to be among the largest firms in the economy, so this sample safely captures them, though slightly biasing the results toward state ownership.[23]

In contrast to China, where many of the largest SOEs are unlisted, nearly all of Malaysia's GLCs are publicly listed. As of 2010, the only large unlisted GLCs were the Petronas group and the Felda plantation group; Felda, however, was privatized in 2012. Figure 6.2 shows the relative importance of SOEs across industries. Firms in which the state has at least a 5 percent stake are identified. If the state is the largest ultimate owner, it is considered the dominant owner. The figure identifies construction as well as finance and real estate as having the largest number of firms with state

---

[20] *Nikkei Weekly*, October 28, 2002.   [21] Ibid.
[22] The data for 1996 come from Claessens, Djankov, and Lang (2000); the data for 2008 come from Carney and Child (2013).
[23] See Menon and Ng (2013) for a detailed overview of Malaysian GLCs.

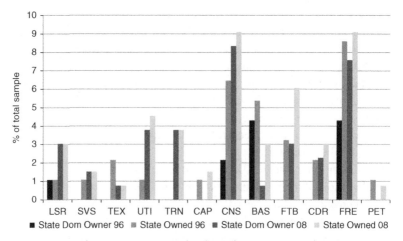

Figure 6.2 Malaysian state ownership by industry, 1996 and 2008.
Note: State Dom Owner 96 and *State Dom Owner 08* indicate firms for which the state was the dominant owner for each year. *State Owned 96* and *State Owned 08* indicate firms for which the state was a minority or nondominant owner for each year. LSR = leisure; SVS = services; TEX = textiles; UTI = utilities; TRN = transportation; CAP = capital goods; CNS = construction; BAS = basic industry; FTB = food and tobacco; CDR = consumer durables; FRE = finance and real estate; PET = petroleum. Industry categories are based on those defined in Campbell (1996).

ownership, followed by utilities, transportation, and food and tobacco. Each of these industries is important to Malaysia's economy, and each has played an instrumental role in the strategic allocation of resources to Bumiputera firms. In this regard, we can observe that the state shifted its ownership profile toward that of a dominant owner, especially in the finance and construction industries, granting it greater control over these firms.[24]

State Intervention in the Banking Sector

In July 1999, initial plans were announced to rationalize the banking sector from the existing fifty-five domestic financial institutions to just six anchor banks. Unsurprisingly given the pattern of state rescues, this announcement raised concerns about political intervention. The lack of

---

[24] See Menon and Ng (2013) for a detailed overview of Malaysia GLCs and their economic dominance.

transparency about how the anchor banks would be selected suggested that Daim's commercial interests would be privileged at the expense of some of Malaysia's more efficient and dynamic banks, many of which were associated with Anwar. Public criticism and negative market reactions forced the government to abandon the original plan, leading to a new proposal for ten anchor banks by the end of 2000. However, the merger process was long and politicized, resulting in politically connected banks being more likely to become acquiring banks.[25] For example, Bank Utama – Malaysia's smallest financial institution – ended up controlling the country's third-largest bank, RHB Bank, which was owned by Rashid Hussain, one of "Daim's boys" and eight times bigger than Bank Utama. Speculation ensued that the merger was politically motivated because Utama's parent, Cahya Mata, was controlled by the family of Sarawak state's Chief Minister Abdul Taib Mahmud, who helped Mahathir's ruling coalition secure an important victory in the Sarawak state election in 2001.[26] Analysts were concerned that the government would use the new bank to pump funds into Sarawak as payback. Ultimately, all ten of the anchor banks were politically connected – four of them were state owned, four were directly tied to Mahathir or UMNO, and the remaining two were linked to Daim.[27]

State Intervention in the Construction Industry

The construction industry has played a vital role for the ruling party coalition to build and maintain a loyal base of support among its Bumiputera base. A leaked US diplomatic cable cited a 2007 internal Works Ministry report that details how this works.[28] "The current system of awarding lucrative government contracts to bumis provides them with a strong economic incentive to simply act as agents, turning over as many projects as possible and taking a cut before handing each one off to a competent non-bumi implementer," the cable said. "This 'bumi agent' system is firmly entrenched in Malaysia," the cable continued. "Any effort to make reforms is likely to be resisted not only by well-established bumis, but also by the non-bumi implementers who have built up a network of well-oiled agent partnership." The cable

---

[25] Shari (2001); Ahmad, Ariff, and Skully (2007).
[26] *Dow Jones International News*, April 23, 2002.
[27] Ahmad, Ariff, and Skully (2007).
[28] *Business Times Singapore*, September 21, 2011.

also said that the study revealed that many Bumiputera contractors commonly sold off their tenders for quick money, often to finance expensive cars and houses. According to the report, 85 percent of government contracts awarded to Bumiputera contractors were sold off to others for completion.

However, only a fraction of the contracts were ever completed. According to the National Audit Department's 2004 report on the 5,208 projects allocated under the Eighth Malaysia Plan (8MP) to improve rural water supplies between 2001 and 2004, 68.3 percent of the RM854.92 million allocated for the projects had been spent, but only 36.4 percent of the projects were implemented.[29] An Auditor General's report further showed that between 2001 and 2005, 99.7 percent of the money had been spent, but only 41.6 percent of 360,000 homes had water supply.[30]

As the data in Figure 6.2 show, a large number of these Bumiputera-owned firms were acquired by the government. One of the largest firms in this area was United Engineers Malaysia (UEM), a subsidiary of the Renong group, Malaysia's biggest conglomerate at the time. In July 2001, the government announced a takeover bid for UEM by Khazanah. The struggle for UEM/Renong, Malaysia's largest corporate debtor, was the most high-profile move made by the government in 2001 as it sought to accelerate restructuring and boost standards of corporate governance. As the former business arm for UMNO, it – perhaps more than any other firm – represented the unhealthy, opaque cronyism that was routinely condemned by Malaysia's opposition and numerous foreign analysts. Following the takeover, Halim Saad, another one of "Daim's boys," resigned from the company, and a new group of professional managers stepped in. Mahathir looked to them to resolve the lingering corporate debt problems.

In the period following the 2004 election, examined in part B of Table 6.1, we will see how the government turned to GLCs to manage the construction of new megaprojects – the economic growth corridors as well as the new Iskandar Project. The old system of awarding government contracts to Bumiputera agents had simply changed hands such that GLCs would now administer them.

---

[29] *Malaysian Business*, November 16, 2006.   [30] Ibid.

Other Indicators of Heightened State Intervention

In addition to the shift toward greater dominant ownership, the government may control firms either as a direct owner or indirectly via intermediate firms. While indirect ownership expands the reach of the state, enabling it to leverage scarce resources, direct ownership reduces the space for managers to act independently of the owner's interests.[31] Table 6.2 indicates that the proportion of firms with direct ownership nearly doubled between 1996 and 2008, from 40.8 to 76.4 percent, while those with indirect ownership fell by over half, from 59.2 to 23.6 percent. Also note that the proportion of firms with state ownership, either direct or indirect, increased by nearly 15 percent, from 32 to 46.7 percent, further magnifying the state's control over the corporate sector.

Changes to state ownership may occur in a variety of ways, such as through mergers, privatization, or because of acquisitions of firms previously owned by nonstate actors. Each of these mechanisms entails a conscious decision on the part of government policymakers to change the state's ownership profile. Because the sample is restricted to the 200 largest listed firms, firms may enter or leave the sample due to changes to their market capitalization. While this may be partially attributable to government policies affecting firm valuations, it is unlikely that policymakers are explicitly targeting firm valuation when making and implementing their decisions. Table 6.3 summarizes the alternative political and market mechanisms contributing to changes in state ownership.

The first political mechanism regards state-owned firms acquiring non-state-owned firms, which indicates that the state purchased stakes above a 5 percent ownership level in 15.5 percent of all listed firms in the sample (for 1996). This is far higher than the proportion for post-1997 democratic regimes (1.5 percent) and also higher than the proportion for Singapore[32] (6.5 percent), indicating that the Malaysian government was highly aggressive and sweeping in its acquisition of corporate assets. The second political mechanism is newly listed SOEs (or GLCs), which indicates that the state retains an ownership stake in these newly listed firms. The data indicate that 10 percent of all firms in the 2008 sample have been newly listed compared

---

[31] Fan et al. (2011).
[32] DPARs refers to Singapore and Malaysia firms combined.

Table 6.2 *Changes to Direct and Indirect Ownership of Malaysian State-Owned Companies*

| | 1996 | | | | 2008 | | | |
	Total N	Proportion state owned (%)	Direct (%)	Indirect (%)	Total N	Proportion state owned (%)	Direct (%)	Indirect (%)
Malaysia	200	32	40.8	59.2	154	46.7	76.4	23.6
Singapore	200	50.4	67	33	131	20.6	96.3	3.7

Table 6.3 *State Ownership Changes: Distinguishing between Political and Market Mechanisms*

	Political mechanisms				Market mechanisms	
	State buys stakes in non-SOE firms (% of total 1996 firms)	Newly listed SOEs in 2008 (% of total 2008 firms)	M&As by the state (% of total 1996 firms)	State sells stakes in SOEs (% of total 1996 firms)	Market valuation of GLCs rises (% of total 2008 firms)	Market valuation of GLCs falls (% of total 1996 firms)
Malaysia	15.5	10	6.5	1	22.5	7
Singapore	6.5	7.6	5	6	12.9	7.5
Post-1997 democracies	1.5	3.4	0.16	0.6	3.5	0.58

with 3.4 percent for post-1997 democratic regimes and 7.6 percent for Singapore. This high proportion of newly listed firms with state ownership is indicative of the Malaysian government's practice of engaging in partial privatization in order to retain control rights.[33] The third political mechanism by which the state can change its ownership stakes is through mergers and acquisitions (M&As). The data indicate that 6.5 percent of all 1996 firms in the sample were involved in mergers and acquisitions. Compared with the sample of firms in post-1997 democratic regimes at 0.16 percent or Singapore (at 5 percent), Malaysia's score is clearly higher. This gain illustrates the state's highly interventionist role in the corporate sector and the effort to consolidate state ownership of corporate assets. Finally, the state can sell its ownership stakes in SOEs – the table shows that this happened far less frequently in Malaysia (1 percent) than in Singapore (6 percent); democracies exhibit a low value on this dimension (0.6) because the state owns few firms to begin with.

Turning to market mechanisms, Table 6.3 indicates the proportion of firms entering (22.5 percent) or leaving (7 percent) the top 200 sample by market capitalization. The proportion entering and leaving is considerably higher than that for post-1997 democracies (3.5 and 0.58 percent, entering and leaving, respectively) and also higher than that for Singapore (12.9 and 7.5 percent, respectively). This disproportionately high figure is very likely due to the beneficial performance effects associated with being government owned in Malaysia.[34]

The state's renationalization, restructuring, and other related activities in the corporate sector indicate that far greater centralized state

---

[33] Another means by which the Malaysian state would retain control is through the use of a golden share, especially among infrastructure companies that were privatized in the late 1990s. The share allowed the government, through the minister of finance, to ensure that certain major decisions affecting the operations of the companies as GLCs were consistent with government policies. The government has been attempting to gradually eliminate rights attached to golden shares that impede value creation. For example, in the case of postal services, a government's golden share usually seeks to ensure that basic postal services reach rural areas without being subordinated to purely profit motives. However, in Malaysia, the golden share frequently grants the state the right to appoint top management and to influence capital expenditure. Concerns over the rights of the golden share in Pos Malaysia delayed and complicated the divestiture of Khazanah's 32 percent stake in 2010 (*The Star Online*, October 11, 2010).

[34] Menon and Ng (2013).

control became a defining feature, especially in construction and banking, with the major beneficiaries of government credit shifting toward the large SOEs and government agencies.[35] This enhanced the state's capacity to deny resources and influence to political challengers. Coupled with the state's increasing controls over the corporate sector were greater levels of state-sector opacity.

Increasing Opacity

Complementing the aggressive state interventions designed to bail out firms allied with the ruling party coalition's leader, Mahathir, was an equally zealous targeting of government critics. For example, the government would actively stifle criticism of its bailouts through laws such as the Sedition Act, the Printing Presses and Publications Act, and the Official Secrets Act (OSA). The Sedition Act criminalizes speech that would "bring into hatred or contempt or to excite disaffection against" the government or engender "feelings of ill-will and hostility between difference races."[36] It has been routinely used against critics of the government's pro-Malay policies. The Printing Presses and Publications Act makes the publication of "malicious news" punishable with jail terms and empowers authorities to ban or restrict the circulation of local publications. It is often used to deter criticism of government officials and policies. The Official Secrets Act prohibits the dissemination of information classified as an official secret, which many criticize as being used to classify documents that "cannot by any stretch of the imagination be reasonably confidential or secret."[37] It acts to stifle dissent and reduces transparency in government workings. It was introduced by the British to restrict and impose penalties on the release of unauthorized information. The OSA's mandate was broadened with amendments in 1972, 1984, and 1986, making it so expansive that it became an offense simply to receive information deemed an "official secret." Investigative reporters and whistle-blowers have therefore faced considerable risks.

The pursuit of antigovernment activists with these acts has surged when UMNO's political position is threatened. For example, following the 1999 election, four prominent opposition figures were charged with

---

[35] Gomez (2006); Carney and Andriesse (2013).   [36] Wu and Hickling (2003).
[37] Wu and Hickling (2003).

sedition in January 2000, and another was arraigned for violating the OSA. All the alleged offenses involved condemnation of UMNO over the treatment of Anwar. US officials described the move against the five as a "transparent and cynical attempt to intimidate government opponents and stifle legitimate political discourse."[38] In April 2000, the government set up a special panel to check unauthorized access to secret documents and prevent leaks of sensitive information. Foreshadowing future secrecy over the government's tendering process, Bernard Dompok, an official in the Prime Minister's Department, said that this was partially in reaction to "opposition leaders receiving secret government documents and information on tenders that the government had approved and government transactions with banks."[39]

Authorities also severely curbed the circulation of the opposition party newspaper *Harakah* and closed down two smaller publications.[40] Such actions caused other newspapers to impose self-censorship to avoid problems with the government. Ownership of the mainstream newspapers by the ruling coalition allowed them to control the reporting of news. For example, the company that publishes the leading Malay-based newspaper, *Utusan Malaysia*, is owned by UMNO, whereas the Malaysian Chinese Association owns Star Publications, which publishes the best-selling English newspaper, *The Star*. The leading Chinese newspapers are owned by members of the Tiong family of Sarawak, who are closely aligned with Barisan Nasional.[41] These ongoing efforts to manipulate news and silence critics led the New York–based Committee to Protect Journalists to denounce Mahathir as an "enemy of the press" for the third consecutive year in 2001.[42]

In addition to silencing critics and distorting news coverage, the government also exercised political influence over institutions that commonly retain independence from political interference, including the central bank and the judiciary. For example, Bank Negara's governor, Ahmad Mohamed Don, and deputy governor, Fong Weng Phak, resigned in 1998 because they could not oppose decisions reached by the National Economic Action Council (NEAC). The NEAC was

---

[38] *Agence France-Presses*, April 19, 2000. [39] Ibid.
[40] *Agence France-Presses*, May 3, 2001. [41] Vithiatharan and Gomez (2014).
[42] *Agence France-Presses*, May 3, 2001.

established in late 1997 under the Prime Minister's Department with Daim Zainuddin as executive director. Its purpose was to decide all economic policies in response to the crisis[43] and ended up becoming a channel through which the politically connected could directly influence policy.[44] The judiciary also lacked independence, having been stripped of its autonomy by Mahathir in the late 1980s, particularly in cases of political or economic importance.[45]

Unsurprisingly, then, neither the Anti-Corruption Agency (ACA), the most powerful institution for fighting corruption, nor the Securities Commission (SC), which is responsible for market surveillance and enforcement of listing requirements, could act independently.[46] The ACA was subordinate to the Prime Minister's Department and was often accused of influencing the ACA's enforcement actions, while the SC reports to the minister of finance.[47] During the crisis, both the ACA and the SC were criticized for engaging in selective investigations and prosecutions of Anwar and his allies. For example, Anwar ally Mohamed Ezam Mohamed Nor was charged under the OSA for allegedly leaking secret government documents to the media about corruption linked to senior government figures.[48] Additionally, in July 1999, former assistant governor of Bank Negara and Anwar associate Abdul Murad Khalid was charged with failure to declare assets worth RM24 million.[49] However, nothing transpired from investigations begun in October 1996 into alleged misappropriation of funds by government politicians associated with the Perwaja Steel scandal.[50] The politicization of the ACA was publicly acknowledged when its former head, Shafie Yahaya, admitted in court that investigations into complaints by Anwar were stopped on the instruction of Mahathir.[51]

Corporate-Sector Challenges

Shortly after the crisis struck, the government implemented a series of initiatives designed to strengthen confidence in Malaysian securities

---

[43] Mahani (2002, 25–26).   [44] Pepinsky (2009).
[45] *Economist Intelligence Unit*, May 5, 2000; Slater (2003).
[46] Liew (2007); Siddiquee (2011).   [47] Ho (1999); Siddiquee (2005).
[48] Rodan (2004).   [49] *Asian Wall Street Journal*, September 17–18, 1999.
[50] It is alleged to have lost RM2.56 billion, though Mahathir admitted in 2002 that it lost RM10 billion (Lim 2002; Wain 2009).
[51] Elegant (2000).

markets. The initiatives included comprehensive corporate governance reforms that were published in the *Report on Corporate Governance* in February 1999. The KLSE, SC, Bank Negara, and Danaharta followed shortly after with additional reforms designed to strengthen transparency and investor protections.[52]

Despite efforts by the government to appear committed to transparency reform, these measures were deemed inadequate in the eyes of foreign investors, especially as politically motivated rescues continued without interruption. For example, Manu Bhaskaran, Singapore Securities' managing director observed in 2000 that "[t]hey're going backwards as the world is going forward. The unwillingness to embrace global trends such as globalization, corporate transparency, and disclosure means the economy may not grow in the optimal way."[53]

To address the continuing unwillingness of foreign investors to return to Malaysia, the government embarked on a new series of reforms from the beginning of 2001. The Code of Corporate Governance finally began its staged implementation in January. Under the Code, at least one-third of the board of directors of listed companies had to comprise independent, nonexecutive directors, and audit, remuneration, and nomination committees must have no less than two independent, nonexecutive directors.[54] Also unveiled, in late February, was the Capital Market Master Plan that contained 152 recommendations, including ten to enhance the dissemination of company information useful to shareholders. The KLSE also required disclosures from directors on the state of internal controls, the independence of the board in annual reports, and attendance at corporate governance training programs. Where found negligent, listed companies as well as individual directors could be investigated and fined by the KLSE.[55] By mid-2001, the KLSE had conducted nearly 500 investigations had taken more than 100 enforcement actions.[56]

Despite this spate of new initiatives, investors remained skeptical about the government's commitment to protect shareholders' interests above those of the politically connected. It became clear that Daim's consistent support for Malay executives such as Halim Saad was

---

[52] Salim (2011).   [53] *Financial Times*, August 16, 2000.
[54] *Asian Wall Street Journal*, July 20, 2001.   [55] Case (2005).
[56] Economic Analytical Unit (2002).

costing the government political support and provoking an erosion of confidence in the economy. "In order to head off a devaluation, [Mahathir] had to restructure because that is the only way that you can increase confidence, locally as well for (international) investors," according to Arnold Lim, head of Malaysia research at ING Barings.[57] In mid-2001, Mahathir finally acknowledged the need to distance himself and his government from the bailouts. This placed Daim, the architect of the crony-based system, in the firing line. Removing him would signal the government's seriousness about changing course. On June 1, and without any stated reason, Daim resigned all his official positions, including finance minister, minister of special functions, and executive director of the NEAC, as well as his party post of UMNO treasurer. The proximate cause often pointed to was his criticism of Mahathir's children's business interests, which had apparently adversely affected Daim's own interests during a bank merger in 2000.[58] Daim's departure marked a critical turning point.

At the end of 2001, a final series of financial regulations was implemented. In September, the SC announced updates to its guidelines on listing, fund-raising, and restructuring of companies listed on the KLSE. In the view of some analysts, they were among the best in East Asia and similar to the London Stock Exchange's rules.[59] The Malaysian Accounting Standards Board also approved twenty-four new standards for accounting and reporting that were considered to exceed US standards. Finally, a variety of new NGOs was set up to promote corporate transparency and the protection of investor interests, including the Minority Shareholders' Watchdog Group and a Malaysian chapter of Transparency International.

Following Daim's exit, the KLSE benchmark Composite Index bucked the global trend and rose by 16 percent from its lowest point in June to the end of July 2001.[60] Morgan Stanley Singapore's managing director, Michael Dee, observed: "We're seeing the beginning of a system of discipline that didn't exist before. It's the beginning of a culture which says 'We're not going to bail you out; there's going to be more accountability, more responsibility and more deadlines.'"[61] In describing the transformation, a report by Credit Suisse First Boston

---

[57] *South China Morning Post*, August 23, 2001.   [58] Gomez (2004).
[59] Case (2005).   [60] *Business Times Singapore*, July 30 2001.
[61] *Business Times Singapore*, September 11, 2001.

declared, "Goodbye cronies, hello professionals."[62] At the end of 2001, Salomon Smith Barney and Merrill Lynch raised their sovereign ratings on Malaysia, citing improved governance and restructuring developments as the main factors.[63] Moody's and Standard & Poor's followed by upgrading the country's ratings in early 2002.

In June 2002, Mahathir made the surprise announcement that he would step down as prime minister in October 2003. But even this only produced a temporary dip in the stock market.[64] Finally, in 2003, the Asian Corporate Governance Association (ACGA) released its regional ranking of countries' corporate governance practices. It profiled Malaysia as staging the biggest improvement since 2001.[65]

State-Sector Opacity

Despite progress for corporate transparency, such reforms did not yet extend to key segments of the state sector. As of 2003, the five major funds – the EPF, SOCSO, LTAT, PNB, and Tabung Haji – accounted for nearly 40 percent of the market capitalization of the KLSE, yet major concerns persisted about their transparency. For example, the PNB together with KWAP and Khazanah launched a new RM10 billion investment fund, ValueCap, in October 2002.[66] The former investment chief of the EPF, Sharifatu Laila Syed Ali, was its new head.[67] According to the Finance Ministry, ValueCap was intended to buy undervalued shares and improve liquidity in the stock market; nevertheless, investors were concerned about the lack of clarity in the fund's investment objectives. Some foreign investors were particularly concerned that it could be used to support ailing firms with strong political connections, leading to long-term economic damage.[68]

Additionally, major GLCs and GLICs continued to be exempt from meaningful public scrutiny. Khazanah, for example, continued to report to the prime minister and not parliament, despite investing huge amounts of taxpayers' money.[69] Similarly, the national oil company, Petronas, reported directly to the prime minister's office and not parliament. Instead of full annual reports, it only released abbreviated financial information.[70] Very little information about contracts,

---

[62] *Asia Times*, December 22, 2001.
[63] *Business Times Singapore*, April 22, 2002.
[64] *Business Times Singapore*, July 4, 2002.   [65] CLSA and ACGA, 2003.
[66] *Business Times*, August 1, 2003.   [67] *The Edge*, January 10, 2003.
[68] Ibid.   [69] Jayasankaran (2000).   [70] Jayasankaran (1999).

agreements, revenue redistribution and usage, and negotiated terms for exploration and production was made publicly available.[71]

The terms and conditions of numerous privatizations and megadeals also remained closed to public scrutiny despite the new emphasis on transparency. For example, requests from NGOs and opposition members of parliament for information about the cost of the Bakun Dam project, the tendering process, and why Ekran Berhad Hydroelectric Corporation received RM950 million in compensation were ignored.[72] Similar requests in relation to other government-funded projects also hit a wall of silence. And although GLICs agreed to launch the Minority Shareholders Watchdog Group to help raise corporate governance standards, critics questioned its independence from political influence. Moreover, the dominance of these funds stunted the growth of private mutual funds, which many financial analysts considered to be a better way to promote corporate governance.[73]

Part A Conclusion

The evidence of this first episode is consistent with the theoretical expectations regarding a weak ruling party in a DPAR. Specifically, transparency for the state sector fell as the state rescued favored firms, state ownership increased for the largest firms, Khazanah began to play a central role in Malaysia's political economy, and through it the state implemented a highly aggressive acquisition initiative. Soon this aggressive behavior would extend to foreign markets.

Part B. Relatively Stronger Ruling Party: 2004–7

The Political Context

Abdullah began his prime ministership in October 2003 following Mahathir's long-planned departure. With Malaysia's economy now clearly recovering, the BN's popular standing was strengthened – the top priority was ensuring victory in the upcoming general election. In the context of a DPAR with an increasingly strong ruling party, I expect transparency to improve, state intervention to decline, and relative in attention to crowding-out effects.

[71] Lee (2013).   [72] Rodan (2004).   [73] *Financial Times*, November 1, 2002.

Abdullah engaged in a variety of measures to further strengthen BN's popularity ahead of the March 2004 election. Building on the efforts initiated by Mahathir to clamp down on cronyism and corruption, Abdullah introduced a National Integrity Plan and gave it form with a Malaysian Institute of Public Ethics.[74] The Anti-Corruption Agency, closely tied to the prime minister's office, brought charges against a sitting cabinet member, Khasitah Gaddam, minister of land and cooperative development, as well as a tycoon, Eric Chia, who was once head of Perwaja Steel. These were soon followed by charges of fraud against the former head of PNB, Shaharin Shaharudin,[75] as well as eighteen additional investigations of high-level politicians, bureaucrats, and business elites.[76] Several megaprojects, a primary means by which patronage was doled out but also an important method for reducing the newly important crowding-out effects of GLCs, were put on "indefinite hold."[77] Instead, Abdullah introduced programs to nurture small and medium-sized enterprises, including cottage industries dealing with halal products and dominated by poor rural Malays, as well as Islamic-based financial services.[78] Abdullah also announced that all sizable state contracts would be issued through open-tender bidding. To further reduce "the dominance of tycoons," he proposed that mutual funds be created.[79]

These efforts proved highly successful. In the 2004 general election, held on March 21, the BN secured a remarkable 90 percent of parliamentary seats and 64 percent of the popular vote. This strong showing was interpreted as a mandate to continue with transparency reforms and also gave the ruling party coalition the freedom to claim a larger share of the economy for its newly acquired GLCs.

---

[74] Case (2010).   [75] *Wall Street Journal*, February 18, 2004.   [76] Case (2005).
[77] Case (2004).
[78] Gomez (2016). The 2005 census revealed that SMEs constituted about 99.2 percent of all business establishments; they employed 5.6 million workers and contributed about 32 percent of real GDP. Eighty-seven percent of SMEs were in the services sector, 7.2 percent in manufacturing, and 6.2 percent in agriculture. Key subsectors within services included those related to Islamic financial products, including banking and insurance. See Malaysia (2006, 166–67) for further details about public programs to aid SME development.
[79] *New York Times*, March 19, 2004.

State Intervention

Despite the electoral mandate from the 2004 election, Abdullah largely failed to deliver on his pledge to foster entrepreneurial small and medium-sized enterprises and thereby reduce crowding-out effects due to the practice of selective patronage.[80] For example, when the government created links between small and medium-sized enterprises (SMEs) and multinational companies (MNCs), Chinese firms were seldom allowed access to the domestic and overseas markets that these foreign enterprises offered. But because local firms left out of these SME-MNC associations could produce better-quality products at cheaper rates, this denied domestic entrepreneurial companies the prospect of expanding. Selective patronage thereby undermined the relationship between MNCs and SMEs when the latter produced poor-quality products.

At the same time, GLCs became increasingly dominant in certain sectors. Based on their share of revenue in 2012, GLC dominance was greatest in utilities (93 percent) and transportation and warehousing (80 percent). GLCs also accounted for over 50 percent of revenue in agriculture, banking, information communications, and retail trade.[81] "When the GLC share of sales in an industry exceeds 60 per cent, there is a strong negative impact on private investment in that industry," according to an Asian Development Bank (ADB) study of Malaysian GLCs. GLCs have greater access to government procurement, making it easier for them to increase investment in sectors where they are already dominant. Additionally, GLCs have total assets almost nine times greater than non-GLCs, on average, and are more likely to invest a higher proportion of their earnings.[82]

As a result, the crowding-out factor "almost certainly" caused investors, including GLCs, to search for better investment returns overseas according to Menon, the lead economist in trade and regional cooperation at the ADB.[83] Menon argued that Malaysia was also the only Association of Southeast Asian Nations (ASEAN) country that was a net exporter of capital, claiming that total outflows exceeded US$40 billion (RM124 billion) between 2006 and 2009, almost double that of inflows. Khazanah's activist behavior shows how this occurred for

[80] Gomez and Saravanamuttu (2013).   [81] Menon and Ng (2013).
[82] Menon and Ng (2013).
[83] Interview with Menon published in *Malay Mail*, June 27, 2013.

GLCs, though it was of a much more modest scope during the 2004–7 period in comparison with the post-2007 period when the ruling party confronted serious threats to its hold on power. I begin with an examination of Khazanah's domestic interventions.

Khazanah's Domestic Interventions

Khazanah is unique among Malaysia's GLICs because its beneficial owner is the government. Hence the political pressures facing the executive are most clearly revealed via Khazanah's initiatives compared with the other GLICs. Four notable examples of Khazanah's domestic interventions reflect the changing political pressures that the ruling party coalition confronted, corresponding to modest activist behavior on the part of Khazanah.[84]

The first example regards Pantai Holdings, a Malaysian healthcare provider. Singapore's Parkway Holdings acquired a controlling stake in Pantai in November 2005, violating conditions for the continuing delivery of government services – 51 percent Malaysian and 30 percent Bumiputera shareholding. Khazanah was directed to create a special-purpose investment vehicle, Pantai Irama, that would meet the conditions and to which Parkway could shift its ownership stake.[85] The solution appeased domestic political concerns about redistributive aims as well as foreign investors who were concerned with firm performance. This intervention, however, did not involve a new Khazanah acquisition (indicative of potentially activist behavior) but instead involved Khazanah finding a solution to a legal, and political, problem.

The second example is Iskandar Malaysia – a major initiative launched in 2006 to develop the region bordering Singapore. It was projected to take twenty to thirty years and would involve the creation of a new state administrative center, an education hub, a biotechnology hub, and various tourism projects. Megaprojects have offered an effective means for the Malaysian government to disburse large contracts to favored business allies and this project would allow Prime Minister Abdullah to answer critics who pointed to an absence of megaprojects during his administration.[86] Khazanah was directed to lead the execution of the project as well as become a major investor.[87]

---

[84] See Lai (2012) for additional details.
[85] *Business Times Singapore*, August 29, 2006.
[86] *Straits Times*, February 9, 2006.
[87] It acquired a 60 percent equity stake in the agency Iskandar Investment in conjunction with a 40 percent stake held by the EPF and the Johor state government. Khazanah was owned by UEM, an unlisted holding company that

The third example regards Malaysia's national car manufacturer, Proton. To restore competitiveness, a partnership with Volkswagen was negotiated by Khazanah as the principal shareholder at the end of 2007. However, this deal was canceled at the last minute due to the negative implications for a large network of Bumiputera-owned SMEs that supplied parts to Proton.[88] The imminent election was a key factor. This last-minute cancellation due to fears of a poor electoral result reveal the willingness to privilege redistributive priorities above national welfare objectives when the ruling party faces a threat to its political dominance.

The final example regards the political challenges that Khazanah faced in dealing with Tenaga Nasional, Malaysia's power generator and distributor.[89] Despite Khazanah's efforts to improve profitability, the strong political opposition of business owners on the demand side prevented price increases, while the political influence of power producers prevented increases in supply. The unwillingness of the government to intervene was influenced by concerns about its electoral popularity.

Overall, Khazanah's role in the domestic market was relatively modest compared with the previous as well as the subsequent period, as discussed in the next section. Only in the case of Iskandar did Khazanah display a need to invest, but even in this situation it was not involved with acquiring any corporate assets or intervening in corporate strategy.

Khazanah's Foreign Interventions

Following the 2004 election, Khazanah began to venture into foreign markets in order to promote select GLCs as "regional champions."[90] For example, in 2005, Khazanah acquired a 52 percent stake in Lippo Bank, Indonesia's ninth-largest bank lender by assets. Indonesia was an attractive market both because of its significant potential and because it shares a common religious majority with Malaysia. In 2006, however,

---

owned two-thirds of the land where the development would occur. The project was expected to require over RM60 billion in financing (*Malaysian Business*, October 16, 2010).

[88] *The Edge Malaysia*, May 28, 2007.
[89] *The Edge Malaysia*, March 27, 2006.
[90] *The Edge Malaysia*, December 1, 2008.

Indonesia passed a law preventing dominant ownership in more than one commercial entity by a single foreign entity.[91] Khazanah violated this new law because of its direct ownership of Bank Lippo, as well as its indirect ownership of Bank Niaga, through Bumiputera Commerce Holdings Berhad (BCHB), which, in turn, owned CIMB Berhad. The latter acquired a 62 percent stake in Bank Niaga in 2002. To meet the new legal requirements, Khazanah had three choices – reduce its holdings in one of the banks, merge them, or create a holding company to control the banks. It ultimately chose to merge them. This was an activist response, but one that aligned with the market opportunities and that its domestic political audience would approve of (due to shared religious beliefs). The new bank became known as Bank CIMB Niaga, the fifth-largest bank in Indonesia by asset size at the time. The merger also helped CIMB become Southeast Asia's largest banking group (based on the number of retail branches), thereby fulfilling the Malaysian government's goal of developing regional champions. Additionally, BCHB became the largest single holding in Khazanah's portfolio and one of the largest companies in Malaysia (by market capitalization).

In addition to Indonesia, Khazanah expanded its investments into China and India. In China, Khazanah bought a 9.9 percent stake in the initial public offering (IPO) of the country's largest retail group, Parkson Retail, in December 2005. And in August 2005, it acquired a 13.2 percent stake in Apollo Hospitals, one of India's biggest healthcare companies. Altogether, Khazanah had twelve foreign investments as of August 2007.[92]

Later, around the time of the 2008 election, Khazanah began to privilege investments that would more clearly cater to its domestic political audience. Specifically, Khazanah began focusing on financial-sector investments in the Middle East in an effort to promote Malaysia as an international Islamic financial center. To this end, it bought a 10 percent stake in Jadwan Investments based in Saudi Arabia in 2008 and a 25 percent stake in Dubai-based Islamic investment firm Fajr Capital Limited in 2009, and it also invested in Singapore-based Asia Capital Reinsurance Group in 2006, with which it later established an Islamic reinsurance company in Malaysia in 2008.

---

[91] Single Presence Policy.   [92] *Asiamoney*, August 20, 2007.

While Khazanah clearly exhibited a growing appetite for foreign acquisitions, its tactics remained relatively less aggressive than what would occur after the 2008 election, when it rapidly developed regional business groups in healthcare, telecommunications, and financial services.

Improving Corporate and SWF Transparency

When the ruling party is strongly dominant, I expect elites in DPARs to be more likely to implement transparency-enhancing reforms. This occurred in Malaysia following the 2004 election when Abdullah initiated the GLC Transformation Program. The program laid out a ten-year plan designed to strengthen the competitiveness of GLCs. Khazanah spearheaded the efforts to reform GLCs in its portfolio by increasing their transparency and shareholder accountability. It hired a new managing director, Azman Mokhtar, to lead the transformation. Khazanah introduced key performance indicators, performance-linked compensation, reforms to board composition, and senior management changes for several major GLCs.[93] Although Khazanah's initiatives were part of a broader effort to reform the state's role in the corporate sector, each GLIC was responsible for its own reform efforts. Khazanah's far-reaching reforms served as a model for the other GLICs.

In 2006, major GLCs unveiled their business targets through key performance indicators, demonstrating the new commitment to transparency.[94] Nevertheless, the broader execution of the GLC Transformation Program disappointed many observers. According to a report by Credit Suisse, "Poor execution may be a result of ... politics."[95] The two areas that drew the scrutiny of investors included the appointment of key officials in GLCs as well as their procurement process, where preference was given to Bumiputera companies, although they may not be in the particular line of business. Moreover, observers generally regarded PNB, Petronas, LTAT, and the EPF as remaining essentially the same as before Abdullah took office.[96]

---

[93] *The Edge*, August 8, 2005; Putrajaya Committee (2006).
[94] *The Edge Financial Daily*, March 21, 2006.
[95] *The Edge Malaysia*, February 6, 2006.
[96] *The Edge Malaysia*, March 12, 2007.

After the sweeping victory in the 2004 election, thanks, in part, to Abdullah's crackdown on corruption, observers warned of a powerful "old guard" in UMNO that was merely biding its time. Many speculated that "the crackdown seems almost certain to produce a backlash within [the] party."[97] At the party's general assembly election in 2004, for example, Abdullah was impelled to lift a ban on campaigning by candidates that he had earlier imposed in order to deter "money politics." This early reversal was a harbinger of later events.

The longer that time passed following the 2004 election, the weaker the prime minister became, leading to greater privileging of redistributive, crony-based outcomes. For example, in 2007, the bureaucratic officials and lone tycoon charged with corruption were acquitted.[98] In the same year, the director of the ACA was revealed to have acquired undisclosed residences and businesses.[99] Later in 2007, a video was made public that showed a conversation where appointments of judges were brokered by a senior lawyer and the Supreme Court's chief justice. Instead of pursuing the offenders in the video, the ACA threatened to jail two opposition leaders if they did not reveal the whistle-blowers behind the video tape. Finally, Abdullah's brother, Fahim Ibrahim Abdullah, was involved in the acquisition of a majority stake in government-controlled MAS Catering, which he later sold to Lufthansa's LSG Skychef at a huge profit. Additionally, Abdullah's son and son-in-law were revealed to have received privatizing contracts with an Iraqi oil-for-food program and the Scomi Precision Engineering nuclear scandal that enriched both of them.[100]

Despite these scandals, signals grew stronger that Abdullah might call a general election for the end of 2007. To prepare for it, the government launched several multibillion-ringgit regional development projects in the Ninth Malaysia Plan (9MP) of 2006, including the Ipoh-Padang Besar double-track railway (RM10 billion), the Trans-Peninsular Oil Pipeline (RM25 billion), extension of the light rail transit system in the Klang Valley (RM10 billion), the West Coast Highway (RM4 billion), the Penang monorail (RM3 billion), Bakun undersea cable (RM10 billion), and the Pahang-Selangor Inter-State Water Transfer (RM5 billion). These were soon accompanied by the Northern Corridor Economic Region in July and the Eastern Corridor

---

[97] *New York Times*, March 19, 2004.   [98] *New York Times*, June 26, 2007.
[99] Lee (2008).   [100] Vithiatharan and Gomez (2014).

Economic Region in September. The government also anticipated spending billions more in the next ten to twenty years on the Iskandar Development Region. These would funnel money to SMEs and reduce GLCs' crowding-out effects.

In addition to growing concern over how the megaprojects would impact the public budget deficit into the future, there was growing frustration about how the government tendered these projects. For example, even before an open-tender process was begun for the mega-projects, there were reports that UEM World (a Khazanah GLC) would build the second bridge to Penang together with a mainland Chinese firm (involving a soft loan of US$900 million). In the Iskandar Development Region, Malaysian Resources Corp. (an EPF GLC) was tipped to secure a RM1 billion highway project. With regard to the northern corridor, Sime Darby (a PNB GLC) was tapped to do its master plan and therefore likely to receive a lion's share of its projects. For the eastern corridor, Petronas prepared an initial infrastructure plan signaling that it would be the likely recipient.[101]

When the GLC Transformation Program was launched, Abdullah announced that a key objective in reforming GLCs was the reduction of the government's holdings in these companies. But such reductions were very slow to occur because of objectives they served beyond pure profit maximization.[102] Highlighting the government's political influence over GLCs, the World Bank report pointed to criticisms about the speed and effectiveness of enforcement efforts by Malaysian regulators. For regulators to perform their duties effectively, they "must be independent in fact and appearance so their actions are objective, they maintain public credibility, and are free from political pressure."[103]

Thus, while Abdullah's abandoning his pledges to contain corruption might have eased tensions among UMNO politicians, non-Malays and a growing segment of Malays grew increasingly incensed. The Chinese and Indian communities became increasingly angry at the various perceived or real disadvantages they faced in the economy, education, and other areas where Malays enjoyed privileges conferred on them by the government. Price increases in food and fuel, as well as worsening corruption, stoked their anger.

[101] *New Straits Times*, July 11, 2007.
[102] *The Edge Financial Daily*, June 13, 2005.
[103] *Business Times Singapore*, January 13, 2007.

Two huge public protests occurred in November 2007. These, in combination with the release of the video suggesting that judiciary appointments were fixed, forced the general elections to be postponed to March 2008. In a poll conducted by the Merdeka Center in late February 2008, more than 60 percent of Malay respondents agreed that in the tendering of state contracts, UMNO politicians benefited the most.[104] Unsurprisingly, Abdullah's promise to improve Malaysia's Transparency International Corruption Index ranking from thirty-seven in 2003 to thirty in 2008 utterly failed; the country's corruption rank dropped to forty-three in 2007 and forty-seven in 2008.

The reinitiation of megaprojects was an acknowledgment of the need to restore, at least partially, the old crony-based model of redistribution ahead of the general election. Yet the scale of the patronage involved pales in comparison with that used following the 2008 election when the ruling party was significantly weakened. Likewise, corruption continued to mount, as indicated in the Corruption Perception Index (CPI) score in Figure 6.3, as the BN opaquely directed a growing volume of funds to development projects run by GLCs in a concerted effort to hold onto power.

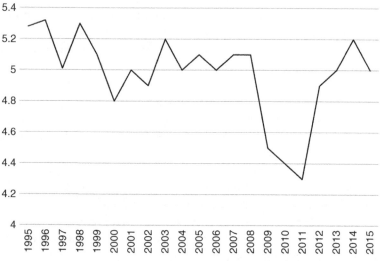

Figure 6.3 Malaysia's Corruption Perceptions Index (CPI) score, 1995–2015. *Source:* Transparency International.

[104] Case (2010).

Part B Conclusion

As the ruling party of a DPAR becomes stronger, I predict that state ownership of large firms will moderate, crowding-out effects will not be effectively addressed, corporate transparency will improve, and SWF investment behavior will be less aggressive in comparison with when the ruling party is relatively weaker. The BN's resounding victory in the 2004 election gave the ruling party a strong mandate to reduce cronyism and improve transparency of the state sector. Critical to these efforts was Khazanah – Malaysia's savings SWF – through its implementation of the GLC Transformation Program. It engaged in modest interventionist activities as it sought to restructure GLCs in an effort to improve their performance and initiated foreign investments in an effort to promote Malaysian regional champions. But these interventions were relatively modest in comparison with those in the post-2008 period when the ruling party was badly weakened.

Part C. Relatively Weaker Ruling Party: 2008–15

The time period from 2008 to 2015 coincides with the prime minister-ship of Najib. The 2008 election results delivered a major blow to BN, jolting its leaders into action to recapture lost electoral support. For a weak ruling party, I predict that transparency will decline, state ownership will increase for large firms, while efforts to reduce crowding-out will also occur for SMEs, savings SWFs will play a central role, and state intervention will become more aggressive.

During this time period, the Malaysian federal government increased the centralization of control over finances away from the states to preserve the prime minister's power to distribute patronage and deny resources to opponents. 1MDB, a savings SWF, was newly established in the wake of the 2008 election, and it engaged in aggressive invest-ments in the domestic market. Meanwhile, Khazanah and its GLCs became far more active in foreign markets. At the same time, state-sector opacity increased. 1MDB is emblematic of this trend. The use of nontransparent tenders of megaprojects to GLCs became an increas-ingly important mechanism by which funds were diverted to favored groups, and this also helped to reduce crowding-out effects for Bumiputera firms.

Weakening Ruling Party Coalition

The 2008 Political Tsunami

In the 2008 election, the BN's parliamentary presence fell nearly 30 percentage points, to 63 percent. In state-level elections, the opposition secured a majority in five states for the first time, including Kelantan, Kedah, Penang, Selangor, and Perak. It was a "political tsunami" according to *The Sunday Star*.[105] The result shook the confidence of UMNO to its core. Intraparty competition for resources was blamed. While internal party reforms and the renationalization of GLCs together centralized the prime minister's control and may have helped to prevent the rise of elite challengers, UMNO party members resorted to sabotaging their own candidates out of concern that if the candidate ascended in the party, they would channel state rents to themselves.[106] Due to this disastrous result, Abdullah was forced to step down as prime minister.

When Najib replaced Abdullah as prime minister in April 2009, he was confronted with both a political crisis and a profound economic downturn. The stock market plummeted by 40 percentage points over the period July 2008 to February 2009, while GDP contracted by a shocking 6.25 percent in the first quarter of 2009. The recession prompted renewed efforts to attract foreign investment and stimulate domestic investment – the latter had fallen continuously since 2000. A new series of initiatives was rolled out, including the Government Transformation Plan (GTP), the New Economic Model (NEM) (I and II), and the Economic Transformation Plan (ETP). These reports acknowledged that the economy continued to be plagued by rent seeking and cronyism, which Najib promised to end. He also sought to minimize state ownership of major corporations through privatization, core features of the NEM and the ETP. The GTP was the first of these to be announced, in January 2010, and it outlined seven national key results areas that the government would address, one of which included corruption, particularly in relation to government procurement and regulatory agencies. However, there was no specific mention of moving oversight of the regulatory agencies out of the executive and to the parliament, revealing the conflicting objectives of growing the economy via improvements to investor risk while also controlling the

[105] *The Star*, March 9, 2008.   [106] Gomez (2016).

disbursement of patronage in order to retain the BN's political supremacy. This schizophrenic approach was displayed in the Tenth Malaysia Plan (10MP), 2010–15, when the government revealed that it would persist with "market-friendly" affirmative action, but details of how this would be accomplished were lacking.

2013 Elections: Clinging to Power

In the 2013 elections, UMNO barely held onto power by regaining sufficient support from rural constituencies after being overwhelmingly rejected by the urban middle class. The BN secured only 133 parliamentary seats compared with the 140 it had obtained in 2008. Corporate scandals continued to occur despite the pledge to curb patronage (e.g., the Port Klang Free Zone, Sime Darby, and the National Feedlot Corporation).[107] Major projects also continued to be selectively awarded, such as lucrative state contracts to George Kent, a company owned by Najib's ally, Tan Kay Hock. Additionally, Syed Mokhtar Al-Bukhary, aligned with Mahathir, received projects such as the Penang Port and Proton Holdings. Selective patronage to Bumiputera SMEs also worsened, leading to the alienation of Chinese business owners. Despite these problems, rural voters opted for BN because of a new initiative of direct cash transfers with the BN's pledge of more handouts if returned to power. These cash transfers were referred to as BR1M (Bantuan Rakyat 1Malaysia or 1Malaysia Peoples Aid), and they reached 7 million people at a cost of RM4.6 billion. The vast majority of the rural poor were ethnic Malays, but because BR1M was based purely on income rather than ethnic status, it assisted minority ethnic groups such as Indians whose vote could swing marginal seats in BN's favor.[108]

False Hope for Improving Corporate Transparency

My argument predicts that a weak ruling party will implement stronger controls over the largest firms coupled with a decline in the state's overall presence in the economy in order to create more opportunities for private capital. Immediately following the 2008 election, the evidence strongly supports these predictions.

---

[107] Ibid. [108] Ibid.

Four initiatives sought to renew growth and create opportunities for private capital, including: (1) reducing state restrictions on investment, (2) privatization, (3) strengthening corporate governance codes, and (4) boosting the bond market. To spur investment, equity ownership regulations were liberalized for key economic sectors. In April 2009, the 30 percent Bumiputera equity requirement was removed for twenty-seven subsectors within services. This was a major policy shift because services represented about 55 percent of GDP and nearly 57 percent of total employment in 2008. The government also liberalized equity ownership regulations within the financial sector for foreign firms only. The limit for equity ownership was raised from 49 to 70 percent for investment banks, Islamic banks, insurance companies, and Islamic insurance firms, but the 30 percent limit for commercial banks was retained. However, foreign investors could only take minority stakes in companies in the telecommunications and energy sectors because these were regarded as strategic industries.[109] At the end of 2009, the government also removed the requirement that companies looking to publicly list offer 30 percent of their equity to Bumiputeras. Additionally, the requirement that Bumiputeras hold a combined 30 percent stake in quoted firms was reduced to 12.5 percent, which could be reduced further if companies later issued more shares.

In September 2010, Najib unveiled the ETP, which aimed to turn Malaysia into a high-income economy by 2020. To accomplish this without creating unsustainably high debt, the government sought to attract 92 percent of the RM1.4 trillion in investments from the private sector, both domestic and foreign.[110] To further assure foreign investors of Malaysia's commitment to protecting their rights and enhancing the country's attractiveness as an investment destination, the SC launched a five-year Corporate Governance Blueprint in July 2011. This was followed by the Malaysian Code on Corporate Governance 2012 (MCCG-2012) in March, which advocated the adoption of standards that go beyond the minimum set by regulation. While it would not be mandatory for companies to observe the MCCG-2012 recommendations, listed companies would be required to explain in their annual reports how they have complied and justify reasons for nonobservance.[111]

---

[109] *The Economist*, June 5, 2009.
[110] The Edge Malaysia, September 27, 2010.
[111] *PwC Alert*, Issue 201, August 2012.

These measures to revitalize the capital markets were supplemented with guidelines for GLICs to divest their shareholdings in major companies listed on BM to increase liquidity, thereby enabling GLICs to increase their investments in overseas markets. In 2012, two of the world's three largest IPOs that year were Malaysian GLCs – Felda Global Ventures and Integrated Healthcare Holdings (IHH). The SC also issued three more stock-brokering licenses in addition to launching *sukuk* (Islamic bonds) and conventional bonds to boost the bond market.[112]

According to the CLSA's *CG Watch 2014* report, Malaysia increased its score from forty-nine in 2007 to fifty-eight in 2014, achieving fourth place in the region behind Singapore, Hong Kong, and Japan. It was also the only market to consistently improve its score in each survey since 2007: forty-nine in 2007, fifty-two in 2010, fifty-five in 2012, and fifty-eight in 2014. The ACGA attributed this to "the state's efforts to require domestic institutional investors to take corporate governance seriously" via gradually improving enforcement and reforms such as the recommendations made in the MCCG-2012.[113] Together with the liberalization of equity ownership and the financial sector, foreign investment sharply increased in 2010, but only back to the level prior to the global financial crisis.

Continuing State-Sector Opacity

Despite the general improvements in corporate governance, notable problems arose in relation to GLCs. This is consistent with the argument's predictions, specifically, that declining transparency emerges as the ruling party becomes politically weaker. CLSA head of Malaysia research, Anand Pathmakanthan, wrote that many GLCs fell short when it came to discipline and independence. With such companies, he argued, minority shareholders could easily be held hostage to the state's strategic agendas. "By virtue of their state-sponsorship (including support by government-linked investment companies such as EPF and PNB), GLCs are less obliged to market discipline and prone to being vehicles to satisfy political or social priorities," he added.[114]

State-sector opacity also worsened in order to hide the increasing use of patronage to buy off strategically important groups. The continuing reliance on nontransparent tenders for megaprojects was an important

---

[112] *The Edge Malaysia*, October 18, 2010.   [113] CLSA and ACGA, 2014.
[114] CLSA and ACGA, 2014.

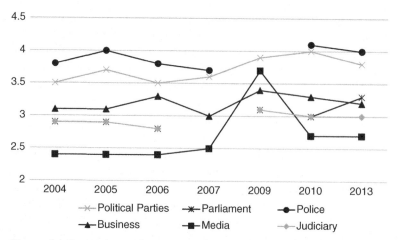

Figure 6.4 Perceptions of corruption in key Malaysian institutions/sectors, 2004–13 (1 = not corrupt; 5 = very corrupt).
Sources: Global Corruption Barometer 2004–7, 2009–10, and 2013.

factor. Only low-value procurements were disclosed on the government's e-procurement portal. Big-ticket projects were still negotiated and signed behind closed doors.[115] For example, in 2014, a consortium comprising SIPP Energy Sdn Bhd (owned by the Sultan of Johor), YTL Power International Bhd (a GLC), and Tenaga Nasional Bhd (a GLC) was given the right to develop the 1,400-MW power plant on a direct-negotiation basis instead of via an open competitive tender.[116]

As mentioned in relation to the 1997–2003 episode, exposing corruption is fraught with risk. Whistle-blowers, anticorruption activists, and investigators who seek to present government documents as evidence of corruption could face severe penalties under the Official Secrets Act, especially since the definition of what constitutes "secret" or "confidential" includes government tender documents.[117]

Figure 6.4 shows the perceptions of corruption across several Malaysian institutions and sectors. After the police, political parties

[115] *Bernama Daily Malaysian News*, August 29, 2013.
[116] *The Edge Malaysia*, August 25, 2014. YTL Power eventually pulled out amid widespread discontent over the way the award was decided.
[117] For example, the Court of Appeal ruled that the concession agreement between the federal government and one of the private water supply companies in Selangor should be kept secret and not divulged to the public (*Malaysian Insider*, February 25, 2011). Also see Jomo and Tan (2011, 358).

have been consistently regarded as the most corrupt, with this perception increasing in the wake of the 2008 election.

An additional reason for the ongoing decline in the perception of corruption is due to the regulatory agencies. In December 2008, Abdullah introduced a bill that replaced the ACA with the Malaysian Anti-Corruption Commission (MACC). The new agency was ostensibly modeled on Hong Kong's highly regarded Independent Commission against Corruption (ICAC), but it could only recommend cases to the Attorney General's Chambers, which would still report in turn to the prime minister rather than parliament.[118] During the beginning of 2009, the commission recommended the prosecution of a number of government and opposition politicians, the most notable of whom was the tourism minister, Azalina Othan Said. However, expectations that the MACC would target political opponents were soon confirmed when the MACC began targeting nearly all the executive council members of the People's Pact government in Selangor in February. In July 2009, an aide to a Democratic Action Party state executive councilor was summoned to a late-night interrogation and found dead the next afternoon on a rooftop nine floors beneath the MACC headquarters.

GLICs continued to remain nontransparent about various key pieces of information.[119] For example, the EPF did not provide a full set of quarterly investment reports on its website as of December 2011, and further details about its equity investments were missing, such as the geographic distribution of its foreign equities, and separate data on returns derived from equity dividends and those from trading profits.[120] Also, PNB's annual report offered no details on its various investments in properties, fixed-income securities, and equities in terms of their geographic spread, sectors, or returns.[121] Khazanah released its portfolio of listed companies at annual briefings but would not reveal its bottom line. ValueCap's financial statements were available on its website but did not offer details of the investments it made.[122]

---

[118] *Malaysiakini*, December 16, 2008.
[119] One exception appears to be Equinas. When Equinas was first established in 2009, many feared that it would become a vehicle to bail out ailing Bumiputera companies. But it has since appeased its critics by being highly transparent, regularly distributing information about its investments, targets, and returns.
[120] *The Edge*, December 26, 2011.   [121] *The Edge*, July 6, 2009.
[122] What was available was the fair value of the investments.

But worst of all has been 1MDB, which amassed a debt of RM36 billion within four years, raising concerns about the risks to Malaysia's sovereign rating.[123] These concerns have been heightened due to the opacity of numerous transactions. For example, the Kuala Lumpur International Financial District (later known as Tun Razak Exchange) is a joint property development between 1MDB and the Mubadala Development Company, but there were no explanations for why a unit of the Abu Dhabi government was chosen over Malaysian developers.[124] Similar concerns arose with regard to the redevelopment of the Sungasi Besi airport (later known as Bandar Malaysia), which did not go through an open tender to determine the price of the land.[125] The redevelopment was to be carried out by 1MDB and the Qatar Investment Authority.

Tabung Haji also engaged in questionable opaque transactions with 1MDB.[126] In 2015, Tabung Haji purchased a small plot of land from 1MDB for what many consider to have been an inflated purchase price.[127] By selling just 2.2 percent of the seventy acres that 1MDB owns in Tun Razak Exchange, 1MDB recouped 97 percent of what it paid for the seventy acres of land, excluding debt service charges. Moreover, the purchase price paid by Tabung Haji was similar to the next half-yearly payment for 1MDB debt. Concerns have arisen over potential conflicts of interest because Tabung Haji's group CEO is a director of 1MDB, while a member of Tabung Haji's investment panel is on 1MDB's advisory board. Tabung Haji's CEO is also chairman of 1MDB subsidiary Edra Global Energy Bhd.

Finally, a new weapon was added to the state's arsenal for silencing critics, whistle-blowers, and investigators. As Najib faced mounting criticism in relation to the multibillion-dollar 1MDB scandal, a new National Security Council Act was implemented on August 1 2016. It would allow the prime minister to designate any area as a "security area," where he can deploy forces to search any individual, vehicle, or premise without a warrant. It also allows investigators to dispense with formal inquests into killings by the police or armed forces in those areas.

---

[123] *The Edge Malaysia*, August 25, 2014.   [124] *The Edge*, August 8, 2011.
[125] *The Edge*, December 5, 2011.
[126] *Malaysiakini*, May 11, 2015; *The Edge Malaysia*, May 18, 2015.
[127] *The Edge*, May 11, 2015.

The State's Reliance on Large GLCs

As part of the GLC Transformation Program and the broader Economic Transformation Program adopted in 2010, the government recommitted itself to divesting of noncore and noncompetitive GLCs. As of December 2014, the government had successfully divested thirty-two companies out of a planned thirty-three.[128] However, the largest GLCs remain state owned because, as Deputy Prime Minister Muhyiddin Yassin said, "they play important roles other than generating revenues that can be used for the country's development."[129] But how these development goals are achieved was and remains a political exercise. For example, in the wake of the 2008 elections, the federal government moved quickly to bypass the opposition-led state governments and rechannel those funds to federally controlled agencies, departments, or GLCs instead.[130] One illustration of this concerns RM25 million allocations to both Penang and Malacca in the 2009 budget for conservation works, but Penang, unlike Malacca, had not received its share. Subsequently, it was discovered that the grant had been channeled to Khazanah.[131] As reflected in the 2013 election results, a major concern among Malaysian voters regarded the non-transparent awarding of megaprojects, which has been used frequently as a disguised form of patronage.

An important contributor to this was the five economic growth corridors proposed in the 9MP, 2006–10.[132] Although the 9MP was scheduled to begin in 2006, the budgeting, infrastructure, and institutions for four of the five economic corridors were not allocated until after the 2008 election.[133] Iskandar is the one that started in 2007, with Khazanah taking the lead role. Recall from part B that GLCs were the primary beneficiaries for the other corridors, largely winning them via negotiation rather than open tenders. This became an ongoing point of concern to Malaysian voters. These concerns were amplified with the 10MP, 2011–15, which unveiled fifty-two "high-impact" projects with GLCs being the major beneficiaries.[134]

---

[128] Economic Transformation Program, annual Report, 2014.
[129] *The Malaysian Insider*, June 25, 2011.   [130] Hutchinson (2014).
[131] *New Straits Times*, August 30, 2009.
[132] They were budgeted at RM145 billion.   [133] *The Edge*, January 26, 2009.
[134] *The Edge*, June 14, 2010. The total development allocation from the 10MP was RM230 billion, of which RM62.7 billion was earmarked for the fifty-two "high-impact" projects.

More recently, the government's 2014 budget would continue to disproportionately benefit the construction sector, with GLCs playing an outsized role.[135] The major construction projects included the five corridors, as well as the implementation of other significant projects, including the Klang Valley Mass Rapid Transit (KVMRT) 2 line, the West Coast Expressway, and the double-tracking rail projects from Ipoh to Padang Besar and from Gemas to Johor Baru. Additionally, rural development initiatives included the building and upgrading of dams and water treatment plants, upgrading of rural roads, and the construction of the Pan-Borneo Highway. Contractors' earnings for 2014 were estimated to increase by 43 percent, while new contracts were projected to be awarded that would be 24 percent higher than 2013's new contract awards.[136] "The RM200 billion worth of jobs in the pipeline for the next 20 years have been carrots for investors and driven up valuations" of construction companies.[137] Over the twelve months from May 2013, when the election occurred, to May 2014, the KL Construction Index climbed 20 percent.[138] Recall that construction firms constitute the sector with the largest number of state-owned firms of the 200-firm sample in 2008 (see Figure 6.2).

Following the 2013 elections, the oil and gas sector also spiked due to the contracts to be awarded by Petronas's huge five-year RM300 billion capital expenditure, including a RM5 billion project in the KL city center named Cititower.[139] The PNB also initiated the construction of a new skyscraper, KL118, with a projected cost of RM2.5 billion to RM3 billion.[140] Even the LTAT (the Armed Forces Fund), which was largely absent from government intervention during the 1997 crisis, initiated the construction of a new base for the air force amounting to RM2.8 billion after "winning" it on a direct-negotiation basis from 1MDB.[141]

Thus, contrary to the initial divestment promise with the GLC Transformation Program launched in 2004, GLCs are increasingly dominant. For example, an analysis of all firms listed on the KLSE from 2007 to 2011 shows that the median control of assets by GLCs was RM5.4 billion compared with only RM100 million for non-

---

[135] The allocation for development in the 2014 budget was RM46.5 billion.
[136] *The Edge*, February 3, 2014. The new 2014 contracts were worth RM22 billion.
[137] *The Edge*, May 5, 2014.   [138] Ibid.   [139] *The Edge*, September 6, 2015.
[140] *The Edge*, June 3, 2013.   [141] *The Edge*, June 20, 2011.

GLCs. The sample of firms included thirty-four GLCs and 914 non-GLCs, confirming that GLCs dominated the largest firms. Despite their small number, they accounted for approximately 36 percent of the KLSE's market capitalization. Due, in part, to their privileged access to government resources, the ratio of investments over fixed assets for GLCs was 0.18 versus only 0.1 for non-GLCs.[142] GLCs also displayed far better performance, with median returns on assets (ROAs) of 7.19 percent versus 4.1 percent for non-GLCs and median returns on equity (ROEs) of 14.36 percent versus 7.6 percent for non-GLCs. A group of GLCs, dubbed the "G20," which is the top twenty performing companies in the government's portfolio, has seen their market capitalization triple over the same period of the initial 2004 divestment promise.

Efforts to Reduce Crowding-Out Effects

To compensate for the growing presence of GLCs and concomitant crowding-out effects, I predict the state will offer assistance to SMEs in order to maintain popular support. In the case of Malaysia, ethnic divisions have dominated how this assistance is administered. Specifically, the BN has chosen to give handouts directly to poor Malays via BR1M instead of implementing programs to assist SMEs, which are heavily dominated by ethnically Chinese Malays. This has alienated Chinese voters, who are suffocating not only from the squeeze of GLCs but also from the slowdown in private investment. Private investment grew by 21.4 percent in 2012, 12.8 percent in 2013, and then 11 percent in 2014. In the first half of 2015, it only grew 7.5 percent.[143]

Before the 2013 elections, the Chinese business elite supported the BN because they reaped considerable profits from pro-Bumiputera policies, often via government contracts sold off to them. But GLCs' unrelenting crowding-out pressures coupled with handouts to poor Malays via BR1M significantly reduced the Chinese share of state-directed benefits. This disaffection was manifested by direct contributions from businesses, which typically favor BN candidates, that went instead to opposition parties, who emphasized curbs on corruption, open tender for government contracts, social equality, and clean

---

[142] Menon and Ng (2013).   [143] *The Edge*, September 28, 2015.

government.[144] As a result, the Malaysian Chinese Association, a member of the BN coalition, saw its vote collapse. Most Chinese (who make up about 25 percent of the population) voted instead for the opposition DAP party, which won an unprecedented thirty-eight seats in the federal parliament, up ten from the 2008 elections. Even the victorious Prime Minister Najib spoke of a "Chinese tsunami" that had hit his coalition.[145] The BN is counting on demographics favoring them over the long run as the Chinese population declines while that of Malays increases.

Domestic Corporate Interventions

My argument predicts that a weak coalition-oriented DPAR will engage in increasing intervention in the corporate sector. We have already seen that the government increased its control over the largest, best-performing GLCs. State intervention extended beyond this select group, of course. For example, in 2013, EPF critics suggested that it was being tapped to support the local equity market as foreigners pulled out. The EPF's investments in equities grew from 25.7 percent of total investment assets in 2008 to 43 percent in 2013, which was up from 38.7 percent in 2012. And in April 2015, Najib announced that ValueCap would be tasked with a RM20 billion fund to boost the stock market.[146]

1MDB

Perhaps the most widely publicized example of the Malaysian state's activist corporate intervention is 1 Malaysia Development Berhad (1MDB). The origins of 1MDB can be traced to the 2008 general election when the head of the executive branch for the state government of Terengganu was changed due to the alleged misuse of oil royalty money that comes from Petronas. To prevent unaccounted-for spending of oil royalties, the Sultan created the Terengganu Investment Authority (TIA) in March 2009. The federal government issued a RM5 billion guaranteed bond to kickstart TIA as part of a "settlement" for unaccounted-for oil royalties.[147]

[144] Weiss (2016).   [145] *The Economist*, May 6, 2013.
[146] *The Edge*, April 6, 2015.   [147] *The Edge*, December 14, 2009.

TIA was originally intended to be modeled after Mubadala, the SWF of Abu Dhabi; the CEO of Mubadala sits on the board of 1MDB.[148] The fund size was initially targeted at RM11 billion, comprising RM5 billion from the federal government and another RM6 billion to come from the securitization of future oil royalties. But after the initial RM5 billion was raised with a thirty-year bond issue that came with a federal government guarantee, there was a dispute over control of the funds, and the agency became a federal entity renamed 1MDB. It was now intended to be a strategic development company reporting to the minister of finance, who was also the Prime Minister Najib, and who had the sole power to approve investments and hire and fire board members and managers. Since 2009, it quickly grew in size with RM45 billion as of March 2013, nearly rivaling the size of Khazanah at RM64 billion.

1MDB's first major investment occurred with PetroSaudi International in September 2009, a Saudi Arabian company, hired to explore for oil and gas.[149] In 2012, 1MDB initiated its first corporate acquisition, which was also Malaysia's biggest-the purchase of Tanjong Energy from tycoon T. Ananda Krishnan.[150] The complex financial deal nearly fell apart until Najib stepped in to secure a co-guarantee of a bond issue from the Abu Dhabi royal family's International Petroleum Investment Company.[151] The aggressive acquisition by 1MDB for Tanjong Energy (renamed Powertek Energy) occurred due to 1MDB's need for a stable cash flow to service its large debt load, amounting to RM6.8 billion at the end of March 2011. The other major investments at the time included the Run Tazak Exchange (in the Kuala Lumpur financial district) and Bandar Malaysia real estate development projects. Soon after, 1MDB acquired two more power-generation facilities – Kuala Langat and Jimah Energy. As a result of its heavy investments in property development and power generation, it competed directly with the private sector. Its

---

[148] A key advisor to the Sultan was Low Taek Jho, or Jho Low, who had strong ties to the Middle East.

[149] *The Edge*, April 1, 2013. The investment was worth RM5.7 billion. According to the US Department of Justice, the deal was merely a "pretense" for "the fraudulent transfer of more than 1 billion USD from 1MDB to a Swiss bank account" controlled by Jho Low – a "29-year-old with no official position with 1MDB or PetroSaudi."

[150] The purchase amounted to 8.5RM billion. [151] *The Edge*, June 4, 2012.

defenders have claimed that its property-development projects promote "Bumiputera empowerment" – but at what cost?[152]

A troubling feature of 1MDB was its high leverage, which raised
concerns that it could emerge as a serious contingent liability for the
government.[153] Unlike other typical SWFs, which invest funds from
central bank reserves, fiscal surpluses, or natural resources, 1MDB's
aggressive expansion is financed largely by debt. Its total liabilities were
larger than those at Khazanah or the EPF, as were its total current
liabilities.[154]

1MDB began reducing its debt burden by various means, including
selling its power plants to a Chinese company.[155] But a politically
explosive problem was the billions in missing funds that appear to
have been siphoned off illegally via a global network of shell
companies. Swiss investigators estimated that about US$4 billion van-
ished from 1MDB's coffers. Separately, Malaysia's parliamentary
Public Accounts Committee concluded in April 2016 that around
US$3.5 billion had disappeared into a company based in the British
Virgin Islands that has since been closed. The US Department of Justice
filed a civil suit to seize over US$1 billion in assets, naming as bene-
ficiaries Riza Aziz, stepson of Najib, and Jho Low, a close friend of
Riza.[156] It also accused Najib of receiving US$681 million in cash from
1MDB – a claim he denied.[157]

Aggressive Foreign Investments

The large size of many GLCs in relation to the domestic market,
coupled with the need to generate positive returns due to the link
between GLCs and Malaysian voter-investors, has contributed to the
push for aggressive foreign investments. More aggressive foreign
investments would also alleviate crowding-out effects.

---

[152] *The Rakyat Post*, December 11, 2015.
[153] Based on the latest accounts ended March 31, 2013, 1MDB has total liabilities
of RM42 billion, including RM36 billion in borrowings and an annual debt
service of RM1.6 billion.
[154] *The Edge*, May 12, 2014. 1MDB's total liabilities were RM42 billion;
Khazanah's total liabilities were RM37.4 billion; the EPF's total liabilities were
RM4.4 billion.
[155] *Wall Street Journal*, November 23, 2015.
[156] *Wall Street Journal*, July 21, 2016.   [157] *The Guardian*, July 28, 2016.

Of Malaysia's GLICs, Khazanah has been the most aggressive in its pursuit of foreign acquisitions and other investments. The approach that has guided Khazanah's domestic activities applies equally to its foreign investments. Indeed, Azman insists that his staff play an active role in monitoring *any* investments they make.[158] "We took up and lived the mantra of execution: 'Execute or be executed,'" Azman said. "We changed CEOs – not too often, but often enough and at the right times." Moreover, Khazanah has preferred to take a majority stake in its overseas investments so that it can have adequate board representation to influence business direction.[159] Khazanah is still heavily focused on Malaysia, but its objective has been to turn many of its GLCs into regional champions. This goal was specified in the GLC Transformation Program and so applies to other GLICs too.

Of all of Malaysia's GLICs, Khazanah has the largest foreign presence. Table 6.4 shows Khazanah's portfolio by domicile of companies and by industry. Between 2008 and 2015, Khazanah rapidly increased its foreign investments from 15.7 to 44.9 percent of its portfolio in comparison with Temasek's increase from 67 to 72 percent over the same time period. With regard to industries, financial services and telecommunications have remained among Khazanah's top four, whereas these have remained the top two for Temasek since 2004. In 2015, healthcare became an important industry for Khazanah.

I survey those GLCs owned by Khazanah that are regarded as Malaysia's regional champions in order to demonstrate its aggressive investment behavior. The regional champions include Axiata (telecommunications), IHH Healthcare (healthcare), and CIMB (financial services). Maybank (a financial services firm owned by PNB), Sime Darby (plantation firm owned by PNB), and RHB Bank (financial services firm owned by EPF) are also regarded as regional champions, but PNB and EPF have been far less aggressive, leaving foreign market entry to the CEOs.[160] Indeed, Khazanah has served as a training ground for managers to learn the methods by which to aggressively implement restructuring activities in an effort to boost performance – the CEOs of Maybank and RHB Bank both learned from restructuring exercises in Khazanah-owned Telekom Malaysia before assuming their new positions. But a clear difference between Khazanah relative to the EPF and

---

[158] *Institutional Investor Magazine*, May 6, 2015.
[159] *The Edge Malaysia*, March 13, 2006.   [160] *Business Times*, July 24, 2015.

Table 6.4 *Khazanah and Temasek Portfolios by Geographic Exposure and Industry*

Year	Temasek		Khazanah	
2004	Singapore 52% OECD (ex-Korea) 31% Asia (ex-Japan) 17%	Telecom 36% Financial services 21%		Media and communications 22.2%
2008	Singapore 33% OECD 23% Asia 41% Other regions 3%	Financial services 40% Telecom 24%	Malaysia 86.3% Indonesia 4.5% Singapore 2.7% Other countries 6.5%	Infrastructure and construction 20% Financial services 19.3%
2015	Singapore 28% OECD 26% Asia 42% Other regions 4%	Financial services 28% Telecom 24%	Malaysia 55.1% Singapore 12.1% Turkey 7.4% China 6.5% Indonesia 5.7% Other countries 13.6%	Telecom 22% Healthcare 17.2% Power 15.3% Financial services 13.7%

PNB is that the latter two have not acted as active partners in developing their firms into regional champions. Khazanah has been far more activist in four ways: (1) taking controlling stakes in target firms in order to implement major changes as part of a longer-term regional plan, (2) bargaining with the foreign government on behalf of its firms, (3) enabling mergers, demergers, and other types of restructuring, and (4) co-investing in target firms. As mentioned earlier, the aim has been the dual purpose of generating positive returns in ways that conform with the government's policy objectives, particularly maintaining its electoral popularity among the domestic Bumiputera voter base.

Axiata

When the GLC Transformation Program was initiated in 2005, Wahid was CEO of Telekom Malaysia (TM). He oversaw the firm's overseas expansion, which began when it entered the Indonesian market in 2004 with an initial 27.3 percent stake in Excelcomindo, Indonesia's third-largest mobile phone company. This ownership stake was increased over the years into a controlling stake. Khazanah played a vital role in clinching the deal because negotiations with the Indonesian authorities took on a government-to-government stance.[161] Around this time, TM also invested in MTN Networks of Sri Lanka (wholly owned by TM) and Telekom Malaysia International (TMI) Bangladesh (a joint venture), in addition to purchasing a large stake in a Pakistani company, Multinet.[162] But to become a truly regional player, it would be necessary to have a foothold in Singapore.

In 2005, TM, in an 80:20 joint venture with Khazanah, acquired a stake of more than 5 percent in MobileOne (M1).[163] The joint venture, SunShare Investments, Ltd., bought another 12.06 percent from Hong Kong's PCCW and Britain's Cable & Wireless (which founded M1), giving SunShare a 17.7 percent stake in M1. Any purchase above 12 percent of a telecom required the approval of Singapore's telecommunications regulator Infocomm Development Authority (IDA), making Khazanah's participation potentially quite helpful. Many prospective bidders backed away for this reason.[164] Khazanah and TM subsequently indicated that they intended to increase their stake to just under 30 percent, the trigger point for making a general offer under

---

[161] *The Edge*, December 20, 2004.   [162] *The Edge*, February 25, 2005.
[163] *The Edge*, August 22, 2005.   [164] *The Edge*, December 5, 2005.

Singapore's securities laws. TM indicated that it did not intend to breach the 30 percent stake, but at that level, TM would be in a good position to assume board control. Market observers suggested that there could be discussions on a government-to-government basis where a tradeoff takes place: "Both [Singapore Press Holdings] and Keppel [Telecommunications & Transportation] are [Singapore] government-linked entities and so are Khazanah and TM. You could have a scenario of TM at the helm of M1, while, say, SingTel is allowed to buy into a company like Time dotCom Bhd in Malaysia." Singapore Press Holdings and Keppel T&T were two other major shareholders of M1.[165] By December 5, TM had acquired a 25 percent stake, and by July 2006, Telekom Malaysia and its parent Khazanah had a controlling 29.8 percent stake.[166]

In 2006, TMI also bought a 40 percent stake in Spice, India's number ten cellular provider.[167] In the same year, Khazanah bought a stake in India's Idea Cellular, which TMI had earlier failed to acquire in its joint effort with Singapore Technologies Telemedia due to regulatory issues.[168] TMI later acquired a 19 percent stake in Idea Cellular, which entailed merging Spice into Idea Cellular.[169] To do this, TMI sold a stake to Khazanah to finance a bridging loan that would enable the purchase of Idea Cellular.[170] Idea Cellular was highly attractive to TMI because it would expand its presence in India beyond just 80 million people in two circles – Punjab and Karnataka – to thirteen circles covering 70 percent of the Indian population.[171]

TMI was spun off from Telekom Malaysia in 2008 and renamed Axiata. Prior to the demerger, TM consolidated its foreign businesses by divesting interests in several South African countries to focus on markets closer to Malaysia.[172] Azman specifically indicated the objective of making Axiata into a regional champion by 2015.[173] By 2015, Axiata's regional units included Hello in Cambodia, Robi in Bangladesh (formerly TMI Bangladesh), Dialog in Sri Lanka (formerly MTN Networks), Multinet in Pakistan, Celcom in Malaysia, XL Axiata in Indonesia (formerly known as PT Excelcomindo), and M1 in Singapore.[174] In 2015, it entered Myanmar with a stake in Digicel.

---

[165] Ibid.   [166] *The Edge*, July 24, 2006.   [167] *The Edge*, January 30, 2006.
[168] *The Edge*, April 17, 2006, and June 20, 2005.
[169] *The Edge*, June 26, 2008.   [170] *The Edge*, November 3 and 5, 2008.
[171] *The Edge*, June 26, 2008.   [172] *The Edge*, December 27, 2010.
[173] *The Edge*, January 18, 2010.   [174] *The Edge*, March 8, 2010.

Integrated Healthcare Holdings

Khazanah's entry into the healthcare sector began with a US$44.23 million investment in Apollo Hospitals Enterprise in August 2005, the largest private hospital group in India. In November 2006, it acquired IMU Education, which owned and managed the International Medical University in Malaysia. In May 2008, it acquired an 18.3 percent stake in Parkway Holdings, a Singapore-based healthcare provider with the largest regional network of private hospitals and healthcare facilities. Building on its preexisting joint venture with Parkway Holdings via Pantai (a Khazanah-owned Malaysian healthcare provider), Khazanah became the second-largest shareholder in Parkway. The largest shareholder at the time was the US private equity firm TPG. But in March 2010 TPG sold its stake in Parkway to Fortis Healthcare, an India-based corporation. Fortis's post-acquisition behavior was regarded as "aggressive" by Khazanah, as detailed in Chapter 1, leading to Khazanah's announcement in May that it wanted to take control of Parkway through a partial offer.[175] This led to a two-month-long takeover battle between Khazanah and Fortis that has been cited as a "rare example of a hostile move by a sovereign wealth fund."[176] Khazanah eventually won and, by the end of 2010, had acquired all of Parkway's shares, which were subsequently consolidated with those in Pantai, Apollo, and its education business to produce "Asia's premium regional healthcare platform" subsequently named Integrated Healthcare Holdings (IHH).[177]

In 2011, Khazanah entered into talks with Almond Holding, a joint venture between Dubai-based private equity group Abraaj Capital and Turkish family Aydinlar, to buy a stake in Turkish hospital group Acibadem.[178] The Aydinlar family and Almond Holding ultimately sold 60 percent of Acibadem shares to IHH and 15 percent to Khazanah, a 75 percent stake in total. The Aydinlar family would retain a 25 percent stake.[179]

After the takeover, Khazanah restructured IHH and put all its healthcare assets into the company. IHH's core businesses would now consist of Parkway Pantai, Ltd., Acibadem, IMU Health, Parkway Life REIT, and Apollo Hospitals. In July 2012, IHH dually

---

[175] *Business Times Singapore*, July 28, 2010.
[176] *Asian Wall Street Journal*, July 27, 2010.
[177] *Business Times*, May 28, 2010.   [178] *TradeArabia*, September 24, 2011.
[179] Reuters, December 13, 2011.

listed on the Malaysia and Singapore stock exchanges to become the world's third-largest IPO after Facebook and Felda Global Ventures (also a Malaysian GLC) that year. IHH would become the world's second-largest listed healthcare provider after HCA Holdings (based in the United States) by market capitalization. As of April 2016 Khazanah owned a 43.59 percent stake in IHH through its special-purpose vehicle Pulau Memutik Ventures. Other major shareholders include Mitsui (20 percent via its subsidiary MBK Healthcare Partners) and the EPF (7.26 percent).

CIMB

Following the Asian financial crisis, new guidelines on foreign bank ownership were relaxed quite significantly across the region.[180] In 2005, Khazanah-owned CIMB purchased GK Goh Holdings, Ltd., the second-largest stock-brokering business in Singapore. This was viewed as an effort to create a regional investment bank because GK Goh also had a strong presence in Indonesia.[181] By 2006, CIMB had become the second-largest banking group in Malaysia and the largest investment bank in Southeast Asia.[182] In that same year, the CIMB group completed a restructuring that involved the delisting of CIMB Bhd and the integration of the investment and commercial banking arms of the group under a new holding company CIMB Group Sdn Bhd. CIMB Group thus became a wholly owned subsidiary of Bumiputera Commerce Holdings Bhd (BCHB) and would lead the charge in transforming the banking group into a universal bank.

CIMB then acquired BNP-Paribas Peregrine Securities in Thailand and Bank Niaga in Indonesia, giving the group a presence in Malaysia, Singapore, Indonesia, Thailand, and Hong Kong. In 2008, Bank Niaga was merged with Bank Lippo, which was 93.6 percent owned by Khazanah, creating an enlarged platform for CIMB's regional growth. The new Indonesian bank PT Bank CIMB Niaga would become the fifth-largest banking group in Indonesia.[183]

In 2009, CIMB acquired a 19.99 percent stake in China's Bank of Yingkou Co., Ltd., and a majority stake in Bank Thai PBL (subsequently known as CIMB Thai Bank PCL).[184] In 2010, it set up a subsidiary in

---

[180] *The Edge*, May 2, 2005.   [181] *The Edge*, January 17, 2005.
[182] *The Edge*, June 12, 2006.   [183] *The Edge*, June 9, 2008.
[184] *The Edge*, August 30, 2010.

Cambodia, CIMB Bank plc, and in 2012, it acquired a 60 percent stake in Bank of Commerce of the Philippines in addition to acquiring the Asian investment banking business of the Royal Bank of Scotland, including the Royal Bank franchise in Australia.[185] These acquisitions have been possible due to its strong domestic banking business, opportunities to purchase banking assets following the 2008 Global Financial Crisis, in addition to support from Khazanah to become a regional player.[186] In 2014, CIMB Thai opened a branch in Vientiane, Laos.

Part C Conclusion

During the time period from 2008 to 2015, the ruling party coalition BN remained weakly dominant. My argument predicts that state ownership of the largest firms will rise as the ruling party exerts greater control over the allocation of state resources, while efforts will be made to reduce crowding-out effects through support to SMEs; transparency will also decline as the state directs support for favored groups; and SWF activism will increase in an effort to improve the performance of GLCs and the financial returns to voter-investors. Although the state followed through with its privatization initiative, the largest GLCs increased their dominance over their respective sectors, leading to expanded state control over the economy. The accompanying crowding-out effects were addressed along ethnic lines as part of the BN's long-term strategy to remain in power due to demographics that indicated higher birth rates for ethnic Malays in comparison with Chinese Malays. This led the BN to direct transfers (via BR1M) to the rural poor, who were primarily ethnic Malays. Neglect for the urban SMEs contributed to the Chinese Malays' abandoning the BN in the 2013 election. Their disaffection with the BN was magnified by the BN's increasing reliance on selective patronage via GLCs, which were the primary beneficiaries of large government contracts, decided via opaque tenders. More explicit manifestations of the diversion of resources to ethnic Malays occurred via the creation of two investment funds shortly after the 2008 elections – Equinas and 1MDB. The former was created to cater to the Bumiputera business community; the latter has been more directly tied to the prime minister and used largely to promote his personal interests, including the support of projects that

[185] *The Edge*, February 27, 2012. [186] *The Edge*, August 30, 2010.

would preserve his power and enrich favored allies. At the same time that the state engaged in increasingly aggressive intervention in the domestic market, Khazanah implemented an aggressive regionalization initiative. Its regional champions in healthcare (IHH), telecommunications (Axiata), and financial services (CIMB) rapidly entered foreign markets, fulfilling Khazanah's ambitions.

Altogether, the striking pattern that emerges is that of a more centralized and aggressive state sector that increasingly engaged in the distribution of patronage via GLCs awarded through opaque tendering procedures. The Malaysian state's aggressive investment behavior has also transformed a few of its GLCs into regional powerhouses with the support of Khazanah.

Chapter Conclusions

Since the Asian financial crisis, Malaysia's ruling party coalition has experienced enduring weakness as political challengers have mounted strong and persistent opposition. In the context of this sustained weakness, national elections have generated swings that magnify or dampen the BN's declining popularity. The four state-sector characteristics – state ownership of large GLCs, state-sector transparency, the reliance on savings SWFs, and state investment behavior – exhibited corresponding shifts, though they are modest in relation to the more sizable differences between Malaysia and Singapore. The one point of divergence between theory and evidence regards policies to address the crowding-out effects of large GLCs. Due to Malaysia's politically important ethnic divisions, the BN implemented policies directed to the predominantly Malay rural poor rather than urban SMEs, which are heavily represented by Chinese Malaysians.

The most notable feature of the country's changing political–corporate-sector characteristics regards the aggressive foreign intervention displayed by Khazanah and its GLCs. This is due to the need to reduce crowding-out effects at home in combination with the need to produce strong performance for its GLCs, in which a large fraction of Malaysians has their savings invested (via GLICs such as the EPF and PNB). This latter feature distinguishes DPARs from SPARs – the other regime with the greatest capacity for public-private co-investment. Malaysia clearly illustrates that the *motivation* for DPARs to engage in aggressive corporate interventions increases as the ruling party's political standing weakens.

While this link may have originally been intended as a means for the ruling party to co-opt the support of ordinary Malaysians, it has also served to discipline the ruling party into prioritizing the financial interests of voter-investors. Chapter 7 offers additional evidence for this tight link between voter-investors and ruling party performance in the context of another DPAR – Singapore.

7 | Dominant Party Authoritarian Regime with a Strongly Dominant Ruling Party: Singapore

State-owned enterprises (SOEs) are integral to Singapore's political economy. Their origin and evolution stem from the ruling party's (the People's Action Party [PAP]) strategy to remain in power. The city-state's independence was racked with instability, throwing into question Singapore's very existence. Growth, via export-oriented industrialization, was pursued as the means by which to secure the nation's future. By successfully delivering on its early promises, the PAP established its legitimacy.

But the capacity to simultaneously sustain its mass appeal through growth while co-opting elite rivals has depended on the control of SOEs, or government-linked corporations (GLCs). At the beginning, GLCs enabled the PAP to attract investment in the absence of strong institutions while funneling capital to the state. These funds could be used toward public goods that would further boost growth, primarily through improvements to the efficient use of factors of production. GLCs could simultaneously provide the PAP with lucrative positions to co-opt elites. By retaining control over the corporate sector, the PAP could open the economy to trade and foreign investment while minimizing risks to the regime's stability that would arise from increasingly powerful private business owners (as emerged in South Korea and Taiwan).

Although the PAP has enjoyed uninterrupted government control since 1959, its popular support has varied over time. As shown in Figure 7.1, the PAP's seat share has remained relatively stable; its vote share, however, has been far more variable. The vote share matters with regard to the public's perception about the PAP's strength and legitimacy. As the PAP's vote share declines, challengers sense opportunity, forcing the PAP to respond to protect its hold on power.

While the PAP has maintained a strongly dominant hold on power, as indicated by its parliamentary seat share, I nevertheless expect the PAP's policies toward GLCs and sovereign wealth funds (SWFs) to display

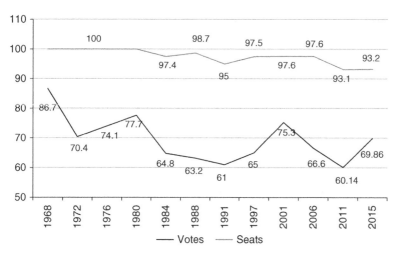

Figure 7.1 The PAP's vote and seat shares: 1968–2015.

some variation as a reflection of the ruling party's vote share. Specifically, a relatively weaker (stronger) ruling party is predicted to increase (reduce) state ownership for the largest firms while reducing (neglecting) crowding-out effects for small and medium-sized enterprises (SMEs) and engage in more (less) aggressive intervention primarily via a savings SWFs. As displayed in table 7.1, this chapter is broken into three parts corresponding to the PAP's varying electoral performance: (part A) 1984–96 when it first encountered threats to its political dominance, (part B) 1997–2011 when its dominance was restored, and (part C) 2011–15 when its dominance was threatened again. Before turning to part A, I review the origins of Singapore's GLCs and SWFs that emerged in the 1960s and 1970s.

The Origins of Singapore's GLCs and SWFs

Government-Linked Corporations

Singapore's GLCs came both from the handover of assets from the departing British following independence in 1967 and from the need to provide basic infrastructure, necessary to attract foreign investment and improve living conditions.[1] By acting as a substitute for the lack

---

[1] See Low (2006, 210–212) for a list of early GLCs and statutory boards. Also see Rodan (1989); Huff (1994); Worthington (2003); Tsui-Auch (2005); Yeung

Table 7.1 *Theoretical Expectations and Case Evidence*

Theoretical expectations	Case evidence	Case evidence
Relatively weaker ruling party	**Part A: 1984–96**	**Part C: 2011–15**
Transparency: lower	Heightened PAP vigilance about negative publicity; high corporate and SWF opacity relative to post-2001 period	Lack of enforcement for new corporate governance code; decline in press freedom
State ownership: higher for large firms; less crowding-out	Large firms remain heavily state owned; SMEs get more opportunities	Large firms remain state dominated; new initiatives to support SMEs
SWF: savings	Temasek becomes more dominant owner of GLCs	GIC engages in more large, long-term holdings
Investment behavior: more aggressive	Temasek invests overseas	Temasek and GIC adopt activist foreign investment strategies
Relatively stronger ruling party	**Part B: 1997–2010**	
Transparency: higher	Numerous improvements to corporate governance and SWF transparency	
State ownership: lower for large firms; more crowding-out	Consolidation in banking only; other sectors see decline in state ownership; few initiatives to aid SMEs	
SWF: savings	Temasek dominates	
Investment behavior: less aggressive	Temasek backtracks quickly on activist foreign investments	

of private entrepreneurs, GLCs helped to overcome investment risk, especially in areas deemed strategically important to national development. For example, the Economic Development Board (EDB) began operations with equity interest in seven manufacturing firms because "many of these projects would not have started if the EDB had not been prepared to share in the risk."[2] A conscious effort was made to ensure that they would be profit oriented, with civil servants monitoring them from the board but otherwise leaving managers to make decisions independently.[3] Consequently, they contributed capital to state coffers and became integral to the development and maintenance of the PAP's political dominance. Many state-controlled statutory boards – a variant of the GLC – were established to oversee and promote industrial investment (EDB), electricity (Public Utilities Board [PUB]), housing (Housing Development Board [HDB]), construction (Jurong Town Corporation [JTC]), communications (Singapore Telephone Board [STB]), and port operations (Port of Singapore Authority [PSA]).[4] The Development Bank of Singapore (DBS) was established in 1968 to take over the development finance section from the EDB. It helped to finance entrepreneurs who needed venture capital because the established banks had no experience outside trade financing and were reluctant to lend to new, untested firms.[5]

(2005); Cheng-Han et al. (2015). Formerly British assets included Sembawang naval dockyard (Sembawang Shipyard Pte, Ltd., established in 1968 as a commercial ship repairer), Keppel Harbour (Keppel Shipyard Pte, Ltd.), and the Royal Air Force Changi Air Base (site of Singapore's international airport managed by Changi Airport Group [Singapore] Pte, Ltd.). But the government soon expanded its involvement in the corporate sector beyond those bequeathed by the British. Other important GLCs that were established around this time include Chartered Industries Pte, Ltd. (1967), which was established to make ordnance for the Singapore Armed Forces; Singapore Shipbuilding & Engineering Pte, Ltd. (1968), now known as ST Marine Limited, which was established to support the Singapore Navy; and Neptune Orient Lines (1968), which was the national shipping company.

[2] Dhanabalan (2001), quoted in Yeung (2011).   [3] Yeung (2011).
[4] Statutory boards are legislated under individual acts of parliament that define their functions, scope, and powers; they are formed under various ministries and are accountable to them through parliament. GLCs are incorporated under the Companies Act and do not come under the direct purview of parliament. Both GLCs and statutory boards can form their own subsidiaries and associated companies.
[5] Lee Kuan Yew (2000, 77).

Many of the early companies were also joint ventures with foreign investors. For example, the Singapore Refining Company (1973), which provided the catalyst for the growth of the oil refining industry, was a joint venture with Caltex and British Petroleum.[6] The Petrochemical Corporation of Singapore (1977), which launched Singapore's entry into the petrochemicals industry, was a joint venture with Shell and a Japanese consortium.

The Singapore government was not unaware of the risks of relying on GLCs. Lee Kuan Yew wrote of his fear that the GLCs would become subsidized and loss-making nationalized corporations, as had happened in many new countries. However, given the lack of a domestic market, many GLCs were compelled to adhere to market disciplining forces from the start and to compete in a global market. "They [were] expected to yield proper economic returns ... SIA [Singapore Airlines], for instance, was told at the beginning that it was not flying the national flag for reasons of national pride. While it does play an important role in maintaining Singapore as a global hub, it has, and it knows it has, to survive against global competition."[7] If they were not profitable, they would be shut down.[8]

The state also had a vested interest in ensuring the continual growth and profitability of these GLCs so that their financial contributions to the state could be sustained; later this would extend to returns for ordinary Singaporean shareholders. As long as GLCs prospered and grew under the PAP government, the ruling party would be assured of its political legitimacy and popular support. Thus, once an enterprise that received assistance from the EDB became stable and profitable, it was corporatized via a public listing, at which time the government would sell off a portion of its shares but continue to hold a controlling stake. This would deepen market discipline of the firm, which would now be accountable to private investors while preserving the state's control.[9] The government's preference for GLCs to be publicly listed has persisted so as to ensure that the pursuit of efficiency and profitability is integrated into their operations.[10] In 2007, for example, only 18 percent of Temasek's

---

[6] Ramirez and Tan (2004).
[7] As recounted by Temasek Holdings Chairman Dhanabalan (2001) in Yeung (2011).
[8] Lee (2000, 87).   [9] Huat (2015).
[10] Sim, Thomson, and Yeong (2014); Ministry of Finance (2002).

assets were unlisted.[11] Like Malaysia, almost all large GLCs have been publicly listed, thus resembling the second tier of China's GLCs.[12]

Initially, civil servants were appointed to manage GLCs.[13] But soon the main method by which the government exercised control was through the appointment of top civil servants to GLC boards. They would be appointed by the Directorship and Consultancy Appointments Council (DCAC), which was responsible to a Coordinating Board, which, in turn, reported to the prime minister.[14] The DCAC consisted of leading ministers and civil servants.

Civil servants appointed to the boards of GLCs served a monitoring function but would not normally interfere in the management of the firm.[15] GLC boards would act as policy boards rather than serving a functional/managerial purpose,[16] a model that has largely endured to the present, though with Temasek acting on behalf of the state.

The PAP's control over the corporate sector not only generated financial contributions to the state but also prevented the emergence of assertive private capitalists, as in Taiwan and South Korea or in Malaysia prior to the Asian financial crisis. This was due, in part, to the PAP's conscious effort to contain and circumscribe the development of private capitalists as a matter of political strategy.[17] The pervasiveness of statutory boards and GLCs denied opportunities for private capitalists to develop sources of economic and political power autonomous of government oversight and control.

The SWFs: Temasek and GIC

The rapid growth of the GLCs prompted the establishment of Temasek Holdings on June 25, 1974. The equity invested in thirty-five companies by the EDB, and placed under the control of the Ministry of Finance, was transferred to it.[18] The rationale was to separate the Finance Ministry's budgetary and fiscal policy functions from its

---

[11] Temasek Holdings, Ltd. (2007).
[12] Unlisted GLCs, all owned by Temasek, include PSA International, Singapore Power, Surbana Corp, Wildlife Reserves Singapore, Singapore Technologies Telemedia, Mediacorp, and Pavilion Energy.
[13] Cheng-Han et al. (2015).   [14] Mauzy and Milne (2002, 29).
[15] Lee (1976). Because certain top civil servants sat on the boards of numerous GLCs, such interlocking directorates would permit control and coordination with government policies; see Ow (1976); and Pillai (1983).
[16] Pillai (1983, 116).   [17] Rodan (1989, 98).   [18] *Temasek Review*, 2009.

administration and management of large public enterprises.[19] Temasek would serve as a holding company to monitor and inform the minister for finance and the cabinet about the performance of these companies.

A former Temasek chairman, S. Dhanabalan, explained that "there was no supervisory function [for Temasek]. Each company had its own management who were accountable to its own board ... The Government's main interest was to make sure the right people were in charge and after that the management was to chart its own course."[20] However, state officials did insist on the capacity to veto any business proposals that were not aligned with the national interests.[21] GLCs were expected to operate as for-profit commercial entities on the same basis as private-sector companies; they did not receive any subsidies or preferential treatment from the government. The main advantage of government ownership was the positive signal it sent to the markets.[22] A GLC manager explained that "[b]eing linked to the Government is of course useful. It gives the company credibility and nobody will think you are a fly-by-night operation. But the company has to justify itself and earn its keep by marketing right products at the right time as no favors are given or expected."[23]

Unlike Temasek, which was focused on domestic investments, the Government Investment Corporation (GIC) has focused on foreign markets. It was created in 1981 to manage the surplus funds generated by the government and the "excess" reserves of the central bank (the Monetary Authority of Singapore [MAS]). The surplus funds came from each year's annual budget surplus and the high rates of compulsory social security savings of every wage earner in the Central Provident Fund (CPF). The existing practice of buying foreign government bonds with very low but secure interest was, according to the first finance minister, Goh Keng Swee, too conservative for an economy undergoing the kind of rapid growth that Singapore was experiencing.[24] It was set up at a time when the state was facing increasing financial commitments as part of its restructuring of industry and the economy, creating a need to earn higher returns on its reserves.[25] In 2006, however, Lee Kuan Yew stated that the GIC was

[19] Elson (2008).   [20] *The Straits Times,* June 25, 1999.   [21] Huat (2015).
[22] Ramirez and Tan (2004).   [23] Quoted in Low (1991, 65).   [24] Huat (2015).
[25] Rodan (1989, 153).

created "to protect the value of our savings and earn a fair return on capital."[26]

Part A: 1984–97, Relatively Weaker Ruling Party

I begin this section with an overview of the emerging threat to the PAP's political dominance in the early to middle 1980s. The reaction was to announce a new privatization drive, as well as to bolster support for SMEs via a variety of new policy initiatives. These would simultaneously reduce the crowding-out effects of the state sector in order to create more opportunities for private business while also generating a vested interest in the success of GLCs among Singaporeans via the sale of shares to a large swath of the electorate. The level of transparency in the state-owned corporate sector was not high to begin with, so it is not clear that this became worse. However, it is clear that improvements to the disclosure of information were not forthcoming – these would have to wait until after the Asian financial crisis, which coincides with a turnaround in the PAP's electoral strength. This will be discussed in part B. Finally, Temasek led a new regionalization initiative with its activist behavior increasing as it sought new growth opportunities beyond Singapore's shores.

The PAP's Weakening Dominance

A by-election held in 1981 drastically altered the perception of the electability of opposition parties when the head of the Working Party, J. B. Jeyeratnam, won a seat. In the 1984 general election, Jeyeratnam was reelected along with another opposition candidate from the Singapore Democratic Party. The election also registered a dramatic decline in the PAP's vote share, which fell from 77.66 percent in the 1980 election to 64.83 percent but did not translate into significant gains in seats by the opposition because of the "first-past-the-post" electoral system. In the 1991 election, opposition candidates made further gains by winning four seats – their best performance prior to the 2011 election. The downward swing in the PAP's vote share was finally arrested in the 1997 election when only two opposition members were elected.

---

[26] Quoted in Clark and Monk (2010, 438).

Tightening Information Controls

In response to the 1984 election results, the PAP began tweaking the electoral rules with changes designed to bolster the PAP's electoral dominance.[27] These rules changes were supplemented with additional devices to ensure the PAP's electoral dominance, such as intimidation of opposition candidates, censorship of the media, and even blatant threats to the electorate. From the mid-1980s, "the legal system became pivotal to the political persecution of the PAP's most formidable opponents and to the intimidation of the international and independent media."[28] Meanwhile, a wide range of existing and new laws and regulations covering licenses and permits for public rallies, the dissemination of political materials, and other matters were applied to further impair the activities of political opponents. Case observes that "political activism in Singapore [risked] blacklisting, shunning, lawsuits, tax investigations, lost business opportunities, and detention without trial."[29] These threats were amplified in the buildup to the 1997 election, when the electorate "were given a stark choice: return government candidates and benefit from a range of expensive new public programs, or have this withheld or delayed in retaliation for electing PAP opponents ... Threats by Goh concerning multimillion dollar housing upgrading program caused special concern. Given that around 86 percent of Singaporeans live in government built flats, the electorate is highly vulnerable to such intimidation. The announcement of a new system of vote counting enabling the government to ascertain voting preferences down to precinct levels of 5,000 voters reinforced the threat."[30]

Given the importance of GLCs to the PAP's political control, sensitivities about the disclosure of certain information are especially acute when the PAP's political position is threatened. Mirroring the political clampdown in response to the decline in the PAP's vote share, a hard line was taken with regard to the disclosure of sensitive economic information about the state sector. For example, in June 1991, the *Business Times* reported official "flash estimates" of economic growth

---

[27] The electoral rules changes included the introduction of nonconstituency members of parliament (NCMP) in 1984, the establishment of group representation constituencies (GRC) in 1988, and the creation of nominated members of parliament (NMP) in 1991. Jeyaretnam (1989); Thio (1997); Chua (1995, 176); Haggard and Kaufman (1992).
[28] Rodan (2008).   [29] Case (2002, 89).   [30] Rodan (1989, 179).

in April and May of that year failing to meet the first-quarter rate of 5.1 percent. While the reporting of such seemingly harmless information revealed a possible gap in the government's information controls, PAP elites used the opportunity to illustrate how seriously they regarded such leaks. This led to a MAS official, the editor and a journalist from the *Business Times*, and two economists from a stock-brokering firm to be found guilty of violating the Official Secrets Act and fined.[31] The episode also sent a clear warning to those who might consider revealing sensitive government information, especially when the PAP's political opponents were making electoral gains, as was then the case.

The implication for corporate transparency, especially in relation to GLCs, is that information has remained withheld from public scrutiny. As Linda Low remarked with regard to GLCs, "working on the subject is fraught with lack of transparency, information and statistics until sometime in the early 2000s."[32] It is therefore unsurprising that David Mason, a partner in an international accounting firm in Singapore for fourteen years, said in 1999 that "Singapore has the reputation of being one of the worst places in Asia for corporate disclosures, despite its overall good record on governance rules."[33]

Reducing Crowding-Out Effects

By 1983, the state had directly invested in fifty-eight companies, which, in turn, held ownership stakes in 490 Singaporean firms.[34] This aggressive expansion encroached on SMEs, alienating the local business community and contributed to declining popular support, as witnessed by the PAP's most dramatic fall in its vote share in history, from 77.7 percent in 1980 to 64.8 percent.

[31] Seow (1998, 218). The MAS official was the economics director, Tharman Shanmugaratnam. The editor and journalist were Patrick Daniel and Kenneth James, respectively. The two economists from stock-brokering firm Crosby Securities were Manu Bhaskaran and Raymond Foo.
[32] Low (2006, 208).   [33] Quoted in Rodan (2004, 57).
[34] Yeung (2011); Huff (1995, 1428). In addition to Temasek, there were three other state-owned holding companies, including Sheng-Li Holdings (restructured into Singapore Technologies in 1989), MinCom Holdings, and MND Holdings (merged into Temasek Holdings in 1998). Today, only Temasek continues to operate as a state-owned holding company.

In 1984, signs of a slowing economy were evident, but a booming construction industry bolstered the overall numbers. Singapore's first recession since 1959 occurred in 1985. Although negative economic growth was not registered until the second quarter of 1985, SMEs were already reeling in the latter half of 1984, contributing to the loss of electoral support in the December 22 election. As mentioned earlier, the PAP could no longer afford to ignore the local business community, which accounted for over 30 percent of Singapore's employment by the mid-1980s.[35]

The government sprang into action with a privatization initiative, announced by Tony Tan, then finance minister, in parliament on March 8, 1985.[36] Its main purpose was to allow the private sector to play a greater role in the Singapore economy and to promote the corporatization of GLCs.[37]

Efforts to reorient the economy toward the local private sector were reinforced by an Economic Committee created in response to the recession and headed by Lee Hsien Loong.[38] It was comprised of numerous subcommittees, including one for local business. It highlighted that GLCs were given preferential treatment, competed directly with the private sector, and denied it opportunities to expand. It recommended privatization of GLCs in which local business had the potential to expand and to refrain from forming new GLCs. The subcommittees on entrepreneurship and manufacturing also concluded that privatization would create more opportunities for local business and that the government should "confine itself to providing general incentives or facilities."[39]

This reorienting of economic policy in the wake of the 1984 election and 1985 recession coincided with a PAP leadership transition already underway since the start of the decade, yielding a second generation of more technocratic leaders culminating in Goh Chok Tong becoming prime minister in 1990. Goh had some experience in business (with the GLC Neptune Orient Line), unlike most of the first-generation leadership. He also favored more participation of civil society, which would presumably include the local private sector.[40]

---

[35] Harvie and Lee (2002).
[36] Following this announcement, the government set up the Public Sector Divestment Committee in 1986 to prepare guidelines for privatizing GLCs.
[37] Yeung (2011); Milne (1991).   [38] Singapore (1986)
[39] Singapore (1986, vii).   [40] Low (1998, 60–64).

In the drafting of the 1991 Strategic Economic Plan, the private sector was granted the opportunity to participate.[41] Detailed surveys and studies of a number of economic clusters further bolstered the conclusion that supporting industries were necessary for the creation of agglomeration economies, thus providing a new impetus for the development of local firms. Complementing this recommendation was the recognition of the increasing size of a number of local private firms that had grown as supporting industries or service providers. This led to the announcement of the Promising Local Enterprise (PLE) Program in 1995, which sought to nurture strong local enterprises into multinational corporations. The aim was to produce 100 PLEs with at least SGD100 billion sales turnover by 2005.[42]

Despite these initiatives, crowding-out effects remained a serious problem. International Monetary Fund (IMF) economists analyzed a sample of listed manufacturing firms and found that GLCs had median assets of SGD944 million, whereas non-GLCs had median assets of SGD0.71 million, illustrating that GLCs were predominantly large firms, granting them economies of scale and scope.[43] Crowding-out effects were most clearly evident from the ratio of investment over fixed assets – the median for GLCs was 0.1, whereas the median for non-GLCs was 0.04. When looking across fourteen industries, GLCs consistently outperformed non-GLCs.

More Active Foreign Investment

In response to its weakening political dominance, I predict that the ruling party will engage in more activist corporate interventions, which is observed most clearly starting in the 1990s. Complementing the domestic initiatives to reduce crowding-out effects was an effort to regionalize the Singapore economy more generally, with Temasek-linked GLCs playing a leading role. This was initially pursued via the development of industrial estate parks. The creation of industrial estates was an attempt to offer Singapore-like facilities to both domestic and foreign companies looking to invest in developing Asian

[41] Strategic Economic Plan, Singapore, Ministry of Trade and Industry (1991).
[42] Low (2001).
[43] The sample included seventeen listed GLCs and ninety-two listed non-GLCs for 1994–98. The manufacturing industry was selected because of the high number of GLCs. Ramirez and Tan (2004).

markets but concerned about the poor investment climate (i.e., weak institutions). The Singapore government, in collaboration with a consortium of Singapore-based and foreign firms, invested in the infrastructure and management of these estates. They were constructed in Indonesia (Batam in 1991 and Bintan in 1993), China (Suzhou and Wuxi both in 1994), India (Bangalore in 1994), and Vietnam (1996). SembCorp, a Temasek-owned GLC, was responsible for the planning, marketing, and management of the parks.

In addition to creating more opportunities for local private business, the regionalization initiative was also initiated to tap into the growth potential of other countries following the collapse of the Soviet Union. Singapore's small size placed an upper limit on the growth potential of large domestic businesses; to continue to grow, GLCs would need to go abroad. Additional overseas investments were initiated by Temasek-linked companies in the early to middle 1990s, notably by Singtel into the Philippines, Thailand, and Norway.[44]

Partial Privatization and the Prevalence of State Ownership

As the ruling party's dominance declines, I expect it to react by tightening controls over the largest GLCs. This is reflected in the fact that the total number of GLCs actually increased almost twofold from 1985 (361) through 1994 (720) despite the privatization initiative following Tony Tan's announcement in 1985.[45] The increase was due, in part, to GLCs taking on a number of new functions, such as the regionalization policy and the effort to complement foreign investment in certain technology and capital-intensive sectors (e.g., semiconductor fabrication).[46] The state's role as a catalyst in such high-technology areas was considered necessary to instill multinational corporation (MNC) confidence. Local enterprises adopted by MNCs and GLCs could also benefit through a Local Industry Upgrading Program initiated in 1986 to improve their operational efficiency, introduce new processes, and jointly develop products.

To the extent that privatizations did occur, they were usually partial. For example, the privatization of Singapore Telecommunications, Ltd.

---

[44] Low (2006, 229–32).
[45] Low (1998, 161). A modest decline occurred in 1996 (to 592).
[46] See Haggard and Low (2001) for details; also see McKendrick et al. (2000).

(Singtel) in 1993 left the government with a controlling bloc of shares – 78.2 percent of equity in the case of Singtel – with the remainder fragmented among small holders. Retaining government control not only allowed the political elite to continue to exercise control over major segments of the economy, but it also provided opportunities for senior members of the PAP to advance their careers. Worthington, for example, shows in considerable detail that the GLC sector is very clearly under the control of the top political leadership.[47] The boards of directors and management were, until the mid-1990s, appointed by the DCAC under the Ministry of Finance, and appointments were drawn heavily from the civil service. Retired politicians and civil servants would enter as consultants or in nonexecutive positions to strengthen government-business ties, resulting in complex interlocking directorships.

Politically, privatization and corporatization would serve three purposes. First, they would reduce the crowding-out effect of GLCs, thereby creating more opportunities for private business. The Singapore state, via Temasek, had acquired a reputation as "an all-pervasive government which cannot stay away when there is profit to be made."[48] Temasek's ownership stakes in nearly 500 firms by the early 1980s even extended to GLCs that went into tourism as well as the retailing of televisions and VCRs.[49]

Second, privatization would occur via the issuing of shares, often at a discount, to a large swath of the electorate, thereby generating a vested interest in the success and growth of GLCs among Singaporeans. A 1986 investment scheme, for example, enabled a percentage of Singaporeans' retirement savings to be invested in "trustee stocks," which were shares listed on the Singapore Exchange that were approved by the Central Provident Fund board.[50] While a Public Sector Divestment Committee issued a report in 1987 that identified over 500 companies and forty statutory boards to be divested over a ten-year period,[51] its implementation was "slow and cautious, suggesting the government's reluctance to surrender complete control,"[52] especially in companies managing critical resources and pursuing public policy objectives.

[47] Worthington (2003).
[48] Quote from Dhanabalan, former chairman of Temasek, as quoted in Huat (2015).
[49] Yeung (2004, 46).   [50] Mauzy and Milne (2002, 85).   [51] Sam (2010).
[52] Low (1993, 176).

Finally, corporatization of GLCs presented an opportunity to further enhance growth and financial contributions to the state by strengthening their profit-oriented incentives via a public listing, but without relinquishing state control. This initially occurred via the separation of regulatory functions and business activity among former statutory boards. For example, Singapore Telecom (SingTel) was hived off from the Telecommunication Authority of Singapore (TAS) and publicly listed in 1993. The TAS later formed part of the Infocomm Development Authority of Singapore, a regulator of information technology and telephony.[53] Likewise, the regulatory role of the Port Singapore Authority was transferred to the Maritime Authority of Singapore, while the business side was incorporated and publicly listed as PSA Corporation in October 1997.[54]

Although economic performance came at the cost of democratic processes, Singaporeans have indicated a willingness to forgo democratic reforms in favor of economic development. As reported by the Asian Barometer Survey, economic development was regarded as "definitely or somewhat more important" than democracy by 64.6 percent of the population in 2006 and by 64.5 percent in 2012. One can only surmise that this ratio would have been even higher when the city-state was at a lower level of development. By bolstering the PAP's commitment to growth-oriented policies, corporatization and privatization would strengthen the PAP's legitimacy in the eyes of Singaporeans, even if it came at the cost of democratic processes.

Part A Conclusion

Following the PAP's formative years in which it established and consolidated its political supremacy, the 1980s revealed that it was vulnerable to political opponents. Faced with weakening political dominance, my argument predicts a reduction in the transparency of the state sector, efforts to reduce crowding-out effects while maintaining state control of the largest firms, and state intervention becoming more assertive.

---

[53] Yeung (2011).
[54] PSA International, established in 2003, is the unlisted holding company of PSA Corporation.

In response to the rising threat of political opponents in the 1984 election, the PAP's reaction was swift. A new initiative that emphasized greater participation of private capital in the economy was announced. Simultaneously, GLCs would be privatized and corporatized – an effective method for bolstering public support for the PAP's economic policies. However, the state would retain a controlling stake. Transparency of GLCs remained low, and the state demonstrated its willingness to attack those who revealed sensitive information about them, mirroring its repressive actions against political opponents and critics more generally. Finally, the state engaged in greater activism with rising investments into foreign markets, both through industrial estates and via direct foreign acquisitions through Temasek-linked companies. While these reactions by the PAP to threats to its political dominance match the theoretical predictions, a clearer sense of the relative magnitude of its response can be gleaned from its reactions when its political dominance was restored.

Part B: Relatively Stronger Ruling Party, 1997–2011

The January 2, 1997, general election yielded an increase of 4 percent of the popular vote (from 61 to 65 percent) and four parliamentary seats for the PAP (resulting in eighty-one of eighty-three contested seats) compared with the 1991 election. The November 3, 2001, elections further strengthened the PAP's support with a popular vote of 75.3 percent – its best result since 1980 – in addition to winning eighty-two of the eighty-four contested seats.

I begin this section with a discussion of how the restoration of the PAP's political dominance translated into political liberalization, as well as relaxation of the tight controls governing information availability with regard to GLCs and SWFs. I then survey changes to the state's ownership of GLCs across time and industries – the evidence reveals that the number of large enterprises in which the state is a significant owner declined from before the crisis to after, which is consistent with my argument. I then turn to an examination of the investment activism displayed by Temasek and offer a direct comparison with that displayed by Khazanah as they both entered the banking and telecommunications industries in Indonesia. The cases clearly demonstrate that Temasek engaged in less activist behavior than

Khazanah, especially when the Malaysian ruling party faced serious political challenges around the time of the 2008 election.

Strengthening Transparency

Given the tight links between the government and the corporate sector, it is useful to start with changes to transparency governing the overall political arena before proceeding to corporate and SWF transparency.

Political Transparency

Corruption indicators offer one lens through which to gauge the level of transparency in a country. Generally speaking, high levels of corruption tend to emerge in places with low levels of transparency. Figure 7.2 shows changes to Singapore's Corruption Perception Index (CPI) score since the index was started. Between 1998 and 2010, the time during which the PAP retained its strongly dominant position as indicated by its total vote share, Singapore's CPI score remained relatively high. In 2011 – the election which yielded the PAP's lowest share of the popular vote since 1965 – Singapore's CPI score quickly dropped to its lowest level since the index was first measured.

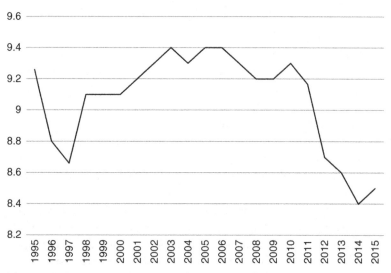

Figure 7.2 Singapore's Corruption Perception Index score, 1995–2015.
Source: Transparency International.

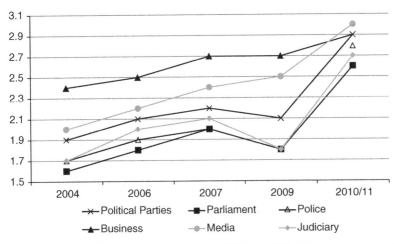

Figure 7.3 Global Corruption Barometer, 2004 to 2010–11 (1 = not corrupt; 5 = very corrupt).
Sources: Global Corruption Barometer 2004–7, 2009–10, and 2013.

Around this time, several high-profile corruption cases were reported that are emblematic of the wider problems ripping through the political establishment. For example, a Corrupt Practices Investigation Bureau (CPIB) official was reported as stealing $1.76 million from a CPIB bank account between 2008 and 2013. Another scandal involved a Ministry of Foreign Affairs official stealing $89,000 by misstating the expenses incurred for visiting foreign delegations in 2013.[55]

It is helpful, however, to look beneath these aggregate numbers to gauge the level of perceived corruption for individual institutions, as with the Global Corruption Barometer (GCB) in Figure 7.3. Three points are of interest. First, the overall level of corruption is lower than that for Malaysia's institutions. The range for Singapore extends from 1.5 to 3 throughout the entire sample; Malaysia's range spans 2.4 to 4.1. Second, business is regarded as engaging in the highest levels of corruption in Singapore, followed by the media, except for 2010–11; in Malaysia, the police and then the political parties were regarded as the most corrupt. Third, there is a sharpened increase in the perceived level of corruption between 2009 and 2010–11 that corresponds to the more modest decline in the overall CPI score but may foretell the subsequent

[55] *Straits Times*, February 17, 2014.

dramatic decline. Notably, political parties, parliament, and the judiciary displayed the largest increases according to the GCB survey between 2009 and 2010–11. It is also noteworthy that Singapore was not included in the 2013 report even though Malaysia was included.

To put the GCB figures in a broader perspective, Prime Minister Lee Hsien Loong initiated several policy changes that enhanced freedom of speech on taking office in 2004. For example, rules governing public speeches and demonstrations at Speakers' Corner were loosened, and indoor political activities were permitted without first acquiring a police permit. In 2008, outdoor political demonstrations were permitted at Speakers' Corner, and in 2009 the ban on political films and videos before elections was lifted. Meanwhile, websites sprouted up permitting expanded opportunities for dissenting and critical opinions. Additionally, changes were implemented that would grant greater opportunities for political opponents to gain representation, including the number of nonconstituency members of parliament, which was increased from six to nine; the number of single-member constituencies was increased from nine to twelve, and the number of GRCs was reduced. But a reversal of these liberalizing reforms occurred following the disastrous 2011 election, which will be discussed in the next section.

Corporate and SWF Transparency
In the wake of the Asian financial crisis, which coincided with strong performance for the PAP in the 1997 election, the ruling elite recognized that there was an image problem for the GLCs. Lee Hsien Loong observed that "regulators, political leaders, the press and local constituents tend to perceive the GLC to be Singapore Government–controlled, operating on an agenda that overrides normal commercial considerations."[56] This perception was fueled, in part, by what Ellis has described as "a merry-go-round of connected interests."[57] Worthington corroborated this impression with systematic, detailed information about these connections.[58] In his analysis of board members of statutory boards and GLCs for 1998, he found that 1.8 percent (twenty-two of 1,235 people) held between twenty-one and forty-four board appointments on statutory boards, and 29.7 percent held five or more board appointments.

[56] Ibid.   [57] *Weekend Australian,* July 28–29, 2001.   [58] Worthington (2003).

Additionally, 59.9 percent of board positions were filled by public-sector appointees – individuals from the Civil Service were the most heavily represented (13.9 percent of the total); members of parliament constituted 5.4 percent. For GLCs, 74 percent of board appointments were from the public sector and predominantly from the higher levels of the Civil Service and statutory boards. However, the density of cross-directorships for GLCs was lower than that for statutory boards, with nine directorships being the highest number of board positions for a single individual. Even as Temasek restructured in response to the Committee on Singapore's Competitiveness Report, it continued to appoint ex-civil servants to GLC boards.[59] This problem was discussed, but not addressed, by the Corporate Governance Committee in 2003: "after deliberating long and hard, the committee decided against any upper limit on directorships."[60] The perception that GLCs lacked independence from the Singapore government created particular problems when they attempted to invest overseas. Failed bids in Hong Kong, Malaysia, New Zealand, and Australia were all due, in part, to concerns about political influence over GLC affairs.[61]

The first initiative promoting greater corporate transparency following the onset of the 1997 crisis was with regard to information about the extent of banks' nonperforming loans. In response to market nervousness, Lee Hsien Loong remarked, "[i]n the absence of information, in times of uncertainty investors fear the worst and tend to overreact. This penalizes sound, well-managed institutions together with weaker institutions facing real problems, and can undermine the financial system."[62] Singapore banks' shares dropped just on the rumor that a lot of money was lost in Indonesia.[63] A Committee on Banking Disclosure was appointed and chaired by Lee Hsien Loong, chairman

[59] *Business Times*, January 4, 2000; Singapore's Competitiveness Report (1998).
[60] *Australian*, January 30, 2003. The chair of the committee, Koh Boon Hwee, was on at least twenty-three directorships himself. Worthington (2003) identifies Koh Boon Hwee as holding twenty director positions on statutory boards and three on GLCs, but Ellis, writing for the *Australian*, identifies him as having forty-seven total directorships.
[61] Singtel failed in its bids in Hong Kong (2001) and Malaysia (2000), Singapore Airlines failed to take a controlling stake in Air New Zealand (1999), and SingTel faced considerable criticism in its takeover bid for Optus Communications in Australia (2001).
[62] Quoted in Rodan (2004, 58).   [63] Rodan (2004, 58–59).

of MAS from January 1998 to August 2004.[64] Its Report on Banking
Disclosure was published in May 1998 with recommendations aimed
at making Singaporean banks' standard of disclosure equivalent to
those of developed countries. The government subsequently accepted
all the committee's recommendations. In 1999, Lee Hsien Loong
declared that "MAS will ensure that our own disclosure and reporting
requirements meet international best practice."[65]

Under Lee Hsien Loong's tenure as MAS chairman, three other
committees soon followed with additional recommendations to
improve corporate disclosures, including the Corporate Governance
Committee (CGC), the Disclosure and Accounting Standards
Committee (DASC), and the Company Legislation and Regulatory
Framework Committee (CLRFC). All the recommendations made by
these committees were accepted by the government starting
in October 2002 and occurring only after the PAP's strong performance in the November 2001 election.[66]

Additionally, the MAS announced in 2002 that (1) issuers of stocks
and bonds must disclose all information that is "reasonably required"
for investors to make informed decisions,[67] (2) all Singaporean banks
would be required to change auditors every five years,[68] and (3) it
would take part in the Financial Sector Assessment Program run by
the IMF and World Bank in order to align it more closely with international best practice.[69]

Temasek also implemented transparency reforms in response to
three different pressures. First, the effort to regionalize GLCs would

---

[64] Lee Hsien Loong became minister of finance from November 2001, a position he
held until December 2007; he was also deputy prime minister
from November 1990 to August 2004 at which time he became prime minister.
[65] Quoted in Rodan (2004, 59).
[66] The CGC's report, published in April 2001, recommended improved disclosure
regarding the composition and remuneration of boards of directors, as well as
auditing procedures and communications with shareholders. However,
adherence to the new code was not mandatory. The DASC's report was released
in late 2001. It stipulated that listed companies should report quarterly results
instead of biannual results, in addition to new regulations to ensure the
independence of auditors, improvements to accounting standards, and ongoing
reviews to strengthen and promote existing corporate governance
arrangements. The CLRFC's report, released in October 2001, primarily
focused on reducing companies' legal compliance costs.
[67] *Business Times*, May 24, 2002.
[68] *Asia Wall Street Journal*, March 14, 2002.   [69] *Business Times*, May 3. 2002.

require allaying foreign concerns about government intervention in corporate affairs, which was magnified by Ho Ching, wife of Lee Hsien Loong, taking over Temasek in 2002.[70] Second, Standard & Poor's published an unsolicited study on Singapore's GLCs, citing the lack of transparency in corporate credit and pointing out that many GLCs were paying a higher bank loan interest rate than that which would occur with a more robust rating exercise.[71] The report also noted that "the financial profile of Temasek is, as with its business profile ... difficult to identify with certainty."[72] Third, the US-Singapore Free Trade Agreement (FTA) signed on May 6, 2003, committed Singapore to "at least annually mak[ing] public a consolidated report that covers, for each entity, the percentage of shares and percentage of voting rights that Singapore and its government enterprises cumulatively own and the name and government title of any government official serving as an officer or a member of the board of directors." Before the signing of the FTA, such information had not been made public.[73]

Lee Hsien Loong became prime minister in August 2004, after which Temasek released for the first time its financial performance and corporate governance structure through the "Temasek Review" in October (its equivalent of an annual report). Officially, Temasek claimed that the release of the information was to allow the company to obtain a credit rating so as to institutionalize its role as a long-term shareholder and an active investor.[74] While the disclosure was an obvious improvement, only the major companies in Temasek's portfolio with direct ownership ties were identified. The compensation of key directors and executives was not disclosed, nor were its numerous indirectly held ownership stakes. Eva Ho, Temasek's director of corporate communications, explained that total transparency is neither possible nor desirable "given the commercial confidentiality and market sensitivities which any commercial company would need to observe."[75]

A similar justification has been used for GIC's opacity. Lee Hsien Loong, who was deputy chairman of the GIC, argued that publishing details about Singapore's reserves would potentially enable currency

---

[70] Haggard and Low (2001) provide some details about her career.
[71] Standard & Poor's 2001.   [72] *Asia Wall Street Journal*, December 26, 2001.
[73] Khanna (2004).   [74] Sam (2010).   [75] *The Straits Times*, March 30, 2004.

speculators to attack the Singapore dollar.[76] GIC Chairman Lee Kuan Yew further argued that "[w]e are a special investment fund. The ultimate shareholders are the electorate. It is not in the people's interest, in the nation's interest, to detail our assets and their yearly returns."[77] But to allay growing concerns about the GIC achieving adequate returns on its investments and that CPF money was used for GIC's offshore ventures, in August 2001 it published an unprecedented amount of information about its successes and failures as well as a list of the individuals on its board.[78] Nevertheless, the GIC continues to forgo routine external reviews, and it only reports to its board, which, until 2011, was chaired by Lee Kuan Yew. Temasek reports to the finance minister and a small parliamentary budget committee.

To further counter concerns about government intervention in the management of GLCs, the government has repeatedly argued that Temasek makes its own investment decisions without government interference. Former Minister for Finance Goh Keng Swee explained: "there is a clear separation of powers of ownership and authority of management. Neither the supervising ministries nor the Boards of Directors can know more of the Government-Linked Companies' business matters than the managers themselves."[79] This independence was enhanced when the DCAC relinquished its responsibility for nominating board members to Temasek's firms in the mid-1990s.[80] Following the debacle with Temasek's investment in Shin Corporation of Thailand in 2006, Second Minister for Finance Tharman Shanmugaratnam explained to parliament that the government chose not to intervene because it was not the government's job to do so.[81] Temasek's board retains the discretion to decide on these types of issues, which, according to Ho Ching, are based on financial returns. Similar arguments were made in front of the House Financial Services Committee in the United States in March 2008, where Temasek Executive Director Claude Israel argued that the commercial focus of Singaporean GLCs was manifested through their compliance with company law like any private corporation and their freedom to follow

---

[76] Rodan (2004, 64).   [77] *Asia Wall Street Journal*, April 26, 2001.
[78] See Rodan (2004, 64–65).   [79] Goh (1995, 46).
[80] This was in response to a rift between then Prime Minister Goh Chok Tong and Lee Kwan Yew and his son, Lee Hsien Loong. See www.newmandala.org/splits-in-the-singapore-elite/ (accessed December 16, 2016).
[81] Sam (2010).

human resource policies and remuneration systems that differ from the civil service.

As further evidence of its independence from government influence, Temasek implemented an internal board and an international panel of about a dozen individuals with diverse management backgrounds and industrial experience from the United States, the United Kingdom, Japan, China, and India. The international panel helps to allay foreign perceptions of excessive government influence on Temasek's management and strengthens its claim that it is commercially and independently run. For example, William J. McDonough, a respected former New York Fed Governor, sat on Temasek's international panel. He played a key role in dealing with Washington during Temasek's purchase of Merrill Lynch stock, worth US$4.4 billion, in December 2007. This impression was bolstered by work comparing data from seventeen Singaporean GLCs and ninety-two private enterprises in a 2004 study by IMF economists that concluded that GLCs competed on a level playing field as far as financing is concerned.[82]

GLCs: A Modest Reduction

My argument predicts a modest decline in state ownership of the largest firms as the ruling party's electoral strength rises because the ruling party does not face pressure to amplify its control over the economy's vital resources to bolster regime stability. However, assessing whether state ownership changed is complicated by the lack of consistent measures of the total size of GLCs.[83] The challenge with obtaining accurate estimates is due, in part, to the lack of information about the extent of the government's shareholdings.[84] For example, Temasek only reports firms in which it has a direct ownership stake.

Hence an important limitation of the existing literature is that it fails to clearly identify changes to Temasek or GLCs over time because they do not reveal second-tier companies. To overcome this problem, it is necessary to start with individual firm's owners and work up to ultimate owners. Figure 7.4 presents the results of this exercise, showing the proportion of state-owned firms with respect to the total number of

---

[82] Ramirez and Tan (2004)
[83] See Peebles and Wilson (2002) for a discussion of this issue.
[84] A related issue is consistency with regard to the ownership level that differentiates a GLC from a non-GLC.

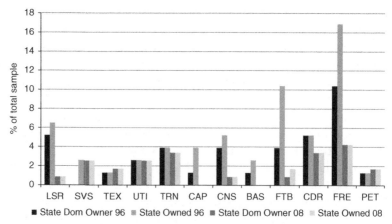

Figure 7.4 Singapore's state ownership by industry, 1996 and 2008.
Note: State Dom Owner 96 and *State Dom Owner 08* indicate firms for which the state was the dominant owner for each year. *State Owned 96* and *State Owned 08* indicate firms for which the state was a minority or nondominant owner for each year. LSR = leisure; SVS = services; TEX = textiles; UTI = utilities; TRN = transportation; CAP = capital goods; CNS = construction; BAS = basic industry; FTB = food and tobacco; CDR = consumer durables; FRE = finance and real estate; PET = petroleum. Industry categories are based on those identified in Campbell (1996).

publicly listed firms for which ultimate ownership could be identified in 1996 and 2008 based on a sample of the 200 largest publicly listed firms in each year.

The results suggest that the state has retreated from its ownership of the largest 200 listed corporations in 1996. This is consistent with an initiative launched in the wake of the Asian financial crisis to rationalize the GLC sector, as articulated in the Report of the Committee on Singapore's Competitiveness (CSC), released in November 1998. Temasek itself was restructured in 1999 to develop more competitive enterprises, leading to the adoption of a number of supervisory changes with regard to the composition of boards and the tenure of directors at any one company, including the separation of the CEO and chairman appointments, more frequent rotation of directors, and specifying corporate performance benchmarks.[85] The aim with the appointments of

[85] Low (2001)

directors was that they should be made so as to avoid the emergence of cliques with control over major groups of GLCs.[86]

However, to assess the scope of change in the GLC sector, it is necessary to examine the details behind these numbers. The evidence indicates that GLCs would either decline in size and no longer appear among the largest 200 listed firms, or they would be merged, yielding larger, more dominant enterprises that would further consolidate the state's control over the corporate sector. For example, the decline in the proportion of GLCs in the food and tobacco (FTB), construction (CNS), capital goods (CAP), and consumer durables (CDR) industries was primarily due to declines in the revenue of these firms, forcing them out of the top 200 by market capitalization in 2008.[87] With regard to the manufacturing-related industries, including consumer durables (electronics), basic industry (e.g., steel), and capital goods (precision and transport engineering), these firms faced rising challenges from other emerging economies with cheaper employment costs that could capitalize on the slowdown in international demand for electronics components following the collapse of the tech sector in the United States. This was compounded by Singapore's declining support for manufacturing-related firms as the PAP shifted toward a greater emphasis on services-related industries. For example, Singapore Technologies Industrial Corporation and Sembawang Corporation were merged in October 1998 to become SembCorp Industries (SCI),[88] which aimed to be a leader in infrastructure, marine engineering, information, and lifestyle. EDB Chairman Philip Yeo was SCI's first chairman. The president of Singapore Technologies Pte, Ltd., Ho Ching, who was Yeo's deputy in EDB, was also his deputy in SCI.[89] Several GLCs in consumer durables also underwent consolidation, such as Keppel Marine, Keppel FELS, and Keppel Singmarine, which merged to form Keppel Offshore and Marine.

Market forces also contributed to declines in the size of GLCs in the construction, food and tobacco, and leisure industries. Although the construction industry played a huge role in the development of Singapore's physical infrastructure, it underwent a major slowdown. For example, in 1999 it contributed to 9 percent of gross domestic

---

[86] Worthington (2003).   [87] Cahyadi et al. (2004).
[88] *Straits Times*, June 2, 1998.
[89] *Business Times* and *Straits Times*, February 3, 1999.

product (GDP), whereas in 2003 this fell to only 5.3 percent. The decline is partly due to negative growth in labor productivity as well as an overdependence on foreign workers that caused slow progress in improving skills and other social problems. The food and tobacco industry experienced a longer-term decline, falling from 4 percent of Singapore's nonoil exports in 1976 to 1.3 percent in 2003. The sudden fall in the number of GLCs in this industry is associated with a decline in the relative market value of these firms between 1996 and 2008, with the state holding minority ownership positions in many of these firms (e.g., Khong Guan Flour Milling, FHTK Holdings, and ABR Holdings). Similar to the food and tobacco industry, the leisure (tourism) industry's contribution to GDP fell over time, from 12.4 percent in 1996 to 8.9 percent in 2008.[90] Consequently, several firms fell out of the top 200, while a few were bought by foreign companies or merged with other firms.

However, the decline in the number of GLCs in the financial services sector, particularly banking, was primarily due to government-led consolidation. In the wake of the regional crisis of 1997–98 and in anticipation of accession to the World Trade Organization (WTO) financial services agreement, the government began to liberalize the domestic financial services sector. This included the removal of the 40 percent foreign ownership limit on domestic banks, paving the way for mergers and greater foreign ownership of domestic banks, as well as placing pressure on local banks to expand into foreign markets. Singapore used the regional financial crisis as leverage to accelerate domestic banking reforms opposed by local private banks. The appointment of Lee Hsien Loong as chairman of the MAS, Singapore's central bank, in 1998 fused the MAS with the top level of Singapore politics. This enabled it to push through reforms against the wishes of local bank owners. In 1998, state-linked Keppel Bank (including both Keppel Bank and Keppel Finance, Ltd.) and the private Tat Lee Bank, purportedly the weakest local bank and the only one to post a loss in 1997, underwent the first bank merger in two decades.[91] Temasek was Keppel Corporation's dominant owner and its only significant one in 2000. DBS was the other major state-owned bank held by Temasek. It acquired the Post Office Savings Bank in 1998. In 1999, the MAS released a five-year plan to liberalize the banking sector that

[90] World Travel and Tourism Council Data (2015).   [91] Hamilton-Hart (2002).

focused on mergers and greater operational freedom for incumbent foreign banks. By increasing their size, bank mergers would facilitate local banks' expansion overseas, while greater competition domestically would incentivize banks to enter foreign markets. In June 2000, United Overseas Finance was merged into United Overseas Bank. In July 2001, OCBC acquired Keppel Tat Lee Bank, which was quickly followed by United Overseas Bank's (UOB's) acquisition of Overseas Union Bank (OUB, including both OUB and Overseas Union Trust, Ltd.), producing Singapore's largest domestic lender. This was soon followed by additional pressures arising from bilateral trade negotiations. Some of the notable changes include Great Eastern Life Assurance merging with Overseas Assurance Corporation to become Great Eastern Holdings in 2000. In 2002, First Capital Corporation merged with its parent company, Guoco Group Limited. After this wave of consolidation, OCBC, UOB, and DBS emerged as the city-state's largest banks, with DBS as the sole state-owned bank.

Surveying the relative importance of political and market mechanisms contributing to changes in the prevalence of GLCs among the top 200 listed firms between 1996 and 2008, as reported in Table 6.3, the Singapore state displayed relatively less activism in comparison with Malaysia, though it was more activist than post-1997 democratic regimes. This largely coincides with the time when the PAP was in a position of relative strength in comparison with Malaysia's ruling party coalition, which faced a period of extreme weakness followed by strength. Each of the political mechanisms indicating various means of changing public-private ownership show that the Singapore state was less aggressive than Malaysia. Specifically, the indicator for the state purchasing a stake in non-SOE firms was 6.5 percent for Singapore versus 15.5 percent for Malaysia; newly listed SOEs in 2008 were 7.6 percent for Singapore versus 10 percent for Malaysia. Mergers and acquisitions (M&As) were 5 percent for Singapore versus 6.5 percent for Malaysia, and the indicator for the state selling stakes in SOEs was 6 percent for Singapore versus 1 percent for Malaysia.

Another view of the state's consolidation and control over the largest firms in the corporate sector can be gleaned from examination of the proportion of firms with direct versus indirect state ownership, as reported in Table 6.2. In Singapore, direct ownership became far more prevalent in 2008 than in Malaysia (96.3 to 67 percent), which is consistent with the view that Singapore consolidated its control over the largest firms in the corporate sector – particularly in industries regarded as strategically important, such as finance. But this has corresponded to a reduction in the state's holdings in the corporate sector more generally, as indirect holdings were shed (from 33 to 3.7 percent).

Modest Activism by Temasek in Foreign Markets

As the ruling party's position strengthens, I predict that state activism will moderate. As mentioned in the preceding section, Singapore's regionalization initiative has followed two strategies – industrial estate parks and direct foreign investments through Temasek and GLCs. Despite significant investment, industrial estate parks yielded limited profitability and have not enabled GLCs to replicate their success in Singapore due to the dependence on foreign governments and corporations.[92] To overcome these limitations, the regionalization initiative shifted to direct foreign investments through GLCs.

Because of the large number of Temasek and GLC overseas investments, a number of challenges with regard to host country investment restrictions have emerged. These challenges have arisen not only among some of Singapore's Southeast Asian neighbors[93] but also with greater force among numerous democratic countries, including New Zealand, India, South Korea, and the United States.[94] Rather than surveying the considerable literature on Temasek's foreign investments, I narrow the focus here to specific investments that yield evidence with regard to my argument about state investment behavior varying with regard to ruling party strength, as displayed by Singapore

---

[92] Yeung (1999).

[93] Brown (1994, 2006); Hamilton-Hart (2002); Jomo (2001); Tipton (2009); Yoshihara (1988).

[94] Goldstein and Pananond (2008). With regard to New Zealand, Singapore Airlines acquired a 25 percent stake in Air New Zealand in 1999. However, problems forced the New Zealand government to intervene, causing SIA to sell most of the investment. In India, Temasek acquired a 7.37 percent stake in ICICI, while GIC held another 2.24 percent stake. A 10 percent limit on foreign ownership in listed Indian companies prevented Temasek from increasing its stake to 10 percent in 2006; however, the Reserve Bank of India permitted a one-time exception to this rule in 2007 by treating the two Singapore investment agencies as separate entities. In South Korea, DBS attempted a failed 10 percent% acquisition of Lone Star Bank in 2007 that may have been due to its government-linked status. ST Telemedia's 61.5 percent purchase of Global Crossing in 2003 required approval by the FBI, CIA, and Pentagon.

versus Malaysia.[95] My argument predicts that Temasek will engage in less activist investment behavior (from 1997 to 2011) than Khazanah, especially from 2008 to 2015, when Malaysia's ruling party endured a period of sustained weakness.

While Table 6.4 shows that the geographic focus of Temasek's investments from 2004 to 2015 expanded far more widely than Khazanah's, Temasek accomplished this with a less aggressive investment strategy. Specifically, Khazanah often teams up with Khazanah-linked companies when making overseas investments, as witnessed with its partnership with Telekom Malaysia when acquiring PT Excelcomindo Pratama in Indonesia and MobileOne in Singapore. Khazanah also prefers to take a majority stake in its overseas investments, granting it adequate board representation to influence business direction as well as safeguard its interests. Khazanah also negotiates on behalf of its linked firms and initiates mergers and demergers among both domestic and foreign firms to enhance the competitiveness of its regional champions.

Temasek, by contrast, has focused its overseas equity investments on revenue-generating companies, preferably those with market-leading positions. Often this occurs independently of Temasek-linked companies. For example, Temasek initiated ownership stakes in Bank Danamon and Bank Internasional Indonesia independently of DBS, in which it has a controlling stake. Temasek also takes minority equity stakes in the vast majority of its overseas investments; consequently, it is not capable of initiating major restructurings, such as mergers or demergers, like Khazanah.[96] In November 2007, Temasek even went so far as to issue three "golden rules" to guide its overseas investments, with the first being the cessation of controlling interests in foreign companies. The second regards cooperation with local partners, and the third emphasizes consideration of the "emotional sentiments" that its acquisitions may provoke in host countries.[97] These offer a clear reflection of Temasek's less activist investment strategy in comparison with Khazanah's post-2008 activities.

---

[95] For literature on Temasek and its investment behavior, see, for example, Alhashel (2015), Dewenter, Han, and Malatesta (2010), Goldstein and Pananond (2008), Yeung (2011), Elson (2008), and Low (2006).
[96] Temasek Annual Reports, various years.
[97] *The Economist*, December 1, 2007.

Evidence for their investment behavior differences can be best obtained from a direct comparison of the two when they invest in the same country and industry and they both have a controlling ownership stake. With such a stake, SWFs have the capacity to engage in aggressive intervention, though they may choose not to. A large stake would more easily allow the SWF (or its GLC) to implement value-enhancing strategies, often through management changes, streamlining operations, or expansion. As shown in Table 6.4, Temaesk and Khazanah have consistently placed a large fraction of their portfolios in financial services and telecommunications. I proceed by comparing their investments in the banking and telecommunications industries in Indonesia in turn.

Temasek and Banking in Indonesia
Temasek's entry into the Indonesian banking sector occurred with a Temasek-led consortium – Asia Financial Indonesia – that directly purchased a 62 percent stake in Bank Danamon in May 2003, the fifth-largest Indonesian bank by assets. The consortium included Temasek and Deutsche Bank. Marking its new control, a new president-director was appointed in June, followed by an increase in the number of commissioners from five to ten.[98]

In October of the same year, another Temasek-led consortium – Sorak Financial – directly purchased a 51 percent stake in Bank Internasional Indonesia (BII), the sixth-largest bank by assets. The consortium included Temasek, Kookmin Bank, Swiss-based ICB Financial Group Holdings, Barclays Bank, and Asia Financial Holdings. One new commissioner and a new board director were appointed soon thereafter.[99]

Finally, in late 2003, Bank Danamon purchased Adira Finance (automobile finance). However, this marked the end of Temasek's banking acquisitions in Indonesia. New foreign ownership rules under the Indonesian central bank's single-presence policy were introduced in 2006 and would take effect in 2010. While protectionist reactions by Indonesian policymakers are partly to blame for Temasek's sudden halt to its activist interventions, Temasek could have merged its new bank holdings so as to reduce the number of financial institutions in which it had a controlling stake. Temasek

[98] *Bisnis Indonesia*, June 17, 2003.   [99] BII, Annual Report, 2003.

chose not to pursue this aggressive restructuring exercise, although this was the path followed by Khazanah. Instead, Temasek sold its stake in BII to Maybank in October 2008[100] and chose to accept a smaller presence in the country's banking sector.

Khazanah and Banking in Indonesia

Khazanah's activism can be broken into two phases. The first phase coincides with Malaysia's ruling party operating from a position of strength. Khazanah's acquisitions of Indonesian banks during this period resemble those of Temasek. The second phase corresponds to the ruling party's significantly weakened position around the 2008 election, when Khazanah engages in more aggressive behavior.

As mentioned in Chapter 6, Khazanah's entry into Indonesia occurred with Commerce Asset Holdings Bhd (CAHB) purchasing a 51 percent stake in Bank Niaga, Indonesia's tenth-largest bank by assets, in November 2002, from the Indonesian Bank Restructuring Agency.[101] In 2004, CAHB's investment banking subsidiary, CIMB, launched CIMB Niaga to participate in the Indonesian capital markets.[102]

In July 2005, Khazanah purchased 52.1 percent of Bank Lippo, Indonesia's ninth-largest bank by assets. To comply with the new single-presence policy, CAHB and Khazanah merged their respective stakes in Bank Niaga and Bank Lippo in 2007.[103] The newly merged Bank Niaga-Lippo would become Indonesia's fifth-largest bank by assets and was renamed CIMB Niaga. This merger coincides with rising

---

[100] *Jakarta Post*, October 2, 2008; *Business Times Singapore*, August 11, 2008. In July, the Malaysian central bank, Bank Negara, stopped an initial deal between the two banks due to concerns that the price for BII was too high. But after a discounted price was offered by Temasek, Maybank acquired a dominant stake in BII in October 2008.

[101] *The Edge Malaysia*, March 19, 2003.

[102] *The Edge Malaysia*, March 10, 2004. CIMB subsidiary CIMB Labuan (an offshore bank) later acquired a 51 percent stake in Niaga Sekuritas, which was 99 percent owned by Bank Niaga. CAHB said it was an internal restructuring to enable the group to establish a foothold in the Indonesian capital markets.

[103] This occurred via the CIMB Group's holding company, Bumiputra-Commerce Holdings Bhd (BCHB), which is the publicly listed arm of CAHB. Khazanah held a 21.42 percent stake in BCHB as of December 31 2006, which in turn owned the CIMB Group. CIMB Group owned 67 percent of Bank Niaga, while Khazanah owned 88 percent of Bank Lippo (*The Edge Financial Daily*, December 7, 2007; *The Edge Financial Daily*, December 28, 2007).

pressure on Malaysia's ruling party coalition ahead of national elections. A period of heightened activism ensued, marking the second phase of Khazanah's activism, which sharply contrasts with Temasek's more passive approach. For example, following the announcement to merge Bank Niaga and Bank Lippo, many changes to Bank Niaga's board of commissioners occurred. Four commissioners left and were replaced by two new people; the president-commissioner was also newly appointed. There was also a new president-director and another two new directors of the six total directors.[104]

In December 2007, CIMB announced that it would merge its asset-management businesses in Indonesia, including CIMB-Principal, CIMB Niaga, and CIMB-GK.[105] The merger would be the first banking merger under the single-presence policy; it was given the government's approval in October 2008.[106] It is worth noting that CIMB-GK Securities topped the Islamic Mutual Fund League Table in assets under management at the end of November 2007, according to BAPEPAM, Indonesia's securities regulator. This success would help the Barisan Nasional appeal to its Bumiputera voters.

At the same time, Malayan Banking Bhd was looking to acquire BII from Temasek and Kookmin Bank.[107] Due to the single-presence policy, the securities regulator was required to make an exception for Maybank because of the Bank Niaga and Bank Lippo merger under the auspices of the CIMB.[108] Maybank finalized its acquisition of BII in September 2008, making it Indonesia's eighth-largest bank by assets.[109]

In summary, the investment behavior of Temasek and Khazanah diverged around 2006, with Khazanah engaging in more activist behavior and Temasek accepting a smaller presence with a far more passive role, resembling the investment pattern of Temasek's investments in other foreign jurisdictions.

---

[104] Bank Niaga, Annual Report, 2003, 2004, and 2007.
[105] The Edge Financial Daily, December 19, 2007.
[106] The Edge Financial Daily, October 17, 2008.
[107] The Edge Financial Daily, April 22, 2008. Khazanah and PNB are CIMB's and Maybank's major shareholders, respectively (with Khazanah having a minority stake in Maybank).
[108] The Edge Financial Daily, September 25, 2008.   [109] Ibid.

Temasek and Telecommunications in Indonesia

Temasek's foray into Indonesia's telecommunications sector mirrors its activities in the banking sector. Specifically, Temasek chose to sell its stakes and restrict its ownership to a single company rather than engage in initiatives to restructure and/or merge its assets.

SingTel, majority owned by Temasek, acquired a 22.3 percent stake in Telkomsel in November 2001 and another 12.7 percent in 2002 for a total 35 percent stake.[110] Telkomsel was Indonesia's largest cellular operator. In December 2002, Singapore Technologies Telemedia (STT), another Temasek-owned firm, acquired 41.94 percent of Indosat, Indonesia's second-largest telecommunications company. However, this second acquisition prompted Indonesia's Business Competition Oversight Committee (KPPU) to express concern about "probable monopoly practices" by Temasek on cellular telecommunications services.[111] KPPU was concerned because Temasek already owned 35 percent of PT Telkomsel, a subsidiary of Telkom, through SingTel. Together, Telkomsel and Indosat controlled about 80 to 90 percent of the highly lucrative mobile phone market.[112] KPPU urged Indonesia's house of representatives to cancel STT's acquisition.[113]

Temasek argued that because the Indonesian government is the majority owner of Telkomsel, collusion was unlikely to have occurred; rather, the attacks suggested political motives by various players.[114] For example, Tanri Abeng, president of Telkom's board of commissioners, said that control of Telkomsel remained very much in Indonesian hands due to its controlling 65 percent stake.[115] Nevertheless, in November 2007, Temasek was ordered to sell one of the two telecommunications companies and pay a fine.[116] The sentence was delivered by Indonesia's antimonopoly watchdog, the KPPU,

---

[110] *Business Times Singapore*, May 22, 2007. Due to a new regulation in August 2000 allowing foreign companies to own up to 95 percent, there were no regulatory restrictions on foreigners owning telecommunications companies. Prior to that, there was a 49 percent limit.

[111] *Bisnis Indonesia*, December 16, 2002.

[112] *Business Times Singapore*, December 14, 2006.   [113] Ibid.

[114] *Business Times Singapore*, June 25, 2007.

[115] *Business Times Singapore*, November 6, 2007.

[116] *Business Times Singapore*, November 20, 2007. The fine was 25 billion rupiah (S$4 million) to Telkomsel, as well as each of its eight affiliate companies, for a total of 225 billion rupiah (S$36 million). Six of the eight affiliate companies include ST Telemedia and companies linked to it; the remaining two are SingTel and SingTel Mobile.

which had repeatedly spoken out against Temasek. Temasek lost on appeal in May 2008 and agreed to pay a fine and sell its stake in Indosat.[117] Temasek has since remained relatively inactive in the Indonesian telecom market, apart from its minority ownership stake in Telkomsel.

Khazanah and Telecommunications in Indonesia

Khazanah's behavior, which led to a growing presence for the SWF in the telecommunications sector, diverged from Temasek's, which exhibited declining activism over time. Khazanah's entry into Indonesia's telecommunications sector occurred via a controlling ownership stake in Indonesia's third-largest cellular telecom company, Excelcomindo (XL).[118] It started with Telekom Malaysia acquiring a 27.3 percent stake in XL in December 2004. Following the purchase by Telekom Malaysia in December 2004 and a shareholders meeting in January 2005, five of the eight commissioners were changed, and the board of directors was reduced from seven to six, with three of the six being new appointments, including the president-director. Telekom said it planned to buy more shares to gain a majority holding,[119] and by February 2008, TM International Bhd (TMI) controlled close to 67 percent of XL and proposed to acquire an additional 16.81 percent from Khazanah. By December 2009, Axiata (formerly TMI) ownership in XL increased to 86.5 percent. Since then, XL has become a member of Axiata's regionalization platform in cellular communications.

Summary

During a period when the PAP retained a strongly dominant political position, Temasek obtained a majority stake in Indonesia's sixth-largest bank and a minority stake in its largest cellular operator. Despite its controlling stake in the Indonesian bank, Temasek did not engage in significant activist interventions, such as mergers or a restructuring of the bank. Likewise, its minority stake in the telecom firm has prevented it from initiating major changes. Khazanah, by contrast, initiated major restructuring and merger activities in its

---

[117] *Business Times Singapore*, January 19, 2011.

[118] As of September 2005, Excelcomindo was the third-largest cellular telecommunication operator in Indonesia (*Bisnis Indonesia*, September 5, 2005).

[119] *The Edge Malaysia*, December 20, 2004.

Indonesian banking-sector holdings, especially since 2007, when the Barisan Nasional (BN) faced a serious political threat. Khazanah also acquired a controlling stake in Indonesia's third-largest cellular firm around this time, enabling it to change management and board members and integrate XL into its regional cellular platform.

Part B Conclusion

During the 1997–2011 period, the PAP's vote share improved. Corresponding to my argument's predictions, the PAP initiated greater liberalization and transparency of GLCs as well as Temasek. A privatization and corporatization initiative was implemented at the beginning of this period, reducing the number of GLCs among the country's largest listed firms. Temasek also exhibited relatively less activist behavior in its foreign investments compared with those of Khazanah, especially following Malaysia's 2008 election. This greater passivity is reflected by its less activist behavior over time in the banking and telecommunications industries in Indonesia.

Part C. Relatively Weaker Ruling Party, 2011–15

My argument predicts that a relatively weaker ruling party will increase its control of information and resources to protect its rule, corresponding to less corporate transparency, increasing controls over the largest firms, initiatives to reduce crowding-out effects, and more activist investment behavior. I begin with an overview of the implications for corporate transparency that resulted from the PAP's worst electoral performance (with regard to vote share) in nearly five decades. The result was a dramatic scaling back of the liberalizing reforms initiated in the years prior to the 2011 election. The implications for corporate transparency included delays regarding the disclosure of directors' remuneration – a critical means by which elites may be co-opted into maintaining loyalty to the PAP. This was indicative of a broader trend regarding the lack of implementation of a new corporate governance code in 2012.

With regard to the dominance of GLCs in the local economy, the proportion of the Singapore Stock Exchange's market capitalization attributable to GLCs increased, rising from around 24 percent in 2003 to around 37 percent for the 2008–13 time period.[120] The top six Singapore-listed GLCs accounted for about 17.3 percent of total capitalization of the Singapore Stock Exchange as of the end of February 2014.[121] At the same time, the PAP initiated several policies to reduce the crowding-out effects and create more opportunities for SMEs. This emphasis on domestic SMEs complements Temasek's and GIC's increasingly activist investment strategy in foreign markets.

The Political Climate and Declining Corporate Transparency

A reversal of the liberalizing reforms initiated by Lee Hsien Loong occurred following the 2011 election when the PAP received its lowest vote share since 1963 – 60.1 percent. The poor result was partly due to the rising income gap. Singapore's Gini coefficient, a measure of income inequality, rose from 0.44 in 2000 to a high of 0.48 by 2013 (one of the highest among developed nations).[122] This growing inequality was further manifested by the disproportionately high ministerial salaries. For example, even after a 28 percent salary cut that was implemented in 2013, Singapore's prime minister remained the highest-paid political leader in the world by a wide margin at US$1.7 million versus the second highest, the US President, at US$400,000. Salaries for other government officials were simply held constant.

Large turnouts for opposition rallies prior to the 2011 election produced a counterreaction from the authorities. A Public Order Act was passed that empowered the police to prevent civil disobedience and mass protest. It was used to prevent an antiracism rally at Speakers' Corner on International Human Rights Day in 2011 by Singaporeans for Democracy. In 2012, the minister, the prime minister, and his brother threatened to sue editors of Temasek Review Emeritus, a website, for defamation. A popular blogger, Alex Au, was forced to apologize in 2012 for questioning the appropriateness of charges against a local surgeon for speeding and giving false information.[123] A cartoonist was subsequently charged with "contempt of court" for

---

[120] For 2003 data, see Ang and Ding (2006). For 2008–13 data, see Sian et al. (2014, 6).
[121] US Department of State (2014).   [122] Singapore statistics.
[123] AsiaOne (2012).

publishing cartoons on his Facebook page that satirized court decisions.[124] In 2013, a new law was passed requiring news websites to apply for licenses, post a bond of S$50,000, and remove any specified content within 24 hours of receiving a government order.[125] The effect of these new measures was to raise the "climate of fear" for Singaporeans supporting an opposition cause.[126] Finally, in 2015, Reporters Without Borders ranked Singapore 153 out of 180 countries for its press freedom due to its highly compliant media.[127]

With regard to corporate-sector transparency, improvements in this domain also stalled. For example, despite the release of a new code of corporate governance in May 2012 that required companies to publish details on the remuneration of directors and senior executives, only 31 percent of firms fully disclosed the required information as of 2014.[128] This issue was flagged by CG Watch in its 2014 report, which ranked Hong Kong above Singapore partly due to the "[d]isclosure of the exact remuneration of directors and senior executives."[129] Matching the lack of compliance on this dimension was Singapore's score for enforcement, which had the biggest drop of any country in the survey, falling from sixty-four in 2012 to fifty-six in 2014. Its score for the political/regulatory environment also had a sharp fall, from seventy-three to sixty-four. Additionally, the definition of "independent director" still did not conform to international standards; companies have been permitted to merely "rigorously review" a director's independence, enabling many individuals to remain on corporate boards despite potential conflicts of interest.[130]

According to Handshakes, which compiled data for a study on Singapore's boards of directors (the Singapore Directorship Report, 2014), the average annual fees for nonexecutive directors for FY2013 was $68,250 for small-cap companies (those with a market capitalization of less than $300 million), $77,806 for midcap companies (market capitalization of between $300 million and $1 billion), and $143,096 for large-cap companies (market capitalization of more than

[124] Human Rights Watch (2014).   [125] *Straits Times*, May 28, 2013.
[126] Loo (2007).   [127] Reporters Without Borders (2013). Malaysia ranks 147.
[128] See sections 9.2 and 9.3 of the Code of Corporate Governance 2012.
[129] CG Watch, 2014.
[130] See CG Watch 2012 for more details on concerns about the lack of independence, particularly in relation to substantial shareholders.

$1 billion).[131] The study also reported that directors of Temasek-linked companies (TLCs) were more than twice as likely to hold multiple director positions (e.g., 36 percent of directors on TLCs held two to four board seats compared with 16.1 percent of directors on non-TLCs) but that nobody was found to sit on more than seven boards, a modest change from that documented by Worthington (nine board seats was the maximum in 1998).[132] With multiple directorships on GLCs (frequently large-cap companies), government officials could reap handsome rewards. The interpenetration by government officials among GLCs alongside the remuneration of potentially multiple director positions may be one reason why transparency of this particular aspect of corporate governance has been among the most resistant to transparency reform.

Moreover, Singapore's Financial Secrecy Index rank increased between 2009 and 2015 from eighth to fifth most opaque among ninety-two countries in 2015. The Tax Justice Network provides a journalistic account of how offshore secrecy and the wider state sector are sustained in Singapore:

"It is impossible to find opinions opposed to the omnipresence of finance on the island. The banks form part of our DNA," says Pritam Singh, one of five opposition deputies among 99 parliamentarians. Former ministers or civil servants make up the boards of the banks. Parliament approves and votes on the executive's decisions, without haggling. "The notion of conflicts of interest does not exist, because everyone is in some form a shareholder of Singapore Inc.," a diplomat says.[133]

Prioritizing the Reduction of Crowding-Out Effects

Singapore's election was held on May 7, 2011. In an effort to boost popular support ahead of the election, the PAP announced a new Productivity and Innovation Credit (PIC) scheme to support investments that would boost innovation and productivity, with special

---

[131] Note that these data reflect only 1,049 of 4,839 non–executive director (independent and nonindependent) seats where specific director remuneration data are available – 21 percent of total board seats.

[132] Worthington (2003).

[133] Quoted in Narrative Report on Singapore, Financial Secrecy Index, Tax Justice Network, 2015, September 23, 2015. Original quote from *Le Temps*, June 18, 2013.

attention paid to SMEs.[134] It would take effect in 2011, with a National Productivity Fund of S$2 billion. In February 2012, the government announced a Special Employment Credit scheme to encourage SMEs to hire older Singaporean workers as a means by which to offset the decline in foreign workers and the rising wage costs.[135] Additionally, a series of new grants and tax reductions was made available to SMEs.[136] In 2014, SMEs accounted for about 70 percent of Singapore's employment and nearly half of its GDP, making them a crucial segment of the electorate.[137]

In advance of the 2015 election, held on September 11, a series of budget initiatives was announced that were specifically targeted at SMEs. The election was particularly important to the PAP in light of the 2011 results. The 2015 budget offered new tax incentives as well as stronger grant schemes for SMEs to internationalize and to engage in mergers and acquisitions, in addition to boosting the PIC scheme. Tharman Shanmugaratnam, deputy prime minister and finance minister, declared: "We have now embarked on a new phase in our nation's economic development ... We are moving from value-adding to value-creation. It means making innovation pervasive in every industry and for firms small and big – so that we can come up with our own products and services, and also to establish Singapore as a leading center for value creation in [the] business strategies of foreign companies." Articulating the importance of SMEs in this new phase, Tharman added: "We can only become an innovative, value-creating economy if a significant segment of our SMEs is driven by innovation. This is a major priority."[138]

More Aggressive Foreign Investments

To boost returns for voter-investors and to reduce crowding-out effects in the context of a weak ruling party, I predict state investment to become more aggressive. Following the 2011 election, more activist behavior was displayed by Temasek and GIC. Prior to 2011, Temasek's

---

[134] *Business Times Singapore*, March 5, 2010; *Channel NewsAsia*, February 22, 2010.
[135] *Channel NewsAsia*, February 17, 2012.   [136] Ibid.
[137] *The Edge Singapore*, February 17, 2014.
[138] *Business Times Singapore*, August 11, 2015.

focus appeared mostly to be financial activism exercised through voicing strategies; this changed after 2011.

Following the 2011 election, Ho Ching was rumored to be stepping down as CEO according to the *Financial Times*.[139] She wound up staying on, but numerous senior executives did depart.[140] This coincides with a reorientation of Temasek's investment strategy. This new activism was manifested in two ways: (1) by actively protecting its interests via board representation and seeking changes to boards of directors and (2) by reorienting its investments toward private firms and private equity placements, which would allow it to intervene without attracting unwanted media attention.

For example, Temasek owned 18 percent of Standard Chartered in 2012 but was not satisfied with corporate governance at the company.[141] Rather than remain silent, Temasek commenced efforts at instituting governance changes, specifically pressuring the bank to appoint more independent directors. As a matter of policy, Temasek does not hold board seats in the companies in which it invests. But it began placing a new emphasis on governance, as indicated by a section about governance in its annual report released in July 2012: "To provide effective oversight of management on behalf of all shareholders, we advocate that boards be independent of management. We do not support excessive numbers of executive members on company boards." Later, in the beginning of 2015, Temasek was reported to be one of the leading shareholders pushing for a boardroom shakeup at Standard Chartered and the appointment of a new CEO. This was in response to the value of its stock plunging since the start of 2014 amid slowing growth in the bank's key Asian and emerging-markets regions.[142]

In addition to more activist behavior as a shareholder, Temasek also modified its investment strategy.[143] It began cutting stakes in big publicly listed companies and put more money into private companies and private equity firms.[144] For example, the percentage of Temasek's unlisted assets increased from 18 percent in 2007 to around 39 percent

---

[139] *Financial Times*, June 8, 2011.   [140] Reuters, January 3, 2012.
[141] *Wall Street Journal*, October 3, 2012.   [142] *Asian Investor*, April 1, 2015.
[143] GIC also placed more emphasis on private placements, though it is difficult to get detailed information about when this began and the extent of its investments. Reuters, September 3, 2014.
[144] Reuters, March 10. 2014.

in 2016.[145] The objective was to improve investment returns, but this new approach also provided a means of exercising greater influence without provoking an outcry since the firms are not publicly listed. As part of this effort, Temasek funded Pavilion Capital in 2013, headed by a former chief investment officer – it invests in closely held SMEs in North Asia. Temasek also funded Seatown in 2010, headed by a former senior Temasek executive. Seatown invests globally with a broad investment mandate. Temasek also funded Astrea II in 2014, a co-investment vehicle with broadly diversified holdings in 36 private equity funds. And in 2015, Temasek co-funded Golden Gate Ventures Fund to invest in new ventures in Southeast Asia. "The investment approach now coming to fruition is a far cry from the multibillion dollar deals Temasek embarked on prior to 2008, garnering significant stakes in leading companies across Asia, Europe and the United States," according to Reuters.[146]

Temasek's shift toward private equity was matched by a comparable shift in GIC's investment strategy toward public equities. Immediately following the 2011 election, Tharman Shanmugaratnam became chairman of GIC. This was followed shortly afterwards by a review of GIC's investment strategy conducted in 2012, which led to a new investment framework for GIC that benchmarks its performance against a reference portfolio comprising 65 percent global equities and 35 percent global bonds. This portfolio "reflects the amount of risk that the government is prepared for GIC to take in its long-term investment strategies."[147] Until the end of the 1990s, GIC maintained a portfolio consisting of 30 percent equities, 40 percent bonds, and 30 percent cash – a "decidedly conservative" investment allocation.[148] In the early 2000s, the GIC began placing a larger allocation of its portfolio into public equities, especially in emerging markets, and alternative asset classes, such as commodities and inflation-linked bonds. This investment approach resembled the endowment approach of many US funds, but with a smaller allocation to equities and alternative asset classes.

---

[145] Nikkei, July 14, 2016.   [146] Reuters, March 10, 2014.
[147] GIC's website, www.gic.com.sg/index.php/newsroom?id=184&Itemid=159 (accessed November 21, 2014). The new portfolio focuses on six core asset classes, including developed market equities, emerging-market equities, nominal bonds and cash, inflation-linked bonds, private equity, and real estate.
[148] GIC Report, available at www.gic.com.sg/index.php/newsroom?id=184&Ite Itemid=159 (accessed November 21 2014).

The new 65:35 reference portfolio represented an explicit willingness by the government to assume greater risk in exchange for higher returns. When considered alongside the changes at Temasek, it is difficult not to think that the timing of GIC's new approach is linked to the PAP's performance in the 2011 election.

Part C Conclusions

Following the plunge in popular support for the PAP in the 2011 election, a series of marked changes occurred with respect to the state's intervention in the corporate sector. Weakening political dominance for the ruling party is predicted to yield stronger controls over the largest firms, reductions in the transparency of the state sector, initiatives to reduce crowding-out effects, and more activist SWFs. With regard to transparency, the threat to the PAP's political control led to a clampdown on opportunities for government critics to voice their views, as well as delays to the enforcement of transparency-related corporate governance measures. Specifically, enforcement about the reporting of remuneration for directors was lacking, loose definitions regarding independent directors were kept in place, and TLCs preserved opportunities for holding multiple directorships, frequently held by government or ex-government officials.

At the same time, PAP weakness led to the promotion of even stronger initiatives for SMEs. These were implemented in line with the PAP's conventional prioritization of growth (via improvements to innovation and productivity), the key issue with which it retains its legitimacy. With regard to SWF activism, Temasek initiated a more activist role in the boardroom of large listed firms in addition to rebalancing its portfolio toward private placements. Investments with unlisted firms would enable Temasek to exercise greater influence without attracting unwanted media attention while also potentially boosting its investment returns. At the same time, the GIC boosted its portfolio allocation to riskier asset classes.

Chapter Conclusions

In contrast to Barisan Nasional in Malaysia, Singapore's ruling party – the PAP – has maintained a strongly dominant position relative to its political opponents. Nevertheless, the PAP's intervention in the corporate sector has exhibited modest variance over time in response to the severity of the threat to the ruling party's political dominance. Political pressures emanating from crowding-out effects that embolden private capital coupled with economic liberalization that enhances its autonomy, in addition to the need to provide good financial returns for GLCs and voter-investors, have together contributed to the rapid expansion of foreign investments in listed firms. But the greater political strength of the PAP relative to the BN has permitted the former to take a more passive approach to its foreign holdings in comparison with Malaysia's SWFs and GLCs.

8 | Conclusions

This chapter proceeds in three sections. In the first section I summarize the argument and evidence. The second section elaborates on the book's theoretical contributions to several literatures, including the role of the state to spur economic development in the presence of weak institutions, the stability and growth of dominant-party authoritarian regimes (DPARs), comparative corporate governance, and the global diffusion of liberalizing reforms. The third section points to directions for future research, including additional work on sovereign wealth funds (SWFs), the role of SWFs as institutional intermediaries, state-owned business groups both within and between countries, the nature of state investment between countries with large state sectors, and extending the framework developed here to other dimensions of "economic statecraft."

Summary of This Book's Argument and Evidence

Economic globalization is theorized to reduce state intervention in the corporate sector, yet state ownership remains pervasive across the world's largest corporations. This book argues that this disconnect between theory and empirics can be resolved, in part, by considering how varying types of political regimes spur (or dampen) state intervention in the corporate sector. I focus on four regime types, including narrow authoritarian regimes (NARs), single-party authoritarian regimes (SPARs), dominant-party authoritarian regimes (DPARs), and democracies. The prevalence of these regimes has changed in recent times. DPARs, for example, have staged a spectacular rise since the end of the Cold War and now account for one-third of all regimes in the world. Yet the existing literature on state intervention in the corporate sector has overlooked this important fact.

I argue that political regimes possess distinctive capacities and motivations for intervening in foreign listed firms as a result of their political institutions. Regimes with institutions that promote political competition and reduce investment risk create more opportunities for private capital. In NARs, these institutions are nonexistent or totally ineffective; hence the largest firms are commonly wholly state owned, and transparency is very low. In democracies, these institutions are highly effective; hence private capital dominates and transparency is high, while state ownership is usually minimized. SPARs and DPARs are in the middle. SPARs permit intraparty competition and host modestly effective legislatures that offer limited reductions to investment risk for private capital. DPARs, however, permit intra- and restricted interparty competition and host legislatures with more heterogeneous representation. Consequently, both of these one-party regimes are likely to host firms with public-private ownership and meet minimum transparency thresholds necessary to invest in many foreign jurisdictions, though DPARs will be able to enter more foreign markets than SPARs because of more balanced public-private arrangements and greater state-sector transparency. Both regimes are also likely to host savings SWFs, which can facilitate entry into foreign markets as well as large share purchases of listed firms.

With regard to the motivation to intervene, DPARs face stronger motivations than SPARs because ruling parties in the former permit political opponents to compete in regular elections but are unwilling to hand over power. Because DPARs and SPARs rely on state ownership of large firms to support their rule, two sources of threat are of particular salience to the stability of these regimes: (1) rising crowding-out effects associated with economic development and (2) economic liberalization. Both of these enhance the power of private capital. To preserve their hold on power, incumbent rulers in DPARs will turn to aggressive state intervention in domestic and foreign firms in an effort to consolidate their control over vital resources and to generate better returns for voter-investors. Although these sources of threat also affect rulers of SPARs, their motivation to intervene is less intense because they do not face regular elections, and opposition parties are explicitly forbidden.

Global and East Asia Patterns

Authoritarian regimes are predicted to have more centralized control over resources and information, and this will be manifested by a greater reliance on state-owned enterprises (SOEs) and lower state-sector transparency than in democracies. Additionally, savings SWFs are predicted to be more common to authoritarian regimes.

Global patterns are consistent with these predictions. SOEs comprise a larger share of the economy among all types of authoritarian regimes, with DPARs displaying a lower reliance on SOEs in comparison with SPARs and NARs. Likewise, Corruption Perception Index (CPI) scores – a rough proxy for political transparency – are lower for authoritarian regimes, with DPARs again displaying higher CPI scores (higher transparency) than either SPARs or NARs. Interestingly, these patterns are stronger for the post-2000 period, suggesting that the global spread of liberalizing reforms may have generated a backlash that has resulted in stronger domestic political influence on the manifestation of state-sector characteristics. Tests on corporate and SWF transparency measures (for 2015 and 2010, respectively) are broadly consistent with the CPI score patterns. Additionally, savings SWFs are more common to authoritarian regimes, even after controlling for oil rents of gross domestic product (GDP), suggesting that they are an extension of authoritarian political arrangements.

The global data draw on relatively coarse indicators to assess the predicted patterns. I therefore narrow the focus to countries in the East Asia region in order to assess the argument with more precise measures. These more detailed data permit more fine-grained distinctions to be drawn among the different types of authoritarian regimes. In contrast to the global data, which failed to clearly distinguish between NARs and SPARs, the corporate ownership data for East Asia indicate that DPARs and SPARs have a greater prevalence of mixed public-private ownership than NARs and that SPARs privilege state ownership more than DPARs. Although the transparency indicators again vary according to the specific variable being measured – political, corporate, or SWF transparency – the overall pattern indicates that NARs have the lowest transparency, followed by SPARs, DPARs, and then democracies. Additionally, the distribution of SWF types shows that savings SWFs are located primarily in authoritarian regimes and more frequently initiate large, long-term corporate ownership positions.

Finally, the East Asia data also offer evidence for the extent of foreign state ownership of large listed corporations. In this regard, Malaysia and Singapore (both DPARs) and their respective savings SWFs, Khazanah and Temasek, display the greatest propensity to acquire sizable ownership stakes in the region's largest listed firms. Although China is not far behind, its foreign ownership positions are primarily due to SOEs; China lacks a savings SWF with the capacity to coordinate SOE acquisitions in foreign markets.

To explore these differences in greater detail and to identify the motivations driving states' varying investment behaviors, I examine individual country cases representing each regime type. Table 8.1 shows the predictions and some illustrative evidence from the corresponding cases.

Narrow Authoritarian Regime: Brunei

Brunei has had a constitutional monarchy since independence in 1984. Political opposition is strictly forbidden, and there is no functioning legislature that can either constrain executive decisions to reduce expropriation risk or act as a forum for private capital owners to bargain with one another to reduce contracting risk. These regime characteristics have contributed to an economy dominated by wholly state-owned enterprises. Additionally, martial law has been in effect since 1962, the media is totally controlled by the sultan, and there is no stock market for firms to list on. Thus state-sector transparency is very low.

A clear manifestation of these arrangements is the country's SWF, the Brunei Investment Agency (BIA). It is under the total control of the sultan, and officials working for it are explicitly forbidden from revealing information about its activities. The BIA sends a large fraction of its endowment to professional managers who then invest in a diversified portfolio that does not attract foreign attention by exceeding key ownership thresholds. Additionally, the sultan remains one step removed from revealing his identity by going through professional managers. But the lack of checks and balances in the government leaves the BIA open to abuse, which is precisely what happened in the years before the collapse of Amedeo in 1998. Despite the loss of around one-third of BIA's funds, little changed following the crisis in terms of transparency or the capacity for the sultan to use BIA funds as he pleases. Likewise, the BIA continues to remain a highly secretive and passive investor. The persistence of these arrangements reflects the continuity of the regime's institutional structure that underpins them.

Table 8.1 *Regime Types and State Investment Behavior: Predictions and Evidence*

Regime type and country example	Explanatory variables — Regime Characteristics		Intervening variables: state capacity to intervene — SOE and SWF Characteristics			Intervening variables: state motivation to intervene		Dependent variable
	Institutions that promote political competition	Institutions to reduce investment risk	SOE and SWF transparency	Public-private ownership: prevailing type of SOE	Prevailing type of SWF	Risks due to crowding-out effects	Risks due to economic liberalization	State investment behavior
NAR	None: no ruling party structure	None: no legislature	Low	Public dominance: dominant state ownership, often unlisted	Savings	Low	Low	Mostly passive
Brunei	None	None	Low	Wholly state-owned (e.g., Petroleum-BRUNEI)	Savings (Brunei Investment Agency)	Low (very little private capital)	Low (1998 crisis had little impact)	Passive (mostly through professional investment firms)
SPAR	Modest: highly restricted competition (intraparty only)	Weak: populated by ruling party members	Moderately low	Public-oriented: state ownership dominates for strategically important firms	Savings	Moderately low	Moderately Low	Occasional displays of aggression
China	CCP intraparty competition only	Weak (National People's Congress)	Low to moderate for top tier; moderate for lower tiers	Wholly state owned or state ownership dominates for listed SOEs	FX reserve (SAFE and CIC), pension (NSSF) and savings (if SASAC regarded as one)	Major risk to CCP has been lack of oil and gas to meet growth targets		Aggressive investments in oil and gas firms in authoritarian regimes

DPAR	Limited: restricted competition (intra- and interparty)	Moderate: legislatures with modest party heterogeneity	Moderate	Public-private balance: hybrid SOEs	Savings	Potentially high	Potentially high	More frequent displays of aggression
Singapore and Malaysia	Ruling parties dominant since independence, but opposition parties compete	Opposition parties represented in legislature	Moderate (Malaysia) to moderately high (Singapore)	Relatively balanced public-private ownership of SOEs	Savings (Temasek, Khazanah, 1MDB) and FX reserve (GIC)	Moderate (Singapore) to moderately high (Malaysia)	Moderately low (Singapore) to high (Malaysia)	Frequent aggressive (Malaysia) and moderately aggressive (Singapore) behavior
Democracy	Extensive: competitive	Strong; legislature can effectively constrain executive	High	Private dominance: relatively few SOEs	Mostly specific purpose (macro-stability, FX reserve, pension)	Low	Low	Mostly passive
Taiwan	Competitive (KMT versus DPP)	Strong	Moderately high and improving	Few SOEs	Macro-stability (National Stabilization Fund)	Low (very small state sector)	Low (change of political party rather than regime change)	Passive

Single-Party Authoritarian Regime: China

In comparison with Brunei, China has modestly stronger institutions governing political competition and the reduction of investment risk. Specifically, the Chinese Community Party (CCP) permits intraparty competition for coveted positions, and the National People's Congress grants limited access to the policymaking process to private capital, thereby expanding access to state resources and reducing investment risk. This is manifested by the ownership structure of SOEs as one descends from the top tier, where state ownership dominates; to the middle tier, where hybrid public-private ownership is common; to the bottom tier, where private ownership prevails. But it is important to emphasize that the corporations that the CCP regards as the most vital to regime survival are located in the top tier. These include the largest companies, most of which are listed on one of the country's stock markets, though many remain unlisted. Because state ownership is so dominant, transparency remains relatively low. Together these two features limit the foreign jurisdictions that would welcome large investments in listed companies. Additionally, China lacks a savings SWF like Temasek or Khazanah that can help to coordinate and promote state-led investments in foreign firms.

Finally, China's motivation to intervene has been driven primarily by holistic threats to the CCP's hold on power; specifically, its capacity to deliver economic growth. This has led to aggressive foreign investments in oil and gas firms located primarily in authoritarian regimes with low transparency requirements. These dominant ownership positions then enable the diversion of petroleum sales to China. Recently, however, China's energy supplies have caught up to demand, enabling China's oil majors to focus on other, more commercially oriented priorities. As a result of the dampening of this threat to CCP rule, large ownership stakes in foreign listed firms have declined and shifted toward minority positions among services-oriented firms in advanced democracies.

Dominant-Party Authoritarian Regimes: Malaysia and Singapore

Although Malaysia and Singapore are dominated by a single ruling party like China, there are important differences. First, Singapore and Malaysia hold regular, semicompetitive elections. Second, opposition parties frequently hold some fraction of seats in the legislature. Together these political characteristics expand access to the resources and information controlled by the state and further reduce investment risk for private capital compared with that in China. These features result in more balanced public-private ownership of SOEs and improved transparency of the state sector. A third difference is that Malaysia and Singapore have savings SWFs, which enable centralized state control over sprawling corporate assets and facilitate investments into foreign corporations. Together these three features have enhanced the capacity of Singapore's and Malaysia's SOEs and SWFs to intervene aggressively in foreign corporations in comparison with China's SOEs.

Additionally, Singapore and Malaysia have also faced strong, and rising, motivations to aggressively intervene in foreign markets and corporations. In both economies, crowding-out effects have impinged on the opportunities for private capital, especially small and medium-sized enterprises (SMEs). These firms employ a large fraction of the work force; hence the People's Action Party (PAP) and Barisan Nasional (BN) cannot ignore them. Their influence is magnified by economic liberalization, which enhances their access to capital outside the regime's control, increases opportunities to grow their business, and generates an implicit threat of exit should a crisis occur. Together these have generated pressures for the largest SOEs to head overseas to grow. At the same time, citizens in both countries want positive returns on their savings, which are often invested in the shares of these hybrid SOEs. This magnifies the pressure for these SOEs (and the SWFs that own them) to profitably enter into and compete in foreign markets and to employ aggressive tactics if necessary.

Because Malaysia and Singapore hold elections but the ruling parties are unwilling to give up power, their SWFs and SOEs engage in stronger interventions as threats to their ruling parties increase. Malaysia's ruling party coalition, the BN, has faced greater threats to its rule than Singapore's ruling party, the PAP, contributing to more frequent displays of aggressive state intervention. This has been manifested by the rapid expansion of regional champions in telecommunications (Axiata), finance (CIMB), and healthcare (IHH), all of which are owned by Khazanah. Aggressive interventions also occurred domestically, notably by 1MDB. Under the direct control of the prime minister, it was created after the abysmal 2008 election through the sale of Malaysian sovereign bonds and subsequently led to purchases of domestic power companies (that acted as cash cows) to service its debt payments.

Democracy: Taiwan

Taiwan's regime characteristics include strongly institutionalized political competition between two major political parties, the Kuomintang and the Democratic Political Party. Additionally, Taiwan's legislature has emerged as a strong, independent base of power with the capacity to effectively constrain the executive. Together these institutional features have strongly reduced investment risk for private capital and contributed to the state sector's retreat. Additionally, the transparency of the state sector has dramatically increased, and a macro-stability SWF (the National Stabilization Fund) was created that focuses exclusively on a passive investment strategy that involves taking small, short-term positions to stabilize Taiwan's stock market. Altogether, Taiwan's SOEs and SWF have a minimal capacity for taking large ownership positions in foreign listed firms.

Contributions

In addition to the literatures on SOEs and SWFs mentioned in Chapter 1, this book contributes to theories about institutions and the role of the state in economic development, the stability and growth of DPARs, comparative corporate governance, and the global diffusion of liberalizing reforms.

Institutions and the Role of the State in Economic Development

The conventional approach to thinking about institutions and firms regards the effect of state ownership on firm performance and how country-level features affect transactions costs and incentives for productive efficiency.[1] Countries with a low level of institutional development are likely to display "voids" in product, labor, and financial markets.[2]

---

[1] North (1990).   [2] Khanna and Palepu (2000).

State capital can be deployed to fill in these voids, as occurred with the early industrial development of many countries.[3]

I advance this theoretical approach by differentiating among types of authoritarian regimes in a way that generates implications for the aggressiveness with which state capital is deployed. I identify DPARs as the most likely type of political regime to have SWFs that can take large ownership positions in listed firms. I further specify the conditions that yield a strong motivation for incumbent rulers to aggressively intervene in the corporate sector – when they face a strong threat to their rule. Such conditions arise most frequently in the context of DPARs because they hold regular elections with multiple political parties, but incumbent rulers are unwilling to give up power. Thus SWFs (and SOEs) respond to electoral threats by targeting specific projects that will result in stronger support for incumbent rulers and/ or deny resources to challengers. Additionally, SWFs (and SOEs) aggressively intervene in firms that are likely to yield positive performance boosts because DPAR leaders depend on the support of voter-investors at election time. This, of course, raises the question of whether SWFs possess a competitive advantage that would enable them to boost the performance of target firms. The existing literature with regard to institutional voids has focused its attention on the domestic marketplace of emerging economies, but SWFs are likely to possess a particular advantage in filling institutional voids in a regional or international context, which is an area for future research discussed below.

Theories about DPAR Stability

The spread of DPARs has generated considerable academic interest, and scholars have shown that compared with other types of authoritarian rule, DPARs last longer[4] and suffer fewer coups.[5] However, the mechanisms by which this stability is achieved remain open to debate. While it is widely recognized that authoritarian rulers must distribute rents in order to co-opt potential rivals,[6] as well as sustain popular

---

[3] Wade (1990); Haggard (1991); Evans (1995); Amsden (2001); Rodrik (2007); Aghion (2011).
[4] Huntington (1968), Geddes (2003), Magaloni (2008).   [5] Geddes (2008).
[6] Wintrobe (1998); Bueno de Mesquita et al. (2005).

support,[7] by illuminating the influence of hybrid SOEs in comparison with crony-based patronage, my argument offers new insights into how stability is achieved and maintained. These insights are relevant to three sets of challenges that authoritarian leaders face in their attempt to co-opt elite opponents and maintain mass support.

First, incumbent leaders confront difficulties in buying off potential rivals with transfers because there is no clear mechanism by which to prevent rivals from using them to mount a challenge against the leaders.[8] This threat is heightened in the context of an open, liberalized economy that allows rivals to use those assets to raise additional funds overseas.[9] Hybrid SOEs offer a mechanism by which authoritarian leaders can address this challenge because the incumbent leaders retain ultimate ownership over the assets while placing rivals in high-paying executive positions. This allows the leader to share the rents and thereby co-opt rivals without abdicating control over the assets.

A second challenge regards establishing a credible commitment to share power with potential opponents when incumbent elites face threats to their survival. The existing literature suggests that incumbent leaders can use institutions governing succession and access-to-power positions within the ruling party to make credible intertemporal power-sharing deals with potential elite rivals.[10] These elites will choose to support the regime rather than challenge it only if they have confidence that they will be promoted into rent-paying positions. SOEs offer a mechanism by which to increase the number of rent-paying positions while minimizing government expenditures, such as would occur by relying solely on government posts.[11] SOEs expand the state's institutional capacity for supporting elites' career prospects and can foster more formalized mechanisms for career advancement, which enhances confidence that elites will be promoted into rent-paying positions.

The third challenge for authoritarian leaders to share power with rivals regards accurate information about regime threats from elites and citizens. Accurate information about elite threats can be difficult to

---

[7] Magaloni and Kricheli (2010).   [8] Haber (2006); Magaloni (2008).
[9] Work on the international and domestic factors influencing authoritarian stability includes Solinger (2001) and Bjornlund (2004).
[10] Lazarev (2005); Brownlee (2007); Gehlbach and Keefer (2011); and Magaloni (2008).
[11] Lust-Okar (2005); Magaloni (2006).

obtain because elites often have an incentive to misrepresent the degree of power and control the incumbent leader actually holds both among elites and in relation to citizens' support.[12] Trade and financial liberalization can complicate the acquisition of accurate information as actors are constantly adapting to market forces. SOEs can reduce these information asymmetry problems by providing an alternative source of information about citizen concerns and a means by which to monitor elites. Additionally, SOEs offer a means by which the party can attract and retain new members and thereby expand its information-gathering resources.[13] "The denser the party's organizational networks to monitor and sanction citizens, and the more it monopolizes valuable resources, the more capable a one-party regime is of trapping citizens into supporting the system."[14]

Theories about DPARs' Rapid Growth

An additional reason for DPARs' greater stability in comparison with other types of authoritarian rule is their stronger economic growth.[15] The mechanisms to account for their higher growth also remain unsettled. Some argue that the greater stability of these regimes, for reasons independent of growth, lengthens rulers' time horizons and reduces their incentives to engage in rent-seeking activities.[16] Others argue that they grow more because they have more effective institutional constraints than other types of authoritarian regimes, lowering the risk of expropriation.[17]

I make two contributions to this literature. First, I argue that institutional constraints are more effective in DPARs due to the reliance on hybrid SOEs. SOEs with mixed public-private ownership give the state a vested interest in a well-functioning marketplace, creating strong incentives for the executive to participate in legislative negotiations to protect property rights, to abide by those which are struck, and to enforce them. Additionally, the rents that accrue to the state from

[12] Tullock (1987); Schatzberg (1988); Wintrobe (1998).
[13] Geddes (1999, 121–34). [14] Magaloni and Kricheli (2010).
[15] On stronger growth contributing to more authoritarian stability, see Haggard and Kaufman (1995) and Geddes (2008). On one-party regimes exhibiting high economic growth, see Keefer (2007), Gandhi (2008), Gehlbach and Keefer (2011); and Wright (2008).
[16] Olson (1993); Wright (2008).
[17] Gandhi (2008); Gehlbach and Keefer (2011); Wright (2008).

these enterprises give the ruling party a vested interest in protecting the property rights of private asset holders. As a result, hybrid SOEs help to reduce both contracting and expropriation risk.

Second, partial state ownership has two features that distinguish it from cronyism and that enhance the stability of property rights protections and reduce the scope for corruption. The first feature is that rents flow to the state entity charged with administering state ownership positions, such as a SWF (controlled by the ruling party) rather than an individual political patron, as with NARs. Such arrangements exist with more stability because they are tied to the ruling party rather than being contingent on the political fortunes of an individual patron. The second feature is that hybrid SOEs tend to be more transparent about the government's investment stakes because the state normally applies a set of uniform rules to its investments. Additionally, hybrid SOEs are publicly listed, requiring public disclosure of firms' financial information. Together these dual features yield greater certainty and uniformity in the application of property rights, thereby reducing investment risk.

Comparative Corporate Governance

Considerable research has been conducted on the influence of national institutions on corporate governance practices and outcomes across advanced economies.[18] I extend this approach to emerging economies by developing a model that differentiates among types of authoritarian regimes with clear implications for the extent of state versus private ownership. The corporate governance implications associated with these regime types can be derived by considering the extent to which they adhere to transparent decision-making processes. NARs, for example, prefer an environment of high opacity. SPARs are slightly more transparent in that they widen access to the governing institutions to members of the ruling party. DPARs are even more transparent because they permit political opponents to hold seats in the legislature. Consequently, the corporate governance of SOEs is expected to reflect these increasingly transparent political arrangements and to exhibit a corresponding improvement in the protection of minority shareholders as one moves from NARs to DPARs, *ceteris paribus*.

[18] Aguilera and Jackson (2010); Filatotchev et al. (2013).

The difference in corporate governance between firms in NARs and SPARs is immediately clear. NARs often do not have a stock exchange (e.g., Brunei). As a result, large firms do not need to disclose any information to satisfy the demands of investors. In SPARs, stock markets tend to be more common (e.g., China and Vietnam). Although corporate governance tends to be weak in these countries, the simple fact that companies are more likely to be publicly listed means that a minimum corporate governance standard is adhered to. DPARs are expected to adhere to even stronger corporate governance rules because private investors are more influential (e.g., Singapore and Malaysia). Finally, democracies will have the potential for the strongest corporate governance codes.

SWFs can play an important role in implementing and enforcing these corporate governance standards. For example, Khazanah, Malaysia's SWF, was charged with improving the corporate governance standards of government-linked companies that it owned after the Asian financial crisis. Temasek, Singapore's SWF, is also responsible for ensuring that the companies in its portfolio adhere to a specified corporate governance code.

The Global Diffusion of Liberalizing Reforms

Recent literature has identified various mechanisms by which liberalizing reforms have diffused across the world, contributing to a highly liberal economic and financial landscape.[19] However, the evidence presented in this book indicates that the diffusion of these reforms varies across types of authoritarian regimes. Indeed, the cases of Brunei, China, Singapore, and Malaysia in particular show that the state can play a significant role in deciding the specific form that these liberalizing reforms take and that they are subject to the institutional mechanisms by which incumbent rulers hang on to power, especially as they pertain to leaders' control over resources and information (the public-private ownership balance of the largest corporations and the transparency of the state sector).[20]

---

[19] Elkins and Simmons (2004); Simmons, Dobbin, and Garrett (2006); Büthe and Mattli (2011); Bach and Newman (2010).

[20] The mechanisms include social construction, coercion, competition, and learning. For an overview on the diffusion of liberalization, see Simmons, Dobbin, and Garrett (2006).

Additionally, the extent and nature of compliance further vary across DPARs, depending on the strength of the ruling party. As political opponents pose a greater threat to the ruling party's dominance, the regime will increase opacity, thereby reducing its level of compliance with liberalizing reforms (e.g., Singapore's delayed enforcement of new rules regarding the disclosure of directors' remuneration). Thus "insincere" or "mock" compliance may be used, in part, to appear compliant with a liberalizing reform agenda in order to attract foreign direct investment (FDI) and promote growth (to boost the ruling party's popular appeal) while deviating from it in practice in order to maintain regime stability.[21]

Finally, the shift in the global balance of power toward China will likely result in more international arrangements that reflect the political priorities of the CCP. This, in turn, will result in the diffusion of authoritarian-oriented reforms. The argument of this book suggests that this diffusion will vary across types of authoritarian regimes but that a clear difference will emerge between the reforms adopted by advanced democracies versus the emerging authoritarian world. An important area of research concerns how the diffusion of these statist-authoritarian-led reforms differs from that of their liberal predecessors.

Areas for Future Research

The framework developed in this book points to a number of areas for future research. A few of these include additional work on SWFs, the role of SWFs as institutional intermediaries, state-owned business groups both within and between countries, entrepreneurship, the nature of state investment between countries with large state sectors, and various dimensions of "economic statecraft" such as trade agreements and foreign exchange rate policy.

Sovereign Wealth Funds

Work in the finance literature has found that SWF investments are not heavily driven by political considerations.[22] The model developed in this book points to the mechanism underlying this finding. Specifically,

---

[21] Walter (2008).   [22] Megginson and Fotak (2015).

SWFs that engage in aggressive interventions do so for financial rather than political considerations because financial returns are often a political objective in their own right. Public-private ownership is common in DPARs, with shares widely held by the country's citizens. Because DPARs hold elections, share ownership offers a way to strengthen the loyalty of citizens to the ruling party, to ensure their continuing support for the ruling party's economic policies and the regime's continuing stability. Thus future research could assess whether financial returns under- or outperform when the ruling party faces a strong challenge and the wider management implications for SWFs and SOEs as a result. For example, when ruling parties in DPARs face strong political opposition, do hybrid SOEs exhibit a higher level of debt (leverage), or issue more equity, or engage in more acquisitions?

SWFs as Institutional Intermediaries

Institutions decide the "rules of the game" that govern economic interactions (Ostrom 1990; Williamson 1990; North 1990), whereas firms behave within the confines of those rules (Delios and Henisz 2000; Henisz 2000; Henisz and Delios 2001; Peng 2003). However, the research in this book shows that institutions and firms are not necessarily distinct. Through their capacity to establish ownership stakes in firms and implement governance strategies, SWFs can actively apply the "rules of the game" by participating in the market themselves on behalf of the institutions they represent. In this manner, SWFs can act as *institutional intermediaries*.[23] Furthermore, SWFs can actively apply institutional rules to firms located in both local and foreign markets, thereby leading to the potential for institutional transplantation, mixing, or even competition. *Institutional transplantation* occurs when a SWF applies the institutional rules of the home country to a foreign environment. *Institutional mixing* happens when home country rules are combined with those of a foreign country. *Institutional competition* refers to institutional rules originating from different countries competing for dominance in deciding how firms behave. The role of SWFs as institutional intermediaries sheds new light on how institutional environments are shaped and yields fresh insights into how institutions can influence organizational strategies.

---

[23] I would like to thank Sam Park for suggesting this idea.

To investigate institutional transplantation, research can examine whether SWFs and their affiliated firms successfully recreate the institutional environment of the home country in a host country with institutional voids. Notable examples of this phenomenon include the creation of industrial parks of Singapore throughout Asia. These parks aim to recreate the institutional environment of Singapore in a foreign country with institutional voids so as to extend the scope of the domestic operations of Singapore companies and to move toward attracting foreign multinational corporations. Temasek-linked companies have played an instrumental role in establishing these parks. The examination of how Temasek-linked corporations transplant institutional rules into the context of a foreign country can be sharpened by drawing comparisons with family-owned business groups that establish significant foreign bases of operation or campuses in the same locations.

The topic of institutional mixing can also be examined through a comparative analysis of these parks. Singapore has established industrial parks in a number of countries across the region, including China, India, Indonesia, the Philippines, Thailand, and Vietnam. Thus comparisons can be made with regard to how Temasek-linked firms mix home-country rules differently depending on the environment of the host country.

In some cases, these parks have encountered competition from the host country. For example, Singapore's Suzhou Industrial Park faced considerable difficulties after the Suzhou local government built its own version of an industrial park next door, the Suzhou New District. In this case, competition from the local park led to the failure of the Singapore state-owned park.

Institutional competition can also be examined in the context of regional markets, such as telecommunications and financial services. Khazanah and Temasek have increased their presence in these arenas. Dewenter et al. found that Temasek-linked firms benefit from network transactions.[24] The benefits that arise from these network transactions increase as the density of Temasek-linked firms increases across different industries at the regional level. An ecosystem of Temasek-linked firms can be recreated at the regional level and can mimic the benefits to

---

[24]   Dewenter et al. (2010).

family-owned business groups that Khanna and Palepu identified in the domestic context.[25]

State-Owned Business Groups

The business-group literature has focused its attention almost exclusively on family-owned groups.[26] State-owned business groups have received relatively little attention, although they now occupy an increasingly important space in some emerging economies, such as China, Singapore, and Malaysia. By 2006, for example, there were 2,856 officially recognized Chinese business groups, which held 27,950 first-tier subsidiaries. They employed around thirty million people directly and had grown at a remarkable pace along many dimensions.[27] Beneath this first tier of firms, many further tiers of participating firms that were not recorded in official statistics also existed. As such, the influence and reach of state-owned business groups are of considerable importance, in addition to the agency – often a SWF – that administers ownership of them.

But business groups have emerged not only in the context of domestic markets but also in regional and international contexts. State-owned business groups, often administered by a SWF, possess two advantages in comparison with privately owned business groups. First, SWFs can more easily call on political leaders to negotiate access to foreign markets. Second, SWFs have access to a greater supply of capital at lower cost due to the sovereign backing of the SWF. As a consequence, state-owned business groups may be better at developing capital-intensive regional businesses in areas such as healthcare, telecommunications, and financial services. The advantages of state-owned entities are magnified in these regional and international contexts because institutional voids are likely to be particularly high. In Southeast Asia, for example, both Khazanah and Temasek illustrate how SWFs and their affiliated companies can successfully develop regional businesses that lack comparable privately owned business group competitors. Evidence from Temasek also suggests that such firms benefit from related-party transactions by gaining access to

---

[25] Khanna and Palepu (2000).
[26] Morck and Nakamura (2007); Morck, Wolfenson, and Young (2004); Yiu et al. (2005); Keister (2000).
[27] Sutherland and Ning (2015).

business opportunities from other firms in the SWF network.[28] This success suggests that such SWF business networks may have a competitive advantage in building business groups that span national jurisdictions.

Entrepreneurship

A critical hindrance to the development of new innovations is for entrepreneurs to access stable financing to develop their ideas into commercial products.[29] SWFs may have a competitive advantage in this regard, especially in markets that have substantial institutional voids. Indeed, SWFs are entering into this arena in Southeast Asia (and elsewhere) where they have more experience and knowledge than venture capitalists based in Silicon Valley. Having the state as a strategic partner can provide entrepreneurs with capital and complementary resources such as improved infrastructure, a trained workforce, and cutting-edge research centers where previously there was none.[30] The framework developed in this book indicates that savings SWFs from DPARs may be the most likely to provide venture capital–style financing for entrepreneurs in developing countries because these SWFs can bridge the gap between private ownership and a public listing. Moreover, these SWFs may be well suited to funding entrepreneurs not only in their own domestic markets but also in a regional context. Indeed, the relatively greater ease of building a regional business network may also create opportunities for entrepreneurs that previously did not exist (e.g., mobile phone apps tailored to the ethnic group of a specific region).

State Investment between Countries with Large State Sectors

An additional line of inquiry regards the nature of foreign investments between regimes. I have argued that states will be more capable of purchasing large stakes in a foreign listed company if it is located in a country with equal or lower transparency requirements. An additional possibility to examine is whether countries that are home to large state sectors are more welcoming of investments by SWFs and SOEs while controlling for transparency. For example, one

---

[28] Dewenter et al. (2010).   [29] Barr et al. (2009); Markham et al. (2010).
[30] Agarwal, Audretsch, and Sarkar (2010); Kogut (1991).

might expect that DPARs would be more welcoming of SWF investments from other DPARs if they recognize that these investments are not motivated by politics to the exclusion of their commercial soundness. Thus the opening anecdote about Khazanah's hostile takeover of Parkway may have occurred because Singapore's leaders (and the public) are not fearful of acquisitions by SWFs and SOEs. The story would likely by quite different if the hostile takeover occurred in the United States, for example. Thus, as SOEs and SWFs from emerging economies engage in more foreign investments, are they likely to preferentially target other countries with large state sectors?

Economic Statecraft

The implications arising from differences among authoritarian regimes also extend to areas of "economic statecraft." Norris, for example, looks at the role of foreign economic policy as a means by which to achieve national security objectives in the context of China.[31] But the framework developed in this book suggests that DPARs are even more likely to engage in aggressive foreign policies to achieve domestic political goals, *ceteris paribus*. Ruling parties in DPARs are just as likely as those in SPARs, such as China, to face holistic threats to their hold on power, but they are more likely to encounter threats from political opponents in the domestic political arena with implications for foreign policy. Russia is a prime example. To what extent are DPARs more likely to engage in aggressive forms of economic statecraft than their SPAR counterparts?

[31] Norris (2016).

References

Abinales, P. N. and Amoroso, D. J. (2005). *State and Society in the Philippines*. Lanham, MD: Rowman & Littlefield.

Abubakar, M. (2010). Towards World Class Corporations, (online) Indonesian Minister of State-Owned Enterprises, available at www.eu romoneyconferences.com/downloads/Asia/2010/Indonesia10/SOE.pdf (accessed November 15, 2016).

Acemoglu, D. and Johnson, S. (2005). Unbundling institution. *Journal of Political Economy* 113(5), pp. 949–95.

Acharya, V. V., Gottschalg, O. F., Hahn, M., and Kehoe, C. (2013). Corporate governance and value creation: Evidence from private equity. *Review of Financial Studies* 26(2), pp. 368–402.

Adams, B. (2012). Speak truth to Cambodia's dictator. *Financial Times*, September 18.

Ades, A. and Di Tella, R. (1997). National champions and corruption: Some unpleasant interventionist arithmetic. *Economic Journal* 107(443), pp. 1023–42.

Agarwal, R., Audretsch, D., and Sarkar, M. (2010). Knowledge spillovers and strategic entrepreneurship. *Strategic Entrepreneurship Journal* 4(4), pp. 271–83.

Aghion, P. (2011). Some thoughts on industrial policy and growth. In O. Falck, C. Gollier, and L. Woessmann (eds.), *Industrial Policy for National Champions*, 1st edn. Cambridge, MA: MIT Press, pp. 13–30.

Aguilera, R. V. and Jackson, G. (2010). Comparative and international corporate governance. *Academy of Management Annals* 4(1), pp. 485–556.

Aguilera, R., Capapé, J., and Santiso, J. (2016). Sovereign wealth funds: A strategic governance view. *Academy of Management Perspectives* 30(1), pp. 5–23.

Ahmad, R., Ariff, M., and Skully, M. (2007). Factors determining mergers of banks in Malaysia's banking sector reform. *Multinational Finance Journal* 11(1–2), pp. 1–31.

Aizenman, J. and Glick, R. (2009). Sovereign wealth funds: Stylized facts about their determinants and governance. *International Finance* 12(3), pp. 351–86.

Alhashel, B. (2015). Sovereign wealth funds: A literature review. *Journal of Economics and Business* 78(March–April), pp. 1–13.

Al-Hassan, A., Papaioannou, M., Skancke, M., and Sung, C. (2013). Sovereign wealth funds: Aspects of governance structures and investment management. IMF *Working Papers* 13, p. 231.

Allen, J. (2014). The state of corporate governance. In *2014 CARE Conference in HK Polytechnic University*. Hong Kong: Asian Corporate Governance Association.

Allen, F., Qian, J., and Qian, M. (2005). Law, finance, and economic growth in China. *Journal of Financial Economics* 77(1), pp. 57–116.

Amsden, A. H. (1979). Taiwan's economic history: A case of etatisme and a challenge to dependency theory. *Modern China* 5(3), pp. 341–79.

(2001). *The Rise of "The Rest": Challenges to the West from Late-Industrializing Economies.* Oxford: Oxford University Press.

Andrews-Speed, C. P. (2004). *Energy Policy and Regulation in the People's Republic of China*, vol. 19. The Hague: Kluwer Law International.

Ang, J. S. and Ding, D. K. (2006). Government ownership and the performance of government-linked companies: The case of Singapore. *Journal of Multinational Financial Management* 16(1), pp. 64–88.

Anwar, D. F. (1994). *Indonesia in ASEAN.* Singapore: Institute of Southeast Asian Studies.

Arian, A. and Barnes, S. H. (1974). The dominant party system: A neglected model of democratic stability. *Journal of Politics* 36(3), pp. 592–614.

Armour, J. and Cheffins, B. (2011). The past, present, and future of shareholder activism by hedge funds. *Journal of Corporate Law* 37, pp. 1–58.

Aspinall, E. 2013. The triumph of capital? Class politics and Indonesian democratisation. *Journal of Contemporary Asia* 43(2), pp. 226–42.

Astami, E. W., Tower, G., Rusmin, R., and Neilson, J. (2010). The effect of privatisation on performance of state-owned-enterprises in Indonesia. *Asian Review of Accounting* 18(1), pp. 5–19.

Australian High Commission (1994). *Country Economic Brief: Brunei Darussalam.* Bandar Seria Begawan: Australian High Commission, pp. 24–25.

Bach, D. and Newman, A. (2010). Transgovernmental networks and domestic policy convergence: Evidence from insider trading regulation. *International Organization* 64(3), pp. 505–28.

Bagnall, A. and Truman, E. (2013). *Progress on Sovereign Wealth Fund Transparency and Accountability: An Updated SWF Scoreboard.* Peterson Institute for International Economics, No. PB13-19. Available at https://piie.com/publications/pb/pb13-19.pdf (accessed March 14, 2014).

Bai, C. E. and Xu, L. C. (2005). Incentives for CEOs with multitasks: Evidence from Chinese state-owned enterprises. *Journal of Comparative Economics* 33(3), pp. 517–39.

Balding, C. (2012). *Sovereign Wealth Funds: The New Intersection of Money and Politics*. New York: Oxford University Press.

Barr, S., Baker, T., Markham, S., and Kingon, A. (2009). Bridging the valley of death: Lessons learned from 14 years of commercialization of technology education. *Academy of Management Learning & Education* 8(3), pp. 370–88.

Barraclough, S. (2000). The politics of privatization in the Malaysian health care system. *Contemporary Southeast Asia* 22(2), pp. 340–59.

Barros, R. (2011). On the outside Looking in: Secrecy and the study of authoritarian regimes. Unpublished paper. Buenos Aires: Universidad de San Andrés. Available at www. udesa. edu.ar/files/UAHumanidades/ EVENTOS/PaperBarros31111.pdf.

Baron, D.P. (1995). Integrated strategy: Market and nonmarket components. *California Management Review* 37(2), pp. 47–65.

(1997). Integrated strategy and international trade disputes: The Kodak-Fujifilm case. *Journal of Economics & Management Strategy* 6(1), pp. 291–346.

Batalla, E. V. (2012). Continuity and change in the Philippine business landscape.*Journal of International Cooperation Studies* 20(1), pp. 1–30.

Bebchuk, L. and Neeman, Z. (2009). Investor protection and interest group politics. *Review of Financial Studies* 23(3), pp. 1089–119.

Beck, T., Demirgüç-Kunt, A., Laeven, L., and Maksimovic, V. (2006). The determinants of financing obstacles. *Journal of International Money and Finance* 25(6), pp. 932–52.

Bernstein, S., Lerner, J., and Schoar, A. (2013). The investment strategies of sovereign wealth funds. *Journal of Economic Perspectives* 27(2), pp. 219–38.

Bird-Pollan, J. (2012). The unjustified subsidy: Sovereign wealth funds and the foreign sovereign tax exemption. *Fordham Journal of Corporate & Financial Law* 17(4), 987–1021.

Bjornlund, E. (2004). *Beyond Free and Fair: Monitoring Elections and Building Democracy*. Washington, DC: Woodrow Wilson Center Press.

Blaydes, L. (2006). Who votes in authoritarian elections and why? Determinants of voter turnout in contemporary Egypt. In *2006 Annual Meeting of the American Political Science Association*. Philadelphia, PA: APSA. Available at http://citeseerx.ist.psu.edu/view doc/download?doi=10.1.1.457.5619&rep=rep1&type=pdf (accessed June 15, 2014).

Bluedorn, J., Duttagupta, R., Guajardo, J., and Topalova, P. (2013). Capital flows are fickle: Anytime, anywhere. *IMF Working Papers* 13(183), p. 1.

Boardman, A. and Vining, A. (1989). Ownership and performance in competitive environments: A comparison of the performance of private, mixed, and state-owned enterprises. *Journal of Law and Economics* 32(1), pp. 1–33.

Boix, C. and Svolik, M. (2013). The foundations of limited authoritarian government: Institutions, commitment, and power-sharing in dictatorships. *Journal of Politics* 75(2), pp. 300–16.

Bortolotti, B. (2014). Trends and challenges in sovereign investment: The SWF discount. In *Paris Nanterre Workshop on Sovereign Investment*. Available at https://economix.fr/pdf/workshops/2014_Sovereign_Weal th_Funds_and_globalization/Bortolotti-SWF-Nanterre.pdf (accessed September 5, 2015).

Bortolotti, B., Fotak, V., and Megginson, W. L. (2015). The sovereign wealth fund discount: Evidence from public equity investments. *Review of Financial Studies* 28(11), pp. 2993–3035.

Bortolotti, B., Fotak, V., Megginson, W., and Miracky, W. F. (2010). Quiet leviathans: Sovereign wealth fund investment, passivity, and the value of the firm. Unpublished working paper. University of Oklahoma and Sovereign Investment Lab.

Boubakri, N., Cosset, J., Guedhami, O., and Saffar, W. (2011). The political economy of residual state ownership in privatized firms: Evidence from emerging markets. *Journal of Corporate Finance* 17(2), pp. 244–58.

Boyson, N. and Mooradian, R. M. (2007). Hedge funds as shareholder activists from 1994–2005. Working paper. Northeastern University, Boston, MA.

Brav, A., Jiang, W., Partnoy, F., and Thomas, R. (2008). Hedge fund activism, corporate governance, and firm performance. *Journal of Finance* 63(4), pp. 1729–75.

Brown, R. (1994). *Capital and Entrepreneurship in South-East Asia*. Basingstoke: Macmillan.

Brown, R. A. (2007). *The Rise of the Corporate Economy in Southeast Asia*. London: Routledge.

Brownlee, J. (2007). *Authoritarianism in an Age of Democratization*. Cambridge: Cambridge University Press.

Bruton, G. D., Peng, M. W., Ahlstrom, D., Stan, C., and Xu, K. (2015). State-owned enterprises around the world as hybrid organizations. *Academy of Management Perspectives* 29(1), pp. 92–114.

Buckley, P. J., Clegg, L. J., Cross, A. R., et al. (2007). The determinants of Chinese outward foreign direct investment. *Journal of International Business Studies* 38(4), pp. 499–518.

Bueno de Mesquita, B. (2005). *The Logic of Political Survival*. Cambridge, MA: MIT Press.

Burton, J. (2013). Singapore issues rules to prevent "crony capitalism." *Financial Times*. Available at www.xn–singapore–window-0z2j.org/sw04/040501ft.htm (accessed October 23, 2014).

Bushman, R., Piotroski, J., and Smith, A. (2004). What determines corporate transparency? *Journal of Accounting Research* 42(2), pp. 207–52.

Büthe, T. and Mattli, W. (2011). *The New Global Rulers: The Privatization in the World Economy*. Princeton, NJ: Princeton University Press.

Cahyadi, G., Kursten, B., Weiss, M., and Yang, G. (2004). *Singapore's Economic Transformation* (Global Urban Development, Singapore Metropolitan Economic Strategy Report). Prague: Global Urban Development, pp. 1–28. Available at www.globalurban.org/GUD%20Singapore%20MES%20Report.pdf (accessed October 24, 2014).

Cameron, R. (1961). *France and the Economic Development of Europe, 1800–1914*. Princeton, NJ: Princeton University Press.

Campbell, J. (1996). Understanding risk and return. *Journal of Political Economy* 104(2), pp. 298–345.

Caprio, G., Hanson, J. A., and Litan, R. E. (eds.) (2005). *Financial Crises: Lessons from the Past, Preparation for the Future*. Washington, DC: Brookings Institution Press.

Carey, J. M. and Shugart, M. S. (1995). Incentives to cultivate a personal vote: A rank ordering of electoral formulas. *Electoral Studies* 14(4), pp. 417–39.

Carney, M. and Andriesse, E. (2013). Malaysia. In M. A. Witt and G. Redding (eds.), *Oxford Handbook of Asian Business Systems*, 1st edn. New York, NY: Oxford University Press.

Carney, R. W. (ed.) (2009). *Lessons from the Asian Financial Crisis*. New York, NY: Routledge.

Carney, R. W. (2012). Political hierarchy and finance: The politics of China's financial development. In A. Walter and X. Zhang (eds.), *East Asian Capitalism: Diversity, Continuity, and Change*, 1st edn. Oxford: Oxford University Press, p. 159.

Carney, R. W. (2014). The stabilizing state: State capitalism as a response to financial globalization in one-party regimes. *Review of International Political Economy* 22(4), pp. 838–73.

(2017). Business-government relations and corporate governance reforms. In X. Zhang and T. Zhu (eds.), *Business, Government, and Economic Institutions in China*. Basinstoke: Palgrave Macmillan.

Carney, R. W. and Child, T. B. (2013). Changes to the ownership and control of East Asian corporations between 1996 and 2008: The primacy of politics. *Journal of Financial Economics* 107(2), pp. 494–513.

Carney, R. W. and Hamilton-Hart, N. (2015). What do changes in corporate ownership in Indonesia tell us? *Bulletin of Indonesian Economic Studies* 51(1), pp. 123–45.

Case, W. (2002). *Politics in Southeast Asia: Democracy or Less*. London: Psychology Press.

(2004). Malaysia. In A. Karatnycky and S. Repucci (eds.), *Countries at the Crossroads*, 1st edn. New York, NY: Freedom House.

(2005). Malaysia: New reforms, old continuities, tense ambiguities. *Journal of Development Studies* 41(2), pp. 284–309.

(2010). Transition from single-party dominance? New data from Malaysia. *Journal of East Asian Studies* 10(1), pp. 91–126.

Chan, H. (2009). Politics over markets: Integrating state-owned enterprises into Chinese socialist market. *Public Administration and Development* 29(1), pp. 43–54.

Chang, H. J. (2000). The hazard of moral hazard: Untangling the Asian crisis. *World Development* 28(4), pp. 775–88.

Chang, S. J., 2006. *Business Groups in East Asia: Financial Crisis, Restructuring, and New Growth*. New York, NY: Oxford University Press.

Chao, V. Y. (2010). Three judges, prosecutor held on graft charges. *Taipei Times*. Available at www.taipeitimes.com/News/front/archives/2010/07/15/2003477968 (accessed January 18, 2015).

Chee, H. L. and Barraclough, S. (eds.) (2007). *Health Care in Malaysia: The Dynamics of Provision, Financing and Access*. New York, NY: Routledge.

Cheffins, B. and Armour, J. (2011). The past, present, and future of shareholder activism by hedge funds. *Journal of Corporate Law* 37, pp. 51–58.

Cheibub, J., Gandhi, J., and Vreeland, J. (2010). Democracy and dictatorship revisited. *Public Choice* 143(1–2), pp. 67–101.

Chen, C. L. (2000). Why has Taiwan been immune to the Asian financial crisis? *Asia-Pacific Financial Markets* 7(1), pp. 45–68.

Chen, J. J., Liu, X., and Li, W. (2010). The effect of insider control and global benchmarks on Chinese executive compensation. *Corporate Governance: An International Review* 18(2), pp. 107–23.

Chen, S. M. S., Lin, C. C., Chu, C. C., et al. (1991). *Disintegrating KMT-State Capitalism: A Closer Look at Privatizing Taiwan's State- and Party-Owned Enterprises*. Taipei: Taipei Society.

Chen, X., Harford, J., and Li, K. (2007). Monitoring: Which institutions matter? *Journal of Financial Economics* 86(2), pp. 279–305.

Chen, Y., Li, H., and Zhou, L. (2005). Relative performance evaluation and the turnover of provincial leaders in China. *Economics Letters* 88(3), pp. 421–25.

Cheng, S. H. (1991). Economic change and industrialization. In E. Chew and E. Lee (eds.), *A History of Singapore*, 1st ed. Singapore: Oxford University Press, pp. 182–216.

Cheng, T. J., and Hsu, Y. M. (2015). Long in the making: Taiwan's institutionalized party system. In A. Hicken, E., Kuhonta and M. Weiss (eds.), *Party System Institutionalization in Asia: Democracies, Autocracies, and the Shadows of the Past*, 1st ed. New York, NY: Cambridge University Press, p. 108.

Cheng-Han, T., Puchniak, D. W., and Varottil, U. (2015). State-owned enterprises in Singapore: Historical insights into a potential model for reform. *Columbia Journal of Asian Law* 28(2).

Cheung, Y. W. and Qian, X. (2009). Empirics of China's outward direct investment. *Pacific Economic Review* 14(3), pp. 312–41.

Cheung, Y., de Haan, J., Qian, X., and Yu, S. (2012). China's outward direct investment in Africa. *Review of International Economics* 20(2), pp. 201–20.

Chong, A. and Lopez-de-Silanes, F. (2005). *Privatization in Latin America: Myths and Reality*. Washington, DC: World Bank and Stanford University.

Chu, Y. H. (1994). The realignment of business-government relations and regime transition in Taiwan. In A. MacIntyre (ed.), *Business and Government in Industrialising Asia*, 1st edn. Ithaca, NY: Cornell University Press, pp. 113–41.

Chua, B. H. (1995). Building the political middle ground. In *Communitarian Ideology and Democracy in Singapore*. New York, NY: Routledge, pp. 169–83.

Chuen, D. L. K. and Gregoriou, G. N. (eds.) (2014). *Handbook of Asian Finance: Financial Markets and Sovereign Wealth Funds*, vol. 1. Burlington, MA: Academic Press.

Claessens, S., Djankov, S., and Lang, L. (2000). The separation of ownership and control in East Asian corporations. *Journal of Financial Economics* 58(1–2), pp. 81–112.

Clark, G. L. and Monk, A. (2010). Government of Singapore Investment Corporation (GIC): Insurer of last resort and bulwark of nation-state legitimacy. *Pacific Review* 23(4), pp. 429–51.

Clark, G. L., Dixon, A., and Monk, A. (2013). *Sovereign Wealth Funds*. Princeton, NJ: Princeton University Press.

Clifford, C. (2008). Value creation or destruction? Hedge funds as shareholder activists. *Journal of Corporate Finance* 14(4), pp. 323–36.

CNOOC's Bid for Unocal (2005). Is CNOOC's bid for unocal a threat to America? November 21, Knowledge@Wharton. Available at http://kno

wledge.wharton.upenn.edu/article/is-cnoocs-bid-for-unocal-a-threat-to-america/ (accessed January 31, 2016).

Coase, R. H. (1937). The nature of the firm. *Economica* 4(16), pp. 386–405.

Coates, M. (2015). Chinese investment in the U.S. will grow in 2016. *Forbes*, December 10. Available at www.forbes.com/sites/forbesleadership forum/2015/12/10/chinese-investment-in-the-u-s-will-grow-in-2016/#4d f01371a8ab (accessed November 12, 2016).

Commission on Growth and Development (2008). *The Growth Report: Strategies for Sustained Growth and Inclusive Development.* Washington, DC: World Bank Publications.

Confederation of Indian Industries and McKinsey (2002). *Healthcare in India: The Road Ahead.* New Dehli: Confederation of Indian Industry and McKinsey & Company.

Conyon, M. J. and He, L. (2011). Executive compensation and corporate governance in China. *Journal of Corporate Finance* 17(4), pp. 1158–75.

Cui, L. and Jiang, F. (2012). State ownership effect on firms' FDI ownership decisions under institutional pressure: A study of Chinese outward-investing firms. *Journal of International Business Studies* 43(3), pp. 264–84.

Cumming, D. J. and MacIntosh, J. G. (2006). Crowding out private equity: Canadian evidence. *Journal of Business Venturing* 21(5), pp. 569–609.

Cunningham, E. (2007). China's energy governance: Perception and reality. In *MIT Center for International Studies Audit of the Conventional Wisdom.* Cambridge, MA: MIT Press, pp. 4–7.

Das, U. S., Lu, Y., Mulder, C., and Sy, A. (2009). Setting up a sovereign wealth fund: Some policy and operational considerations (IMF Working Paper 09/179). International Monetary Fund, Washington, DC.

De Dios, E. (2007). Local politics and local economy. In A. Balisacan and H. Hill (eds.), *The Dynamics of Regional Development: The Philippines in East Asia*, 1st edn. Northampton, MA: Edward Elgar, pp. 157–203.

Deacon, R. T. (2009). Public good provision under dictatorship and democracy. *Public Choice* 139(1–2), pp. 241–62.

Delios, A. and Henisz, W. I. (2000). Japanese firms' investment strategies in emerging economies. *Academy of Management Journal* 43(3), pp. 305–23.

Deng, G. S. and Kennedy, S. (2010). Big business and industry association lobbying in China: The paradox of contrasting styles. *China Journal* 63, pp. 101–25.

Dewenter, K. L., Han, X., and Malatesta, P. H. (2010). Firm values and sovereign wealth fund investments. *Journal of Financial Economics* 98(2), pp. 256–78.

Dhanabalan, S. (2001). Role of government ownership of business in the era of globalisation and role of Temasek (speech to Foreign Correspondents Association), Singapore, December 12.

Dharwadkar, B., George, G., and Brandes, P. (2000). Privatization in emerging economies: An agency theory perspective. *Academy of Management Review* 25(3), pp. 650–69.

Diamond, D. W. (1984). Financial intermediation and delegated monitoring. *Review of Economic Studies* 51(3), pp. 393–414.

(1991). Monitoring and reputation: The choice between bank loans and directly placed debt. *Journal of Political Economy* 99(4), pp. 689–721.

Dickson, B. J. (2008). *Wealth into Power*. Cambridge: Cambridge University Press.

Dinc, I. S. (2005). Politicians and banks: Political influences on government-owned banks in emerging markets. *Journal of Financial Economics* 77(2), pp. 453–79.

Dixit, A. (2002). Incentives and organizations in the public sector: An interpretative review. *Journal of Human Resources* 37(4), p. 696.

Djankov, S., Lopez de Silanes, F., La Porta, R., and Shleifer, A. (2008). The law and economics of self-dealing. *Journal of Financial Economics* 88(3), pp. 430–65.

Doner, R., Ritchie, B., and Slater, D. (2005). Systemic vulnerability and the origins of developmental states: Northeast and Southeast Asia in comparative perspective. *International Organization* 59(2), pp. 327–61.

Doraisami, A. (2015). Has Malaysia really escaped the resource curse? A closer look at the political economy of oil revenue management and expenditures. *Resources Policy* 45, pp. 98–108.

Dow Jones (2010) Parkway Holdings: Mohammed Azlan bin Hashim appointed chairman. *Dow Jones International News*, August 25.

Downs, E. (2010). Who's afraid of China's oil companies. *Energy Security*, pp. 74–78.

Economic Analytical Unit (2002). *Changing Corporate Asia: What Business Needs to Know*, vol. 2: *Regional Economy Studies*. Canberra: Department of Foreign Affairs and Trade.

Economist (2012). The state advances. *The Economist*, October 6, pp. 39–40.

(2013). Nice to see you, EU. *The Economist*, April 20.

(2014). State-owned assets: Setting out the store. *The Economist*, January 11.

Economist Intelligence Unit (2014). *Economist Intelligence Unit Country Report 2014*. Brunei: Economist Intelligence Unit.

Elegant, S. (2000). Malaysia Uncensored. *Far Eastern Economic Review*, July 6, p. 26.

Elkins, Z. and Simmons, B. (2004). The globalization of liberalization: Policy diffusion in the international political economy. *American Political Science Review* 98(1), pp. 171–89.

Elson, A. (2008). The sovereign wealth funds of Singapore. *World Economics* 9(3), pp. 73–96.

Engerman, S. L. and Sokoloff, K. L. (2006). *The Persistence of Poverty in the Americas: The Role of Institutions*. Princeton, NJ: Princeton University Press, pp. 43–78.

Epstein, R. E. and Rose, A. M. (2009). The regulation of sovereign wealth funds: The virtues of going slow. *University of Chicago Law Review* 76(1), pp. 111–34.

Evans, D. (2015). Sovereign wealth funds weekly news roundup: SWFs eye new private equity strategies, Institutional Investor's Sovereign Wealth Center, February 27. Available at www.sovereignwealthcenter.com/Article/3431 517/Sovereign-Wealth-Fund-Weekly-News-Roundup-SWFs-Eye-New-Pri vate-Equity-Strategies.html#/.Vlusz78WD (accessed November 30, 2015).

Evans, P. (1995). *Embedded Autonomy: States and Industrial Transformation*. Princeton, NJ: Princeton University Press.

Fama, E. F. (1985). What's different about banks?. *Journal of Monetary Economics* 15(1), pp. 29–39.

Fama, E. F. and Jensen, M. C. (1983). Separation of ownership and control. *Journal of Law & Economics* 26(2), pp. 301–25.

Fan, J. P., Wei, K. J., and Xu, X. (2011). Corporate finance and governance in emerging markets: A selective review and an agenda for future research. *Journal of Corporate Finance* 17(2), pp. 207–14.

Fearon, J. D. and Laitin, D. D. (2003). Ethnicity, insurgency, and civil war. *American Political Science Review* 97(1), pp. 75–90.

Fell, D. (2002). Party platform change in Taiwan's 1990s elections. *Issues and Studies: An International Quarterly on China, Taiwan, and East Asian Affairs* 38(2), pp. 31–60.

(2012). *Government and Politics in Taiwan*. New York, NY: Routledge.

Fernandes, N. (2009). Sovereign wealth funds: Investment choices and implications around the world, IMD and European Corporate Governance Institute.

Fields, K. (1998). KMT, Inc. Party capitalism in a developmental state, Japan Policy Research Institution Working Paper No. 47. Available at www .jpri.org/publications/workingpapers/wp47.html (accessed January 12, 2015).

Filatotchev, I., Jackson, G., and Nakajima, C. (2013). Corporate governance and national institutions: A review and emerging research agenda. *Asia Pacific Journal of Management* 30(4), pp. 965–86.

Firth, M., Fung, P. M., and Rui, O. M. (2006). Corporate performance and CEO compensation in China. *Journal of Corporate Finance* 12(4), pp. 693–714.

(2007). How ownership and corporate governance influence chief executive pay in China's listed firms. *Journal of Business Research* 60(7), pp. 776–85.

Fitriningrum, A. (2006). Indonesia experiences in managing the state companies, presentation given at the OECD Roundtable on Corporate Governance, Network on Corporate Governance of State Owned Enterprises, Singapore, May 15. Available at www.oecd.org/daf/ca/cor porategovernanceprinciples/37339611.pdf.

Ford, M. Brunei: Profligate Prince Jefri. *Newsweek*, April 10, 2000.

Fort, T. C., Haltiwanger, J., Jarmin, R. S., and Miranda, J. (2013). How firms respond to business cycles: The role of firm age and firm size. *IMF Economic Review* 61(3), pp. 520–59.

Frazier, M. W. (2015). The evolution of a welfare state under China's state capitalism. In B. Naughton and K. S. Tsai (eds.), *State Capitalism, Institutional Adaptation, and the Chinese Miracle*, 1st edn. Cambridge: Cambridge University Press, pp. 223–39.

Freeman, N. J. and Than, T. M. M. (eds.) (2002). *Regional Outlook: Southeast Asia 2002–2003*. Singapore: Institute of Southeast Asian Studies.

Fuller, T. (2014). Cambodia steps up crackdown on dissent with ban on assembly. New York Times, January 5.

Gandhi, J. (2008). *Political Institutions under Dictatorship*. New York, NY: Cambridge University Press

Gandhi, J. and Przeworski, A. (2006). Cooperation, cooptation, and rebellion under dictatorships. *Economics & Politics* 18(1), pp. 1–26.

(2007). Authoritarian institutions and the survival of autocrats. *Comparative Political Studies* 40(11), pp. 1279–301.

Garrett, G. (1998). *Partisan Politics in the Global Economy*. New York, NY: Cambridge University Press.

Geddes B. (1999). What do we know about democratization after twenty years? *Annual Review of Political Science* 2(1), pp. 115–44.

(2003). *Paradigms and Sand Castles: Theory Building and Research Design in Comparative Politics*. Ann Arbor, MI: University of Michigan Press.

(2005). Why parties and elections in authoritarian regimes? In *Annual Meeting of the American Political Science Association*. Washington, DC: APSA, pp. 456–71. Available at www.daniellazar.com/wp-con tent/uploads/authoritarian-elections.doc (accessed January 10, 2014).

(2008) Party creation as an autocratic survival strategy. In *Dictatorships: Their Governance and Social Consequences*. Princeton, NJ: Princeton University Press.

Gehlbach, S. and Keefer, P. (2011). Investment without democracy: Ruling-party institutionalization and credible commitment in autocracies. *Journal of Comparative Economics* 39(2), pp. 123–39.

Gelb, A., Tordo, S., and Halland, H. (2014). Sovereign wealth funds and long-term development finance. Policy Research Working Paper 6776, World Bank, Washington, DC.

Gelpern, A., (2011). Sovereignty, accountability, and the wealth fund governance conundrum. *Asian Journal of International Law* 1(2), pp. 289–320.

Gerschenkron, A. (1962). *Economic Backwardness in Historical Perspective*. Cambridge, MA: Harvard University Press.

Gillan, S. and Starks, L. T. (1998). A survey of shareholder activism: Motivation and empirical evidence. *Contemporary Finance Digest* 2(3), pp. 10–34.

Gilson, R. J. and Milhaupt, C. J. (2008). Sovereign wealth funds and corporate governance: A minimalist response to the new mercantilism. *Stanford Law Review* 60(5), pp. 1345–70.

Göbel, C. (2004). Beheading the hydra: Combating corruption and organized crime. *China Perspectives* 56 (Oct–Nov), pp. 14–25.

(2015). Anticorruption in Taiwan: Process-tracing report.

Goh, K. S. (1995). Experience and prospect of Singapore's economic development: Strategy formulation and execution. In L. Low (ed.), *Wealth of East Asian Nations: Speeches and Writings by Goh Keng Swee*, 1st edn. Singapore: Federal Publications, pp. 34–55.

Golder, M. (2005). Democratic electoral systems around the world, 1946–2000. *Electoral Studies* 24, pp. 103–21.

Goldstein, A. and Pananond, P. (2008). Singapore Inc. goes shopping abroad: Profits and pitfalls. *Journal of Contemporary Asia* 38(3), pp. 417–38.

Gomez, E. T. (2004). Introduction: Politics, business and ethnicity in Malaysia: A state in transition? In E. T. Gomez (ed.), *State of Malaysia*, 1st edn. New York, NY: Routledge, pp. 1–29.

(2006). Malaysian business groups: The state and capital development in the post-currency crisis period. In S. J. Chang (ed.), *Business Groups in East Asia: Financial Crisis, Restructuring, and New Growth*, 1st edn. Oxford: Oxford University Press, pp. 119–46.

(2009). The rise and fall of capital: Corporate Malaysia in historical perspective. *Journal of Contemporary Asia* 39(3), pp. 345–81.

(2016). Resisting the fall: The single dominant party, policies and elections in Malaysia. *Journal of Contemporary Asia* 46(4), pp. 570–90.

Gomez, E. T. and Jomo, K.S. (1999). *Malaysia's Political Economy: Politics, Patronage, and Profits*. New York, NY: Cambridge University Press.

Gomez, E. T. and Saravanamuttu, J. (eds.) (2013). *The New Economic Policy in Malaysia: Affirmative Action, Horizontal Inequalities and Social Justice*. Singapore: National University of Singapore Press.

Governance Commission for GOCCs (2016). *The GCG Legacy Report: October 2011–March 2016*. Manila: GCG.

Greene K. F. (2002). Opposition party strategy and spatial competition in dominant party regimes: A theory and the case of Mexico. *Comparative Political Studies* 35(7), pp. 755–83.

(2007). *Why Dominant Parties Lose*. New York, NY: Cambridge University Press.

Greenwood, R. and Schor, M. 2009, Hedge fund investor activism and takeovers. *Journal of Financial Economics* 92(3), pp. 362–75.

Gunn, G. C. (2001). Brunei. In P. Heenan and M. Lamontagne (eds.), *The Southeast Asia Handbook*, 1st edn. London: Fitzroy Dearborn.

(2008). Trophy capitalism, jefrinomics, and dynastic travail in Brunei, *Asia Pacific Journal: Japan Focus* 6(3). Available at http://apjjf.org/-Ge offrey-Gunn/2696/article.pdf (accessed November 3, 2015).

Guthrie, D., Wang, J., and Xiao, Z. (2007). Aligning the interests of multiple principals: Ownership concentration and profitability in China's publicly-traded firms. NYU-Stern Working Paper EC-07–32.

Gwartney, J., Lawson, R., and Hall, J. C. (2015). Economic freedom data set. In *Economic Freedom of the World: 2015 Annual Report*. Vancouver, BC: Fraser Institute. Available at www. freetheworld.com/ datasets_efw. html (accessed November 2, 2015).

Haber, S. H. (2002). *Crony Capitalism and Economic Growth in Latin America: Theory and Evidence*. Washington, DC: Hoover Institution Press.

(2006). Authoritarian government. In B. R. Weingast and D. Wittma (eds.), *Handbook of Political Economy*, 1st edn. New York: Oxford University Press, pp. 693–707.

Hadenius, A. and Teorell, J. (2007). Pathways from authoritarianism. *Journal of Democracy* 18(1), pp. 143–56.

Haggard, S. (1988). The Philippines: Picking up after Marcos. In R. Vernon (ed.), *The Promise of Privatization*, 1st edn. New York: Council on Foreign Relations, pp. 91–121.

(1990). *Pathways from the Periphery: The Politics of Growth in the Newly Industrializing Countries*. Ithaca, NY: Cornell University Press.

(2000). *The Political Economy of the Asian Financial Crisis*. New York, NY: Peterson Institute.

Haggard, S. and Kaufman, R. R. (1992). *The Politics of Economic Adjustment: International Constraints, Distributive Conflicts, and the State*. Princeton, NJ: Princeton University Press.

(1995). *The Political Economy of Democratic Transitions*. Princeton, NJ: Princeton University Press.

Haggard, S. and Low, L. (2001). State, politics, and business in Singapore. In E. T. Gomez (ed.), *Political Business in East Asia*, 1st edn. New York: Routledge.

Hamilton, G. G. (1997). Organization and market processes in Taiwan's capitalist economy. In M. Orru, N. W. Biggart, and G. Hamilton (eds.), *The Economic Organization of East Asian Capitalism*. Thousand Oaks, CA: Sage, pp. 237–93.

Hamilton-Hart, N. (2002). *Asian States, Asian Bankers: Central Banking in Southeast Asia*. Ithaca, NY: Cornell University Press.

Hanemann, T. and Gao, C. (2016). China's global outbound M&As in 2015. Rhodium Group Online Note. Available at http://rhg.com/notes/chinas-global-outbound-ma-in-2015 (accessed November 4, 2016).

Hart, O. D., Shleifer, A., and Vishny, R. W. (1997). The proper scope of government: Theory and an application to prisons. *Quarterly Journal of Economics* 112(4), pp. 1127–61.

Harvie, C. and Lee, B. C. (eds.) (2002). *The Role of SMEs in National Economies in East Asia*, vol. 2. Northampton, MA: Edward Elgar.

Hegre, H. and Sambanis, N. (2006). Sensitivity analysis of empirical results on civil war onset. *Journal of Conflict Resolution* 50(4), pp. 508–35.

Helleiner, E. (2009). The geopolitics of sovereign wealth funds: An introduction. *Geopolitics* 14(2), pp. 300–4.

Henisz, W. J. (2000). The institutional environment for economic growth. *Economics & Politics* 12(1), pp. 1–31.

Henisz, W. J. and Delios, A. (2001). Uncertainty, imitation, and plant location: Japanese multinational corporations, 1990–1996. *Administrative Science Quarterly* 46(3), pp. 443–75.

Hewison, K., Robison, R., and Rodan, G. (1993). *Southeast Asia in the 1990s: Authoritarianism, Democracy and Capitalism*. Melbourn: Allen & Unwin Australia.

Hillman, A. J., Keim, G. D., and Schuler, D. (2004). Corporate political activity: A review and research agenda. *Journal of Management* 30(6), pp. 837–57.

Ho, K. L. (1999). Public accountability in malaysia: Control mechanisms and critical concerns. In H. Wong and H. S. Chan (eds.), *Handbook of Comparative Public Administration in the Asia Pacific Basin*, 1st edn. New York, NY: Marcel Dekker, pp. 23–45.

Hong, T. and Biallas, M. (2007). Vietnam: Capital market diagnostic review, International Finance Corporation, World Bank, Washington, DC.

Houser, T. (2008). The roots of Chinese Oil Investment Abroad. *Asia Policy* 5(1), pp. 141–66.

Hu, Y. W. (2010). *Management of China's Foreign Exchange Reserves: A Case Study on the State Administration of Foreign* (No. 421), Directorate

General Economic and Monetary Affairs (DG ECFIN), European Commission, Brussels. Available at http://ec.europa.eu/economy_fi nance/publications/economic_paper/2010/pdf/ecp421_en.pdf (accessed December 12, 2016).

Huat, C. B. (2015). State-owned enterprises, state capitalism and social distribution in Singapore. *The Pacific Review*, pp. 1–23.

Huff, W. G. (1994). *The Economic Growth of Singapore: Trade and Development in the Twentieth Century.* Cambridge: Cambridge University Press.

(1995). What is the Singapore model of economic development?. *Cambridge Journal of Economics* 19(6), pp. 735–59.

Huifen, C. (2010). Why the Parkway bride is so much in demand. *Business Times Singapore.* Available at http://news.asiaone.com/News/The%2BBu siness%2BTimes/Story/A1Story20100528-219004.html (accessed August 21, 2015).

Hun, F. M. (2010). Khazanah's pre-emptive strike on Parkway. *The Edge Malaysia* (weekly). Available at www.theedgemarkets.com/arti cle/corporate-khazanah%E2%80%99s-pre-emptive-strike-parkway (accessed September 3, 2015).

Huntington, S. P. (1968). *Political Order in Changing Societies.* New Haven, CT: Yale University Press.

(1991). Democracy's third wave. *Journal of Democracy* 2(2), pp. 12–34.

Hurst, G. (2014). The world's largest sovereign wealth funds go private. *Institutional Investor.* Available at www.institutionalinvestor.com/arti cle/3382248/investors-sovereign-wealth-funds/the-worlds-largest-sover eign-wealth-funds-go-private.html#.WIdis7Z9634 (accessed March 27, 2015).

Hutchinson, F. E. (2014). Malaysia's federal system: Overt and covert centralisation. *Journal of Contemporary Asia* 44(3), pp. 422–42.

International Monetary Fund (2005). IMF Executive Board Concludes 2005 Article IV Consultation with Brunei Darussalam. International Monetary Fund, Public Information Notice No. 05/137, September 30, 2005.

(2007). *Global Financial Stability Report.* Washington, DC: IMF.

(2008). *Sovereign Wealth Funds: A Work Program.* Washington, DC: IMF.

(2012). *Global Financial Stability Report.* Washington, DC: IMF.

International Working Group of Sovereign Wealth Funds (2008). *Generally Accepted Principles and Practices: "Santiago Principles."*

Jacobs, J. B. (2012). *Democratizing Taiwan.* Leiden: Brill.

Jayasankaran, S. (1999). Saviour complex. *Far Eastern Economic Review* 162(32), pp. 10–13.

(2000). National interest. *Far Eastern Economic Review* 163(27), p. 77.

(2002). Malaysia turns around. *Far Eastern Economic Review* 23, pp. 40–41.

(2003). Lasting achievements. *Far Eastern Economic Review* 166(4), pp. 32–34.

Jensen, M. C. and Meckling, W. H. (1976). Theory of the firm: Managerial behavior, agency costs and ownership structure. *Journal of Financial Economics* 3(4), pp. 305–60.

Jensen, N., Malesky, E., and Weymouth, S. (2014). Unbundling the relationship between authoritarian legislatures and political risk. *British Journal of Political Science* 44(3), pp. 655–84.

Jeyaretnam, J. B. (Anson SMC) (1989). Speech during the second reading of the Constitution of the Republic of Singapore (Amendment) Bill. In *Singapore Parliamentary Debates, Official Report (July 24, 1989)*, vol. 44, pp. 1754 and 1757–58.

Jiang, F. and Kim, K. A. (2015). Corporate governance in China: A modern perspective. *Journal of Corporate Finance* 32, pp. 190–216.

Jiang, J. and Ding, C. (2014). Update on overseas investments by China's national oil companies: Achievements and challenges since 2011. International Energy Agency, Paris. Available at www.iea.org/publica tions/freepublications/publication/PartnerCountrySeriesUpdateonOversea sInvestmentsbyChinasNationalOilCompanies.pdf (accessed November 22, 2017).

Jiang, J. and Sinton, J. (2011). Overseas investments by China's national oil companies: Assessing the drivers and impacts. Information Paper, International Energy Agency, Paris. Available at www.iea.org/publica tions/freepublications/publication/overseas-investments-by-chinese-nat ional-oil-companies.html (accessed November 22, 2017).

Jiang, J. S. (2003). *The National People's Congress of China*. Beijing: Foreign Languages Press.

Johan, S. A., Knill, A., and Mauck, N. (2013). Determinants of sovereign wealth fund investment in private equity vs. public equity. *Journal of International Business Studies* 44(2), pp. 155–72.

Johnson, S. and Mitton, T. (2003). Cronyism and capital controls: Evidence from Malaysia. *Journal of Financial Economics* 67(2), pp. 351–82.

Jomo, K. S. (1998). Financial liberalization, crises, and Malaysian policy responses. *World Development* 26(8), pp. 1563–74.

(ed.) (2001). *Southeast Asia's Industrialization*. Basinstoke: Palgrave.

Jomo, K. S. and Tan, J. (2011). Lessons from privatization. In *Malaysia: Policies and Issues in Economic Development*, 1st edn. Kuala Lumpur: Institute of Strategic and International Studies.

Jomo, K. S. and Tan, W. S. (2003). Privatization and renationalization in Malaysia: A survey. Available at www.jomoks.org/research/research.htm (accessed November 15, 2015).

Judd, E. (2008). *Good Guanxi: Managing Government Relations in China.* Washington, DC: Foundation for Public Affairs.

Kaldor, N. (1980). Public or private enterprise: The issue to be considered. In W. J. Baumol (ed.), *Public and Private Enterprises in a Mixed Economy,* 1st edn. New York: St. Martin's Press, pp. 1–12.

Kang, D. C. (2002). *Crony Capitalism: Corruption and Development in South Korea and the Philippines.* New York, NY: Cambridge University Press.

Kato, T. and Long, C. (2006). CEO turnover, firm performance, and enterprise reform in China: Evidence from micro data. *Journal of Comparative Economics* 34(4), pp. 796–817.

Kay, R. (2009). Sultan of Brunei buries the hatchet with his playboy brother. *Mail Online,* September 28. Available at www.dailymail.co.uk/news/arti cle-1216520/Sultan-Brunei-buries-hatchet-playboy-prince-brother.html (accessed November 22, 2017).

Keefer, P. (2007). Governance and economic growth in China and India. In A. Winters and S. Yusuf (eds.), *Dancing with Giants: China, India, and the Global Economy.* Washington, DC: World Bank Publications, pp. 211–42.

Keefer, P. and Vlaicu, R. (2008). Democracy, credibility, and clientelism. *Journal of Law, Economics, and Organization* 24(2), pp. 371–406.

Keister, L. A. (1998). Engineering growth: Business group structure and firm performance in China's transition economy. *American Journal of Sociology* 104(2), pp. 404–40.

(2000). *The Structure and Impact of Interfirm Relations during Economic Development.* Oxford: Oxford University Press.

Kennedy, S. (2008). *The Business of Lobbying in China.* Cambridge, MA: Harvard University Press.

Kern, H. L. and Hainmueller, J. (2009). Opium for the masses: How foreign media can stabilize authoritarian regimes. *Political Analysis* 17(4), pp. 377–99.

Khaitan, A. (2014). Chinese super majors: Tilting the global oil and gas playing field. *The China Analyst,* pp. 12–14. Available at www.thebeijingaxis.com/ Newsletter/April_2014/PDF/The_China_Analyst_April_2014_Chinese_Su per_Majors.pdf (accessed April 14, 2015).

Khalik, S. (2011). Changes at the top for Parkway Group. *Straits Times,* January 26.

Khanna, T. (2000). Business groups and social welfare in emerging markets: Existing evidence and unanswered questions. *European Economic Review* 44, pp. 748–61.

Khanna, T. and Palepu, K. (2000). Is group affiliation profitable in emerging markets? An analysis of diversified Indian business groups. *Journal of Finance* 55(2), pp. 867–91.

Khanna, T. and Yafeh, Y. (2007). Business groups in emerging markets: Paragons or parasites? *Journal of Economic Literature* 45, pp. 331–72.

Khanna, V. (2004). The USSFTA: The impact on government-linked companies and Singapore's corporate scene. In T. Koh and L. L. Chang (eds.), *The United States and Singapore Free Trade Agreement: Highlights and Insights.* Singapore: Institute of Policy Studies and World Scientific Publishing Company.

Khazanah (2005). Media briefing: One-year review. Khazanah Nasional. Available at www.khazanah.com.my/Media-Downloads/Downloads (accessed November 15, 2015).

(2006). Media briefing—second year review. [pdf] Khazanah Nasional. Available at http://www.khazanah.com.my/Media-Downloads/Downloads (accessed November 15, 2015).

(2008). Media briefing: Fourth-year annual review 2007–2008. Khazanah Nasional. Available at www.khazanah.com.my/Media-Downloads/Downloads (accessed November 15, 2015).

Khoo B. T. (2003). *Beyond Mahathir: Malaysian Politics and Its Discontents.* London: Zed Books.

Kim, W., Nam, I. C., and Cuong, T. T. (2010). On the governance of state-owned economic groups in Vietnam. SSRN. Available at https://ssrn.com/abstract=1729093 (accessed December 19, 2016).

Klein, A. and Zur, E. 2009, Entrepreneurial shareholder activism: Hedge funds and other private investors. *Journal of Finance* 64(1), pp. 187–229.

Koch-Weser, I. N. and Haacke, O. D. (2013). China Investment Corporation: Recent developments in performance, strategy, and governance. *US-China Economic and Security Review Commission,.* Available at www.uscc.gov/sites/default/files/Research/China%20Investment%20Corporation_Staff%20Report_0.pdf (accessed November 22, 2017).

Kogut, B. (1991). Country capabilities and the permeability of borders. *Strategic Management Journal* 12(1), pp. 33–47.

Kolstad, I. and Wiig, A. (2012). What determines Chinese outward FDI? *Journal of World Business* 47(1), pp. 26–34.

Kondo, M. (2014). Philippines. In M. Witt and G. Redding (eds.), *Oxford Handbook of Asian Business Systems,* 1st edn. New York, NY: Oxford University Press.

Kornai, J. (1979). Resource-constrained versus demand-constrained systems. *Econometrica* 47(4), pp. 801–19.

Kotter, J. and Lel, U. (2011). Friends or foes? Target selection decisions of sovereign wealth funds and their consequences. *Journal of Financial Economics* 101(2), pp. 360–81.

Kowalski, P., Buge, M., Sztajerowska, M., and Egeland, M. (2013). State-owned enterprises: Trade effects and policy implications. OECD Trade Policy Papers No. 147, OECD Publishing, Brussels.

Krause, L. B., Koh, A. T. and Tsao, Y. L. (1990). *The Singapore Economy Reconsidered*, vol. 73. Singapore: Institute of Southeast Asian Studies.

Krugman, P. (2000). Fire-sale FDI. In S. Edwards (ed.), *Capital Flows and the Emerging Economies: Theory, Evidence and Controversies*. Chicago, IL: University of Chicago Press, pp. 43–58.

Kuczynski, P. P. (2003). *After the Washington Consensus: Restarting Growth and Reform in Latin America*. Washington, DC: Peterson Institute.

Kunzel, P., Lu, Y., Petrova, I., and Pihlman, J. (2011). Investment objectives of sovereign wealth funds: A shifting paradigm, IMF Working Paper 11/19, Washington, DC.

Kuo, C. T. (2000). New financial politics in Taiwan, Thailand and Malaysia. In *Annual Meeting of the American Political Science Association*. Washington, DC: APSA.

La Porta, R., Lopez-de-Silanes, F., Shleifer, A., and Vishny, R. (1998). Law and finance. *Journal of Political Economy* 106(6), pp. 1113–55.

La Porta, R. and López-de-Silanes, F. (1999). The benefits of privatization: Evidence from Mexico. *Quarterly Journal of Economics* 114(4), pp. 1193–242.

La Porta, R., Lopez-de-Silanes, F., and Shleifer, A. (1999). Corporate ownership around the world. *Journal of Finance* 54(2), pp. 471–517.

(2007). The economic consequences of legal origins. NBER Working Paper Series No. w13608, National Bureau of Economic Research, Cambridge, MA. Available at www.nber.org/papers/w13608 (accessed November 14, 2015).

La Porta, R., Lopez-de-Silanes, F., Shleifer, A., and Vishny, R. (2000). Investor protection and corporate governance. *Journal of Financial Economics* 58(1), pp. 3–27.

Lai, J. (2012). Khazanah Nasional: Malaysia's treasure trove. *Journal of the Asia Pacific Economy* 17(2), pp. 236–52.

Lardy, N. R. and Subramanian, A. (2012). *Sustaining China's Economic Growth after the Global Financial Crisis*. Washington, DC: Peterson Institute.

Lawson C. (2002). *Building the Fourth Estate: Democratization and the Rise of a Free Press in Mexico*. Berkeley, CA: University of California Press.

Lazarev, V. (2005). Economics of one-party state: Promotion incentives and support for the Soviet Regime1. *Comparative Economic Studies* 47(2), pp. 346–63.

Lazear, E. P. and Rosen, S. (1981). Rank-order tournaments as optimum labor contracts. *Journal of Political Economy* 89(5), pp. 841–64.

Leckie, S. and Pan, N. (2007). A review of the national social security fund in China. *Pensions: An International Journal* 12(2), pp. 88–97.

Lee, E. (2013). Scope for improvement: Malaysia's oil and gas sector. Research for Social Advancement. Available at http://refsa.org/wp/wp-content/uploads/2013/07/OG-Scoping-Report-Malaysia-final-201307 01.pdf (accessed November 15, 2015).

Lee, H. G. (2008). Malaysia in 2007: Abdullah administration under siege. In D. Singh and T. Than (eds.), *Southeast Asian Affairs in 2008*, 1st edn. Singapore: Institute of Southeast Asian Studies, pp. 187–206.

Lee K. Y. (1998). *The Singapore Story: Memoirs of Lee Kuan Yew.* Singapore: Prentice-Hall.

(2000). *From Third World to First: The Singapore Story: 1965–2000.* New York, NY: HarperCollins.

Lee, S. Y. (1976). Public enterprise and economic development in Singapore. *Malayan Economic Review* 21(2), pp. 49–73.

Leng, J. (2009). *Corporate Governance and Financial Reform in China's Transition Economy*, vol. 1. Hong Kong: Hong Kong University Press.

Levitsky, S. and Way, L. A. (2010). *Competitive Authoritarianism: Hybrid Regimes after the Cold War.* New York, NY: Cambridge University Press.

Li-Ann, T. (1997). An i for an I: Singapore's communitarian model of constitutional adjudication. *Hong Kong Law Journal* 27, pp. 152–405.

Li, Q. (2009). Democracy, autocracy, and expropriation of foreign direct investment. *Comparative Political Studies* 42(8), pp. 1098–127.

Li, H. and Zhou, L. A. (2005). Political turnover and economic performance: The incentive role of personnel control in China. *Journal of Public Economics* 89(9), pp. 1743–62.

Liao, J. X. (2015). The Chinese government and the national oil companies (NOCs): Who is the principal?. *Asia Pacific Business Review* 21(1), pp. 44–59.

Lieberthal, K. and Herberg, M. (2006). China's search for energy security: Implications for US policy. National Bureau of Asian Research, Washington, DC.

Liew, P. K. (2007). Corporate governance reforms in Malaysia: The key leading players' perspectives. *Corporate Governance* 15(5), pp. 724–40.

Lijphart, A. (1999). *Patterns of Democracy.* New Haven, CT: Yale University Press.

Lim K. S. (1998). An obstinate silence: Trade union reps on EPF board should exert their power. *Aliran Monthly* 18(3), pp. 6–8.

(2002). DAP calls for royal commission of inquiry into RM10 billion Perwaja scandal with former ACA Director-General Zaki Husin appointed to assist the inquiry to ensure that Malaysia does not get into the *Guinness Book of Records* in having the most heinous mega scandals without criminals. Lim Kit Siang. Available at www.limkit siang.com/archive/2002/feb02/lks1473.htm (accessed November 14, 2015).

Lin, J. Y. and Tan, G. (1999). Policy burdens, accountability, and the soft budget constraint. *American Economic Review* 89(2), pp. 426–31.

Liu, Q. (2006). Corporate governance in China: Current practices, economic effects and institutional determinants. *CESifo Economic Studies* 52(2), pp. 415–53.

Liu, Q. and Lu, Z.J. (2007). Corporate governance and earnings management in the Chinese listed companies: A tunneling perspective. *Journal of Corporate Finance* 13(5), pp. 881–906.

Liu, X., Buck, T., and Shu, C. (2005). Chinese economic development, the next stage: Outward FDI? *International Business Review* 14(1), pp. 97–115.

Londregan, J. B. and Poole, K. T. (1990). Poverty, the coup trap, and the seizure of executive power. *World Politics* 42(2), pp. 151–83.

Loo, D. (2007). Climate of fear hurts Singapore. *Sydney Morning Herald*. Available at www.smh.com.au/world/climate-of-fear-hurts-singapore-author-20071214-1h5t.html (accessed January 23, 2016).

Lord, N. (2004). Khazanah's quiet revolution. *Finance Asia*, November, pp. 58–62.

Love, V. and Zicchino, L. (2006). Financial development and dynamic investment behavior: Evidence from panel VAR. *Quarterly Review of Economics and Finance* 46(2), pp. 190–210.

Low, L. (1991). *The Political Economy of Privatisation in Singapore: Analysis, Interpretation and Evaluation*. Singapore: McGraw-Hill.

(1993). The public sector in contemporary Singapore: In retreat?. In G. Rodan (ed.), *Singapore Changes Guard*, 1st edn. Melbourne: Longman Cheshire, p. 176.

(1998). *The Political Economy of a City-State: Government-Made Singapore*. Singapore: Oxford University Press.

(2001). The Singapore developmental state in the new economy and policy. *Pacific Review* 14(3), pp. 411–41.

(2006). *The Political Economy of a City-State Revisited*. Singapore: Marshal Cavendish Academic.

Lust-Okar E. (2005). *Structuring Conflict in the Arab World: Incumbents, Opponents, and Institutions*. Cambridge: Cambridge University Press.

Lyall, K. (2004). PM's graft war right on money. *The Weekend Australian*, February 14–15, p. 12.

Mackenzie, W. (2010). *Chinese NOC's Step Up International Expansion*. London: Wood Mackenzie Corporate Service.

Magaloni, B. (2006). *Voting for Autocracy*. New York, NY: Cambridge University Press.

(2008). Credible power-sharing and the longevity of authoritarian rule. *Comparative Political Studies* 41(4–5), pp. 715–41.

Magaloni, B. and Kricheli, R. (2010). Political order and one-party rule. *Annual Review of Political Science* 13(1), pp. 123–43.

Mahani Z. A. (2002). *Rewriting the Rules: the Malaysian Crisis Management Model*. Petaling Jaya: Pearson Malaysian Sdn Bhd.

Malaysia (2006). *Third Industrial Master Plan, 2006–2020*. Kuala Lumpur: Government Printers.

Malesky, E. and Schuler, P. (2010). Nodding or needling: Analyzing delegate responsiveness in an authoritarian parliament. *American Political Science Review* 104(3), pp. 482–502.

Maremont, M. (2009). Royal dispute over billions in Brunei nears a resolution. Wall Street Journal. Available at www.wsj.com/articles/SB125375281010136095 (accessed August 13, 2014).

Markham, S. K., Ward, S. J., Aiman-Smith, L., and Kingon, A. I. (2010). The valley of death as context for role theory in product innovation. *Journal of Product Innovation Management* 27(3), pp. 402–17.

Marshall, A. R. C. (2012). Tenth out of ten. *The Economist*, November 17, 2012.

Mathew, J. C. (2010). Fortis readies to battle Khazanah. *Business Standard*. Available at www.business-standard.com/article/companies/fortis-readies-to-battle-khazanah-110052900021_1.html (accessed November 15, 2015).

Mauzy, D. K. and Milne, R. S. (2002). *Singapore Politics under the People's Action Party*. London: Psychology Press.

Mayhew, D. R. (1974). *Congress: The Electoral Connection*. New Haven, CT: Yale University Press.

Mazzucato, M. (2011). *The Entrepreneurial State*. London: Demos.

McAllister, I. (2016). Democratic consolidation in Taiwan in comparative perspective. *Asian Journal of Comparative Politics* 1(1), pp. 44–61.

McBeath, G. A. (1997). Taiwan privatizes by fits and starts. *Asian Survey* 37(12), pp. 1145–62.

McCahery, J. A., Sautner, Z., and Starks, L. T. (2016). Behind the scenes: The corporate governance preferences of institutional investors. *Journal of Finance* 71(6), pp. 2905–32.

McCoy, A. W. (1993). *An Anarchy of Families: State and Family in the Philippines*. Madison, WI: University of Wisconsin Press.

McDermott, G. A. (2003). *Embedded Politics: Industrial Networks and Institutional Change in Postcommunism*. Ann Arbor, MI: University of Michigan Press.

McKendrick, D., Doner, R. F., and Haggard, S. (2000). *From Silicon Valley to Singapore: Location and Competitive Advantage in the Hard Disk Drive Industry*. Stanford, CA: Stanford Business Books.

McKinnon, R. and Pill, H. (1998). International overborrowing: A decomposition of credit and currency risk. *World Development* 26(7), pp. 1267–82.

McNally, C. (2002). Strange bedfellows: Communist Party institutions in the corporate governance of Chinese state holding corporations. *Business and Politics* 4(1), pp. 91–115.

Megginson, W. L. (2013). Privatization trends and major deals of 2012 and 1H2013. In *Privatization Barometer 2012 Report*. Privatization Barometer, Milan. Available at www.privatizationbarometer.net.

—— (Forthcoming). Privatization, state capitalism, and state ownership of business in the 21st century. *Foundations and Trends in Finance*.

Megginson, W. L. and Fotak, V. (2015). Rise of the fiduciary state: A survey of sovereign wealth fund research. *Journal of Economic Surveys* 29(4), pp. 733–78.

Megginson, W. L. and Netter, J. M. (2001). From state to market: A survey of empirical studies of privatization. *Journal of Economic Literature* 39(2), pp. 321–89.

Mendoza, R. U., Beja, E. L., Jr, Venida, V. S., and Yap, D. B. (2012). Inequality in democracy: Insights from an empirical analysis of political dynasties in the 15th Philippine Congress. *Philippine Political Science Journal* 33(2), pp. 132–45.

Menon, J. and Ng, T. H. (2013). Are government-linked corporations crowding out private investment in Malaysia? ADB Economics Working Paper Series No. 345, Asian Development Bank.

Mietzner, M. and Schweizer, D. (2014). Hedge funds versus private equity funds as shareholder activists in Germany: Differences in value creation. *Journal of Economics and Finance* 38(2), pp. 181–208.

Migdal, J. S. (1988). *Strong Societies and Weak States: State-Society Relations and State Capabilities in the Third World*. Princeton, NJ: Princeton University Press.

Milne, R. S. (1991). The politics of privatization in the ASEAN states. *ASEAN Economic Bulletin* 7(3), pp. 322–34.

Ministry of Finance (2002). Budget Speech 2002, Singapore.

Mokhtar (2004): www.khazanah.com/docs/speech20041004-KLBCKL.pdf (accessed November 14, 2015).

Moore, J. (1991). British privatization: Taking capitalism to the people. *Harvard Business Review* 70(1), pp. 115–24.

Morck, R. and Nakamura, M. (2007). Business groups and the big push: Meiji Japan's mass privatization and subsequent growth. NBER Working

Paper Series No. 13171, National Bureau of Economic Research, Cambridge, MA. Available at www.nber.org/papers/w13171 (accessed October 12, 2015).

Morck, R., Wolfenzon, D., and Yeung, B. (2004). Corporate governance, economic entrenchment and growth. NBER Working Paper Series No. 10692, National Bureau of Economic Research, Cambridge, MA. Available at www.nber.org/papers/w10692 (accessed August 8, 2015).

Morrison, K. M. (2009). Oil, nontax revenue, and the redistributional foundations of regime stability. *International Organization* 63(1), pp. 107–38.

Moustafa, T. (2014). Law and courts in authoritarian regimes. *Annual Review of Law and Social Science* 10, pp. 281–99.

Muno, W. (2010). Conceptualizing and measuring clientelism. In *The Workshop on Neopatrimonialism in Various World Regions*. Hamburg: GIGA German Institute of Global and Area Studies.

Musacchio, A. and Lazzarini, S. (2014). *Reinventing State Capitalism*. Cambridge, MA: Harvard University Press.

Naughton, B. (2008). Market economy, hierarchy and single party rule. In J. Kornai and Y. Y. Qian (eds.), *Market and Socialism Reconsidered*, 1st edn. London: Macmillan, pp. 135–61.

(2015). The transformation of the state sector: SASAC, the market economy, and the new national champions. In B. Naughton and K. S. Tsai (eds.), *State Capitalism, Institutional Adaptation, and the Chinese Miracle*, 1st edn. Cambridge: Cambridge University Press, pp. 46–72.

(2016). State enterprise reform: Missing in action. *China Economic Quarterly* 20(2), pp. 15–21.

Naughton, B. and Tsai, K. S. (eds.) (2015). *State Capitalism, Institutional Adaptation, and the Chinese Miracle*. Cambridge: Cambridge University Press.

Ngiam, T. D. and Tay, S. S. (2006). *A Mandarin and the Making of Public Policy: Reflections*. Singapore: NUS Press.

Nguyen, D. T., Nguyen, T. P., and Nguyen, J. D. (2012). Vietnam's SCIC: A gradualist approach to sovereign wealth funds. *Journal of the Asia Pacific Economy* 17(2), pp. 268–83.

Nikomborirak, D. and Cheevasittiyanon, S. (2006). Corporate governance among state-owned enterprises in Thailand. In S. Montreevat (ed.), *Corporate Governance in Thailand*, 1st edn. Singapore: Institute of Southeast Asian Studies.

Nograles, P. C. and Lagman E. C. (2008). Understanding the "Pork Barrel." Philippines House of Representatives. Available at www.congress.gov .ph/pdaf/news/pork_barrel.pdf (accessed March 28, 2016).

Norris, P. and Inglehart, R. (2009). *Cosmopolitan Communications: Cultural Diversity in a Globalized World*. New York, NY: Cambridge University Press.

Norris, W. J. (2016). *Chinese Economic Statecraft: Commercial Actors, Grand Strategy, and State Control*. Ithaca, NY: Cornell University Press.

(1991). Institutions. *Journal of Economic Perspectives* 5(1), pp. 97–112.

North, D. C. and Weingast, B. (1989). Constitutions and commitment: The evolution of institutions governing public choice in seventeenth-century England. *Journal of Economic History* 49(4), pp. 803–32.

OECD (2009). *Privatisation in the 21st Century: Recent Experiences of OECD Countries*. Paris: Corporate Affairs Division, Directorate for Financial and Enterprise Affairs, Organisation for Economic Co-operation and Development. Available at www.oecd.org/corporate/ca/corporategovernanceofstate-ownedenterprises/48476423.pdf (accessed August 12, 2015).

(2009). *State-Owned Enterprises in China: Reviewing the Evidence*. Paris: OECD Working Group on Privatisation and Corporate Governance of State-Owned Assets. Available at www.oecd.org/daf/ca/corporategovernanceofstate-ownedenterprises/42095493.pdf (accessed August 23, 2016).

(2013). Structural policy challenges for Southeast Asian countries. In *Southeast Asian Economic Outlook 2013: With Perspectives on China and India*, 1st edn. Boulogne-Billancourt: OECD Development Centre.

Oehlers, A. (2005). Corruption: The peculiarities of Singapore. In N. Tarling (ed.), *Corruption and Good Governance in Asia*, 1st edn. London: Routledge Curzon.

Olson, M. (1965). *The Logic of Collective Action*. Cambridge, MA: Harvard University Press.

Olson, M. (1993). Dictatorship, democracy, and development. *American Political Science Review* 87(3), pp. 567–76.

Ow, C. H. (1976). Singapore. In N. Truong (ed.), *The Role of Public Enterprise in National Development in Southeast Asia: Problems and Prospects*, 1st edn. Singapore: Regional Institute of Higher Education and Development.

Pao, H. W., Wu, H. L., and Pan, W. H. (2008). The road to liberalization: Policy design and implementation of Taiwan's privatization. *International Economics and Economic Policy* 5(3), pp. 323–44.

Park, J. (2009). Lessons from SOE management and privatisation in Korea. KDI School of Public Policy and Management Working Paper (09–10), Sejong-si.

Paulson, H. (2015). *Dealing with China: An Insider Unmasks the New Economic Superpower*. New York, NY: Twelve.

Pearson, M. M. (2015). State-owned business and party-state regulation in China's modern political economy. In B. Naughton and K. S. Tsai (eds.), *State Capitalism, Institutional Adaptation, and the Chinese Miracle*, 1st edn. Cambridge: Cambridge University Press, pp. 27–45.

Peebles, G. and Wilson, P. (2002). *Economic Growth and Development in Singapore*. Northampton, MA: Edward Elgar.

Peng, M. W. (2003). Institutional transitions and strategic choices. *Academy of Management Review* 28(2), pp. 275–96.

Peng, M. W., Sun, S. L., Pinkham, B., and Chen, H. (2009). The institution-based view as a third leg for a strategy tripod. *Academy of Management Perspectives* 23(3), pp. 63–81.

Peng, W. Q., Wei, K. J., and Yang, Z. (2011). Tunneling or propping: Evidence from connected transactions in China. *Journal of Corporate Finance* 17(2), pp. 306–25.

Pepinsky T. (2007). Autocracy, elections, and fiscal policy: Evidence from Malaysia. *Studies in Comparative International Development* 42(1–2), pp. 136–63.

(2009). *Economic Crises and the Breakdown of Authoritarian Regimes*. New York, NY: Cambridge University Press.

Petrova, I., Pihlman, J., Kunzel, M. P., and Lu, Y. (2011). Investment objectives of sovereign wealth funds: A shifting paradigm (No. 11–19). International Monetary Fund, Washington, DC.

Pillai, P. N. (1983). *State Enterprise in Singapore: Legal Importation and Development*. Singapore: NUS Press, pp. 117 and 202–4.

Pistor, K. and Xu, C. (2005). Governing stock markets in transition economies: Lessons from China. *American Law and Economics Review* 7(1), pp. 184–210.

Prasetiantono, T. (2004). Political economy of privatisation of state-owned enterprises in Indonesia. In P. van der Eng (ed.), *Business in Indonesia: New Challenges, Old Problems*. Singapore: Institute of Southeast Asian Studies, pp. 141–57.

Preqin (2016). *2016 Preqin Sovereign Wealth Fund Review*. Available at www.preqin.com/swf (accessed September 12, 2016).

(2016). *2016 Preqin Global Private Equity & Venture Capital Report*. Available at www.preqin.com/privateequity (accessed September 12, 2016).

(2016). *2016 Preqin Global Hedge Fund Report*. Available at www.preqin.com/hedge (accessed September 12, 2016).

Przeworski, A., Alvarez, M., Cheibub, J., and Limongi, F. (2000). *Democracy and Development: Political Institutions and Material Well-Being in the World, 1950–1990*. New York, NY: Cambridge University Press.

Puchniak, D. W., Cheng-Han, T., and Varottil, U. (2016). State-owned enterprises in Singapore: Historical insights into a potential model for reform. *Columbia Journal of Asian Law* 28(2), p. 61.

Putrajaya Committee (2006). *The Green Book: Enhancing Board Effectiveness*. Kuala Lumpur: Putrajaya Committee on GLC High Performance.

Qian, M. and Yeung, B. Y. (2015). Bank financing and corporate governance. *Journal of Corporate Finance* 32, pp. 258–70.

Quah, J. S. (2010). *Public Administration Singapore-Style*, vol. 19. Singapore: Emerald Group Publishing.

Rahman, K. and Ahmed, M. (2000). *Towards Islamic Banking Experiences and Challenges: A Case Study of Pilgrims Management and Fund Board, Malaysia*. Islamabad: Institute of Policy Studies.

Ramirez, C. D. and Tan, L. H. (2004). Singapore Inc. versus the private sector: Are government-linked companies different?. *IMF Staff Papers*, pp. 510–28.

Rasiah, R., Noh, A., and Tumin, M. (2009). Privatising healthcare in Malaysia: Power, policy and profits. *Journal of Contemporary Asia* 39(1), pp. 50–62.

Rodan, G. (1989). *The Political Economy of Singapore's Industrialization: National, State and International Capital*. London: Macmillan.

(2004). *Transparency and Authoritarian Rule in Southeast Asia: Singapore and Malaysia*. London: Routledge.

(2008). Singapore "exceptionalism"? Authoritarian rule and state transformation. In E. Friedman and J. Wong (eds.), *Political Transitions in Dominant Party Systems: Learning to Lose*. London: Routledge, p. 231.

Rodrik, D. (2006). Goodbye Washington consensus, Hello Washington confusion? A review of the World Bank's economic growth in the 1990s: Learning from a decade of reform. *Journal of Economic Literature* 44(4), pp. 973–87.

(2007). *One Economics, Many Recipes: Globalization, Institutions, and Economic Growth*. Princeton, NJ: Princeton University Press.

(2008). The disappointments of financial globalization. In *International Symposium, Bank of Thailand*. Available at www.bot.or.th/Thai/Mon etaryPolicy/ArticleAndResearch/DocInterconference/01_Keynote_Rod rik.pdf (accessed October 12, 2015).

Rodrik, D. and Subramanian, A. (2009). Why did financial globalization disappoint?. *IMF Staff Papers* 56(1), pp. 112–38.

Rose, P. (2013). Sovereign shareholder activism: How SWFs can engage in corporate governance. In *Harvard Law School Forum on Corporate*

Governance and Financial Regulation. Available at https://corpgov.law .harvard.edu/2014/08/07/sovereign-shareholder-activism-how-swfs-can-engage-in-corporate-governance/ (accessed October 12, 2015).

Rutkowski, R. (2014). *State-Owned Enterprise Reform: The Long Wait for a Chinese Temasek Continues …* Washington, DC: Peterson Institute for International Economics.

Saleh, A. and Ndubisi, N. 2006. An evaluation of SME development in Malaysia. *International Review of Business Research Papers* 2(1), pp. 1–14.

Salim, M. R. (2011). Corporate governance in Malaysia: The macro and micro issues. In C. A. Mallin (ed.), *Handbook on International Corporate Governance*, 1st edn.Northampton, MA: Edward Elgar.

Sam, C. Y. (2010). Globalizing partially privatized firms in Singapore: The role of government as a regulator and a shareholder. *Journal of Asian and African Studies* 45(3), pp. 258–73.

Samphantharak, K. (2017). Economic development of Southeast Asia. Manuscript in progress, University of California San Diego.

Sauvant, K. P., Sachs, L. E., and Jongbloed, W. P. S. (2012). *Sovereign Investment: Concerns and Policy Reactions.* Oxford: Oxford University Press.

Schatzberg M. G. (1988). *The Dialectics of Oppression in Zaire.* Bloomington, IN: Indiana University Press.

Schwab, K. (ed.) (2010). *The Global Competitiveness Report 2010–2011.* Geneva: World Economic Forum. Available at www3.weforum.org/do cs/WEF_GlobalCompetitivenessReport_2010–11.pdf (last accessed November 22, 2015).

(2014). *The Global Competitiveness Report 2014–15.* Geneva: World Economic Forum. Available at www3.weforum.org/docs/WEF_Global CompetitivenessReport_2014-15.pdf (last accessed November 22, 2017).

Seow, F. T. (1992). *To Catch a Tartar: A Dissident in Lee Kuan Yew's Prison.* New Haven, CT: Yale University Press.

Shari, M. (2001). Malaysia's not-so-masterful bank plan. *Business Week Online.* Available at www.bloomberg.com/bw/stories/2001–03-11/ma laysias-not-so-masterful-bank-plan (accessed November 14, 2015).

Sharpe, S. A. (1990). Asymmetric information, bank lending, and implicit contracts: A stylized model of customer relationships. *Journal of Finance* 45(4), pp. 1069–87.

Shih, V. C. (2008). *Factions and Finance in China.* Cambridge: Cambridge University Press.

(2009). Tools of survival: Sovereign wealth funds in Singapore and China. *Geopolitics* 14(2), pp. 328–44.

Shirley, M. and Nellis, J. (1991). *Public Enterprise Reform: The Lessons of Experience*. Washington, DC: Economic Development Institute of the World Bank.

Shleifer, A. (1998). State versus private ownership. *Journal of Economic Perspectives* 12(4), pp. 133–50.

Sian, I., Thomsen, S., and Yeong, G. (2014). *The State as Shareholder: The Case of Singapore*. Singapore: Chartered Institute of Management Accountants (CIMA) and Centre for Governance, Institutions and Organisations (CGIO). Available at https://bschool.nus.edu.sg/Portals/0/docs/FinalReport_SOE_1July2014.pdf (accessed September 16, 2015).

Siddiquee, N. A. (2005). Public accountability in Malaysia: Challenges and critical concerns. *International Journal of Public Administration* 28(1–2), pp. 107–30.

(2011). Approaches to fighting corruption and managing integrity in Malaysia: A critical perspective. *Journal of Administrative Science* 8(1), pp. 47–74.

Sidel, J. T. (1999). *Capital, Coercion, and Crime: Bossism in the Philippines*. Stanford, CA: Stanford University Press.

Sim, I., Thomson, S., and Yeong, G. (2014). The state as shareholder. In *The Case of Singapore*, Centre for Governance, Institutions and Organizations, NUS Business School.

Simmons, B., Dobbin, F., and Garrett, G. (2006). The international diffusion of liberalism. *International Organization* 60(4), pp. 781–810.

Singapore (1986). *The Singapore Economy: New Directions. Report of the Economic Committee*, February.

Slater, D. (2003). Iron cage in an iron fist: Authoritarian institutions and the personalization of power in Malaysia. *Comparative Politics* 36(1), pp. 81–101.

Smith Diwan, K. (2009). Sovereign dilemmas: Saudi Arabia and sovereign wealth funds. *Geopolitics* 14(2), pp. 345–59.

Social Weather Stations (2007). *The 2006–2007 Surveys of Enterprises on Corruption*. Quezon City: Asia Foundation.

Solinger, D. J. (2001). Ending one-party dominance: Korea, Taiwan, Mexico. *Journal of Democracy* 12(1), pp. 30–42.

Song, T. K. and Bhaskaran, M. (2015). The role of the state in Singapore: Pragmatism in pursuit of growth. *Singapore Economic Review* 60(3), pp. 51–82.

Soon, L. C. and Koh, P. T. (2006). Corporate governance of Banks in Malaysia. In S. W. Nam and C. S. Lum (eds.), *Corporate Governance of Banks in Asia*, 1st edn. Tokyo: Asian Development Bank Institute, pp. 243–314.

Sovereign Wealth Fund Institute (2016). *Sovereign Wealth Fund Rankings.* Available at www.swfinstitute.org/fund-rankings/ (accessed September 12, 2016).

Spence, M. (2008). *The Growth Report: Strategies for Sustained Growth and Inclusive Development.* Washington, DC: Commission on Growth and Development. Available at https://openknowledge.worldbank.org/han dle/10986/6507 (accessed September 10, 2015).

Standard & Poor's (2001). Singapore: Government-Linked Enterprises, December 15.

Stasavage, D. (2002). Credible commitment in early modern Europe: North and Weingast revisited. *Journal of Law, Economics, and Organization* 18(1), pp. 155–86.

Stenson, M. R. (1970). *Industrial Conflict in Malaya: Prelude to the Communist Revolt of 1948.* London: Oxford University Press.

Sudan Divestment Task Force (2007). PetroChina, CNPC, and Sudan: Perpetuating genocide, April 15. Available at www.sudandivestment.org/docs/petrochina_cnpc_sudan.pdf (accessed December 10, 2016).

Sutherland, D. and Lutao, N. (2015). The emergence and evolution of Chinese business groups: Are pyramidal groups forming?. In B. Naughton and K. S. Tsai (eds.), *State Capitalism, Institutional Adaptation, and the Chinese Miracle*, 1st edn. New York: Cambridge University Press, p. 102.

Svolik, M. W. (2009). Power sharing and leadership dynamics in authoritarian regimes. *American Journal of Political Science* 53(2), pp. 477–94.

(2012). *The Politics of Authoritarian Rule.* Cambridge, MA: Cambridge University Press.

Szamosszegi, A. and Kyle, C. (2011). *An Analysis of State-Owned Enterprises and State Capitalism in China.* Washington, DC: Capital Trade, Incorporated for US-China Economic and Security Review Commission, p. 89.

Tamamura, H. 2004. The actual state and effect of privatization in Japan. In *The 11th Technical Training Course on the Antimonopoly Act and Competition Policy.* Available at www.jftc.go.jp/eacpf/05_05_01_ma in.html (accessed December 9, 2016).

Tan, N. (2013). Manipulating electoral laws in Singapore. *Electoral Studies* 32(4), pp. 632–43.

Tanner, M. S. (1999). *The Politics of Lawmaking in Post-Mao China: Institutions, Processes, and Democratic Prospects.* Oxford: Oxford University Press.

Teehankee, J. C. (2013). Clientelism and party politics in the Philippines. In D. Tomsa (ed.), *Party Politics in Southeast Asia: Clientelism and*

Electoral Competition in Indonesia, Thailand and the Philippines, 1st edn. London: Routledge, p. 186.

Thio, L. A. (1997). Choosing representatives: Singapore does it her way. In G. Hassall and C. Saunders (eds.), *The People's Representatives: Electoral Systems in the Asia-Pacific Region*. Sydney: Allen & Unwin.

Thu, Prak Chan (2013). Analysis: Punished at the polls, Cambodia's long-serving PM is smiling again. Reuters, September 18.

Tipton, F. (2009). Southeast Asian capitalism: History, institutions, states, and firms. *Asia Pacific Journal of Management* 26(3), pp. 401–34.

Tolentino, P. E. (2010). Home country macroeconomic factors and outward FDI of China and India. *Journal of International Management* 16(2), pp. 102–20.

Tranoy, B. (2009). Flexible adjustment in the age of financialisation: The case of Norway. *Geopolitics* 14(2), pp. 360–75.

Truex, R. (2014). The returns to office in a "rubber stamp" parliament. *American Political Science Review* 108(02), pp. 235–51.

(2016). *Making Autocracy Work*. 1st edn. New York: Cambridge University Press.

Truman, E. M. (2011). *Sovereign Wealth Funds: Threat or Salvation?*. Washington, DC: Peterson Institute for International Economics.

Tsui-Auch, L. S. (2005). Unpacking regional ethnicity and the strength of ties in shaping ethnic entrepreneurship. *Organization Studies* 26(8), pp. 1189–216.

Tullock G. (1987). *Autocracy*. Boston: Kluwer Academic.

Turnbull, C. M. (1977). *A History of Singapore, 1819–1975*. New York, NY: Oxford University Press.

(2009). *A History of Modern Singapore, 1819–2005*. Singapore: NUS Press.

US Department of State. (2014). 2014 Investment Climate Statement. June 2014.

Varkkey, H. (2015). Natural resource extraction and political dependency: Malaysia as a renter state. In L. W. Meredith (ed.), *Routledge Handbook of Contemporary Malaysia*, 1st edn. Londres: Routledge, Taylor and Francis, pp. 189–99.

Vasudeva, G. (2013). Weaving together the normative and regulative roles of government: How the Norwegian sovereign wealth fund's responsible conduct is shaping firms' cross-border investments. *Organization Science* 24(6), pp. 1662–82.

Venkat, P. R., Holmes, S., and Tudor, A. (2010). Khazanah wins Parkway. *Wall Street Journal Asia*, July 27.

Vickers, J. and Yarrow, G. (1988). *Privatization: An Economic Analysis*. Cambridge, MA: MIT Press.

Vieira, Paul. 2012. Canada approves big energy mergers. *Wall Street Journal*, December 8.

Vietor, R. H. K. and Thompson, E. J. (2008). *Singapore Inc.* Harvard Business School Case 703–040, February 2003, Cambridge, MA.

Vithiatharan, V. and Gomez, E. (2014). Politics, economic crises and corporate governance reforms: Regulatory capture in Malaysia. *Journal of Contemporary Asia* 44(4), pp. 599–615.

Wade, R. (1990). *Governing the Market: Economic Theory and the Role of Government in East Asian Industrialization*. Princeton, NJ: Princeton University Press.

Wain, B. (2009). *Malaysian Maverick: Mahathir Mohamad in Turbulent Times*. New York, NY: Palgrave Macmillan.

Walter, A. (2008). *Governing Finance: East Asia's Adoption of International Standards*. Ithaca, NY: Cornell University Press.

Wang, C. (2005). *The Political Economy of Privatization: A Comparative Study of Indonesia, the Philippines and Taiwan*. DeKalb, IL: Northern Illinois University Press.

Wang, J. (2014). The political logic of corporate governance in China's state-owned enterprises. *Cornell International Law Journal* 47(3), pp. 631–69.

Wei, W. X. and Alon, I. (2010). Chinese outward direct investment: A study on macroeconomic determinants. *International Journal of Business and Emerging Markets* 2(4), pp. 352–69.

Weiss, M. L. (2016). Payoffs, parties, or policies: "Money politics" and electoral authoritarian resilience. *Critical Asian Studies* 48(1), pp. 77–99.

Whitley, R. (1999). *Divergent Capitalisms: The Social Structuring and Change of Business Systems*. New York: Oxford University Press.

Williamson, J. (1990). What Washington means by policy reform. In J. Williamson (ed.), *Latin American Adjustment: How Much Has Happened?*, 1st edn. Washington, DC: Institute for International Economics, pp. 7–20.

(2012). Is the "Beijing consensus" now dominant?. *Asia Policy* 13(1), pp. 1–16.

Williamson, O. E. (1975). *Markets and Hierarchies: Analysis and Antitrust Implications*. New York, NY: Free Press.

Wintrobe, R. (1998). *The Political Economy of Dictatorship*. Cambridge: Cambridge University Press.

World Bank (2000). *Combating Corruption in the Philippines*. Washington, DC: World Bank. Available at http://documents.worldbank.org/curated/en/826151468776117170/Philippines-Combating-corruption-in-the-Philippines (accessed September 12, 2015).

(2008). *Sovereign Wealth Funds in East Asia*. Washington, DC: World Bank. Available at http://documents.worldbank.org/curated/en/25848

1468023353801/Sovereign-Wealth-Funds-SWFs-in-East-Asia (accessed May 3, 2015).

(2009). *Malaysia Economic Monitor: Repositioning for Growth.* Bangkok: World Bank. Available at http://documents.worldbank.org/curated/en/383361468088737863/Malaysia-economic-monitor-reposi tioning-for-growth (accessed March 5, 2016).

Worthington, R. (2003). *Governance in Singapore.* London: Routledge Curzon.

Wright, C. (2007). What price Malaysia's corporate reconstruction?. *Euromoney.* Available at www.euromoney.com/article/b13226qv79w v2t/what-price-malaysias-corporate-reconstruction (accessed November 22, 2017).

Wright, J. (2008). Do authoritarian institutions constrain? How legislatures affect economic growth and investment. *American Journal of Political Science* 52(2), pp. 322–43.

Wu, M. and Hickling, R. (2003). *Hickling's Malaysian Public Law.* Selangor Darul Ehsan: Longman.

Xu, C. (2011). The fundamental institutions of China's reforms and development. *Journal of Economic Literature* 49(4), pp. 1076–151.

Yeh, Y., Lee, T., and Woidtke, T. (2001). Family control and corporate governance: Evidence from Taiwan. *International Review of Finance* 2(1–2), pp. 21–48.

Yermo, J. (2008). Governance and investment of sovereign and public pension reserve funds in selected OECD countries. OECD Working Papers on Insurance and Private Pensions.

Yeung, H. (1999). The internationalization of ethnic Chinese business firms from Southeast Asia: Strategies, processes and competitive advantage. *International Journal of Urban and Regional Research* 23(1), pp. 88–102.

(2004). *Chinese Capitalism in a Global Era.* London: Routledge.

(2005). Institutional capacity and Singapore's developmental state. In H. E. Nesadurai (ed.), *Globalisation and Economic Security in East Asia: Governance and Institutions*, 1st edn. London: Routledge, pp. 85–106.

(2011). From national development to economic diplomacy? Governing Singapore's sovereign wealth funds. *Pacific Review* 24(5), pp. 625–52.

Yiu, D., Bruton, G., and Lu, Y. (2005). Understanding business group performance in an emerging economy: Acquiring resources and capabilities in order to prosper. *Journal of Management Studies* 42(1), pp. 183–206.

Yoshihara, K. (1988). *The Rise of Ersatz Capitalism in Southeast Asia.* Singapore: Oxford University Press.

You, J. S. (2015). *Democracy, Inequality and Corruption*. New York, NY: Cambridge University Press.

Zhong, Y. and Chen, J. (2002). To vote or not to vote: An analysis of peasants' participation in Chinese village elections. *Comparative Political Studies* 35(6), pp. 686–712.

Zou, H., Wong, S., Shum, C., Xiong, J., and Yan, J. (2008). Controlling-minority shareholder incentive conflicts and directors' and officers' liability insurance: Evidence from China. *Journal of Banking & Finance* 32(12), pp. 2636–45.

Index

Made in the USA
Las Vegas, NV
07 March 2021

19051556R20184